The Philippines
a travel survival kit

The Philippines — a travel survival kit

Published by
    Lonely Planet Publications
    PO Box 88, South Yarra
    Victoria 3141, Australia

Printed and bound in Singapore through Hedges & Bell Printing (S.E. Asia) Pte. Ltd.

Colour Photographs by
    Jens Peters — cover, 32AB, 33ABC, 64AB, 65B, 96B, 128AB, 192ABC, 193AB, 224BC,
      225AB, 256AB, 257B, 288AB, 289AB
    Tony Wheeler — 65A, 96A, 97B, 129ABC, 224A, 257A

First Published
    1981

This Edition
    October 1983

Peters, Jens.
    [Philippinen Paradies fur Globetrotter. English].
    The Philippines, a travel survival kit.

    2nd ed.
    Previous English ed. : South Yarra, Vic. :
    Lonely Planet, 1981.
    Includes index.
    ISBN 0 908086 49 0.

    1. Philippine Islands — Description and travel —
    1975- . — Guide-books. I. Title.

915.99'0446

© Jens Peters 1983

Jens Peters studied advertising and communications in Berlin and later taught there before becoming involved in travel writing. Since 1970 he has travelled for several months of each year and the Philippines has become his favourite country in South-East Asia.

Thanks to
In addition to the many German speaking travellers who contributed to the new German language edition of Jens Peters' guide thanks must also go to the following contributors to this guide and to those who have written suggestions and corrections for the Philippines section of *South-East Asia on a Shoestring*. In particular to Mons Michael, Ray Steen (USA), Ola & Anne Holmgren (Sw), Terry Whiteman (Aus), Christopher Jacques (UK), Mary Lippens (B), Joe & Sylvia Weiss (HK), Wendy Fletcher (Aus), Ralph McLintock, ATO Liddell (HK), Stefan Braunwalder (CH), Neil Slavin (Aus), Teresa Howells (Aus), Tony Grey (UK), Godfried & Hilda Sippel (Nl), Piers & Jill Beagley (Aus), William S Weir (USA), Terry Whiteman (Aus), Adrian Rice (M), Bert Jan Schaap, Peter Waldschmidt & Peter Kirkham (UK), G A Orton (Aus), Daver Tirman, Claire Marcoux (C), Helen Bischoff & Ross Melrose (Aus), John Catmuil, Richard Meixsel (USA), Jon Snyder (USA), Alan Jackson (Aus), Ludovica Villa (I), J A Plampin (UK), Mark Watson (UK), Joanne Sweeney (Aus), Claes Carlstrom (Sw), Bruce Mason (NZ), Fritz Balkau (Aus), Ian Park (Aus), Anne Larson, Billy Miller, Carole Harrison, J R Munro (Aus), Alastair Dow (Aus), Brian Hensley (C), P M Clayton (Aus), James Harvey and Eitan Alumi (Isr).

USA - USA, Sw - Sw, Aus - Australia, UK - UK, Nl - Netherlands, M - Malaysia, C - Canada, I - Italy, NZ - New Zealand, Isr - Israel.

Here at Lonely Planet thanks must also go to Neil Kirk and Margit Meinhold who translated the new German edition. Mary Covernton edited, Isabel Carroll typeset, Joy Weideman drew maps, Eveyln Vynhal did the layout and paste-up.

And the next edition
Things change — prices go up, good places go bad, bad ones go bankrupt and nothing stays the same. So if you find things better, worse, cheaper, more expensive, recently opened or long ago closed, please write and tell us. We really appreciate those letters from 'our' travellers out on the road and, as usual, we try to show our appreciation to as many of the good letter writers as possible with free copies of the next edition, or another LP guide if you prefer.

John Peters attained an enduring and communications in birth and later ... until there before becoming involved in travel writing. Since ... he has travelled for several months ... each year and the Philippines has become his favourite country in South-East Asia.

Thanks to

In addition to the many German-speaking travellers who contributed to the new German language edition of this Peters' guide thanks must also go to the following contributors to the guide and to those who have written suggestions and corrections for the Philippine section of South-east Asia on a Shoestring, in particular, to:

Sonia Michael, Kay Sneath (USA), Ola & Anne Holmqvist (Swd), Terry Wheeler (Aus), Christopher Jacques (UK), Marc Laporte (B), Joe & Sylvia Hess (HK), Wendy Melchior (Aus), Ralph McLintock, ATO Lindrel (HK), Stefan Brandvoider (DH), Neil Slavin (Aus), Teresa Lowells (Aus), Tony Grey (UK), Godfried & Linda Spoel (Nfl), Peter & Jill Bentley (Aus), William S Wolf (USA), Terry Whenan (Aus), Adrian Rice (NL), Bert Jan Schaap, Petra Waldschmidt & Peter Kubbenz (DK), G A Orton (Aus), Dave Truman, Glenn Maccoll (C), Helen Bradfield & Russ Melrose (Aus), John Carroll, Richard Mercuri (USA), Bob Snyder (USA), Alex Jackson (Aus), Frederick Villa (I), J A Plumpin (UK), Mark Watson (UK), Joanne Sweeney (Aus), Grace Calderon (Swd), Bruce Mason (NZ), Felix Balkan (Aus), Tza Park (Aus), Anne Larson (UK), Miller Carole Harrison, J R Munro (Aus), Alasdair Dow (Aus), Brian Hensley (C), P M Clayton (Aus), James Harvey and Helen Altman (Isl)

USA – USA, Sw – Sweden, Aus – Australia, UK – UK, NL – Netherlands, M – Malaysia, C – Canada, Isl – Iceland, NZ – New Zealand, HK – Hong Kong

Here at Lonely Planet thanks must also go to Neil Kirk and Margit Meinhold who translated the new German edition, Mary Covernton edited, Isabel Carroll typed and Jay Weinstein drew maps. Elvyla Vunak did the layout and paste-up.

And the next edition

Things change – prices go up, good places go bad, bad ones go berserk, and nothing stays the same. So if you find things better, worse, cheaper, more expensive, recently opened or long ago closed, please write and tell us. We really appreciate those letters from 'out there' travellers out on the read and go to some trouble, to show our appreciation to as many of the good letter writers as possible with free copies of the next edition, or another LP guide if you prefer.

Contents

INTRODUCTION 7

FACTS ABOUT THE COUNTRY History — Economy — Geography — Population — 8
Tribes — Religion — Health — Plants & Animals — Forces of Nature — Fiestas &
Festivals — Language

FACTS FOR THE VISITOR Visas — Climate — Books & Bookshops — Mass Media — 39
Health — Art & Culture — Cinemas — Sports & Games — Nightlife — Film &
Photography — Post — Telephone — Telegrams — Electricity — Time — Business
Hours — Places to Stay — Food & Drink — Information — Security — Filipinos &
Foreigners — National Clothing — Things to Buy — Things to Bring — Diving

GETTING THERE Entering the Philippines — From Australia — From New Zealand — 54
From Asia — From Europe — From the USA — Round the World Fares — Circle
Pacific Fares — Getting Away — Arriving in Manila

GETTING AROUND Trishaws — Tricycles — Calesas — Jeepneys — Taxis — PU-Cabs — 58
Rental Cars — Motorcycles — Bicycles — Air — Long Distance Buses — Local Buses —
Trains — Boats

MANILA Transport from Luzon 66

AROUND MANILA Bataan Peninsula — Corregidor — Olongapo — Las Pinas — 91
Cavite — Los Banos — Pagsanjan — Tagaytay (Taal Volcano) — Matabungkay —
Batangas — San Pablo

NORTH LUZON Baler — Botolan & West Coast — Lucap & Alaminos — Hundred 100
Islands — Bolinao — Lingayen & Dagupan — San Fernando (Pampanga) — Angeles —
Baguio — Bontoc — Sagada — Banaue — Batad — San Fernando La Union —
Bauang — Vigan — Laoag — Claveria & Taggat — Aparri — Tuguegarao — Tabuk —
Lubuagan

SOUTH LUZON Lucena City — Daet — San Miguel Bay — Naga — Iriga — Legaspi — 133
Legaspi to Tiwi — Tiwi — Bulan — Sorsogon — Matnog — Transport from South Luzon

AROUND LUZON 151

BATAN ISLANDS Batan Island — Sabtang Island — Itbayat Island — Transport to & 151
from Batan

CATANDUANES Virac — Getting Around — Transport to & from Catanduanes 154

LUBANG Around Lubang — Transport from Lubang 157

MARINDUQUE Santa Cruz — Gasan — Boac — Around the Island — Transport from 159
Marinduque

MASBATE Transport from Masbate 162

MINDORO Puerto Galera — Calapan — Bongabong & Roxas — Mansalay — San Jose — 164
Mamburao — Transport from Mindoro

THE VISAYAS 175

BOHOL Tagbilaran — Around the Island — Chocolate Hills — Tubigon — Transport from Bohol   175

CEBU Cebu City — Lapu Lapu (Mactan Island) — Cebu Beaches — Talisay — Sogod — Toledo — Moalboal — Matutinao — San Sebastian, Talisay & Bato — Argao & Santander — Sumilon Island — Transport from Cebu   182

LEYTE Tacloban — Ormoc — Baybay — Bato — Maasin — Liloan — Transport from Leyte   200

NEGROS Bacolod — Alcada — Granada — Mambucal — Ma-ao — Valladolid & Guimaras Island — Silay — Victorias — San Carlos — Dumaguete — Kawayan Beach — Malabatay & Zamboanguita — Twin Lake — San Jose — Binalbagan — Kabankalan — Hinobaan — Transport from Negros   207

PANAY Iloilo — Guimaras Island — Sicogon & Gigante Islands — Roxas — Kalibo — Boracay — The South Coast — San Jose de Buenavista — Transport from Panay   220

ROMBLON Romblon Island — Romblon — Tablas Island — San Augustin — Odiongan — Looc — Tugdan — Sibuyan Island — Transport from Romblon   235

SAMAR Allen — Catbalogan — Getting Around — Transport from Samar   239

SIQUIJOR Larena — Siquijor — San Antonio — Lazi — Salang Do-Ong — Transport from Siquijor   244

MINDANAO & PALAWAN   246

BASILAN Isabela — Lamitan — Maluso — Transport from Basilan   246

CAMIGUIN Mambajao — Hibok-Hibok Volcano — Katibawasan Waterfall — White Island — Around the Island — Transport from Camiguin   250

SULU ISLANDS Jolo — Siasi — Bongao — Sitangkai — Transport from the Sulu Islands   255

MINDANAO Surigao — Siargao Island — Butuan — Balingoan — Cagayan de Oro — Malaybalay & Kibawe — Iligan — Lake Lanao & Marawi — Pagadian — Ozamiz — Oroquita, Dapitan & Dipolog — Zamboanga — Davao — Around Davao — General Santos City (Dadiangas) — Lake Sebu — Cotabato — Transport from Mindanao   263

PALAWAN Puerto Princesa — Brooke's Point & Ursula Island — Quezon & the Tabon Caves — Iwahig — Balsahan — Santa Lucia — Baheli — Tagburos & Honda Bay — Nagtabon Beach — San Rafael — Roxas — Taytay — Liminangcong — Port Barton — San Vicente — Transport from Palawan   292

INDEX   307

Introduction

Despite a massive increase in tourism in Asia, the Philippines are still a paradise for globetrotters. Modern mass tourism has certainly changed the land and people of the Philippines but so far the changes have not gone too far and have been relatively limited in their scope. To get out and explore the 7000-plus islands of the Philippines still requires a little effort and energy.

It is the contrasts which make this country so interesting for the traveller. The bustling capital of Manila contrasts with lonely islands fringed with superb beaches and gardens of coral. There are towns which consists practically only of bars but there are also mountain tribes who still live according to their own laws. There are huge rice terraces built eons ago with the most primitive tools; or wide sugarcane fields still harvested by age old methods. Active volcanoes and hall-size caves with subterranean rivers and lakes. Shadowy palm forest groves and dense jungle.

Nor should the extraordinarily friendly people be forgotten — this is, the Filipinos like to remind you, 'where Asia wears a smile'. For the traveller the Philippines offer the further advantages of reasonable accommodation and food at pleasantly low prices. The myriad islands of this island-nation are connected by such frequent boat services that island hopping is a real pleasure. Have a nice time!

Facts about the Country

HISTORY

Philippine history is classified as beginning somewhere between 150,000 and 30,000 years ago. From this epoch stems the stone artefacts (paleoliths) which have been found together with fossils of long extinct mammals in Solano, Cagayan. They were probably used by hunters who immigrated over a then-existing landbridge from the Asiatic mainland. The oldest human bones which have so far been excavated have been dated as being 50,000 years old. However, many historians consider the Negritos or Aetas who arrived about 25,000 years ago from the Asian continent, as the aboriginal inhabitants of the Philippines. They were later driven back by several waves of immigrants from Indonesia.

In about 5000 BC the last landbridge sank into the ocean. Between 1500-500 BC five immigration periods from Indo-China were recorded. The last of these groups to arrive in their long canoes brought the first copper and bronze artefacts, and they are also credited with building the gigantic rice terraces at Banaue, North Luzon. The immigration of Malaysian peoples from 500 BC to 1500 AD brought further cultural changes, particularly in house construction (they built on piles), agriculture (with introduced plants and trees) and husbandry (use of the water buffalo).

Indian influences came from the Buddhist-Hindu empire of Sri-Vijaya (800-1377 AD) in Sumatra and Mojopajit (1293-1478) in Java. In this period trade also began with Indo-Chinese states. In particular the merchants of the Sung Dynasty (960-1280) visited the main island, Luzon, and the islands of the Visayas with their merchant ships. They mainly exchanged Chinese products like porcelain for native wood and gold.

In 1380 the Arab-taught Makdum arrived in the Sulu Islands to the south of the Philippines and began the 'Propagation of Islam'. His mission was most successful in Bwansa, the old Sulu capital, and Tapul Island. A powerful Islamic mission was finally achieved in 1475 by Sharif Mohammed Kabungsuwan, a Moslem leader from Johore. He married the very influential native princess Putri Tunoma, converted many tribes and was the first sultan of Mindanao.

The Moslems had already extended their power to a part of Luzon, when Ferdinand Magellan, a Portuguese seafarer in the service of Spain, arrived on the scene on the 16 March, 1521. His first landfall was on Homonhon, an uninhabited island near Leyte. But it was on Mactan that he erected a cross and claimed the whole land for Spain — with the blissful disregard typical of early colonisers for the local inhabitants' claim to their country. Lapu-Lapu, a proud Filipino Chief, opposed the Spanish authority, which led to a battle in which Magellan was killed.

Ruy Lopez De Villalobos was the next to try and claim the islands for Spain. With an expedition he reached the island realm in 1543 and named it 'Filipinas' after King Philip II of Spain. The permanent Spanish colonial occupation of the Philippines began in 1565. In November of that year Miguel Lopez de Legaspi landed with his fleet at Bohol. In Tagbilaran he sealed a blood friendship with the island ruler Rajah Sikatuna, conquered Cebu a short time later, and erected the first Spanish fort in the Philippines here. A very energetic type it would appear.

In 1571 Legaspi conquered Manila and a year later the whole country, with the exception of the strictly Islamic Sulu Islands and Mindanao, was under the domination of Spain. With the zeal typical of the Spanish at the time, churches were built and the propagation of Catholicism began. Until 1821 the Philippines were

8

administered from Mexico, and attempts by the Dutch, Portuguese and Chinese to set foot in the Philippines were successfully repelled by the Spanish, though the British had occupied Manila for a short time in 1762 during the Seven Years' War. They reluctantly handed it back to Spain under the conditions of the Treaty of Paris signed in 1763.

After the opening of the Suez Canal in 1869 many young Filipinos left their country to study in Spain and in other European countries. New ideas and thoughts of freedom were brought back by them to their countrymen. In 1872 there was a revolt in Cavite by about 200 Filipino soldiers against their Spanish masters. It was quickly put down but was the signal for the start of a determined struggle for freedom and independence.

The spiritual founders of the independence movement were the Philippine thinkers and patriots Marcelo H Del Pilar, Graciano Lopez Jaena, Juan Luna and Dr Jose Rizal. The critical writings and poems of Rizal inspired many Filipinos in their fight for freedom. When Jose Rizal founded the 'Liga Filipina' in 1892, he was exiled as a revolutionary agitator to Dapitan, Mindanao. Andres Bonifacio then founded the secret organisation 'Katipunan'. In August 1896, the armed struggle for independence broke out, first in Manila and later throughout the country. On 30 December 1896, after an absurd mockery of a trial, Rizal was executed by the Spanish authorities. He spent the last weeks before his death in the dungeon of Santiago in Manila. Emilio Aguinaldo replaced Bonifacio as leader of the revolution in March 1897.

In 1898 the Spanish-American war broke out. Under Admiral Dewey the Spanish fleet was decisively beaten in Manila Bay. The Filipinos, seizing their chance to strike against the Spanish, fought on the side of the Americans, and on 12 June 1898 Aguinaldo declared the Independence of the Philippines. The Americans, however, to show their gratitude for the role the Filipinos had played in the war, chose to ignore this and paid the Spanish 20 million dollars for their expossession. This was ratified by the Paris Peace Treaty, 10 December 1898, and Aguinaldo was not recognised as president of the revolutionary government. The Filipinos had to begin the struggle again against foreign domination — this time the formidable USA.

After President Roosevelt recognised the newly drawn-up Philippine consitution, Manuel L Quezon was sworn in as President of the Philippine Commonwealth. Then came WW II. After the attack on Pearl Harbour, Japanese troops landed on Luzon and conquered Manila on 2 January 1942. The Filipino-American troops suffered defeats with high casualty rates in battles at Corregidor Island and on the Bataan Peninsula. This resulted in the brutal Japanese military rule which lasted until 1944, when General Douglas MacArthur fulfilled his promise to liberate the Philippines from the Japanese. American troops landed at Leyte and under their lead the islands were recaptured from the Japanese forces.

On 4 July 1946 the Philippines received full independence. The first President of the Republic was Manuel Roxas. His successors were Elpidio Quirino, Ramon Magsaysay, Carlos Garcia and Diosdado Macapagal. The current president, Ferdinand E Marcos, was elected to power in 1965 and also, unusually for the Philippines, was re-elected. The Marcos government found the country in a desolate state. Corruption and crime had become the order of the day. People talked of the 'Wild East'. In 1972 Marcos declared martial law and began to implement his concept of the 'new society'. Within a short time some changes were apparent — guns disappeared from the street and crime decreased, land rents were partly abolished through the land reform law of October 1972 and improvements in public health were also made. Martial law was abolished in January 1981 and in the presidential election held in June, Marcos was confirmed as head of state for another six years. Parliamentary elections have been announced for 1984.

Although more overseas companies have been investing in the Philippines due to the availability of cheap labour, not all Filipinos are happy with Marcos' achievements. Despite the sweeping powers Marcos has been given he has not been able to solve the Philippines' pressing economic problems which include, in common with other third world countries afflicted with costly energy imports, low growth. The communist guerillas of the New People's Army (NPA) and members of the Moro National Liberation Front (MNLF) are determined to upset the balance of power through violent means while the opposition parties, the Democratic Socialist Party and the Philippine Democratic Party, are unlikely to have much influence on the political development of the next few years. Democratisation undertaken by President Marcos and his wife Imelda Marcos (First Lady, Governor of Metro Manila and Minister of Human Settlements) should be a significant factor in the internal political development of the 1980s.

ECONOMY

About two-thirds of the Philippine people live by fishing, agriculture and forestry. A significant contribution to their diet comes from ocean, coast and fresh-water fishing. Rice is the most important agricultural product. The development of new varieties of rice at the International Rice Research Institute at Los Banos, improvements in methods of cultivation and enlargement of the area of cultivation have brought the Philippines closer to self sufficiency in food production.

The main produce for exports are coconuts (copra), abaca (Manila hemp), tobacco, sugar cane, bananas, pineapples, and timber. Cattle farming is still relatively undeveloped. Poultry, pigs, sheep and goats are reared as meat animals while buffaloes serve mainly as work animals. The most important minerals are chrome, iron, copper, coal, nickel, gypsum, sulphur, mercury, asbestos, marble and salt. Test drillings for oil have only been semi-successful.

The Philippines, like many other Asian countries, suffers for its oil dependency for energy needs. In 1980 about $2.7 milliard was spent on crude oil imports. Hydro-electric and geothermal power projects are hoped to go some way towards imporoving the energy situation. The Philippines are second only to the US in harnessing geothermal energy sources. Manufacturing industry is located principally in and around Manila and consists mainly of the luxury and food industries, the textile industry and the leatherware industry although the Philippines also manufacture automobile components. Economic analysts are worried that the Filipino passion for grand and impressive projects, often highly capital intensive, may limit the nation's ability to come to terms with its employment problems. There is a minimum wage set by the state but this often exists only on paper. The Philippines has a large pool of skilled but under-utilised labour.

Tourism is a further source of income and from 1970 to 1982 the tourist flow has increased from just 14,000 tourists to one million. Of these approximately 40% are Japanese and 25% American. Manila has had a massive increase in hotel rooms in the '70s but this has not been followed up with a similar development in provincial areas. This lack of development outside Manila may eventually limit the growth of tourism but does make the Philippines more enjoyable for the shoestring traveller!

collecting the coconuts

GEOGRAPHY

The Philippines officially consists of 7107 islands of which only 2000 are inhabited. Only about 500 of the islands are larger than a square km and 2500 of them aren't even named. In order of size the biggest islands are:

Luzon	104,683 square km	Negros	9,225 square km
Mindanao	94,596 square km	Leyte	6,268 square km
Palawan	14,896 square km	Cebu	5,088 square km
Panay	12,327 square km	Bohol	4,117 square km
Mindoro	10,245 square km	Masbate	4,047 square km
Samar	9,949 square km		

The total area of the Philippines is 299,404 square km. From north to south the Philippines stretch for 1850 km and from east to west for 1100 km. The highest mountain is Mt Apo, near Davao in Mindanao, at 2953 metres. Mt Pulong, east of Baguio in North Luzon, is second highest at 2930 metres. There are over 30 volcanoes in the Philippines, 10 of which are classed as being active including the Mayon Volcano near Legaspi in south Luzon. The longest rivers are the Cagayan River, the Rio Grande de Pampanga and the Agno in Luzon; the Rio Grande de Mindanao and the Agusan River in Mindanao.

The islands of the Philippines can be conveniently divided into four groups. First there's Luzon, the largest and northernmost island and the site of the capital,

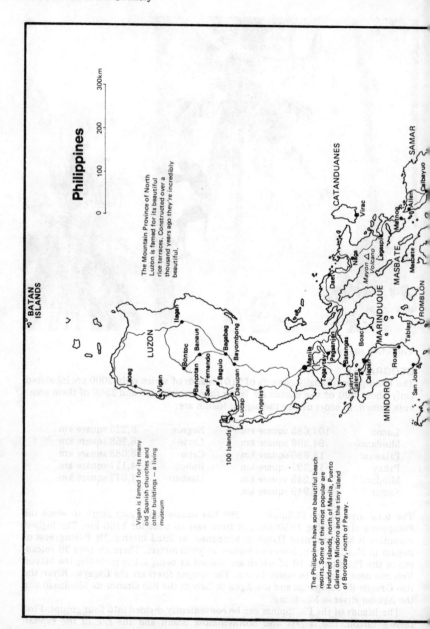

Philippines

The Mountain Province of North Luzon is famed for its beautiful rice terraces. Constructed over a thousand years ago they're incredibly beautiful.

Vigan is famed for its many old Spanish churches and other buildings – a living museum

The Philippines have some beautiful beach resorts. Some of the most popular are Hundred Islands, north of Manila, Puerto Galera on Mindoro and the tiny island of Borocay, north of Panay.

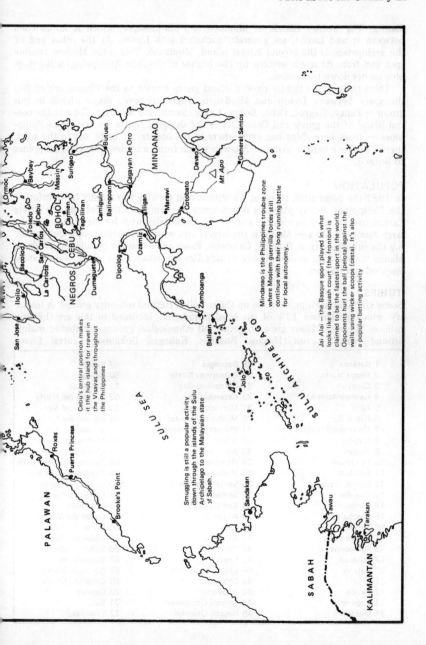

Cebu's central position makes it the hub island for travel in the Visayas and throughout the Philippines

Smuggling is still a popular activity down through the islands of the Sulu Archipelago to the Malaysian state of Sabah.

Mindanao is the Philippines trouble zone where Moslem guerilla forces still continue with their long running battle for local autonomy.

Jai Alai — the Basque sport played in what looks like a squash court (the fronton) is claimed to be the fastest sport in the world. Opponents hurl the ball (pelota) against the walls using wicker scoops (cesta). It's also a popular betting activity

Manila. The nearby islands of Mindoro and Marinduque, which is sandwiched between it and Luzon, are generally included with Luzon. At the other end of the archipelago is the second largest island, Mindanao. This is the Moslem trouble spot and from its south-western tip the islands of the Sulu Archipelago make stepping stones down to Borneo.

Third there is the tightly packed island group known as the Visayas, which fills the space between Luzon and Mindanao. There are seven major islands in this group — Panay, Negros, Cebu, Bohol, Leyte, Samar and Masbate. Cebu is the central island of the group and Cebu City is the shipping centre for the entire Philippines — from here ships run everywhere in the country. Finally, off to the west, there's the long narrow island of Palawan which forms a bridge from the Philippines to Borneo.

POPULATION
In 1982 the population stood at 50 million and growing too rapidly for comfort — the Philippines' family planning programmes are hampered not only by the strong Catholicism of the Filipinos but also by the usual Asian wish for the 'insurance' of a large family in old age. Manila is the largest city with 1.3 million people but including the suburbs such as Quezon, Caloocan, Pasay and so on the population of Metro Manila is over eight million. Other major cities are Davao, Cebu, Iloilo, Zamboanga, Bacolod and Basilan.

TRIBES
Some six million Filipinos make up the so-called cultural minority groups. A minority which comprises 13% of the total population, included in this are the four million Moslems. There are all together 60 ethnological groups distributed mainly around North Luzon (Ifugaos, Bontocs, Kalingas, Ilokanos), Central Luzon

1 Batanes	25 Batangas	49 Bohol
2 Ilocos Norte	26 Camarines Norte	50 Siquijor
3 Cagayan	27 Camarines Sur	51 Camiguin
4 Kalinga-Apayao	28 Catanduanes	52 Surigao del Norte
5 Abra	29 Marinduque	53 Surigao del Sur
6 Ilocos Sur	30 Mindoro Oriental	54 Agusan del Norte
7 Mountain Province	31 Mindoro Occidental	55 Agusan del Sur
8 Isabela	32 Albay	56 Misamis Oriental
9 Ifugao	33 Sorsogon	57 Misamis Occidental
10 La Union	34 Romblon	58 Zamboanga del Norte
11 Benguet	35 Masbate	59 Zamboanga del Sur
12 Nueva Vizcaya	36 Samar, Northern	60 Lanao del Norte
13 Quirino	37 Samar, Western	61 Lanao del Sur
14 Pangasinan	38 Samar, Eastern	62 Bukidnon
15 Zambales	39 Aklan	63 Davao del Norte
16 Tarlac	40 Capiz	64 Davao Oriental
17 Nueva Ecija	41 Antique	65 Davao del Sur
18 Pampanga	42 Iloilo	66 Sultan Kudarat
19 Bulacan	43 Leyte	67 Maguidanao
20 Bataan	44 Leyte, Southern	68 Cotabato North
21 Rizal	45 Cebu	69 Cotabato South
22 Cavite	46 Palawan	70 Basilan
23 Laguna	47 Negros Occidental	71 Sulu
24 Quezon	48 Negros Oriental	72 Tawi-tawi

Provinces

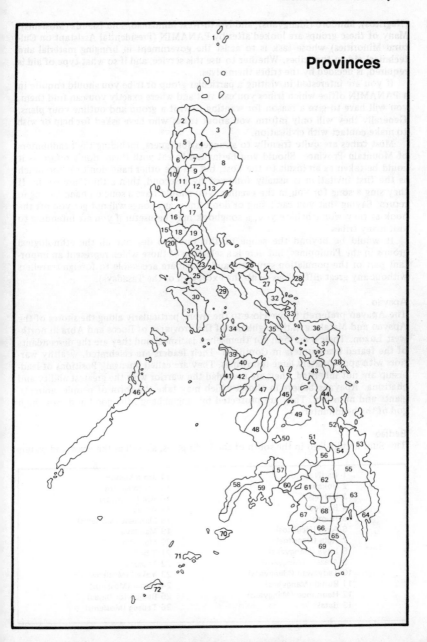

(Negritos), Mindoro (Mangyans), and North-West Mindanao/Sulu Islands (Moslems). Many of these groups are looked after by PANAMIN (Presidential Assistant on Cultural Minorities) whose task is to assist the government in bringing material and technical aid to the tribes. Whether to use this service, and if so what type of aid is required, is decided by the tribes themselves.

If you are interested in visiting a particular group or tribe you should enquire in a PANAMIN office which tribes you can visit and where exactly you can find them, you will have to give a reason for wanting to visit a group and outline your plans. Generally they will only inform you about tribes who have asked for help or wish to make contact with civilisation.

Most tribes are quite friendly to strangers/foreigners, including the headhunters of Mountain Province. Should you be invited to eat with them, don't refuse as it could be taken as an insult to the host, but on the other hand don't eat too much as the first invitation is usually followed by a second, then a third and so on. If they sing a song for you in the evening, you should have a song on hand to sing in return. Saying that you can't sing or don't know any songs will not get you off the hook as they won't believe you, a songbook may be useful if you are intending to visit many tribes.

It would be beyond the scope of this book to describe all the ethnological groups in the Philippines, but here is a selection of those which represent an important part of the population structure and which are accessible to foreign travellers without any great difficulties (with the exception of the Tasadays).

Apayao

The Apayao preferred to live close to the rivers, particularly along the shores of the Apayao and Matalang in the highlands of the provinces of Ilocos and Abra in north-west Luzon. Their own term for themselves is 'isneg' and they are the descendants of the feared headhunters in Cordillera. Their leaders are celebrated, wealthy warriors with appropriately large followings. They are called 'mengal'. Positions of leadership are not inherited, they are accorded the warrior with the greatest ability and charisma. Apayaos believe in ghosts which may take the form of people, animals, giants and monsters. They are protected by 'anglabbang', the good and most high god of the headhunters.

Badjao

The Sulu archipelago in the south of the Philippines, as well as the coast and waters

1 Ita (Negritos)	14 Jama Mapun
2 Ilokano	15 Ati (Negritos)
3 Kalinga	16 Ata (Negritos)
4 Bontoc	17 Waray
5 Ifugao	18 Maranaw (Moslems)
6 Ayta (Negritos)	19 Mandaya
7 Agta (Negritos)	20 Mansaka
8 Iraya (Mangyans)	21 T'boli
9 Alagan (Mangyans)	22 Tasaday
10 Tadyawan (Mangyans)	23 Yakan (Moslems)
11 Buhid (Mangyans)	24 Samal (Moslems)
12 Haunanoo (Mangyans)	25 Badjao (or Bajau)
13 Batak	26 Tausug (Moslems)

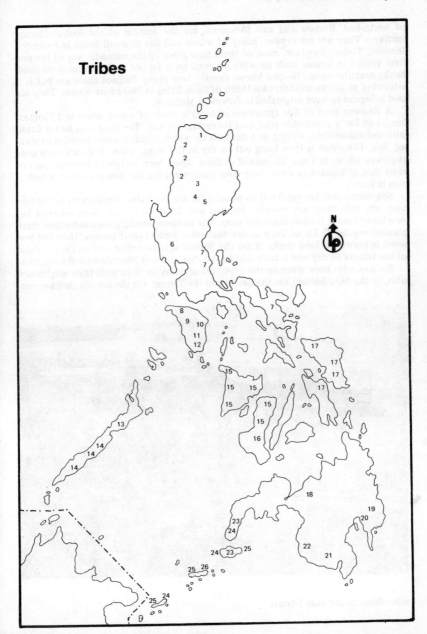

Tribes

of north-east Borneo and east Indonesia, are the domain of the Badjao (Bajau, Badjaw). They are sea-gypsies, many of whom still live in small boats as extended families. Today, however, most of them have given up the nomadic way of life and have settled in houses built on stilts on coral reefs far out in the ocean or on sandbanks near the coast. No-one knows exactly how many Badjaos there are but it is estimated at about 30,000; two thirds of them living in Philippine waters. They are said in legend to have originated in Johore in Malaysia.

A Badjaon boat or lipa (pronounced lepa) is made of wood, seven to 12 metres long, and has a removable roof over its central section. The long thin hull is fitted with individual slats, serving as a flat base on which to stand when spearing or staking fish. The catch is then hung out to dry in the stern. There is a little oven over the stern where fish can be cooked or fried. Apart from seafood a principle part of their diet is kassava, a nourishing stew prepared using the kassava tuber, which is rich in starch.

Sea cucumbers are gathered to be sold for use in Chinese restaurants but before they are sold they are cooked, cleaned and dried. In recent years seaweed has developed into a further tradeable crop. The Badjaos, having grown sedentary, have planted regular fields of crop under the water around their homes. Here the seaweed is grown on long stalks. After the harvest it is stretched out on the platform of the villages to dry and is later sold to the chemical and pharmaceutical industries.

Badjaos who have given up the gypsy life-style try to fit in with their neighbours who, in the Sulu Islands, are the Samal and the Tausug. On the sea the Badjaos con-

stilt village in the Sulu Islands

sider themselves part of a mystical animist world, which is ruled by the great god Tuhan, but closer to land many have adopted Islam. Despite Mecca they are still afraid of *saitan*, the spirit of the winds, the fish, the trees, the hills and so on, because these will cause sickness if they are angy. Only the *jin*, a sort of magician or medicine man, can make contact with them and try to appease them to drive them out and thereby eventually to heal the sick.

A marriage celebration lasts for two days and only takes place on the full moon. The whole village joins in. After much clanging of *kulintangan* (xylophones), *tambol* (drums) and *agung* (gongs) men and women dance the *igal*, a traditional dance. Polygamy is allowed but is seldom practised. Couples rarely have more than five children. The dead are buried on special islands which serve as graveyards and are only visited for burials. Because contact with the spirits of the dead is maintained, the sea people are tied to the land. Before burial the corpse is washed and wrapped in a white sheet. As well as personal treasures, provisions are placed in the grave for the journey to the beyond.

Batak

Bataks are semi-nomadic hunter-gatherers. They live together in numerous little groups in the hills and coastal regions of north-east Palawan. During the rainy season small groups join together to form larger communities. The leaders of the small groups, called 'kapitan', nominate one person, also known as 'kapitan' to lead this larger group during this time. He makes all the important decisions, such as choice of settlement, sharing of work, organisation of gathering activities and so on. During this settled period the Bataks also plant out crops.

Bontocs

The tribes of the Mountain Province (Ifugaos, Kalingas, Bontocs) in Northern Luzon are often classified together as Igorots. Trinidad Pardo de Tavera, a Philippine scholar, interprets this designation as 'People of the Mountains'. But since the 200,000 mountain inhabitants differ culturally quite considerably, it is not correct to regard the different tribes collectively as Igorots. It is remarkable that in the literature on the main ethnological groups of the Mountain Province it is frequently only the Bontocs who are treated in connection with the Igorots.

The Bontocs live in thoroughly organised village communities. Their houses are built close to the ground, and every village (Iti) has two further important accommodation arrangements — Ato and Olog. In the Ato live the village elders, here social and political decisions are made as well as religious ceremonies are prepared. An Ato also serves as a guest house and as sleeping quarters for young bachelors. Women are strictly prohibited from entering.

About 10 girls of marriageable age live in the Olog, a flat house with an extraordinarily small entrance. This building is taboo to married men, only bachelors are allowed to enter an Olog and spend the night with their intended wives. Before they get that far both partners must fulfill certain rules of the game, the man must promise to marry his partner in the event of pregnancy, if he doesn't keep his promise he will be socially isolated and not permitted to enter the Ologs again. The invitation and permission to spend the night together must be issued by the girl, as a sign of her consent, she 'steals' a small item of his property. Every Bontoc understands this hint, and when many tobacco pouches or pipes are purloined during the day in the village, you can bet the Ologs will be crowded that night.

The Bontocs are feared head-hunters, the justice that prevails in the mountains is strictly 'an eye for an eye — a tooth for a tooth', or more appropriately, 'a head for a head'. Tuf-ay (spear), Kalasag (shield), Kaman (head-axe) and Sangi (satchel) comprise the equipment of a warrior. The Sangi serves as a carrier for the enemy's head. When a successful warrior returns from his expedition, there is a great celebration for two days in the village. As a sign of his heroic deed the hero is tattooed on the chest, this is known as Chak-lag and is much coveted, as it symbolises strength and bravery. The tattooing on the arms of male and female Bontocs is called Pango. Fatek simply means tattoo.

Bontocs believe in a better life after death, and their funerals are not sorrowful occasions, only the heads of the family are in mourning. The most important requisite of the several days long ceremony is a death seat, the Sungachil. A short time after its demise, the dead body is placed in an upright position in the death seat, bound fast and placed so as to be visible to all passers by in front of the house, the shroud is selected according to the status of the family. Old women sing Anako, the death song, and a pig is sacrificed and eaten. After nightfall, a sort of recitation begins, called Achog, in which the life history of the dead one is reflected upon, this ritual can be quite merry as it is very difficult to get a coherent, objective account of the deeds accomplished by the deceased during his lifetime. Daybreak or exhaustion of the participants ends this part of the funeral ceremony.

The body of a decapitated warrior will be dumped without ceremony in the vicinity of a track leading to an enemy village. This stands as a reminder to the enemy village that his death will be avenged.

Kalingas

The Kalingas live northwards from the Bontocs. They are also head-hunters. Wars and head-hunting expeditions have been largely restricted through the peace pact, Budong, which they have worked out. This treaty declares above all that a Kalinga whose honour has been impugned does not lose the respect of his tribe, if, instead of beheading his enemy, he accepts a water buffalo (for example) as payment. A significant effect of this ruling is the initiation of social and family ties between different groups.

Like the Bontocs, the Kalingas also have a house for the men and village elders. They call it Dapay. However there is not a typical house for marriageable girls and women, it can be any house which is indistinguishable from the others, from the outside; the Kalinga name for it is the Ebgan. Here the evening courtship takes place, the initiation songs are sung, stories told or flutes played. Successful suitors spend the night with their ladies in the Ebgan and both partners have the opportunity to consider a common future together. If they decide to separate the event of a pregnancy is no hindrance, there are no disadvantages for the parents or the child who is later declared legitimate by the tribal community.

A marriage is prepared for over a long period by different ritual acts. Earthquakes, landslides and other bad omens can draw out the required ceremonies for months. When all the formalities have at last been accomplished, a house is built for the engaged couple. Marriages can only be celebrated in March, September or October, as, according to Kalinga tradition, these months, called Dadawak, are the only times when marriages are allowed.

Ifugaos

The most spectacular of the tribes of the Philippines are the Ifugaos. They are the builders of the gigantic rice terraces of Banaue (Banawe) and the surrounding area. In the last 2000 years they have shaped a technical and architectural masterpiece with bare hands and primitive tools. The imposing terrace landscape was constructed step by step from the bottoms of the valleys up to heights of 1000 metres or more. There are productive rice fields with a perfectly functioning irrigation system on the steep mountain slopes. The boundary walls would, altogether, have a length of about 20,000 km. From this measurement the rice terraces of the Ifugaos exceed by far those of the Bontocs and Kalingas. With justification they are often referred to as the 'eighth wonder of the world'. The life of the Ifugaos is full of ceremonies and celebrations, at which rice wine plays an important part, whether at a funeral or at the carving up of a wild pig brought in by the hunters. They originally learned the rice wine manufacturing process from Chinese traders. Rice harvested by the full moon is preferred and in order to accelerate the process of fermentation, the rice is partly boiled in fresh, clean water. After adding a minimal quantity of sugar, the promising pot contents are emptied into an earthenware vessel, sealed and left for six months to ripen. After this period, the Ifugaos can enjoy themselves over a pleasant-tasting Tapuy, it is also possible that an undrinkable, sour liquid will result from mistakes in the manufacturing process.

Ifugaos build their houses on piles, the windowless space under the pyramid shaped roof is used as a bedroom, kitchen and store room. In order to please the gods, the skull of a sacrificed pig is fixed on the outside of the house. The greatest occasion for the sacrifice of a pig is the return of a successful headhunter. Ifugaos still practice this type of justice, for example in October 1977 an Ifugao youth was run over and fatally injured by a bus, the tribe decided that either the bus driver or a member of his family must die.

The war dance, Bangibang, is a component of this traditional vengeance, equipped with spear, shield and axe the warriors dance on the walls of the rice fields with their heads adorned with the Katlagang, a form of decoration. The person who will carry out the act of vengeance is determined by a chicken. The warriors form a circle, kill a chicken and leave it to die in the circle, the one chosen is the one in whose proximity the chicken comes to rest (dead) after its final hops and death-throes.

Ilokanos

Ilokanos are of Malay ancestry. About 200-300 BC they came through Borneo, Palawan and Mindoro to Luzon where they settled. The most significant part of the group settled the coastal strips and the adjoining mountain regions in northern and north-western Luzon.

Weak, already settled tribes like the Isnega and Tinguians could not resist the new wave of immigration and were pushed into the back lands. Before the Ilokanos were confronted with Christian beliefs they had a multi-tiered and complicated system of gods and spirits but only fragments of their superstitions have persisted and these are mainly external such as amulets and lucky charms which are generally only worn by the inhabitants of outlying Ilokano villages.

Mandayas & Mansakas

The Mandayas live in the north-east and south-east part of Davao del Norte, Mindanao. Mandaya means 'Inhabitant of the Highlands'. The Mansakas are classified ethnologically with the Mandayas, they are originally highland people who settled clearings deep in the mountains, though today many Mansakas live in the eastern coastal regions of Davao Bay.

Animism is strongly practiced by both groups as demonstrated by the many idols carved out of wood which stand in their houses and fields. Also noteworthy are the numerous examples of silver work. Hardly any other tribe of the island realm would use more silver for the production of ornaments than the Mandayas. Even more striking than the ear adornments and finger rings are the large round chain pendants which are worn by men and women and are frequently made from coins.

Mangyans

More than 50,000 Mangyans live on Mindoro. The majority of them live in the difficult to penetrate jungles of the mountainous interior. They are subdivided into the Iraya, Hanunoo, Alagan, Tadyawan, Tawbuid and Buhid. In earlier times the majority of the Mangyans lived along the coast as fishermen but later they retreated to the hills, changed their lifestyle and took up agriculture. They did not go back of their own free will but were driven back by new settlers. In their culture 'land' belongs to everyone. If someone approaches them with deeds of title these peace-loving people simply withdraw.

In the south of Mindoro there are settled Hanunoos who are often referred to as 'true Mangyans'. They have their own form of writing in an elaborate syllabic script. 'Hanunoo' means 'real' and 'true'.

Maranaos

The province Lanao del Sur in the north of Mindanao is the homeland of the Maranaos (Maranaws). They are the 'People of the Lake', of Lake Lanao. Of all the Philippine Moslem groups, the Maranaos were the last to be converted to Islam. They successfully defended themselves against all colonisation attempts by the Spaniards and Americans, for which their natural environment provided a not inconsiderable protection against unwanted foreign influences. Culture and religion have both developed without interference.

Today the Maranaos are concerned to preserve and maintain their cultural identity. Marawi City, lying on the northern tip of Lake Lanao, is an important spiritual centre for Moslems, several Islamic-oriented schools and the Mindanao State University (MSU), a southern branch of the University of the Philippines, are situated here.

Maranaos are skilled artisans and capable merchants. Cloth, wood and metal work is the second most important sector of their economy; only agriculture being more important. They have a leading position in the country in the production of brass work.

By the way — don't refer to Moslems as Moros, it is incorrect. The tag 'Moros' was first used by Spaniards who viewed the Moslems with contempt, probably because the Spaniards resented the fact that they could not bring them under their yoke, as they did with the other population groups.

Negritos

There are approximately 25,000 Negritos in the Philippines. The various tribes give themselves names like Agta, Alta, Ita, Ati, Atta and Aeta, which all mean 'man' or 'person'. They live dispersed over many islands but are principally found in East Luzon. They can readily be distinguished from all other Filipinos by their physical characteristics, they are darker and are rarely taller than 1.5 metres. Their hair is short and woolly-crinkly, often decorated with a bamboo ornament. They wear scanty clothing made out of tree-bark.

Negritos are nomads, only a few of them have settled in one place. Instead of living in solid houses they live in huts built from twigs, branches, foliage and grass. Sometimes they lay out small fields in which they plant sweet potatoes, rice and vegetables; they also hunt and gather fruit. Bows and arrows are their weapons, the arrows being mostly poison tipped.

Negritos don't have laws nor do they feel themselves bound to any authority. When decisions do have to be made, the decision of the chief of the families is accepted and followed.

Pala'wan

The Pala'wan live in the highlands of south Palawan. Their villages consist of from three to twelve houses. They are led by a number of 'panlima', who function as administrators and are meant to help maintain the peace. The Pala'wan's religion has been influenced by Hindu and Islamic elements. The highest deity is 'ampo', who is believed to pass on responsibility for the regulation of the affairs of man to his subordinate lesser gods, the 'diwats'. The practice of the religion also includes social activities such as communal dancing, singing and drinking of rice wine. A marriage is only agreed upon after lengthy negotiations between the two families concerned and is often arranged when the couple are still children.

Tasadays

The Tasadays live in the mountains deep within the tropical rainforest of the South Cotabato province, Mindanao. They were first discovered in the early '60s by a hunter named Dafal but the first 'official' meeting didn't take place until June 1971. Their good health was remarkable; from the earliest time until their discovery these semi-naked cavemen and forest dwellers lived only on the fruit they gathered and the fish, frogs, tadpoles and crabs, etc, which they caught. They had not yet discovered hunting or agriculture and used only primitive stone devices as tools.

Because of their isolation at least 50,000 years of evolution had completely bypassed them. According to some reports the 25 clan members had no contact at all with the outside world until they met Dafal. They did not even know of the existence of other groups of people outside their forest.

PANAMIN wants to protect the living space and customs of the Tasaday, so only a few scientists have, up to now, received permission to study this quite unique tribe. It's worth reading John Nance's book *The Gentle Tasaday*. It's a fascinating eye-witness account with many photos.

Tausug

The majority of Tausug live on the island of Jolo in the Sulu Archipelago. They describe themselves as 'men in the current' and were the first Filipinos to accept Islam both as a religion and as a way of life. Nevertheless traditional customs are still maintained. Thus a Tausug wedding 'pagtiaun' is amongst the richest, most colourful festivals celebrated anywhere on the Sulu Islands. The ceremonies and celebrations last a week. An important part of the activity is the 'pangalag', a wedding dance to the sound of gongs and drums.

Tausugs love freedom and are proud of their bravery. They are renowned as skilled seafarers, diligent traders and excellent businessmen. Prosperity and pride have helped make the Tausug the dominant race from Zamboanga to Sitangkai.

Their cultural wealth is exhibited through their dress, the architecture of their houses and in the style of their brass artifacts, jewellery and weapons.

Tau't Batu

The Tau't Batu are referred to as 'people of the rock'. They live in caves in the Singnapan Basin, north-west of Mount Mantalingajan, the highest peak in Palawan. They only leave their caves to hunt, gather fruit or harvest kassawa and rice in unobtrusive fields. Other forms of nutrition, such as bats and birds, are found inside the caves. Their belief demands that nature must be compensated for the death of one of the animals. Animals which have been killed will, therefore, be replaced through representation in stone or wood.

A particular social custom is 'bulun-bulun', the communal living of several families brought about through the necessity to share nourishment. The Tau't Batu were officially discovered only in 1978. In order to protect the lifestyle and habitat of this peaceful little group the Signapan Basin has been declared off-limits. This must be scrupulously respected.

T'boli woman and child

T'bolis

An estimated 60,000 T'bolis live in about 2000 square km in the south-western corner of Mindanao. The area is known as Tinuray Highlands and their cultural centre is midway between the triangle formed by the villages Surallah, Polomolok and Kiamba near Lake Sebu.

T'bolis do not have a village community structure. They live in houses set well apart from each other along the ridges of the hilly highlands. In some cases, when there are close family ties, three or four houses are clustered together. Called long-houses, or more colloquially gunu bong, they stand on two-metre high posts and are about 15 metres long and 10 metres wide. T'bolis are monogamous people, but polygamy is allowed and is sometimes practised by the more prosperous as a status symbol.

T'bolis women have a passion for decoration. They adorn themselves with or-namental combs, ear-rings, necklaces and chains, arm and foot bracelets, finger and toe rings and heavy, bell belts. You seldom see one without a head covering, either a kayab — originally a turban of abaca, more often today a simple headcloth — or a colourful s'laong kinibang. This is a large, round hat with a diameter of about half a metre. The traditional clothing of both men and women consists of T'nalak. A material woven from abaca it has a dark brown background lightened by red and beige-coloured designs. It takes several months to weave, but the weaving of the kumo, the wedding dress, takes even longer. This typical metre-long T'boli covering has great significance in the wedding ceremony.

Yakan

The Yakan live exclusively on Basilan Island in the south of the Philippines. They are peace-loving Moslems who live by agriculture and cattle breeding. The most im-portant house in a village is the 'langgal' or prayer house which is run by an 'imam'. All larger annual ceremonies take place here too. Absolutely essential elements to any festivity are music and games, a particularly thrilling sport being the water buffalo fights.

Yakan are famous as exceptional weavers. A part of their unusual traditional clothing is the 'kandit', a red belt, several metres long, which is wrapped around the hips to hold up skin-tight trousers. An adornment men wear is a colourful turban known as a 'pis' or a helmet shaped hat called a 'saruk'. Old women can still be found wearing overlong artificial fingernails known as 'suploh'.

RELIGION

The Philippines are unique for being the only Christian country in Asia, over 90% of the population claim to be Christian, over 80% Roman Catholic. The Spanish did a thorough job! Largest of the minority religions are the Moslems who are chiefly on the island of Mindanao and along the Sulu archipelago. When the Spanish arrived, toting their cross, the Moslems were just getting a toehold on the region. In the northern islands the toehold was only a small one and easily displaced but in the south the people had been firmly converted and Christianity was never able to make a strong impression.

About 4% of the Filipinos belong to the Philippine Independent Church, which was founded by Gregorio Aglipay in 1902 as a nationalist Catholic Church. The Iglesia ni Cristo is the largest community of Protestant believers, to which 4% of the population belongs. The 8% of Moslems form the Islamic bloc, principally in the south of the Philippines. Baptists, Methodists, Mormons, Jehovah Witnesses and members of other sects make up about 2%. Except for a tiny percentage of Buddhist believers the remainder of the population are animists.

HEALTH

Much progress has been made in public health since 1975, when the Ministry of

Health started an intensive programme to combat sickness and disease. Preventative measures, production of preservable food and dietary education are key points in this health campaign. Town health centres, mobile centres, mobile sickness-treatment stations, free treatment and issue of necessary medicines support the programme.

There has been a general decline in the mortality rate with the death rate of mothers and babies especially decreasing. The most significant diseases are still pneumonia, tuberculosis, heart diseases, intestinal diseases and bronchitis. Out of a total of 845 hospitals, 570 are run privately. There are 252 hospitals in Metro Manila alone, 34 of which are run by the government. Undoubtedly the best and most well known are the Medical Center and the Philippine Heart Center for Asia. Both have above average quality staff and are equipped with modern technology but the treatment of the population at large is certainly not up to this standard. There are simply too few hospitals, doctors and nurses. An intensive collaboration between the Community Development Planning Council, which has been set up for village sanitation, and the government health service can only be welcomed.

PLANTS & ANIMALS
Over 50% of the Philippine land surface is forested. Thus the Philippines belong to the vegetation-rich lands of the earth. There are some 10,000 species of trees, shrubs and ferns. Pines are dominant (in the North Luzon mountains) as are palms and bamboos (on the coast and in the flat interior).

The tropical spectrum of flowers is unique. Over 900 species of orchids are known. The Cattleys orchid is seductively beautiful. The sweet scented Sampaguita was chosen as the national flower, Filipinos like to wear chains of it about their necks.

There are no powerful predators in the Philippines, so there are a great number of small animals like the 'mouse deer' in South Palawans, a midget deer, the smallest species of red deer in the world. In Lake Buhi, South Luzon, 'sinarapan' are found, the smallest food fish in the world, not even a cm long. The 'tamaraw', a wild dwarf buffalo with relatively short horns, lives in the mountains of Mindoro. The 'tarsius', the smallest primate in existence, and the 'tabius', the second smallest, are likewise at home in the Philippines, which is unfortunate for them because so is the Philippine Eagle, the largest eagle in the world, whose dietary preference is supposed to be for small primates.

Some 850 species of birds are known. Parrots are mainly found in Palawan. Colourful butterflies are all around in Cebu, Mindanao and Palawan. The ubiquitous cockroaches and mosquitoes are also well represented in the Philippines. The latter area a favourite food of the little gecko, which is very popular as a house pet. The largest reptile of the lizard family which will be found in the Philippines is the 'monitor'. Many souvenir shops sell their remains in the form of handbags, belts and shoes.

Crocodiles are rare, though they may still exist on Siargao Island, eastwards of Surigao, in Mindanao. On the other hand there is a great variety of species of snakes, especially noteworthy are the metre-long python and the poisonous water-snake. Fish and corals are present in such a multiplicity that there wouldn't be room to detail them here. The cumbersome water buffalo, carabao, is the most important domestic animal of the Filipinos and is not for nothing called the 'Farmer's Friend'.

FORCES OF NATURE

The earth's crust, the lithosphere, is only about 70 km thick and is composed of several small and large plates. Earthquakes occur depending on the amount of friction between these horizontal plates. Among the six large plates, also called continental plates, are the Eurasian plate and the Pacific plate and in between is squeezed the small Philippine plate. Strong earthquakes are generally fairly rare here but you must reckon with light earth tremors from time to time.

The breaking points in the earth's crust are marked by deep trenches, high mountain ranges and volcanoes. The most prominent volcanic chain leads from Alaska and the Aleutian Islands, past the Siberian Kamchatka Peninsula, the Kuril Islands and Japan to the Philippines, where there are still at least 10 active volcanoes. The Mayon Volcano in south Luzon last erupted in May 1978. On 3 May the eruptions began, the strongest activity was registered on 22 May and over 20,000 people had to be evacuated.

Luzon and the northern Visayas lie in the typhoon-belt. Some of the whirlwinds wandering from the Pacific to the Chinese mainland also affect the Philippines. Typhoons often cut the electricity supply and fires frequently occur with whirlwinds. Violent weather is common in the season from June to November.

FIESTAS & FESTIVALS

There are many town fiestas which take place on the numerous national holidays over the whole year. An expensive festival is held for two or three days in honour of the appropriate patron saint. It is hard to understand how some of the families bear the financial burden as the expenses incurred bear no comparison with everyday life in the Philippines. Food and drink are offered with lavish generosity and at the end of the fiesta some visitors even get the money for their journey home pressed into their hands. One or several bands are engaged and musicians and entertainers add to the atmosphere of a peoples' festival. There is also usually a beauty contest in which the contestants are heavily sponsored. Foreigners and visitors from distant towns get the same royal treatment as friends and relatives.

Here is a selection of the most important holidays.

1 January	*New Year's Day* As in western countries the new year is colourfully and loudly welcomed in, a family day.
1st Sunday in January	*Holy Three Kings Day* This is the official end of the Christmas season. The children receive their last Christmas presents on this day. In Santa Cruz and Gasan, Marinduque, the imitation kings are led on horseback through the town. Spectators throw coins and sweets (candy) to the children who run alongside the procession.
9 January	*Black Nazarene Procession* The largest procession begins early in the afternoon at Quiapo at the Catholic church. Thousands of Catholic believers crowd the streets when the 'Black Nazarene', a life size statue of Christ made of blackwood, is carried through the town.

Ati-Atihan festival in Kalibo

17 January

Constitution Day

in January

Pipigan Harvest festival in Novaliches, Rizal Province.

in January

Manerway Ritual sacrifice festival of the Bontocs in honour of the rain god.

in January

Appey Three-day thanksgiving festival of the Bontocs for a bounteous harvest.

3rd weekend in January

Ati-Atihan This is a spectacular festival in Kalibo, Panay, held in memory of the peaceful reception of the Maraynons (Malay immigrants from Borneo) by the resident Atis (Negritos) in the 13th century AD. The town shakes when the soot-blackened and splendidly costumed 'warriors' dance and whistle to the hollow beat of drums. The huge Santo Nino procession takes place around 5 pm on the Sunday afternoon.

3rd weekend in January
Sinulog — Santo Nino de Cebu The climax at the close of the week long festival of 'Pasundayag sa Sinulog' is the third Sunday in January. Groups of people, all dressed up in costume, gather around the capital building until about mid-day when they make their way to the old Lahug airport, sometimes marching, sometimes dancing the peculiar Sinulog steps and shouting 'Pit Senyor'. Sinulog is the traditional dance of the old women followers, who can also be seen dancing by themselves in front of the Basilica Minore del Santo Nino and Magellan's Cross any day of the week. Hotels are nearly always booked out on the holiday weekend.

4th weekend in January
Dinagyang This Ati-Atihan mixture of festivals takes place in Iloilo City. It is fairly organised with parades and passive spectators.

in January/February
Chinese New Year Depending upon the lunar calendar, Chinese New Year celebrations take place some time between 21 January and 19 February. There are lion dances in Manila's Chinatown.

2 February	*Feast of our Lady of Candelaria* This is a town festival with processions and parades in honour of the patron sain of Jaro, a district of the city of Iloilo.
11 February	*Feast of our Lady of Lourdes* These are celebrations held in memory of the appearance of the 'Lady of Lourdes' in Lourdes, France. They take place in Kanlaon St, Quezon City. There are processions in the evening.
14 February	*St Valentine's Day* This is a day for lovers — an important date for the romantic Filipinos. It is not officially a public holiday.
26 February	*Zamboanga Zamboanga* A festival held by and for Moslems and Christians with cultural offerings, exhibits, regattas and religious ceremonies. This festival used to be held in May and called the Bale Zamboanga Festival.
in February	*Hariraya Haji* This is the time of pilgrimages to Mecca. Moslems predominantly spend the 10th day of the 12th month of their calendar in mosques.
in February	*Saranggolahan* In many villages and towns this is the beginning of the kite-flying season. Children, adolescents and adults take part in competitions with kites of the most varied forms, colours and sizes.
in February	*Kaamulan* A come-together festival in Malaybalay (North Mindanao). Six to seven clans come to this cultural gathering in Pines View Park, dressed in tradition outfits, for dances, music and rituals. If the weather is fine it may be held in November.
in March/ April	*Moriones Festival* Around Easter there are many passion-plays in the Philippines. The most popular and most colourful is the Moriones Festival in Marinduque. The Roman Longinus, not Jesus, is the focus of the one-week play. Longinus is blind in one eye; as he pierces the right side of the crucified Jesus with his spear, blood flows out of his blind eye and suddenly he can see again with both eyes. His first sight is Christ's passage to heaven; Longinus announces the incident and must flee. The Roman warriors want to stop this 'rumour' and capture him on Easter Sunday. His execution by beheading is the climax of the play. Maundy Thursday is also part of the Easter holiday season here. On Thursday and Good Friday almost everything is closed or stops — even PAL flights. They start again on Easter Saturday.
Good Friday	*Crucifixions* The many crucifixions and scourgings which take place throughout the country have grown into a real tourist attraction. Places well-known for this are San Fernando (Pampanga), Marinduque, Manila and Jordan (Guimaras Island). In San Fernando in 1981 three men were nailed to crosses in the midday heat and erected together.

Easter crucifixions in San Fernando (Pampanga)

in March/ April	*Maulod-En-Nabi* This is Mohammed's birthday. It is a Moslem holiday with ceremonial readings from the Koran in all mosques.
9 April	*Bataan Day* This is a national remembrance day to recall the disastrous battle against the Japanese in WW II and the degrading 'Death March' on the Bataan Peninsula.
27 April	*Bahug Bahug* Magellan's landing is acted out on the beach of Mactan, Mactan Island, Cebu. There are fights in the water and so on. Be early, the re-enactment may be dependent on appropriate time factors. In 1981 it kicked off at 8 am and was all over 1½ hours later.
28 April- 1 May	*Binirayan — Handugan* Over 500 years ago 10 Malayan political fugitives from Borneo reached the Panay coast. They were made welcome by the Negrito chief Marikado and were allowed to settle in Malandog near San Jose de Buenavista. The landing and settlement are re-enacted using time-honoured costumes and decorated boats. This festival has been celebrated since 1974 but the date has tended to vary widely.
1 May	*Labor Day* This is a national holiday without any important activities.

Carabao Carroza in Pavia, Panay

3 May	*Carabao Carroza* Water buffalo races are held in Pavia, Panay. The fastest carabaos from the surrounding 18 barrios run off against each other in a final deciding race. The beauty queens are carried to the race track on festively decorated sleds. Be there by 8 am. There is a town fiesta on the following day.
6 May	*Fall of Corregidor* War veterans and other nostalgic people visit the fortified island in Manila Bay in memory of the battle in 1942.
14 & 15 May	*Carabao Festival* Two day celebration in honour of the patron saint of the settlers, San Isidro. Farmers lead decorated water buffaloes to the church square in a long procession on the afternoon of 14 May. There they kneel and are blessed. The next day the Carabao races take place. Festivals take place in Pulitan (Bulacan Province), San Isidro (Neuva Ecija Province) and Angono (Rizal Province).
15 May	*Pahiyas* The patron saint San Isidro is also honoured in Lucban and Sariya, Quezon Province. On the day of the harvest festival the house facades are attractively decorated with agricultural products. There is a procession in the afternoon.
17-19 May	*Fertility Rites* This three-day festival in Obando (Bulacan Province) is dedicated to the three patron saints of the city. The

Obando Festival is well-known for its dancing processions.

1-30 May	*Flores de Mayo — Santacruzan* Throughout the whole country, processions in honour of the Virgin Mary take place in the afternoon and evening. Young girls in white dresses decorate the Mary statues with flowers. An attractive focus of the processions in the flowering month of May are the most beautiful Filipinas of the local villages.
in June	*Davao Tribal Festival* For three days tribes from south-east Mindanao come into the city for parades, dances and cultural events.
12 June	*Independence Day* This is a national holiday with military parades.
24 June	*St John the Baptist Day* The deeds of St John the Baptist are re-enacted on this day in San Juan, Manila. Friends, relatives and curious spectators are 'baptised'. Water is thrown from and at passing cars — keep your camera in a plastic bag!
24 June	*Parade of Lechon* In Balayon, Batangas, St John's Day is celebrated with a 'suckling pig parade'.
28-30 June	*Apalit River Parade* With a boat parade the inhabitants of Apalit (Pampanga) show their reverence for St Peter.
1st Sunday in July	*Pagoda Sa Wawa* This is a river procession with the 'Holy Cross of Wawa' in the pagoda boat. It takes place in Bocaue, Bulacan Province.
4 July	*Fil-American Day* The Philippine-American Friendship Day (formerly Independence Day) is a national holiday.
29 July	*Pateros River Fiesta* Pateros, a suburb of Manila, is the centre of duck breeding. From here Manila is supplied with baluts to eat. The fiesta recalls the killing of a powerful crocodile which threatened the existence of the balut suppliers a long time ago.
1-7 August	*Dance of the Aetas* The first week of August in Bayombong, North Luzon, are characterised by the street dances of the Negritos.

A
B

a & b   Scenes at the Ati-Atihan festival, Kalibo, Panay

26 August   *Cry of Balintawak*   This is the national holiday in memory of the first revolt against the Spaniards in the year 1896.

3rd weekend   *Penafrancia Festival*   The ceremonious and colourful river festival
in September   in Naga City, South Luzon, has become a great tourist attraction. The climax is the spectacular boat parade on the Naga River in honour of the 'Blessed Virgin of Penefrancia'.

2nd weekend   *La Naval de Manila*   This procession goes along the main streets of
of October   Quezon City to the Domingo Church. It commemorates the victorious sea battle against the Dutch plunderers in the year 1646.

19 October   *Turumba Festival*   Turumba means falling, leaping, jumping, skipping or dancing. This is also the behaviour of the participants in the procession in Pakil, Laguna.

1 November   *All Saints' Day*   On this national holiday families meet at the cemetery and stay there the whole night. Numerous lights, candles and flowers on the graves make for an impressive experience.

15-30 November   *Yakan Harvest Festival*   This is a harvest thanksgiving festival of the Yakan tribe on Basilan Island.

23 November   *Feast of San Clemente*   This is a boat parade in Angono, Rizal.

30 November   *Hero Memorial Day*   This national holiday is also known as Bonifacio Day.

in November   *Hari Raya Poasa*   This is a Moslem holiday. The 30 day fasting period of Ramadan is finished.

in November   *Grand Canao*   Festival of the hill clans in Baguio with dances and ritual honouring of victorious warriors. Water buffalo, pigs and chickens are slaughtered and there are agricultural exhibitions and craft demonstrations.

8 December   *Feast of our Lady of the Immaculate Conception*   This is a boat procession held at night on the waters of the fishing village of Malobaon, a suburb of Manila.

12 December   *Pagsanjan Festival*   This well known town festival is another attraction of Pagsanjan in addition to the rapids and the waterfalls.

A	
B	C

Festivals

a   The Philippines — 'where Asia wears a smile'
b   Roman centurion at the Moriones Festival, Marinduque
c   Fire-eater at the Ati-Atihan Festival in Kalibo, Panay

16-25 December	*Simbang Gabi*	One can hear Christmas carols practically all over the Philippines from about the beginning of November. Officially, however, the Christmas season begins on 16 December. Following the old traditions, religious Filipinos go to night masses held before dawn. (nightmass = simbang gabi).
24 December	*Panunuluyan*	Regional nativity plays as in Cavite.
24 December	*Lantern Festival*	The most spectacular lantern parades take place in San Fernando, Pampanga. It is connected with a contest. Some of the coloured paper lanterns are so large they must be drawn by a tractor. Be at the big church by about 8 pm and you won't miss anything. After midnight mass the most beautiful lantern will be chosen.
25 December	*Christmas*	This family day, as in practically all Christian countries, is awaited with great excitement by children.
28 December	*Holy Innocent's Day*	Just as everyone plays April Fool's tricks on 1 April, so do Filipinos try to catch one another out on this day.
30 December	*Rizal Day*	National holiday with street parades in memory of the Filipino national hero Dr Jose Rizal.

LANGUAGE

Historically the waves of immigration of alien peoples (Indonesians, Chinese, Malays, etc) and the structure of the country (a series of islands) have brought about a multiplicity of languages and language groups. Today there are about 80 significantly different dialects spoken. During the period of Spanish occupation, Spanish was taught in schools and since education is mainly a prerogative of the wealthy, it developed as the language of politicians and businessmen. The influence of Spanish on the local language, though small, has not disappeared and is still present today (eg in the numerical system and in the Zamboangan language in Chavacano). Spanish was abolished in 1968 as a compulsory subject in higher schools, but is still used today as the mother tongue of a small percentage of the population, mainly the upper class.

Since in an occupied country the language of the colonial overlord often dominates, English became very important with the beginning of the American era. Since the declaration of total independence from the USA in 1946, English has remained the language of commerce and politics in the Philippines. Newspapers, television, radio announcements and even government statistics are evidence of this.

The concept of a national language was formed after the Spanish-American War in 1898 but it wasn't until 1936, a year after the formation of the Commonwealth of the Philippines, that the Insitute of National Language was established. President Manuel Quezon declared Tagalog to be the national language in that year and the appropriate bill was incorporated into the Philippine constitution in 1946. There were several other contenders for the role of the main language in this multilingual country — among them the speakers of Cebuano, Hiligaynon and Ilocano, none of whom were too happy with anonymity and non-representation in Filipino. The compromises reached during the '70s still hold: the constitution of 1973 confirms Filipino as the main language. It is based on Tagalog but contains certain linguistic elements from the other Philippines languages. Since 1978 Filipino has been taught in schools and universities.

At present Filipino is understood by about 50% of the population, English has remained the language of the elite and Filipino that of the underprivileged. If it is the aim of the Institute of National Language to shape a national linguistic self-awareness, a possible solution may be to use Filipino as the national language used by everyone while English remains the medium for international communication.

It is not vital to know the local language as English will get you through most situations, but locals will be pleased and surprised if you have mastered even a few fragments of Filipino. The following words and phrases may help.

Some Notes on Pronunciation

In Filipino P and F are often interchanged (Filipino = Pilipino). This means that a written P can be pronounced as an F. This interchange is sometimes carried over into English by Filipinos (April = Afril) but it in no way impairs understanding.

A W written in Filipino is often pronounced as a U (Banawe = Banaue, ikaw = ikau). Double vowels are pronounced separately (paalam = pa-alam). The combination 'ng' is pronounced 'nang', 'mga' is pronounced 'manga'.

The syllable 'po' underlines courtesy towards elders and persons of respect (Salamat po, Ginang Santos).

In the words and phrases below a line under the vowel of a syllable means that this syllable is stressed. Alternative forms are given in brackets.

Greetings & Civilities

hello, greetings	mabuhay
good morning	magandang umaga
good day	magandang tanghali
good afternoon	magandang hapon
good night	magandang gabi
goodbye	paalam (adyos)
thank you	salamat
please	paki
yes/no	oo/hindi
OK	sige
only, merely, simply	lang (lamang)
again, similarly	naman
how are you?	kamusta (ka)?
good	mabuti
good thank you, and you?	
	mabuti salamat, at ikaw?
also good	mabuti rin
and	at

People & Pronouns

man	lalaki (lalake)
woman	babae
Mr	Ginoo
Mr Santos	Ginoong Santos
Mrs	Ginang
Mrs Santos	Ginang Santos
Miss	binibini
Miss Santos	Binibining Santos
unmarried (man)	binata
unmarried (woman)	dalaga
I	ako
you	ka (ikaw)
he, she	siya
they	sila
we (I and you)	tayo
we (I and others)	kami
they	kayo

Questions, Commands & Conversation

who? (singular)	sino?
who? (plural)	sinu-sino?
how?	paano?
how many?	ilang?
how much?	gaano?
what?	ano?
when?	kailan?
where?	saan?
why	bakit?
where is the post?	saan ang koreyo?
what is this/that?	ano ito?
when is it ready?	kailan matatapos?
how far is it?	gaano kalayo?
who is there?	sino iyan?
what is your name?	
	anong pangalan mo?
how old are you?	
	ilang taon ka na?
where do you come from?	
	tagasaang bayan ka?
you are beautiful!	maganda ka!
you are ugly!	pangit ka!
I like you	gusto kita
I love you	mahal kita (ini-ibig kita)
never mind	hindi bale
I don't know	aywan ko
	(hindi ko alam)
let's go	tena
	(tayo na, sige na, halika na)
I don't like	ayaw ko
what a pity	sayang

Directions & Places

left/right	kaliwa/kanan
straight on	deretso
back	paurong
here/there	dito/diyan
turn off	lumiko
stop	para
car	kotse
aircraft	eroplano
which bus for Manila?	
	aling bus ang papuntang Maynila?
where is the bus stop?	
	saan ang hintayan ng bus?
what time is it?	
	anong oras?

what town is this?	
	anong bayan ito?
how many km to...?	
	ilang kilometro hanggang....?
village	barrio
town	bayan
city	lungsod/syudad
island	isla
beach	beach
hill	burol
street	kalye
street corner	kanto
bus station	istasyon ng bus
railway station	istasyon ng tren
airport	airport
petrol station	istasyon ng gas
hotel	otel
police station	istasyon ng pulis
embassy	embassi
taxi	taksi
tricycle	traysikel
entrance	pasukan
exit	labasan

Shopping

money	pera
how much is this?	magkano ito?
do you have?	mayroon ba kayong?
expensive/cheap	mahal/mura
too expensive	masyadong mahal
anything cheaper?	
	mayroon bang mas mura?
big/small	malaki/maliit
several/few	konti pa/tama na

Accommodation

hotel	otel
room	kuwarto
bath, toilet	banyo
do you have air-con?	
	mayroon baang air-condition?
there is no water	walang tubig
how much is this?	magkano ito?

Food & Drink

I am hungry	gutom ako
I am thirsty	nauuhaw ako
breakfast	almusal

lunch	pananghalian
dinner	hapunan
delicious	masarap
knife	kutsilyo
fork	tinidor
spoon	kutsara
rice (uncooked)	bigas
rice (cooked)	kanin
fish	isda
meat	karne
soup	sabaw
salad	insalada
vegetables	gulay
potatoes	patatas
onions	sibuyas
eggs	itlog
bread	tinapay
salt	asin
pepper	paminta
sugar	asukal
sweet	matamis
beer	cervesa
wine	alak
water	tubig
coffee	kape
black coffee	kapeng matapang
milk	gatas
tea	tsa
banana	saging
coconut (ripe)	niyog
coconut (unripe)	buko
pineapple	pinya
mango	mangga
hot	mainit
cold	malamig
this is cold	malamig ito
I want rice & fish	
	gusto ko ng kanin at isda
bill	chit
the bill please	
	akina ang kuwenta ko
	(magkano)

Days & Times

Monday	Lunes
Tuesday	Martes
Wednesday	Miyerkoles
Thursday	Huwebes
Friday	Biyernes
Saturday	Sabado
Sunday	Linggo
today	sa araw na ito
tomorrow	bukas
everyday	araw araw
night	gabi
tonight	ngayong gabi
anytime	maski kailan
when?	kailan?
now	ngayon
a day	isang araw
a night	isang gabi
day & night	araw-gabi
every night	gabi-gabi
every day	araw-araw
every Thursday	tuwing Huwebes
every afternoon	tuwing hapon
day before yesterday	
	noong kamakalawa
yesterday	kahapon
today	ngayon
tomorrow	bukas
day after tomorrow	sa makalawa

Weeks

week	linggo
last week	noong nakaraang linggo
this week	ngayong linggong ito
next week	sa linggong darating

Months

month	buwan
January	Enero
February	Pebrero
March	Marso
April	Abril
May	Mayo
June	Hunyo
July	Hulyo
August	Agosto
September	Setyembre
October	Oktubre
November	Nobyembre
December	Disyembre

a month	isang buwan	brown (leather)	kayumanggi
this month	ngayong buwang ito	yellow	dilaw (dilau)
year	taon	grey	gris
a year	isang taon	green	berde
every year	taon-taon	orange	kulay-dalandan
		red	pula
Colours		black	itim
blue	asul	white	puti
brown	kulay-kape		

Numbers

0	sero/wala	70	sitenta, setenta/pitumpu
1	uno/isa	80	osenta/walampu
2	dos/dalawa	90	nobenta/siyamnapu
3	tres/tatlo	100	siyento/isang daan
4	kuwatro/apat	101	siyento uno/
5	singko/lima		isang daan at isa
6	sais/anim	200	dosyentos/dalawang daan
7	siyete/pito	201	dosyentos uno/
8	otso/walo		dalawang daan at isa
9	nuwebe/siyam	500	kiyentos/limang daan
10	diyes/sampu	1000	mil/isang libo
11	onse/labing-isa		
12	dose/labindalawa	1 pound	isang libra
13	trese/labintatlo	2 peso	dalawang piso
20	beynte/dalawampu	3 km	tatlong kilometro
21	beynte uno/	5 litre	limang litro
	dalawampu't isa	10 cubic metres	
22	beynte dos/		sampung metro kibiko
	dalawampu't dalawa		
30	treynta/tatlumpu	1/2	kalahati
31	treynta'y uno/	1/3	isang-katlo
	tatlumpu't isa	1/4	isang-kapat
40	kuwarenta/apatnapu	3/5	tatlong-kalima
41	kuwarenta'y uno/		
	apatnapu't isa	once	minsan
50	singkuwenta/limampu	twice	makalawa
60	sisenta, sesenta/anumnapu	three times	makatatlo
		often	madalas
		seldom	bihira

As well as the spoken and written language, the Filipinos use various gestures and signs. The hand movements which mean 'go away' to us signifies 'come here' in the Philippines. The short raising of the eyebrows is generally meant positively. One hisses to gain attention, for example when calling a waitress. The thumb is not used to indicate numbers, you indicate two beers always with the ring finger and the little finger. Instead of pointing with your finger one indicates discreetly by pointing pursed lips in the particular direction. Turo turo food, incidentally, means 'point point' — there is no menu so you must point out what you want! When you want to pay the bill look out for the waitress and 'draw' a rectangle in the air with index finger and thumb. Should the waitress be looking the other way then just use a short hiss. The bill in a restaurant is the 'chit'.

Facts for the Visitor

VISAS

Visas for the Philippines are somewhat confusing. Basically the story is that most western nationalities do not need visas so long as they are not staying for more than 21 days and they arrive with a ticket out of the Philippines clasped in their hand. If you do want a visa you can get one allowing an initial stay of 59 days. This visa is free if you're American, Australian or a New Zealander but for most European nationalities you have to pay for it and how much it costs depends on where you get it. The cost can vary from as little as US$1 to US$10 or more. In Hong Kong, for example, they're US$3 while in Jakarta the fee is US$13!

An alternative is to extend your 21 day stay while in the Philippines although this is also rather expensive. Initially you're allowed a 38-day extension, to bring you up to the 59-day stay which visa holders are permitted. This costs P82 and involves a bit of paper shuffling at the Commission of Immigration & Deportation, Magallanes Drive, Intramuros, Manila.

Note that you are only able to extend your stay permit or visa in Manila — there is no other office anywhere in the country. If you're unable to return to Manila it is generally possible to apply for an extension by mail — explain your non-appearance in writing (sightseeing tour or whatever) and send this letter together with a photocopy of your passport by registered mail to the immigration department. It helps to have the application letter stamped and signed by some official such as the police or a town mayor. For safety's sake you should also keep a copy of your application for extension.

You can extend again beyond 59 days, by the month for up to a year, but the process is much more complicated and expensive. The first extension costs a total of P175 made up of P25 head tax, P50 alien registration, P80 visa extension fee and P20 for the first month's extension. Each additional month costs a further P20. Once you've had your visa extended you also need an Immigration Clearance which costs a further P52 for more than two months and is checked before you leave the country.

If you stay longer than six months you also need a Court Clearance from the immigration office and after a year you need a Tax Clearance (another P38) which necessitates a trip out to the Bureau of Internal Revenue in Quezon City. Plus you are up for an exit tax of about P600 after one year. You're not allowed to leave the country without all the proper bits of paper and receipts so if you're staying a long time you'd better take it seriously.

At the immigration department the steps for extending your visa are as follows:

Get a form and fill it out.
Have the form stamped in room 105.
Hand over the form and your passport in room 204, wait.
Hand over all the documents at the left counter.
Go away, the next step can take several hours.
Collect the documents later that day or the next.
Pay at the right counter.
Show the payment receipt at the left counter and have your passport stamped.
Get your Immigration Clearance at the right counter.

MONEY

Australia	A$1	= P8.4	P1	=	A$0.12
USA	US$1	= P9.8	P1	=	US$0.10
UK	£1	= P14.7	P1	=	£0.07
Netherlands	fl 1	= P3.5	P1	=	fl 0.28
New Zealand	NZ$1	= P6.4	P1	=	NZ$0.16
Canada	C$1	= P7.9	P1	=	C$0.13
Singapore	S$1	= P4.6	P1	=	S$0.22
Hong Kong	HK$1	= P1.4	P1	=	HK$0.69
Japan	y100	= P4.0	P1	=	y25

The Philippines currency is the peso (P) — correctly spelt piso but always referred to as the peso. It's divided up into 100 centavos (c). There are coins of 1, 5, 10, 25 and 50 centavos and of 1 and 5 peso but the 5 peso coin is rare. Banknotes are available in deonominations of 2, 5, 10, 20, 50 and 100 pesos. At present there are still some old coins in circulation which can be a little confusing since the old 50c coins are very similar in size to the new P1 coin. Take care.

The US dollar is far and away the most recognised foreign currency in the Philippines. Bank of America and American Express travellers' cheques are probably the most widely accepted — you can change them at most banks but especially the Philippine National Bank (PNB). Although the safety consideration with travellers' cheques applies as much in the Philippines as anywhere else, cash (dollars) does, as usual, have its uses. You will often find it easier to change a small amount of cash rather than a cheque.

There is a fairly active black market with a small increment over the official rate. It is usually better for large denomination bills (US$100) than for smaller notes. A US$1 note has no blackmarket value. You also get a better rate through the official money changers than the banks. Note, however, that the rate is best in Manila, dwindling away as you get further from the capital. In some smaller regional towns there may be no bank at all and the only possibility of changing money may be at a hotel and then only at a poor exchange rate. Money changers are often rather faster and more efficient than banks although it's wise to shop around since their rates do vary. When you do change money try to get a reasonable amount of it in smaller denominations. In more remote areas it can be difficult to change even P100 notes.

Pesos can be bought at a good discount in overseas money markets such as Hong Kong or Singapore. Getting money transferred to the Philippines can be a painfully slow process. Even by telex it can take 10 days or more. In Manila use the European Asean Bank in Makati (fast and reliable), American Express or the Philippine National Bank. The Bank of America tends to be slow. Amex card holders can get US$1000 in travellers' cheques every 21 days on their card account. Up to 20% of it can be taken in cash.

On departure you can take up to P500 out with you and unused peso can be reconverted, but only if you have receipts from banks or official money changers to back it up. The bank counter is in the exit hall of the Manila International Airport. One traveller advised keeping enough pesos for taxi fares and departure tax but not arriving at the airport with too much money. In his case on a Sunday night when a PAL and a Qantas flight left for Australia at the same time the bank simply did not have enough Australian dollars to meet demand. In that situation you are probably better changing into US dollars or another hard currency, rather than trying to change peso overseas at a bad rate.

CLIMATE

The Philippines are typically tropical — hot and humid year round. Although the actual weather pattern is fairly complex it can be roughly divided into January to June dry and July to December wet. January is usually the coolest month and May usually the hottest but the temperature is not far off 25°C (80°F) year round.

December to February is the 'cool dry' while March to May is the 'hot dry'. You can count on rain every day in July, August and September. In May Manila usually has daytime temperatures of 35-40°C and at night it doesn't drop much below 27°C. This is the time of year when rich citizens of Manila head for the perpetual spring of Baguio and the mountain provinces.

All in all mid-January to mid-May is probably the best time for travelling in the Philippines but in some places it seems to rain year round and in others hardly at all. The Philippines are subject to typhoons which usually come with the wet, monsoon season from May to November. The south-west Visayas and Mindanao lie beneath the typhoon belt. Typhoons usually blow in from the south-east.

BOOKS & BOOKSHOPS

Manila has a good selection of bookshops — see the Manila section for details. There is a fairly active local publishing industry, mainly in English. Books on the Philippines tend to fall into either the coffee table variety or the rather dry facts and history group.

For a detailed overall look at the Philippines try the *Insight Guide to the Philippines* (Apa Productions, Singapore). It has excellent photographs and an informative text but is much less detailed on the Visayas and Palawan than on Manila and Luzon. Road maps covering the whole of the Philippines are issed by Petron and Mobil. Petron's *The Philippine Motorists' Road Guide* is available from most bookshops and the 7th edition was available in 1981. The map by Heinrich Engeler, available from the National Book Store, is recommended for Manila, Metro Manila and the area within a 50 km radius. Detailed maps and sea charts can be obtained from the Bureau of Coast & Geodetic Survey office.

A handy, easy-to-carry Filipino/English dictionary is *The New Dictionary* by Marie O de Guzman.

Interesting books to look for on specific Filipino topics include *The Truth behind Faith Healing in the Philippines* by Jaime T Licauco. *The Yakans of Basilan Island* by Andrew D Sherfan or *T'boli Art* by Gabriel S Casal will be of interest to those wanting more information on the people of Mindanao and the south.

Amongst the history books is *A Short History of the Philippines* by Teodoro Agoncillo, *The Philippines* by Onofre D Corpuz and *Readings in Philippine History* by Horacio de la Costa — the latter is good if you're not too fond of formal history. *The Philippines — Shattered Showcase of Democracy in Asia* by Beth Day is a good round up of Philippine history from the Spanish days up to martial law, and very sympathetic to Marcos. *For Every Tear a Victory* by Hartzell Spence is said to be the best Marcos biography. *Shadows on the Land — An Economic Geography of the Philippines* by Robert E Huke may also be of interest.

MASS MEDIA

The national daily newspapers with the largest circulation are the *Bulletin Today*, *Philippine Daily Express*, *Times Journal* and *Evening Express*. They appear in the English language and have a combined circulation of about 500,000. They are scarcely distinguishable from one another in content. Uncritical reports of the activities of the government are dominant. International politics are treated as second class news. If you want to know more you can get *Newsweek, Time, Asiaweek* or the *Far Eastern Economic Review*. Up to now Filipino language newspapers have played a subordinate role to the English language ones in range and in circulation.

The number of comics published and read each week is quite phenomenal. Radio and television operate on a commercial basis and the programmes are continually being interrupted by advertisements. After a five-year test phase, colour television was introduced in 1972. Out of a total of 22 television stations, five transmit from Manila. The programmes are predominantly broadcast in English.

HEALTH
In line with other Asian countries smallpox and cholera immunisation is being phased out as an entry requirement, unless you have come from an infected area. You may still feel it is worthwhile to get cholera protection and to be vaccinated against typhoid and tetanus. Malarial mosquitoes are still rife in some area, particularly Palawan and Mindanao, so bring anti-malarials with you and take them regularly. There are various forms of anti-malarial prophylactics now, ask your doctor for advice. They generally have to be taken for a period before you depart and after you return.

As in Bangkok men intent on sampling the Philippines' sexual delights should be aware of the considerable dangers of contracting that well known 'social disease' — VD. It's widely available in the Philippines, particularly in Manila, and in a variety of forms, some of them resistant to normal treatment. Beware of the water in more remote parts of the Philippines. If you have to drink water from rivers, lakes or ponds make sure it is boiled for at least 15 minutes. Or add suitable chemical purifiers.

ART & CULTURE
The Philippines have developed a mixed culture from the historical blending of foreign influences with native elements. The ability of the Filipinos to improvise and copy is very apparent, you need only see how the army jeeps left by the Americans have been converted into colourful, shining-chrome taxis. What would a jeepney be like without 'stereo-disco-sound' and what would a Philippines town be like without jeepneys?

Pop and folk music from the west is perfectly imitated by the local bands, which is one reason why Filipino musicians are in great demand in South-East Asia from Jakarta all the way to Tokyo.

The small gallery shops in the tourist belt of Ermita reflect the high level of Filipino painting; from impressionism to realism virtually all styles are represented. Handicrafts of natural fibres, shells, brass and wood show the technical and formal crafts and abilities of these talented people.

CINEMAS
Cinemas are good value — for a few pesos you get a double feature. There are particular starting times but no fixed entry times, which means there is constant coming and going during the programmes. Disaster movies, murders and vampires are the preferred themes. Watch out for the national anthem — sometimes they play it at the end, sometimes at the beginning, usually not at all. If they do play it all the Filipinos will stand up. It's best to join them.

Filipino films are produced in great number, dealing mainly with variations on the themes of violence and cliched love stories. Productions like *Mababangong Bangungot* by Kidlat Tahimik are rare. This socially critical film was screened overseas under the title *The Perfumed Nightmare*. In 1982 the Manila film festival was held for the first time at the Convention Center but it's unlikely to rival Cannes!

SPORTS & GAMES

The Filipinos are sports enthusiasts but although basketball is their favourite sport (there has been a professional league since 1975), the real passion is reserved for games involving betting. Many pesos are risked at jai-alai and cockfights. Jai-alai (pronounced 'high-aligh') is a frantically fast ball game played in a court rather like a squash court. The players have a shovel-like holder called the 'cesta' with which they hurl a small, hard ball called the 'pelota' against the wall. Their opponent must try to catch the rebounding ball and then hurl it back. The final winner is decided by a knock-out competition and bets are placed on the first place winner. Manila and Cebu have jai-alai courts, which are known as 'frontons', and games are played every evening except on Sundays and public holidays.

Anyone who wants to bet on those days can go to a cockfight, also called a 'sabong'. The fights take place in the wooden arena known as a cockpit and there is great acitivity as early as 8 am. Before each fight several 'kristos' come into the ring to encourage the spectators to part with their money and to take the bets. They use a sign language for betting and, amazingly, nothing is noted down — it's all committed to memory. Four fingers raised means P40, horizontal fingers signify hunders and fingers pointed downwards means thousands — but check this first!

While bets are being taken the very expensive cocks are brought out and stirred up for the fight. Like boxers they fight in different weight classes. Each cock is equipped with a razor sharp spur fastened behind the leg. Bouts last only a few seconds before the loser is crippled or killed.

NIGHTLIFE

The Filipinos are very keen on their nightlife — it certainly does not depend solely on tourists. There are bars, clubs and massage parlours in the provinces where foreigners seldom or never go but in the big cities tourism has certainly contributed to the booming nightlife.

Although they are more enticing after dark you can, of course, frequent the bars during the day, however, a serious drinker will hang on to his money until the happy hour when the price of beer is reduced. Most nightclubs demand a cover charge and/or a table charge. That's your financial contribution towards the entertainment — music or a show. It's justifiable if there's a good programme but it's also advisable to enquire beforehand how much you are likely to be up for in the end. The bars and clubs of the big hotels can be excellent places for meeting people.

There are many bars with 'hospitality girls' always ready for a 'chat' and happy to let you buy them a 'lady's drink' — which is usually little more than cola and four times as expensive as beer! The bar and the girls both profit from this. In an expensive club conversation with one of the hostesses can cost P30 to 50 an hour — not bad for the oratorical abilities of the young 'student'. If men want to take the hospitality girls out of the bar for possible further hospitality there will be a 'bar fine' to be paid. This can range from P50 to much, much more. Western women should not be misled by notices saying 'unescorted ladies not allowed', it only refers to the local professionals.

The private operators are called streetwalkers or, more picturesquely, 'hunting girls' — parks and open-air restaurants are their hunting grounds and they work around the clock. Some of these short-timers have made a lot of money in a short period of time; with the customers the opposite is true. Manila has a somewhat similar reputation to Bangkok and both share a particularly virulent form of VD. Any 'cultural interchange' of an intimate nature should be accompanied by suitable precautions. According to *Bulletin Today* in 1981 a team of specialist doctors had to be flow in from Texas to try to combat a particularly resistant 'unspecified' disease at Angeles — the USAF Clark Air Base.

FILM & PHOTOGRAPHY
Take sufficient film with you, there is not a lot of choice in the Philippines and you certainly won't save any money by buying locally. Take particular note of the 'use by' date if you are forced to buy film locally. Officially you are only allowed to bring five reels of film in with you but the customs people usually turn a blind eye to tourists.

The usual rules for tropical photography apply in the Philippines. Remember to allow for the intensity of the tropical light, try to keep your film as cool and dry as possible, have it developed as soon as possible after exposure. Remember that cameras can be one of the most invasive and unpleasant reminders of the impact of tourism — it's polite to ask people before you photograph them. A smile always helps. Although airport x-ray security equipment is said to be safe for films that doesn't apply to frequent x-rays. If you're going to be passing through airport security checks on a great number of occasions it's wise to remove your film from your bag and have it inspected separately.

POST
The Filipino postal system is generally quite efficient. You can get mail sent to you at poste restantes at the head post office in all the major towns. Make sure your surname is printed clearly and underlined — most missing letters to post office poste restantes are simply misfiled under Christian names. You can also have mail sent to American Express if you're using Amex travellers' cheques or carry an Amex Card. American Express have offices in the Philippines in Manila and Makati and at Angeles City (for the big US base there). The Manila address is Clients' Mail, American Express, Philamlife Building, UN Avenue & Maria Orosa St, Manila.

If you are sending important items out by mail, such as film, it is best to send it by registered post. Parcels have to be wrapped with brown paper and secured with string as well. Although the postal service is usually quite OK it is not recommended that you send money through the mail. Letters with banknotes inside tend to mysteriously disappear, even if they are registered.

Stamp collectors should visit the main post office in Manila where you can get special release stamps from a room at the rear of the building on the left.

TELEPHONE
There are PLDT (Philippines Long Distance Telephone Company) offices at Escolta St and Taft Avenue in Manila as well as at other central locations. You can also make international calls from the Manila Hilton but there is a 25% surcharge for non-guests. Note that it is far cheaper to make station-to-station rather than person-to-person calls from the Philippines. The charges are about 25% less. Phone numbers in the Philippines changes frequently so check them again in a phone book before ringing.

TELEGRAMS
The international telegram service is pretty prompt and reliable. There are several telegram companies. To overseas destinations 12-hour telegrams cost around P4 a word. Within the Philippines a telegram to Cebu from Manila, for example, costs around 65c a word and takes five hours.

ELECTRICITY
Electric current is generally 220 volts, 60 cycles although the actual voltage is often less, particularly in some provinces. In some areas the standard current is US-style 110 volts. Blackouts are common outside the tourist centres, which are usually protected from such inconvenience. An adapter may be needed for Filipino plugs which are usually like the US flat two-pin type.

TIME
The Philippines are eight hours ahead of GMT, two hours behind Australian Eastern Standard Time. Time is not taken too seriously in the Philippines.

BUSINESS HOURS
Businesses and factories open their doors to the public between 8 am and 10 am. Offices, banks and public authorities have a five-day week. Some offices are also open on Saturday mornings. Banks close at 4 pm, offices and public authorities at 5 pm. Large businesses like department stores and supermarkets continue until 7 pm, smaller shops often until 10 pm.

PLACES TO STAY
Have a look at the hotel room before you book in, inspect the showers and toilets and only then pay for the room. There are often cheaper rooms in the inner part of the building without windows.

As there are lots of fires in the Philippines you should check the exits. Having lived through a fire with useless fire equipment, been left hanging between floors in an elevator several times due to power blackouts and having had to evacuate from a hotel due to an earthquake in Baguio, I've developed a preference for rooms on the ground floor. That may perhaps seem to be somewhat wary.

If you do deposit your valuables in the hotel safe get a receipt with an exact account of the details. Also enquire as to whether you can get them back at any time. The night shift is not always entrusted with a key.

If you intend staying anywhere for some time enquire about weekly and monthly rents. For a long stay it is worthwhile taking a furnished apartment. This brings down the expense a lot. Even cheaper accommodation — known as 'bedspacing' — is available on a shared room basis.

Should you have accommodation difficulties in smaller towns go to the mayor or barrio captain. He will quickly arrange some shelter for you, perhaps you could even use the government rest house.

Toilets
The toilets are known as 'comfort rooms' -- 'lalake' means gentlemen and 'babae' ladies in Filipino. The toilets in restaurants and bars are usually dirty and there is seldom toilet paper, but you will always find clean toilets in the lobbies of the larger hotels (Manila Hilton, etc). Shakey's Pizza Parlours, while their pizzas may be rather expensive, certainly have clean toilets.

FOOD & DRINK

Many western travellers regard the Philippine diet as monotonous. Dairy products are lacking and daily fare consists of rice and fish, but if you are flexible you can add some variety. There are dairy products like milk, yoghurt, cheese and ice cream in most supermarkets and meals can be varied by checking out the contents of the cooking pots in restaurants. In a Turo-Turo restaurant there is no other way of knowing exactly what dishes are available as there is no menu. Of course the range of choices is more restricted in the country than in the city. In larger towns there are usually a number of western and Chinese type restaurants.

Progressive Filipinos usually eat with spoon and fork, knives are not often used. The original mode, namely eating with the fingers, seems to be coming back into fashion, so there is no cutlery laid on the table in the *Kamayan Restaurant* in Makati. National and local personages have documented by fingerprints on the wall that they can live 'from hand to mouth'.

The following description of Filipino foods and drinks may make it a little easier to choose when confronted with a menu.

Adobong Pusit Cleaned cuttlefish is prepared with coconut milk, vinegar and garlic. The ink is used as a special seasoning.

Ampalaya con Carne Beef with bitter melon, prepared with onions, garlic, soy-sauce and some sesame oil. Served with rice.

Asado Seasonal smoked meat, served with sour papaya strips.

Aso Dog! Stray mongrel in a piquant sauce. This is a special dish in north and central Luzon.

Balut This is a favourite Filipino snack which can be purchased from street sellers and at markets. A balut is a half-boiled, about to hatch duck egg. You can distinguish a beak and feathers!

Some baluts still contain some liquid so don't break open the whole egg, make a small hole first.

Bangus Milkfish — this is a herring-size fish lightly grilled, stuffed and baked.

Batchoy Beef, pork and liver in noodle soup. A speciality of the western Visayas.

Calamares Fritos Fried squid.

Crispy Pata Pig skin first cooked and then seasoned with garlic, salt, pepper, vinegar, etc, and then baked crisply in oil. There are many ways of seasoning and preparing it. Crispy Pata is often served cut into small pieces. There is usually more crackling than meat!

Halo-Halo Dessert made from crushed ice mixed with coloured sweets and fruits, covered with evaporated milk.

Gambas al Ajillo Raw shrimps without scales. Prepared with olive oil, pepper, salt, some paprika and a lot of garlic. Served with white bread.

Kilawan Pusit Raw cuttlefish (small) is cut and cleaned. The white meat is cut into small pieces and soaked for four to five hours in coconut milk, garlic, salt and peppercorn. Kilawan Pusit is eaten raw.

Lapu Lapu Inihaw Grilled fish, seasoned with salt, pepper, garlic and soy sauce.

Lechon Suckling pig served with a thick liver sauce. Lechon is an important dish at fiestas.

Lechon Kawali Pork leg, crisply baked and seasoned with green papaya, ginger, vinegar and sugar.

Lumpia Shanghai Small spring rolls served with soy sauce.

Mami Noodle soup with chicken is chicken mami, with beef it's beef mami, and so on.

Misua Soup Soup made from rice-noodles, beef, garlic and onions.

Pancit Guisado Dried Chinese white noodles are baked, then mixed with pork, shrimps and vegetables. The pork is cooked in soy sauce beforehand.

Pancit Canton This is a noodle dish like Pancit Guisado but spicier. Thick noodles are used, not thin Chinese ones.

Pork Adobo Baked pork is prepared with white coconut milk, garlic, peppercorns and salt. There is usually more fat than meat. It is served with rice.

Pork Apritada Pork is cut into small pieces and baked. The sauce includes pieces of tomato, onions, potatoes, pepperoni and garlic. It is served with rice.

Shrimp Rebosado Shrimps baked in butter.

Shrimp Sinigang Rice is washed several times and in the last wash shrimps are boiled with cut up tomatoes, onion rings and vinegar. The resulting soup is rather sour.

Sinigang na Baboy Like Shrimp Sinigang except pork is used instead of shrimps.

Siopao A quick snack. A white, steam-heated dough ball with a filling such as chicken or pork.

Tahong Large green mussels cooked or baked in sauce.

Talaba Raw oysters soaked in vinegar and garlic.

Tapa Baked dried beef served with raw onion rings. Tapa is also available as a vacuum packed preserved food but this tastes dreadful — remarkably similar to plastic.

Tropical Fruits

All the tropical fruits are available in the Philippines — pineapples, bananas, mangoes, papayas and so on. The season for yellow mangoes (sweet) is from March to May while lanzones (they look like small potatoes and have a delicious glassy fruit-flesh) are sold principally by street traders in Cebu City during January and February. You can also buy ground-nuts roasted and cooked and green mangoes which taste sour-bitter and are eaten with a strong fish-paste.

Calamansis are small green fruits which look like lemons and are fairly sour. They are well suited to the manufacture of a refreshing fruit drink — calamansi juice hot or cold. Papayas are sweet and ripe when the fruit is orange-yellow inside. There are large pineapple plantations in Mindanao and all fruits can be bought in the San Andres Market, Manila.

Drinks

Only young coconuts are regarded as edible in the Philippines. They are opened at the ready-to-drink stage, in order to enjoy the delicious coconut water. The flesh is still soft and very nourishing. The harder flesh of older coconuts is used for copra. Tuba is a palm wine made from the juice of coconut palms. It is tapped from the crown of the tree. Tuba is drunk fresh or after a fermentation process.

Tapuy (Tapey) is a rice wine and the end of the six-month long fermentation process is eagerly anticipated, only after this period can you discover whether the aimed for taste has been achieved or if the wine has become sour and undrinkable.

San Miguel is the excellent beer from the brewery of the same name. After a monopoly of many years standing it is now in serious competition with the beer houses of the Asia Brewery. Hard drinks — rum, whisky, gin and brandy of local manufacture — are very good value. Try the five year old Tanduay Rum.

Eating & Drinking

As a rule of thumb where the locals eat is generally good and value for money. Also the western dishes aren't always so expensive. In some restaurants you can get a complete meal for just P10.

In the larger cities there are foodstands which sell grilled meats like liver, pork, chicken or seafood at night. They're good value for these delicacies but in the hot months of April and May take the precaution of smelling the food before eating it.

You shouldn't have any health problems in the Philippines; the water is clean and drinkable, at least in the towns. In the country you should be more cautious. It is inadvisable to buy ice-cream from street vendors, preferably buy the packed Magnolia Icecream or go into one of the many Magnolia Dairy Bars.

INFORMATION

You can get up to date news and travel tips about prices, departure times and so on from other travellers. For regional information the representatives of the Ministry of Tourism (MOT) are available. Don't expect too much of them, they are friendly and helpful but not always terribly knowledgeable. As well as the MOT head office in Manila there are various overseas offices and regional field offices scattered around the country.

Overseas offices of the Philippines Ministry of Tourism include:

Australia	Suite 919-920, Tower Building, Australia Square, Sydney 2000 (tel 02 276 991/2)
Hong Kong	Philippine Trade House, D1-D2 1st Basement, Sheraton Shopping Mall, Nathan Rd, Kowloon (tel 3 667 610)
Japan	Philippine House, 11-24 Nampeidai Machi, Shibuya-ku, Tokyo (tel 03 464 3630)
	Room 352, Dojima Grand Building, 5-17 Dojima 1-Chome, Kita-ku, Osaka (tel 06 347 0700/1)
Singapore	Yen San Building, 10th floor, Room C-1, 268 Orchard Rd, Singapore 9 (tel 235 2184/5)
UK	199 Piccadilly, London W1 (tel 01 439 3481)
USA	Suite 1111, 30 North Michigan Ave, Chicago, IL 60602 (tel 312 782-1707)
	Suite 606 FIC Building, 3325 Wilshire Boulevard, Los Angeles, CA 90010 (tel 213 487-4525)
	Philippine Center, 556 Fifth Avenue, New York, NY 10036 (tel 212 575-7915)

447 Sutter St, Suite 523, San Francisco, CA 94018 (tel 415 433-6666)

Around the Philippines the local tourist offices are at:

Angeles	Dau Interchange, Mabalacat, Pampanga (tel 2213, 3016)
Baguio	Ministry of Tourism Complex, Government Pack Rd (tel 7014, 5415, 5416, 6858)
Bacolod	J C Kilayco Building, San Juan St (tel 2 7662, 2 3592)
Cagayan de Oro	Ground Floor, Marcos Sports Center Complex (tel 3340)
Cebu City	Fort San Pedro (tel 9 1503, 8 2329, 9 6518)
Davao	Apo View Hotel, J Camus St (tel 7 4861, 7 1534)
Iloilo	Sarabia Building, General Luna St (tel 7 8701, 7 5411, 7 7054)
La Union	Veterans Building, Capitol Site, San Fernando (tel 2411)
Legaspi	Penaranda Park, Albay District (tel 4492, 4026)
Marawi City	Ford Guest House No 2, Mindanao State University (tel 58 9255 & ask for MSU)
Tacloban	Children's Park, Senator Enage St (tel 2048)
Zamboanga	Lantaka Hotel, Valderosa St (tel 3931, 3247)

In Manila there are tourist offices at Nayong Pilipino, Manila International Airport and by Rizal Park. See the Manila Information section for more details.

SECURITY
Thieves abound in Manila so watch your valuables. Try not to look or act like a wealthy foreigner — a prosperous appearance is practically a provocation to those who would part you from your worldly goods. Some hints on how to guard your possessions and look after your own safety:

Money belongs in your front trouser pockets or in a pouch worn around your neck and under your clothes. Don't make it easy for pickpockets who are often very skilful.

Keep shoulderbags or camera bags in body contact, don't let them out of your sight — and develop the habit of keeping your hand underneath them, Filipino razors are quiet and quick.

At night avoid dark alleys, especially if you have been enjoying San Miguel beer or Tanduay rum.

Don't pay your taxi fare until all of your luggage has been unloaded.

Deposit valuables in the hotel safe — or rent a safe-deposit box at a large bank, it will cost P50 a year. This is recommended if you want to deposit tickets, documents, travellers' cheques, trinkets, etc, for any length of time while travelling around the country.

Look over your hotel room carefully before you check out, anything left behind becomes the property of whoever finds it.

If at any stage you should be held up — eg by a bike in a dark alley — don't try to defend yourself. Filipinos shoot quickly.

Wherever there are tourists there are trick thieves. Pickpockets and transvestites in Ermita, amateur and professional thieves in the buses to Batangas or Puerto Galera, etc. Be particularly cautious around Ermita — Mabini St and Rizal Park.

Recently there appears to have been an upsurge of thieves who specialise in robbing travellers so beware. If a complete stranger hands you a line about remembering you and suggests showing you the town or inviting you to dinner, don't accept. One line which has been used is that somebody comes up to you in Rizal Park and says he was the customs or immigration officer when you arrived at Manila Airport recently. He wasn't. Another is to say 'we're also strangers here but we know people who can show us the town together'. Invitations to a party from such a stranger will usually end up with your being drugged, robbed and abandoned there.

Be wary also of Europeans who either can't or don't want to go home and talk about 'extremely promising' ideas or having good connections. They will tell you that all they need is an investor and can assure you you're not in the least worried about how small or large the investment is. Never join a card game with Filipinos, you'll always lose. If the 'cousin' of your host allegedly works at the casino, and offers to coach you in tricks, don't be taken in. I've met people who after losing three games still haven't realised the syndicate was working against them. Finally remember that there will be new ideas and variations each year. Filipino thieves do not lack ingenuity or imagination. Don't let them spoil your holidays.

FILIPINOS & FOREIGNERS

You couldn't blame the Filipinos if they were sceptical and distant towards foreigners. As history shows, foreigners have generally not come to the Philippines with friendly intentions. In spite of this, every visitor is heartily welcomed, the Filipinos are very sociable and tolerant and their natural openness surprises many visitors.

One way this friendliness manifests itself is not always welcome, however. Since the days of the Americans every male has been tagged 'Joe' and just as in Indonesia where the constant 'hello, where are you going?' becomes a mite irritating, 'Hey Joe' becomes equally wearing. Try not to let it get you down too much, a smile and a nod may help.

One thing which Filipinos and foreigners have in common is the discovery of the Philippines as a country for travel. Since tourists and travellers have been going to the country more and more, the Filipinos' interest in their homeland has suddenly been awoken. Even so imported products are still more revered than the best locally made goods. Until recently the slogan 'See the Philippines First' would not have appealed to Filipinos with the urge and enough money to travel.

NATIONAL CLOTHING

There is no compulsion to wear either tie or suit, even at highly official political receptions. The barong tagalog is the rational alternative. It is a long-sleeved shirt which lets the air through and is worn over the trousers. Underneath it is customary to wear a T-shirt. The short sleeved style is known as a polo barong. Good quality barongs are made from pina, a fabric made from the fibres from pineapple leaves, and they are usually embroidered.

The terno is the typical Philippine dress worn by women, recognisable by its stiff butterfly sleeves. It is only taken out of the wardrobe for formal occasions. The general fashion for women follows the western trends.

THINGS TO BUY

The Philippines have many things to buy, particularly in the handicrafts line. Cane work, woodcarving, clothes and articles made of shells are all popular buys. You can find many items in Manila, particularly around Ermita, in the Quiapo Bridge market or the Shoemart department store in the Makati Commercial Centre, but good shopping opportunities can also be found in Cebu, Davao and Zamboanga.

Clothing The Philippines has become a major manufacturing centre for cheap western-style clothing but many men come away from the Philippines with the shirt which is the Filipino national dress — the long sleeve *barong tagalog* or its short sleeve version the *polo barong*. These cool, semi-transparent shirts with their fine embroidery date from the Spanish era when Filipinos were required to wear their shirts untucked — and the barong became a symbol of national consciousness. Fine barongs are made from pina, a fibre made from the pineapple plant, but cheaper ones are made of ramie.

Woodwork Much of the wood carving is of the tourist-kitsch variety but you can also find some useful articles such as salad bowls. The Ifugao tribespeople in north Luzon's Mountain Province also produces some high quality wood carving.

Cane Work & Basketry In south Luzon abaca products are the main craft; abaca is a fibre produced from a relative to the banana tree. Its best known end product was the rope known as Manila hemp but today it's made into bags, place mats and other woven products. There's some interesting basket work from the Mountain Province and also from the island of Bohol. Mats and cane furniture are also good buys.

Other Shell jewellery, wind chimes and just plain shells are all popular purchases. Zamboanga is a shell centre. The usual 'caveat emptor' applies to Filipino antiques. Brassware is a specialty in Mindanao. Hand woven cottons from the Mountain Province are produced in such limited quantitites they don't even reach Manila - they're much cheaper in Bontoc or Banaue than in Baguio too. Marble eggs and other marble items come from Romblon. Apart from the pineapple fibre fabrics, Iloilo is also noted for *santos*, statues of saints. Cebu is the guitar centre of the Philippines but note that cheap guitars are unlikely to be able to withstand drier, non-tropical climates. Lilang's Guitar Factory on Mactan Island is a good place — nice people and guitars for P60 to P1800.

THINGS TO BRING

Bring as little as possible is the golden rule — it's almost always possible to get things you might need and that's far better than carrying too much with you. A backpack is probably the best way of carrying your gear but try to thiefproof it as much as possible and remember that backpacks are prone to damage, especially by airlines where they easily get caught up on loading equipment.

The Philippines have enough climatic variations to require a fairly wide variety of clothing. At sea level you'll need lightweight gear, suitable for tropical temperatures. Up in the Mountain Provinces or if you intend to scale the odd volcano you'll need warmer clothing — sweaters and a light jacket. Bring thongs for use in hotel bathrooms and showers. A sleeping bag can be particularly useful in the Philippines, especially on overnight boat trips.

If you're a keen snorkeller then bring your mask and snorkel, there are many superb diving areas around the islands. Soap, toothpaste and other general toiletries are readily available but out in the sticks toilet paper can be difficult to find. A padlock is always worth carrying, you can often use it to add security to your hotel room. When it rains in the Philippines it really rains — a raincoat or umbrella can be useful. Other possibilities? — a sewing kit, torch (flashlight), Swiss army knife, travel alarm, mosquito net — the list goes on.

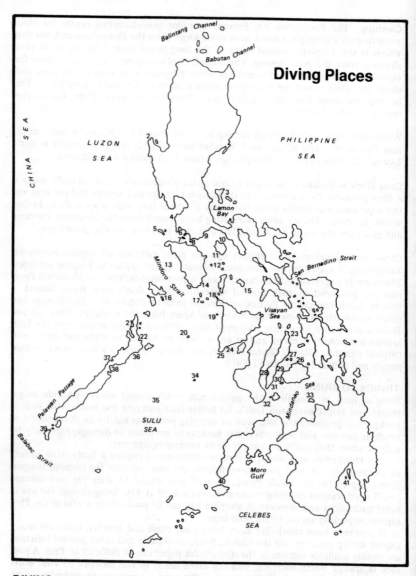

Diving Places

CHINA SEA

LUZON SEA

PHILIPPINE SEA

Balintang Channel

Babutan Channel

1

Lamon Bay

San Bernadino Strait

Mindoro Strait

Visayan Sea

Sulu Sea

Palawan Passage

Balabac Strait

Mindanao Sea

Moro Gulf

CELEBES SEA

DIVING

Diving has become a very popular activity in the Philippines. The MOT quickly recognised this trend and issued the informative *Discover the Philippines through Scuba Diving* guide. It lists 10 dive resorts, 11 dive shops and 16 agencies which

	diving place	diving season	entry point
1	Fuga Island	April-May	Fuga Island
2	Santiago Island	November-June	Bolinao
3	Polillo Island	April-October	Infanta, Jomalig, Balesin
4	Nasugbu	November-June	Nasugbu Town
5	Lubang Islands	March-June	Catalagan (Batangas Province)
6	Balayan Bay	all year	Anilao
7	Puerto Galera	all year	Batangas City
8	Verde Island	all year	Batangas City
9	Sigayan Bay	all year	San Juan
10	Mompog Island	April-October	Lucena City, Gasan
11	Tres Reyes Islands	April-October	Gasan
12	Dos Hermanas Islands	April-October	Gasan
13	Apo Reef	March-June	San Jose (Mindoro)
14	Buyallao	April-October	Mansalay
15	Cresta de Gallo	March-June	Tablas
16	Calamian Island	all year	Coron
17	Semirara Island	March-June	San Jose (Mindoro)
18	Boracay Island	all year	Kalibo
19	Batbatan Island	April-June	San Jose (Panay)
20	Cuyo Islands	March-June & October	Cuyo Town
21	Bacuit Bay	November-June	Liminancong
22	Taytay Bay	April-October	Taytay
23	Capitancillo Island	April-October	Sogod
24	Cresta de Gallo	all year	San Joaquin
25	Nagas Island	all year	San Joaquin
26	Danojan Banks	all year	Mactan
27	Mactan	all year	Cebu City
28	Pescador Island	all year	Moalboal
29	Cabilao Island	all year	Tagbilaran
30	Panglao Island	all year	Tagbilaran
31	Sumilon Island	all year	Dumaguete
32	Apo Island	all year	Dumaguete
33	Mambajao	all year	Balingoan
34	Cagayan Islands	March-June	Cagayancillo
35	Tubbataha Reef	March-June	Puerto Princesa
36	Green Island Bay	April-October	Roxas
37	Ulugan Bay	November-June	Bahile
38	Honda Bay	April-October	Puerto Princesa
39	Balabac Island	all year	Balabac
40	Santa Cruz Island	all year	Zamboanga
41	Talikud Island	all year	Davao

offer excursions. The best known of these firms is Aquaventure which organises trips to the popular Apo Reef, west of Mindoro, and the increasingly popular Tubbataha Reef in the Sulu Sea. This has a diving school connected to it. For more information you can contact the addresses given in the brochure or the Philippine Commission on Sports, Scuba Diving, Tourism Building, Agrifina Circle, Rizal Park, Manila.

Good information is also available from Heinz Pflugfelder, St Moritz Dive Shop, Gorordo Avenue, Cebu City or from Manuel V de la Riva, Dive Adventure Planning, 2169 Agno St Int 4, Malate, Manila. Another new book is *The Diver's Guide to the Philippines* by David Smith and Michael Westlake.

Getting There

ENTERING THE PHILIPPINES

Basically the Philippines has one entry point — Manila. And one entry means — by air. There are no regular shipping services into the Philippines and no regular flights to other points in the Philippines, apart from Manila. Other possible, but improbable, entry points are in Mindanao. From time to time there have been flights between Zamboanga and either Kota Kinabalu, Sandakan or Tawau in Sabah (the Malaysian state occupying the north-east corner of Borneo) or Tarakan in Kalimantan (the Indonesian state occupying the southern part of Borneo). From time to time there have also been flights between Davao in the south of Mindanao and north Sulawesi in Indonesia.

At present none of these possibilities seem to be operating. It's a case of reluctance on both sides. The Filipinos would prefer you to enter through Manila and the Indonesians and Malaysians are not very enthusiastic about you arriving in their countries through these points either. It's kind of a drag because the idea of making your way through Borneo and then making the short hop across to Mindanao in the Philippines has a lot of appeal. Instead you have to backtrack to Kota Kinabalu and make the much longer and more expensive (M\$413) flight from there to Manila. If you want to investigate the current state of play on these routes the airlines which most recently operated between Mindanao and Borneo are Swiftair, Air Mindanao and Air Sabah.

To Manila, on the other hand, you have no trouble flying to from all over. There are flights into Manila from most of the Philippines' Asian neighbours including Japan, Hong Kong, Singapore, Malaysia and so on. Plus from Papua New Guinea, Australia, New Zealand, the USA and Europe.

Arriving by Sea

Although there are so many excellent connections by ship around the Philippine Islands there are very limited possibilities of getting to the Philippines from overseas by ship. You might find a passenger-carrying freight ship out of Hong Kong or Singapore but in these containerised days it is increasingly unlikely. One place where there are regular sea connections is between Borneo and Mindanao but since it is mainly smugglers and pirates operating there you're unlikely to be too popular on arrival.

FROM AUSTRALIA

You can fly from Australia to the Philippines with Philippine Airlines (PAL) or Qantas. Philippine Airlines have one major selling point over Qantas in that if you arrive in the Philippines by PAL you can purchase domestic tickets at a 50% discount on their '1000 Islands Fare' policy. See the Getting Around section for more details. Otherwise fares to the Philippines are identical. Regular one-way economy class fares and 14/28 day excursion fares to Manila are as follows:

	economy one-way	14/28 day excursion
Brisbane	A\$ 977	A\$1047
Sydney	A\$1019	A\$1091
Melbourne	A\$1143	A\$1253

Economy class return fare is double the one-way fare. With the 14/28 day excursion you must stay a minimum of 14 days and a maximum of 28 days in the Philippines.

Alternatively there are Apex tickets both one-way and return. These must be booked and paid for 21 days prior to departure and after that time cancellation penalties apply. You must be away for at least five days and at most 12 months on the return Apex ticket. There are two fare seasons — high and low — but the high season level only applies for one month from mid-December to mid-January. Apex fares are the same from Brisbane, Sydney or Melbourne.

	low season	high season
one-way	A$502	A$608
return	A$772	A$936

FROM NEW ZEALAND

There are no direct flights between New Zealand and Manila so the regular economy fare of NZ$1165 one-way is all there is on offer. If it's any help New Zealand is currently a fairly competitive place for under the counter ticket discounting so you may find some cheaper fares.

FROM ASIA

There are lots of flights to the Philippines from its Asian neighbours. Cheap deals tend to vary these days — one day one country is cheaper, one day another. Currently it appears that Bangkok is no longer the bargain basement and that Hong Kong is the place for really good deals.

From Hong Kong the regular economy one-way fare to Manila is HK$769 and discount returns can be found for around HK$1150. From Japan the one-way is y107,000 but you can find returns for y53,000. Korea is U$401 one-way but discount fares can be found for around US$300 one-way or US$600 return.

Out of Malaysia M$693 is the regular one-way and you can fly return for M$918 with some shopping around. Out of Singapore the regular one-way is S$693 but again discount fares will be available. You can find interesting fares from these two countries via the Philippines to the USA. In Thailand the regular one-way fare from Bangkok is 7860B and discount tickets run around 5500B. From Sri Lanka you pay Rs 9122 for the regular one-way but can find discount tickets for around Rs 6400.

The chart shows typical discount one-way fares around the region in US$.

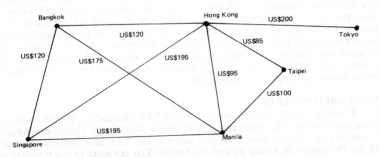

FROM EUROPE

Philippine Airlines and a number of European airlines including British Airways connect London and other major European capitals with Manila. The regular economy one-way fare London-Manila is £317 and 90-day excursion returns cost £587. You can get to Manila from London for much less by shopping around London's numerous bucket shops.

Bucket shops are travel agents who specialise in discounting airline tickets — a practise for which London is probably the world headquarters. To find out what fares are available simply scan the weekly what's on magazine *Time Out* or the give-away newspaper *Australasian Express*. Two excellent places to look for cheap tickets are Trailfinders on Earls Court Rd or STA Travel on Old Brompton Rd. Typical discount fares London-Manila are £220 one-way or £440 return.

You can also get to the Philippines cheaply from London by flying to Hong Kong and continuing from there. Competition on the London-Hong Kong route is cut throat. Although London is probably the major European centre for ticket discounting you can also find good ticket deals in Belgium and the Netherlands where exchange rate advantages help to keep the prices down.

FROM THE USA

From the west coast, Los Angeles or San Francisco, the straight one-way economy fare is US$843. This permits stop-overs en route. There's also a non-stop economy fare at US$759 and two stop-overs can be tagged on to this fare at US$25 a time. Alternatives are the excursion return ticket or Apex return ticket. Excursion returns require a 30-day minimum, 120-day maximum stay. Apex returns are 21-day minimum, 90-day maximum. You're allowed one stop-over on the excursion fare for an extra US$50. No stop-overs are permitted on the Apex ticket and payment must be made 21 days in advance, after which the usual cancellation penalties apply. Both tickets have high or low season levels:

	low season	high season
excursion return	US$1269	US$1380
Apex return	US$1024	US$1126

ROUND THE WORLD FARES

RTW fares, as round-the-world tickets are known, have become all the rage of late. Basically two or more airlines get together and offer a ticket which gets you right around the world using only their own services. You're allowed stop-overs (sometimes unlimited, sometimes not) and you have to complete the circuit within a certain period of time. Philippine Airlines offer a RTW ticket in combination with Canadian Pacific Air which will take you from Australia to the Philippines-Asia-Europe-Canada and back to Australia for A$2200. The usual Apex booking conditions apply and you have 120 days to complete the circuit. In Europe you can buy the same ticket for £1270 or for £956 if you do not include Australia — ie you fly Europe-Asia-the Philippines-Canada-Europe.

CIRCLE PACIFIC FARES

Circle Pacific Fares are really a variation on the RTW idea and once again there's an option that includes the Philippines. Continental Airlines and Philippines Airlines get together on this one which lets you combine the USA, New Zealand, Australia and the Philippines in a loop around the Pacific. You can make as many stop-overs as the two airlines' routes will permit and have up to a year to complete the loop. The ticket must be purchased at least 30 days prior to departure after which the usual cancellation penalties apply. Although you must make all reservations prior to the 30-day cut-off point you can alter flights after departure at no cost so long as a revalidation sticket on your ticket is all that's necessary. In other words you can change your flight date without penalty. If you actually want to change your route, requiring your ticket being rewritten, then there's a US$25 charge. Economy class Circle Pacific Fares are US$1700 from the USA, NZ$2110 from New Zealand or A$1612 from Australia.

GETTING AWAY

The Philippines is no place to look for cheap airline tickets. In fact, reported one traveller, with 300-plus travel agents in Manila the lack of competition is astounding. Discounts are available but you have to be persistent and must shop around. There are lots of agents around the Ermita area, particularly off Roxas Boulevard and in T M Kalaw St, by Rizal Park. You can also try the Philippines student travel association — Ystaphil (tel 52 4277) at Suite 202, Marietta Apartments, 1200 Jorge Bocobo St, almost at the corner of Padre Faura St.

Typical one-way fares available include Bangkok US$200, Hong Kong US$125, Tokyo US$210, Taipei US$130, Singapore US$220. To the US there are budget fares with Pan Am, Northwest, Philippine Airlines, Korean Airlines and China Airlines. To the west coast they cost US$483 in the low season, US$531 in the high. To the east coast low is US$594, high US$654. Advance purchase fares to Australia are the only cheaper tickets available. To European destinations you can fly to London for around US$650.

When you depart Manila there is a P50 airport tax.

ARRIVING IN MANILA

When you arrive at Manila International Airport (MIA) there are the usual passport, health and customs checks. You'll then want some local money and the Comtrust Bank is behind the luggage inspection. Make sure you get some small change for things like taxis. Also behind the luggage inspection area you will find an office of the Ministry of Tourism (MOT). The friendly women there will check with hotels in Manila for room availability.

Watch out for the baggage porters at the international airport. There are lots of them, all eager to carry your luggage through customs. They demand a lot of money for this service.

For transport between the airport and the city see the Getting Around section for Manila.

Getting Around

TRISHAWS
These are bicycles with a side-car for passengers. They are becoming rarer even in the provinces, as transport becomes more motorised.

TRICYCLES
These are small motorcycles or mopeds with side-cars for passengers. They go much better than you might think. The fare must be negotiated — usually around a peso for a short ride,

CALESAS
These two-wheeled horse-cabs are still to be found in Chinatown in Manila, in Vigan, where they blend in nicely with the cityscape, and in Cebu City where they are called Tartanillas. A short stretch costs P2 to 5 per person.

JEEPNEYS
These are the most popular means of transport for short journeys. The good old jeepneys are reconstructed Jeeps which were left in the Philippines by the US Army after WW II. They are colourfully painted and the bonnets (hoods) are decorated with a multitude of mirrors and statues of horses. Jeepneys are outfitted with a seemingly always-playing cassette recorder and belong to the typical Philippine street scene. Newer jeepneys are of the Ford Fiera type — utilitarian locally manufactured pickups. Their travel route is prescribed and the fares start at 65c, more for longer journeys. When you want to get off, just bang on the roof, hiss, or yell 'para'.

TAXIS
Taxis have meters (or at least they are supposed to). Flat fare arrangements will always work out to the driver's advantage although it is said that some meters turn over rather more quickly than normal! When you first arrive in Manila there is a taxi stand in front of the airport terminal. Don't let yourself be grabbed by a porter and taken to a taxi 'just around the corner'. Let the driver know that you are familiar with what is going on, even if you're not. Then he's less likely to make any detours on the way into town. If possible take some change as there is no guarantee that the driver will have change for more than P20.

Flag down charge in taxis is P2.50 followed by 50c for the first km and 50c for each subsequent 300 metres, if it hasn't already gone up. TOMMI, the Taxicab Operators of Metro Manila, would certainly like to see it raised. The BOT, Bureau of Transportation, will agree to an increase but only when all taxis have been fitted with a modern meter which cannot be fiddled with. In spite of fines of up to P5000, countless taxis still have rigged meters. Pay particular attention to the digital price display if the driver honks the horn every few seconds. Sometimes horn and meter are linked up and the meter adds a unit every time the horn is sounded! As with taxis everywhere in Asia make sure the meter is turned on when you start.

PU-CABS
These are small taxis without meters; their minimum price is P3 for a town journey. For longer journeys you pay correspondingly more — negotiated beforehand.

RENTAL CARS

Avis has the widest choice of rent-a-cars in the Philippines and the best cars. You can rent by the day, the week or the month. The Weekender Special (Friday-Sunday) or the Bizweek Special (Monday-Friday) can be advantageous for short trips.

VW 1300s and VW Brasilias are the cheapest, and therefore often unobtainable, although they can be reserved ahead of time. They cost P175 per day plus 65c per km. Avis has several offices in Metro-Manila (eg in the Manila Hilton), in Baguio, in Cebu and in Davao.

MOTORCYCLES

Unlike Thailand or Indonesia there is no organised set-up here to hire motorbikes. If you want to rent a bike you have to ask around. In 1981 there was a German in Paranque, Manila, who leased out a Honda 125 on an hourly or daily basis. He may have acquired others since then so ring 827 4282 for details.

Alternatively look for advertisements under 'Classified Ads — Rent' in *Bulletin Today*. You can also find motorcycles for sale in the same paper, particularly the Sunday edition. You can buy a 125 — the most common bike here — for about P5000. More expensive, but better for touring, is a 350 but outside Manila parts are hard to come by.

If you do buy a bike here make sure you obtain the original:

Bill of Sale — have it drawn up by a notary.

Registration Certificate — pink paper, endorsed by the Land Transportation Commission. A number plate 'Ready for Registration' is sufficient until then.

Official receipt — you need this for the finance office. It is available at the Bureau of Land Transportation. Costs for registration, number plate, etc, amount to about P25.

If you want to sell your motorcycle before leaving the country, you'll be paid in pesos. These can only be exchanged at a loss on the market. It is recommended that you convert dollars into pesos before you buy. You can do this completely officially at the Central Bank which gives you a receipt of the transaction. With this receipt you can change the pesos back into dollars without problems.

Before you set off you should have an owner's manual handy. You should also take a toolset with you. If you buy a 350 you must carry a spare inner tube, puncture repair outfit, spark plugs and chain at the least. You'll also need a helmet — the Highway Police are heavy on this!

A *shipment clearance* is required for island hopping. You can get this from the Highway Police before leaving the island. You'll need a photocopy of the Bill of Sale or Registration Certificate.

BICYCLES

Although it is very dangerous on busy streets, travelling by bicycle can be another interesting way to explore the Philippines, as one traveller reported:

Bringing your own bicycle is fairly easy (Philippine Airlines took mine free) and a good way to meet people and see the country. I bicycled around Luzon and found the riding good. The mountain roads require low gear and good tires but are possible: Baguio-Bontoc took three days. Only in Manila was traffic and air pollution a problem. If taking your bicycle on a boat try to avoid extra freight costs by loading the bicycle on the boat yourself.

William Weir

AIR

Philippine Airlines (PAL) operates an extensive domestic network. Cynics insist that PAL means 'Plane Always Late'; or 'Passengers Always Late' depending on whom you listen to. There used to be a secondary domestic airline, Philippine Aerotransport, operating to smaller towns, but it was taken over by PAL and most of its routes have now been dropped.

PAL operates BAC-111 jets and YS-11 and HS-748 propjets on their routes. There are a variety of price levels. Most expensive are the 'Dayjet' flights. On some routes there will be cheaper 'Nightjet' flights where you can save money so long as you don't mind travelling between 1 and 4 am. Turboprop flights knowns as 'Rolls Royce' (both the YS-11s and HS-748s have Rolls-Royce engines) are cheaper than jet, if there are also jet flights on the same route. Cheapest of all are turboprop flights in the middle of the night, they're known as 'Night Mercury'.

Apart from these price variations there are also a number of cheap deals for domestic flights in the Philippines. In actual fact domestic flights are pretty reasonably priced to begin with. The longest flight you can make (Manila-Davao) is US$88 and there are lots of short flights which cost under US$20. Cebu-Tagbilaran on Bohol is just US$12 for example. Best of the PAL cheap deals is their '1000 Island Fare'. This is available to anybody who arrives in the Philippines from abroad by PAL and it permits you to purchase tickets for any complete loop from Manila to Manila at 50% off the regular fare. You could, for example, fly Manila-Cebu-Zamboanga-Manila.

Students are eligible for a 30% discount on return flights. PAL also have curiously named 'Mr & Mrs' flights where the first person pays the full return fare but his (or her) partner only pays 50%. If you're over 60 you're also eligible for a 30% discount, just like students, on the 'Golden Years Economico Fare'.

The rules applying to student discounts vary greatly. As well as a travel pass and a student card you are generally requested to produce documentation from the university as well (if you argue this point well and persistently you will eventually get by). The student discount is given regardless of age and a photocopy of the student identification must be left with the agent.

There is a security tax on domestic flights included in the ticket price. PAL have been very security conscious ever since a spate of hijackings in the '70s including one which goes down as the longest ever. It took the hijackers a full week to fly to Libya in a BAC-111! Maximum baggage allowance on domestic flights is 18 kg but they tend to be less exacting on tourists. PAL have offices in all the major towns where you must take a number on entry and wait your turn to be served. Even if you have just a simple query you still have to wait for your number so it is often easier and quicker to phone. Bookings can be changed without any charge up to 12 noon on the preceding day. After that you will be charged P50.

Note that the domestic airport in Manila is a seperate terminal but the same airport as Manila International Airport. The two terminals are some distance apart. The chart shows regular PAL fares on some of the main routes. On certain of these routes there will be cheaper night flights also. PAL flight frequencies vary considerably. On some main sectors there will be several flights a day (eight on Manila-Cebu) while on lesser routes there may be just a few flights a week.

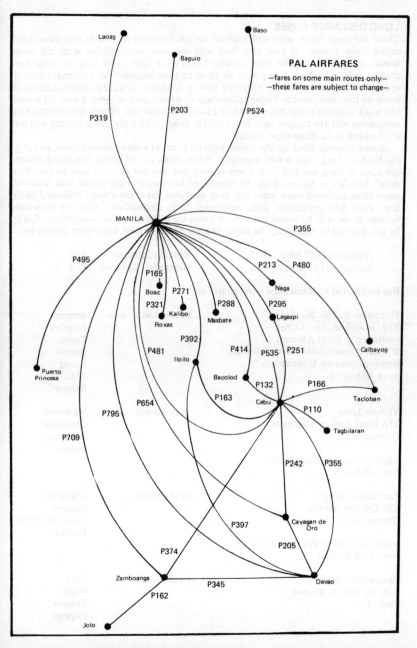

PAL AIRFARES
—fares on some main routes only—
—these fares are subject to change—

LONG DISTANCE BUSES

There are large buses with and without air-conditioning as well as minibuses (also called Baby Buses). If you have long legs the most comfortable seats are those beside the driver. In the large overland buses the back seats may be your best choice, mainly because you get to sit close to your luggage — an important consideration. Like most Asians, Filipinos have a tendency towards travel sickness so being at the back has the further advantage of having no one behind you. Of course the weak stomachs may have something to do with the way drivers from competing companies will try to race each other off the roads, which are often bumpy and not at all suited to Le Mans-type speeds.

Street vendors flock to the buses with all kinds of edibles at each stop, so carrying food on long trips is not necessary. Buses often set off before the listed departure time if they are full — if there is only one bus per day it's wise to get there early! The fare is reckoned by the number of km travelled but gravel road kms cost more than surfaced road kms. On long stretches fares are always collected fairly late. First the conductor asks passengers their destinations, then he dispenses tickets, these will be inspected several times by different chief conductors, finally he gets around to collecting the fares. Typical ordinary class fares from Manila are:

Alaminos (237 km)	P32	Baguio (250 km)	P36
Batangas (110 km)	P15	Olongapo (126 km)	P17

Bus companies in Manila and their routes are:

Philippine Rabbit Bus Lines 819 Oroquieta, Santa Cruz (entrance in Rizal Avenue) & Rizal Avenue Extension, Caloocan *jeepneys towards Monumento* *from Mabini St*	to the north	Balanga Angeles Tarlac Baguio Laoag Vigan Benguet
Victory Liner 713 Rizal Avenue Extension Caloocan City *jeepneys toward Monumento* *from Mabini St*	to the north	Mariveles Olongapo Alaminos Baguio
Pantranco Tours 325 Quezon Avenue Quezon City *jeepneys towards Pelco or Project 8* *from Taft Avenue*	to the north	Alaminos Banaue Cagayan Valley Baguio
Pantranco Tours E de los Santos Avenue Pasay City	to the south	Daet Naga Tabaco Legaspi

jeepneys & buses towards Baclaran from
Taft Avenue or M H Del Pilar St. In or from
Baclaran you must change.

Sorsogon
Matnog

BLTB   to the south   Nasugbu
E de los Santos Avenue   Calamba
Pasay City   Batangas
                                                  Santa Cruz
jeepneys & buses towards Baclaran from   Lucena
Taft Avenue or M H Del Pilar St. In or from
Baclaran you must change.

The Ministry of Transport plans to relocate various bus terminals from the city centre to the edge. This should apply particularly to the terminals near the main post office and opposite the city hall — ie the buses to Batangas, Laguna, Quezon and Cavite. Check!

LOCAL BUSES
As with the long distance buses, the city buses announce only the final destination. In Manila that can be a large complex like the MIA (Manila International Airport) or street names like Ayala (Ayala Avenue in Makati) or a suburb like Santa Cruz. Depending on the distance the trip costs 65c or more.

In Manila the air-conditioned *Love Bus* is very popular. See the Manila Getting Around section for more details on bus travel in the capital.

TRAINS
There are two railway lines — one in Luzon and one in Panay. The one in Panay connects Iloilo with Roxas and is fairly unimportant and very unreliable. The network of the Philippine National Railways (PNR) on Luzon is divided into north and south connections. The northern line leaves the main station in Manila (Tutuban Terminal) past Caloocan, Meycauayan, Malolos, San Fernando Pampanga, Angeles, Tarlac, Paniqui, Bayambang, Malasiqui, San Carlos, Dagupan, San Fabian, Damortis, Agoo, Aringay and Bauang to San Fernando La Union.

The southern line goes from Manila to Calamba, San Pablo, Lucena, Gumaca, Hondagua, Tagkauyan, Ragay, Lupi Viejo, Sipocot, Libmanan, Naga, Pili, Iriga, Polangui, Oas, Ligao and Camalig. Legaspi is no longer the terminus. You can travel De-Luxe, Tourist or Economy Class. In general the trains are quite slow. An additional charge of 25% must be paid for express trains. There is no essential difference in price between trains and buses. Students get a 25% discount.

Some typical economy class fares from Manila include:

Angeles (82 km)	P 9.35	San Fernando La Union (260 km)	P31.90
Naga (443 km)	P49.15	Camalig (539 km)	P59.80

BOATS
Wherever you go there's always a boat ready to take you to the next island. For short distances outrigger boats and pumpboats are used. You get least wet in the front of the boat as the motor is at the back.

The quality of the passenger ships of the inter-island operators varies widely. The flagships of several companies run on the prestige route Manila-Cebu-Zamboanga-Davao. They are punctual and fast and the service is relatively good, some boats even have a disco on board. Third class (deck class) is quite acceptable. Ask for the 'Sun Deck' when you buy your ticket; it is often more pleasant than the cabins and rooms which are under the deck and are cramped and sticky.

The quality of the large passenger ships certainly does vary widely. Some of the boats may even once have been top quality but as with all Asian inter-island boats you must expect:

1. As many people as possible crammed into the smallest possible space.
2. Bunks welded to every available bit of floor space.
3. Absolutely disgusting toilets often overflowing due to no water and over-use.
4. Lousy food, very little drink available and the boat arriving several hours late.
5. Everyone throwing up everywhere if it is slightly rough.

Beware when there are two third classes — we asked what the difference was between third class deluxe and third class ordinary and the answer was 'deluxe has bedding, ordinary doesn't'. It was only P5 extra but who needs sheets and blankets anyhow? We got ordinary to find when we got on board that she meant deluxe had reserved beds. In ordinary you had to fight with thousands of Filipinos to find a square cm of empty floor space not near the toilets. Luckily a friendly Filipino family saved us but make sure to check about reserved beds!

Piers & Jill Beagley

It is a good idea to be on board a couple of hours before the scheduled departure time and buy tickets a couple of days beforehand if possible. Meals, usually just fish and rice, are included in the fare price.

If you want to go long distances by freighter you must count on long, unscheduled stops in the different ports. On small passenger boats over average distances the tickets are also sold on board. Drinks are practically always on sale but other foodstuffs must be brought along. In contrast to the large ships the places on the upper deck are the most expensive.

The major shipping lines include Sweet Lines, William Lines, Sulpicio Lines, Negros Navigation, Aboitiz Lines and George & Peter Lines. You can find the lines you want in the yellow pages under shipping. First class fares are about twice the deck class fare. Some typical deck class fares from Manila include:

Catbalogan, Samar	P 92	Cebu City, Cebu	P104
Davao, Mindanao	P168	Tacloban, Leyte	P 99
Zamboanga, Mindanao	P138		

Filipino transport

a   The ubiquitous jeepney
b   A flat tyre in the Zambales Mountains

Island Hopping

There are all sorts of possible routes around the Philippines. You can head straight off into the Visayas or to Mindanao from Manila. Or you can travel south, via Legaspi and the Mayon Volcano, and hop across from Bulan to Masbate or from Matnog to Allen on Samar. From Masbate you can continue on to Panay, Negros and Cebu. Or from Allen at the north of Samar you can head down through Samar and Leyte and across to other Visayan Islands.

Eventually there will be a road threading together Luzon, Samar, Leyte and Mindanao — joining them together from the north of Luzon to Zamboanga in the south of Mindanao. Already this Japanese aided project has dramatically improved the transport situtation through Samar where the main road used to be terrible. Work is underway to complete the crossing point from south Leyte to Surigao in northern Mindanao.

For more on island hopping see the Visayas island hopping section for details of the interesting route from Puerto Galera to Boracay, one fantastic beach to another!

A
B

Filipino transport

a Tricycles
b A calesa

Manila

Manila was formed by merging 17 towns and communities into Metro Manila — Manila, San Nicolas, Binondo, Santa Cruz, Quiapo and San Miguel form the nucleus of the city. Here you will find the markets (Divisoria Market, Quinta Market), the churches (Quiapo Church, Santa Cruz Church), the shopping streets (Rizal Avenue, Escolta St), Chinatown (Binondo, Ongpin St), the official home of the president (Malacanang Palace in San Miguel) and many, many people,

Rizal Park, better known as the Luneta, is the centre of Manila and the city's most important meeting place. The two most important areas for tourists flank Rizal Park. To the north is Intramuros, the Spanish walled city which was badly damaged during the fierce fighting in WW II. To the south of Rizal Park is the area where the more peaceful modern invaders are drawn — Ermita and Malate. Here you will find most of Manila's hotels, restaurants and active nightspots. Known as the 'tourist belt', the waterfront Roxas Boulevard is the main street here. Ermita is about 10 km from the Manila International Airport.

Manila's business centre is Makati where the banks, insurance companies and other concerns have their head offices as well as the embassies of many countries. At the edge of Makati lies Forbes Park, a millionaire's ghetto with palatial mansions and even its own police force.

At the other end of the scale is Tondo, Manila's chief slum. It is estimated that 1.5 million Filipinos live in slums in Manila and Tondo has 180,000 living in 17,000 huts in just 1.5 square km. Other parts of Manila include Caloocan City, a light industrial engineering and foodstuff preparation centre. Quezon City is the government centre and here

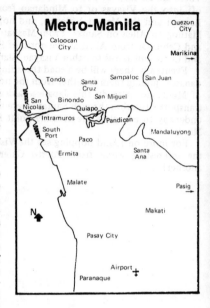

you'll also find the Philippine Heart Center for Asia, the 25,000 seat Araneta Coliseum and the 400 hectare campus of the University of the Philippines (UP).

You can get a good view over central Manila from the revolving restaurant atop the Manila Royal Hotel on Carlos Palanca St near the main post office.

Orientation

Although Manila is a fairly sprawling town it's quite easy to find your way around. Like Bangkok, however, there is no real 'centre' to Manila. Instead there are various different centres — like Makati the business centre or Ermita the tourist centre. The area of most interest to most visitors can be defined by the Pasig River, Manila Bay and Taft Avenue. The river forms the northern boundary of this rectangular area while the bayside and Taft Avenue form the west and east boundaries.

Immediately south of the river you'll find the oldest area of Manila including Intramuros. Here you'll find most of the places of historic interest in Manila. The GPO and the immigration office are also in this area, immediately south of the river. South of this area is the open expanse of Rizal Park, the Luneta, which extends from Taft Avenue to the bayside Roxas Boulevard. This is the central meeting and wandering place in Manila but beware of pickpockets here and in areas like Santa Cruz. South of the park is Ermita the tourist centre. Here you'll find cheaper (and some more expensive) accommodation, restaurants, airline offices, nightlife and pretty much everything else you'll need.

Continuing south again from Ermita is Malate and Pasay City where many of the up market hotels are located, particularly along the bayside on Roxas Boulevard. The modern Cultural Center is built on reclaimed land jutting out into the bay. If you continue down Taft Avenue you'll eventually find your way to the airport while Makati is off to the south-east from this main avenue. North of the river is the crowded and interesting Chinatown area, the sprawling slums of Tondo and the main railway station.

Information

There are three Ministry of Tourism information centres in Manila. A 'Reception Unit' at the international airport, another at the nearby Nayong Pilipino Complex and the main Tourist Information Center, ground floor, Tourism Building, Agrifina Circle, Rizal Park. The phone number there is 50 2384 and 50 1703.

Money Manila is the best place to change money, the rates at money changers are better than at banks and they're better in Manila than anywhere else. Carry lots of change or small bills when you get out into the country, changing P100 notes can be difficult.

Shopping The *Central Market* on Quezon Boulevard in Santa Cruz is a large market hall selling mainly clothes including T-shirts, bags, shoes and so on. *Divisoria Market* on Santo Cristo St in San Nicolas is a particularly nice market, colourful and with pretty well everything which is manufactured in the Philippines on sale at reasonable prices. Beware of pickpockets here.

Try the *San Andres Market* on San Andres St in Malate for a wide choice of vegetables and tropical fruit. *Aurora Gardens* is where the orchid sellers have their stalls, you can get cheap pottery there too. The *Makati Commercial Center*, on the corner of Makati Avenue and Ayala Avenue in Makati, is a modern shopping centre with a very wide choice including imported goods. There's a good bookshop here and between the shops are restaurants and open rest areas. On M Adriatico St in Ermita, *Robinson's* is a modern shopping centre with three cinemas. It's a smaller version of Harrison's Plaza which has been burnt out.

In Ermita *Pistang Pilipino* on the corner of Pedro Gil and M H Del Pilar is a tourist market — fixed prices but 'I give you good discount'. It does have a good display of handicrafts produced in the country. The *Flea Market* on the other side of the street is relatively expensive. *Martin's Products* on M H Del Pilar in Ermita is a place to head for when you've had your fill of rice and burnt toast, they sell 'real' bread here.

The new *Philippine Center for International Trade & Exhibition* on Roxas Boulevard is an interesting place to visit to view most of the Philippine products under one roof. You can buy most things here but the prices are relatively high. Bargain! *Tiangge ng Antik* in

Puerto Real Gardens, Intramuros is an antique market with high prices. It's open the last Saturday of the month, weather permitting.

Duty Free Shopping There are eight duty free shops in Manila, the best is in the Makati Commercial Center on Ayala Avenue. You need your passport and flight ticket when shopping. Other duty free shops are at the Manila Hilton Hotel, Manila International Airport, the Manila Garden Hotel, the Philippine Plaza Hotel, the Manila Hotel, the Hyatt Regency and the Philippine International Convention Center. There are restrictions to how much you can spend in pesos without proof of currency conversion.

Bookshops The *National Bookstore* at 701 Rizal Avenue, Santa Cruz is the largest and best bookshop in the Philippines and has a number of branches in the Metro Manila suburbs.

On UN Avenue in Ermita, *Alemar's Bookshop* has low cost books and also stationery and newspapers. On Padre Faura, between Mabini and Taft, the *Solidaridad Bookstore* is 'an intellectual's delight' with excellent sections on religion (Buddhism especially), philosophy, politics, poetry and fiction. It's complimented by the *Bookmark* nearby on the corner of Mabini St and Padre Faura with plenty of lightweight paperback fiction although it mainly concentrates on scientific literature.

The *Casalindra Bookstore* on the second floor of the San Antonio Plaza (near the Makati Commercial Center) is a small shop with a good section on the Philippines. *Erehwon* on the corner of Postal Arcade and Makati is another good bookshop.

Go to the Bureau of Coast & Geodetic Survey on Barraca St in San Nicolas for detailed maps, including nautical charts. The two-part complete map of the Philippines is far too large to be useful as a touring map.

Embassies & Consulates

Australia	China Bank Building, Paseo de Roxas, Makati, Rizal (tel 87 4961)
Canada	PAL Building, Ayala Avenue, Makati, Rizal (tel 87 6536)
Denmark	JMT Building, Ayala Avenue, Makati, Rizal (tel 89 7511)
Finland	Gilarmi Apartments, Ayala Avenue, Makati, Rizal (tel 88 5551)
Indonesia	Indonesian Embassy, Salcedo St, Legaspi Village, Makati, Rizal (tel 85 5061)
Japan	Sikatuna Building, Ayala Avenue, Makati, Rizal (tel 89 1836)
Korea	Rufino Building, Ayala Avenue, Makati, Rizal (tel 88 6423)
Malaysia	Architectural Center Building, Makati, Rizal (tel 87 4576)
Netherlands	Metro Bank Building, Makati, Rizal (tel 88 7753)
Norway	Bonifacio Drive, Manila (tel 48 3391)
Papua New Guinea	1414 Roxas Boulevard, Manila (tel 58 2354)
Singapore	JMT Building, Ayala Avenue, Makati, Rizal (tel 89 4596)
Taiwan	Pacific Economic & Cultural Centre, BF Home Condominium Building, Intramuros, Manila
Thailand	A Soriano Building, Ayala Avenue, Makati, Rizal (tel 88 8961)
UK	L&S Building, Roxas Boulevard, Manila (tel 59 2461)
USA	Roxas Boulevard, Manila (tel 59 8011)

Photography Mayer Photo on Carlos Palance St, Quiapo, near the Manila Royal Hotel has the cheapest film in Manila. Around the corner in Hidalgo St there are more photo shops.

Rizal Park

A real park in the centre of the city. Flowers, fountains, spacious lawns and, of course, plenty of music to attract thousands of Filipinos every day. On Sundays there are free concerts at 5 pm. Many families spend their whole Sunday here, it is particularly popular on 1st January. You can buy refreshments in the cafeteria, but as the waiters are deaf and dumb orders must be written down. It is interesting to watch the changing of the guard at the Rizal Memorial which is where the national hero, Dr Jose Rizal, was executed on 30 December 1896, by the Spaniards. There is a childrens' playground at the waterfront, a good place to enjoy the colourful Manila Bay sunset. The Japanese Garden and the Chinese Garden adjoin Rizal Park, a popular meeting place for couples.

Hidden between the Rizal monument and the fish pond at the Kalaw St end is the original well from a village near Heidelberg, Germany. The story goes that Rizal used to drink from this well during his Heidelberg student days.

Rizal Park is also popularly known as Luneta Park.

Intramuros

Literally the 'city in walls', Intramuros is the Manila of the past. This is where Legaspi erected a fortress in 1571 after his victory over the Moslems. After attacks by the Chinese fleet and a fire the Filipinos were forced to build the defence wall. A wide moat all around made the bulwark complete. Within the walls, the most important buildings were the numerous feudal lords' houses, 12 churches and several hospitals. Only Spaniards and Mestizos were allowed to live within the walls, Filipinos were settled on what is now the site of Rizal Park. Likewise the Chinese were quartered in range of the canons, about where the City Hall stands today. Neither the Dutch nor the Portuguese could storm this fortress and the attacks of the Sulu pirates were also unsuccessful.

Intramuros was almost totally destroyed by bomb attacks during WW II. The San Augustin Church remained relatively undamaged and the Manila Cathedral was rebuilt after the war. With the restoration, Puerto Isabella and Puerto Real, two of the original seven gates of the city, were also restored.

Fort Santiago

The most important defence location of the Intramuros fortress-city was Fort Santiago. From this strategic location (the mouth of the Pasig River) all activity in Manila Bay could be observed. During the Japanese occupation in WW II innumerable Filipino prisoners lost their lives in the infamous dungeon cells which lay below sea level — at high tide there was no escape. Dr Jose Rizal also spent his last days in a narrow cell at this fort before his execution by the Spaniards in 1896.

Today Fort Santiago is a memorial. There is an open-air theatre, a Rizal Museum and a display of old cars which used to belong to important Philippine personalities. The fort is open daily between 8 am and 11 pm.

San Augustin Church

The first constructions of the San Augustin Church were destroyed by fires in the years 1574 and 1583. In 1599 the foundation stone was laid. The massive church was not damaged by the heavy earthquakes of 1645, 1754, 1852, 1863, 1880, 1968 and 1970 nor by the bombardment in the fight around Manila in February 1945.

It is the oldest existing stone church in the Philippines. In 1879/80, the walls and roofs were masterfully painted by two Italian artists, the crystal chandeliers came from Paris and the choir stalls were carved by hand by the Augustine monks themselves. In a small chapel to the left of the high altar there lie the mortal remains of Legaspi. There is a museum and a contemplative inner yard adjoining the church.

Manila Cathedral
This cathedral with the great cupola is the most significant Catholic church in the Philippines. It is at the Plaza Roma, Intramuros. With the help of the Vatican the building, which was destroyed in WW II, was rebuilt from 1954 to 1958. Some old walls were restored and integrated into the new construction. The large organ, with its 4500 pipes, comes from the Netherlands and is the largest in Asia.

Quiapo Church
This church has become famous because of its large crucifix of black wood. The 'Black Nazarene' was carved in Mexico and brought to the Philippines by the Spaniards in the 17th century. Each Friday hundreds of Catholic believers come to Quiapo Church in order to pay homage to the 'Black Nazarene'. The climax of the adorations is the procession on 9 January and in Passion Week (Monday to Friday).

Chinese Cemetery
As a tourist sight, this 'city of death' simply must not be missed. Here you will find the most incredible tombs in the whole world. There are actual houses with mailboxes and toilets! Some even have an air-conditioner. All solely for the use of the dead. Descendants of those buried here visit the cemetery on 1 November each year for the All Saints Day celebration.

To get there from Mabini St or Taft Avenue in Ermita catch a jeepney towards Caloocan City, terminus 'monumento'. Rizal Avenue in Santa Cruz later becomes Rizal Avenue Extension and you get off where it begins. The Chinese Cemetery is on the right hand side.

It's possible that tourists are no longer permitted here. When I tried to visit it in mid-1981 I was told by MOT officials that it was closed to visitors to keep out squatters. Worth a try though.

Malacanang Palace
The Malacanang Palace is the single most noteworthy attraction in the suburb of San Miguel. It is in Jose P Laurel St, on the bank of the Pasig River. Malacanang is a derivation from the old Filipino description *May Lakan Diyan*, which meant 'Here lives a nobleman'. This referred to the Spanish aristocrat Luis Rocha, who built this palace. In 1802 he sold it to an important Spanish soldier. From 1863 the house of the nobleman was used by the Spaniards to domicile their heads of government. Later the Americans also used the palace as their residence. As the first Philippine head of state, Manuel Quezon entered the palace. Today the Malacanang Palace is the seat of the office of the current president, Ferdinand Marcos.

It's interesting to stroll around the grounds inside — once you get through the barrage of military interrogation at the entrance and if you don't mind being accompanied by a military escort.

Cultural Center
The Cultural Center of the Philippines (CCP) was built under the umbrella administration of the First Lady Imelda Marcos. The 40 million peso project was opened on 10 September 1969. It was designed by Leandro Locsin, a leading Filipino architect. The CCP includes a theatre, art gallery and museum. It was designed as a symbol of national cultural development and is open for viewing

daily between 9 am and 5 pm.

In the vicinity of the CCP are the Folk Arts Theatre, the Philippine International Convention Center, the Film Theatre and the Philippine Plaza Hotel. The Folk Arts Theatre was built in a record time of only 70 days. Anyone who is interested in seeing the conference rooms of the Convention Center can take a tour at 9, 10 or 11 am, 2, 3 or 4 pm; admission is P2. The modern-traditional architecture and the splendid construction of the Plaza Hotel are well worth seeing.

Nayong Pilipino
Nayong Pilipino means 'Philippine Village' and is a miniature version of the whole country — a concept which has become popular in a number of countries in the region. Typical houses and distinctive landscapes have been built on the 35 hectare site. There are six regions: Mountain Province, Northern Province, Bicol Province, Central and South Luzon, the Visayas and the Moslem region. Jeepneys transport you cost-free through the various locations.

Naturally there are also souvenir shops. The museum is highly recommended, see the museum section for more details. Moslem dances are performed on Saturday afternoons in the Mindanao section. Opening hours are Monday to Friday from 7 am to 6 pm. On weekends from 9 am to 7 pm. Admission is P5. To get there take a bus along Roxas Boulevard with the destination marked 'MIA' (Manila International Airport). When returning catch a bus on the same side of the street as you got off — they do a loop around the MIA and do not return via the Nayong Pilipino.

Not everyone is so impressed by Nayong Pilipino. One traveller wrote:

I would quite honestly not recommend anyone the trouble of seeing this. When I was there the museum was closed, there were no jeepneys operating and it was very badly signposted. In fact it's just a collection of souvenir huts. You can get in free simply by walking through the car park.

Teresa Howells

Forbes Park
Such a profusion of opulent mansions and ostentatious displays of wealth as is found in Forbes Park, or in neighbouring Sasmarinas Village, is rare anywhere in the world. They even have their private police troops to watch and protect the 'millionaires' ghetto'. The difference between this luxury and the Tondo slum quarter is so gigantic that further comparison is meaningless.

Forbes Park lies in the southern part of Makati, go by bus from Taft Avenue or from M H Del Pilar St to the Commercial Center, bus sign 'Ayala' (Avenue).

Faith Healers
The unorthodox healing methods of the Philippines faith healers are now world famous. Clearly some of these 'doctors' are no more than money-grubbing charlatans but others are so skilful that even disbelievers gape in wonder.

Many patients travel to Baguio, some to Pangasinan Province, but there are also faith healers in Metro-Manila. Anyone can watch after obtaining the consent of the patient. Ask at the Christian Travel Center at the Bayview Plaza Hotel, Roxas Boulevard, Ermita — the office is right next to reception. There is also Alex Orbito, 9 Maryland St, Cubao, Quezon City.

Other Attractions
Catching a famous Manila Bay sunset is increasingly difficult with all the land reclamation underway. The park created for the film festival, on the waterfront just south of the Philippine Plaza Hotel in the Cultural Center complex, gives you the waterfront, the requisite palm trees and no traffic to interrupt your

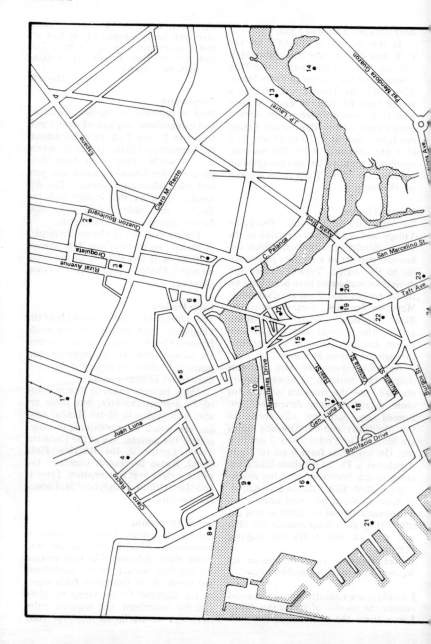

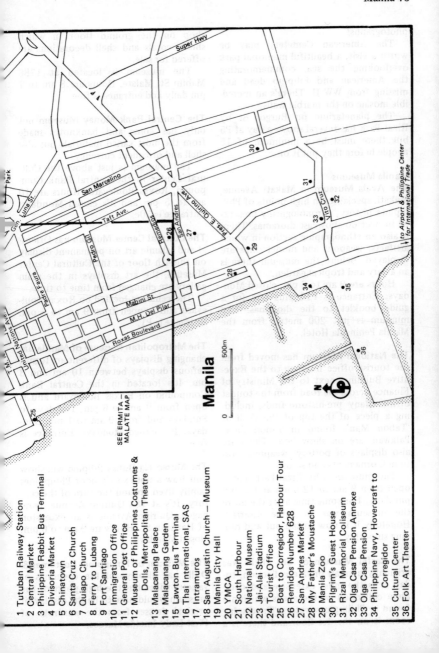

1 Tutuban Railway Station
2 Central Market
3 Philippine Rabbit Bus Terminal
4 Divisoria Market
5 Chinatown
6 Santa Cruz Church
7 Quiapo Church
8 Ferry to Lubang
9 Fort Santiago
10 Immigration Office
11 General Post Office
12 Museum of Philippines Costumes & Dolls, Metropolitan Theatre
13 Malacanang Palace
14 Malacanang Garden
15 Lawton Bus Terminal
16 Thai International, SAS
17 Intramuros
18 San Augustin Church – Museum
19 Manila City Hall
20 YMCA
21 South Harbour
22 National Museum
23 Jai-Alai Stadium
24 Tourist Office
25 Boat to Corregidor, Harbour Tour
26 Remidos Number 628
27 San Andres Market
28 My Father's Moustache
29 Manila Zoo
30 Pilgrim's Guest House
31 Rizal Memorial Coliseum
32 Olga Casa Pension Annexe
33 Olga Casa Pension
34 Philippine Navy, Hovercraft to Corregidor
35 Cultural Center
36 Folk Art Theater

Manila

0   500m

SEE ERMITA – MALATE MAP

to Airport & Philippine Center for International Trade

photographs!

The American Cemetery may be worth a visit, a beautiful memorial park overlooking the sea, commemorating the American and Filipino dead and missing from WW II. There's an incredible mosaic on the marble walls.

The planetarium on Burgos St by Rizal Park has several shows a day at P5 but there must be a minimum of 15 people before they put it on.

Manila Museums

The Ayala Museum in Makati Avenue, Makati, specialises in high points of Philippines history, chronologically presented in over 60 showcase dioramas. There is also an ethnographic section in which artifacts, weapons and model ships are displayed. Behind the museum there is an aviary and tropical garden.

Hours are 9 am to 6 pm, closed Mondays. Entrance is P10 plus 60c for a guide booklet to the dioramas. The museum is just 200 metres from the Manila Peninsula Hotel.

The National Museum has moved from the tourist office building to the Executive Building, next to the Ministry of Finance across the road from the tourist office. Many pre-historic finds, including a piece of the top of the skull of 'Tabon Man' found in Tabon Cave, Palawan, are on show here. There are also displays of pottery, weapons, costumes, ornaments and so on.

The museum is by Rizal Park and is open from 9 am to 12 noon and 1 to 5 pm daily. For some time after the move the museum was in some disarray. Hopefully it is now sorted out and running smoothly.

The Carfel Museum of Sea Shells was originally a small private collection, today it is the most extensive and complete collection of the shells which are found in Philippines waters. The display room is on the 1st floor and there is a shop on the ground floor in which shells, corals and shell decorations are offered for sale.

The museum is located at 1786 Mabini St, Malate. Hours are 8 am to 7 pm daily and entrance is free.

The Central Bank Money Museum not only has coins and banknotes made from the most varied materials but also shell and ornament currency.

The museum is just above the Cultural Center in the Central Bank Compound, Roxas Boulevard. Hours are 10 am to 5 pm and it's closed Mondays. Entrance is 50c.

The Cultural Center Museum has Oriental and Islamic art on permanent display on the 4th floor of the Cultural Center Museum, the art displays in the main gallery are changed from time to time.

The center is located on Roxas Boulevard and is open from 9 am to 6 pm. Entrance is P1.

The Metropolitan Museum of Manila has changing displays of different art forms, various displays between 10 am and 3 pm. It's located in the Central Bank Compound on Roxas Boulevard and is open from 9 am to 6 pm, Tuesdays to Sundays and from 9 am to 1 pm, Sundays. It's closed Mondays. Entrance is free.

The Museo Ng Buhay Pilipino will show you how a not-exactly-poor Philippines family lived around the turn of the century. It's at 784 Quirino Avenue, Paranague. Quirino Avenue is an extension of Harrison St. Hours are 9 am to 6 pm, closed Mondays.

The Museum of Philippines Costumes & Dolls has displays of the costumes of various tribes but the high point of the museum would have to be the display of original dresses from the wardrobe of First Lady Imelda Marcos.

The museum is situated opposite the GPO, Quiapo Bridge (Metropolitan Theatre). Hours are 9 am to 12 noon and 1 to 9 pm. On Saturdays and Sundays, including public holidays, it's open from 9 am to 9 pm. It's closed Mondays. Admission is free.

The Museum of Traditional Philippine Culture at the Nayong Pilipino offers the opportunity to get comprehensive information on the lifestyles of the so-called cultural minority groups. Tools, weapons, musical instruments and items used in daily life are all displayed. Texts and photographs indicate and explain the differences between the various cultural groups. Unfortunately the documentary about the Tasadays is apparently no longer available. It might be worth ringing 83 6755 to enquire.

The museum is part of the Nayong Pilipino complex so for information on getting there see that section. It's open 9 am to 6 pm Monday to Friday and 9 am to 7 pm on Saturday and Sunday.

The Rizal Shrine is a memorial to the national hero, Dr Jose Rizal; besides the display of personal effects you can also see his death cell. The Rizal Shrine is in Fort Santiago, Intramuros. It's open from 9 am to 12 noon and from 1 to 5 pm.

In the same area the Intramuros Exhibition Gallery is a new museum on Magalunes St, across from the Immigration Office. Admission is free.

The San Augustin Museum in the halls of the Augustine monastery has been open since 1973. On display are frescoes, oil paintings, antique choir stalls, valuable robes and other liturgical requisites. The museum is in the San Augustin Church, Intramuros. It's open from 8 am to 5 pm and entrance is P5.

The UST Museum has an extensive collection of historic documents and a noteworthy library with over 180,000 books. This Museum of Arts & Sciences is in the Santo Tomas University, the oldest university in the country. It's on Espana St and hours are 9 am to 12 noon and 2 to 5 pm except on Sundays.

Places to Stay

Manila has a very wide range of accommodation and it shouldn't be too hard to find something to suit. The tourist 'centre' is Ermita, where you will find most of the government offices, while the business 'centre' is Makati. You'll find most of the cheaper places to stay either in or very close to Ermita. At the other end of the price scale a few of the top end hotels are in Ermita but quite a few more are strung out along the bayside, fairly close to Ermita in Malate and Pasay City. Some of the top end places can also be found in Makati.

Places to Stay – bottom end

Hostels There are a lot of hostel-style places around Manila, many offering dorm-style accommodation. You'll find a number of them close to Ermita, generally on or just off Taft Avenue away from the bayside. The *YMCA* (tel 45 5033) is at 350 Arroceros St. It has a wide variety of accommodation from dorm beds at P38, singles/doubles with fan for P45/57 or with air-con at P72/85. Although the main entrance is on Arroceros St the office is round the corner at 1068 Conception St. the YMCA is a big, sprawling place and takes couples as well as men but the cheaper accommodation tends to be practically always booked out. There is also a cafeteria here.

Youth Hostel Philippines (tel 50 9970) at 1572 Leon Guinto St has dorm beds in fan-cooled rooms at P22, P2 less if you're a YHA member. There are also rooms at P45 or doubles from P50. The doors are shut at 12.30 am but it's very noisy. If you want to leave gear here while you're travelling around the country it costs P1 a day.

Remedios at 628 Remedios St is a simple private guest house with a relaxed atmosphere. Singles with fan are P30. *Pilgrims Guest House* (tel 50 7227) at 2456 Taft Avenue used to be the popular Ystaphil Hostel. It's opposite the De La Salle University and has a billiard table, cafeteria, TV and even a gym room! Beds in the fan-cooled dorm are P20, rooms with fan are P40/55 for singles/doubles.

Guest Houses The *Travelers' Pension* at 934 Pedro Gil is a very simple place but with wide beds. Singles with fan are P35, doubles from P40 but it's a bit of a noisy dump according to some travellers. *Manda Pension House* (tel 59 0607) is at 1387 F Agoncillo St on the corner of Padre Faura, Ermita. It's better than the old Manda Pension although toilets and washing facilities are outside the rooms. Singles with fan are P45 and you can get a discount for a week's stay. Very clean report some travellers.

Still in Ermita the *Carnes Inn* on M H Del Pilar St is another simple place. There aren't many rooms and the doors are locked at midnight. Singles with fan cost P50. The *Commodore Pension House* (tel 59 6864) at 422 Arquiza St is a clean, simple, relaxed place with rooms with fan at P50, with fan and bath at P75.

Places to Stay − middle
Particularly around Ermita there are many cheap guest houses a notch up from the lowest price places. They include the *Casa Pension* (tel 58 7647) at 1406 M H Del Pilar St. Singles with fan cost from P55, doubles P65, doubles with fan and bath from P80. It's run by pleasant people and they're quite happy for you to leave your gear here while travelling.

Manila has three other 'Casa Pensions'. The *New Casa Pension* is at 1602 Leon Guinto St on the corner

with Pedro Gil − close to the youth hostels. It looks like a house that's just been demolished. The *Olga Casa Pension Annex* (tel 59 6265) is at 640 Vito Cruz, Malate and has rooms with fan from P55/90, with fan and bath P100/110 or a double with air-con and bath for P130. And there's the *Olga Casa Pension* (tel 59 3113) at 1674 Mabini St where rooms with fan are P60 and 70. It's a nice, clean place with wide beds and a coffee shop.

The *Congress Family Hotel* (tel 50 9696-98) is at 1427 M H Del Pilar St. Singles with fan and bath are P45, doubles P50-60. With air-con rooms are P69/82. This is neither a congress or a family hotel but a good clean place in the lower price category. Unfortunately there are very few singles with fan but luggage can be left here if you're off travelling. When renovations are completed there may be a price hike here.

Pension Conula (tel 58 2334) is at 1445 Mabini St close to the Mabuhay Hotel. Rooms with fan are P60/65 or a double with fan and bath P85. It's clean but the rooms are rather small. *Santos Pension House* (tel 59 5628) is at 1540 Mabini St, about opposite to Kowloon House. Rooms with air-con and bath are P85/95 and there are also some dorm-style rooms with four to six beds at P25 to 30. It's got a good atmosphere and gives discounts to peace corps workers − they may even give you a discount if you ask. There's no problem about storing luggage, leaving messages or making overseas phone calls from here.

The *Malate Pension* (tel 59 3489) at 1771 Adriatico St is a quiet and clean place a little away from the main strip. The atmosphere here is friendly and you can leave your gear here while travelling. Singles with fan are P68, rooms with air-con P85/100, with air-con and bath P125/145. The *Mabini Pension* (tel 59 4853) at 1377 Mabini St has dorm beds at P30 or well kept singles with air-con and bath at P70, doubles from P88 to 98.

At 1250 J Bocobo St the *Ryokan Pension House* (tel 59 8956) is a clean place with good wide beds. Rooms with fan are P70/80, with air-con and bath P145/165.

Pension Filipinas (tel 58 6824 or 59 5583) is at 542 Arkansas St on the corner of Maria Orosa. Rooms with air-con are P90/120, bathrooms and toilets are outside the rooms. It's well kept and has a friendly atmosphere. *Yasmin Pension* (tel 50 5134) at 453 Arquiza St is a clean and quiet place with air-con doubles with bath from P120 to 150. The *Ermita Tourist Inn* (tel 521 8770) is at 1549 A Mabini St on the corner of Soldado St, Ermita. It's a new place with rooms from P140 to 180, all air-con and with bathroom and there's a restaurant.

The *Diamond Executive Inn* (tel 59 9261) at 1217-1219 M H Del Pilar St is also a clean, good place with wide beds but the street is rather noisy. Rooms with air-con and bath are P140/160. *Sandico Apartment Hotel* (tel 59 2036-39) is a good clean place on M H Del Pilar St. The rooms have air-con, bathroom, colour TV and a fridge and cost P155/175. If you stay here often ask about a discount.

The *Iseya Hotel* (tel 59 2016) on M H Del Pilar is clean and good but the live music from the beer garden outside is rather noisy. Rooms with air-con and bath are P110/140. It's possible to leave luggage here. The *Manila Tourist Inn* (tel 59 7721) at 487 Santa Monica St has pleasant, clean, quiet rooms with air-con and bath for P165/210.

At 512 R Salas St (between Mabini St and Adriatico) in Ermita the *Bayview Penthouse* (tel 58 3485) has rooms with fan at P60 to 70, apartments at P150 to 200. It's a nice, clean place but there's no direction sign so ask the porter for Mr or Mrs Prats who own this place. *Euro-Haus Inn* (tel 57 3981 or 3994)

at 1212 Roxas Boulevard has rooms with air-con and bath at P160/180. Ask about the cheaper rooms for P70 and 80 in the *International University* behind.

Hotel Soveiente (tel 59 9123) is on the corner of Bocobo and Flores Sts and is a good, clean, new place. Rooms with air-con and bath are P150/175. *Pensione Virginia* (tel 87 8690) at 816 Pasay Rd in San Lorenzo Village, Makati has air-con doubles with bath at P175. It's a quiet, clean and relatively good value place.

Another very good and relatively cheap place in Makati is the *Robelle House* (tel 88 2583) at 4402 Valdez St. It's opposite the International School and has singles/doubles with air-con and bath at P174/192 as well as an excellent Filipino atmosphere, a good restaurant and a swimming pool.

Apartments If you're going to stay longer in Manila it may be worth investigating apartments instead of taking a hotel room. It's possible to find apartments with cooking facilities, fridge, air-con, TV and so on for P80 to 120 a day. Electricity is extra and rentals are only monthly. You'll find places to rent in the weekend editions of the large daily papers.

Apartments in Makati are very expensive while those in Ermita are seldom free. If you don't mind being further out a reasonably good address in Quezon City is *Broadway Court*, 16 Dona Rodriguez St, New Manila, near the Goethe Institute. Monthly rentals are typically from P1900 to 2800.

Places in Ermita include the apartments of *Mabini Mansions* on Mabini St (by Rizal Park); *Dakota Mansions* on the corner of Adriatico and Malvar Sts; *Dona Petronila Mall* on Mabini St (in the Tempura House across from Shakey's Pizza) and *Casa Blanca* in Adriatico St near Midland Plaza. Rentals at Dona Petronila Mall are available on a

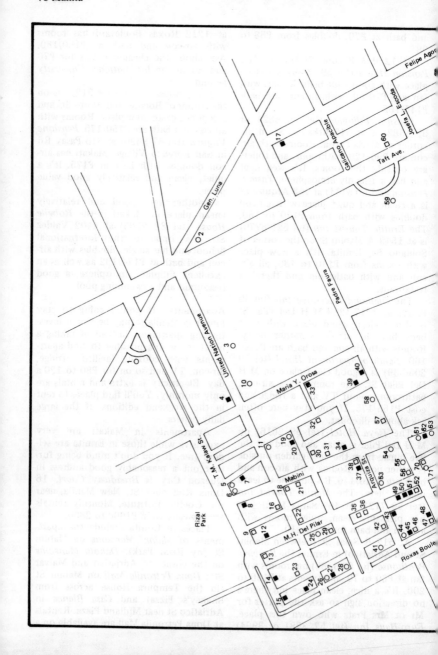

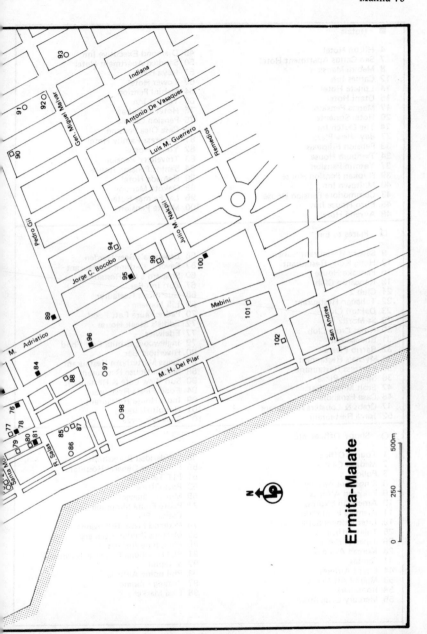

Ermita-Malate

■ Hotels

4 Hilton Hotel
7 San Carlos Apartment Hotel
8 Mabini Mansion
12 Carnes Inn
14 Luneta Hotel
15 Otani Hotel
17 Manda Pension
20 Hotel Soriente
24 The Dutch Inn
27 Bay View Plaza
33 Pension Filipinas
34 Tempura House
37 Yasmin Pension
39 Ryokan Pension House
40 Midtown Inn
43 Commodore Pension House
45 Euro House Inn
48 Aurelio Hotel
49 Diamond Executive Inn
50 Sandico Apartment Hotel
51 Iseya Hotel
62 Tower Hotel
64 Mabini Pension
66 Tourist Inn
75 Hotel Mabuhay
76 Pension Conula
78 Casa Olga Pension
81 Congress Family Hotel
82 Youth Hostel
83 Travellers' Pension
84 Santos Pension House
89 Ramada Hotel
95 Dakota Mansion
96 Las Palmas Hotel
100 Malate Pension

□ Places to Eat

9 Savory Restaurant Luneta
13 Hong Kong Restaurant
16 Pancake House
18 Kangaroo Club
21 Club 2
22 Tahanan Restaurant
23 Daktari Club
29 St Moritz Bar
30 Kings Cross Club
31 Bodega Pub
32 Barrio Fiesta
35 Myrna's Restaurant
36 Fortress Restaurant
38 Shakey's Pizza
42 Stolt Milanie Bar
46 Casa Espanola
47 Crabs & Lobsters Restaurant
52 Iseya Restaurant
56 Espanola's Beer Garden
57 Savory, Kashmir Restaurant
60 Shepard's Inn Restaurant
67 Zuri Inn Bar
68 Guernica's Restaurant
69 Lili Marleen
70 Padre Faura Fast Food
72 Eddie's Steak House
77 Edelwies
79 Inglewood, Ermita Fast Food
80 Riverboat Bar
87 Swiss Matterhorn Restaurant
88 Mabini House Restaurant
90 Sun View Cafe & Restaurant
94 Food Fiesta Restaurant
99 India House Restaurant
101 Hobbit House
102 Shakey's Pizza

○ Shops, Offices, etc

1 Tourist Office
2 Medical Center
3 Police
5 Singapore Airlines
6 Pakistan Airlines
10 American Express
11 Alemars Bookshop
19 International Supermarket
25 Telex Office
26 Japan Airlines
28 Korean Airlines
41 Qantas
44 Egypt Airlines
53 Mabini Art Center
54 Bookmark
55 Mercury Drug Store
58 Solidaridad Bookshop
59 Philippine General Hospital
61 PIT Telegram
63 Post Office
65 Money Changer
71 Padre Faura Shopping Center
73 Cathay Pacific
74 Midland Plaza, Robinsons
85 Martin's Products Bakery
86 Philippine Airlines
91 PLTD — Long Distance Telephone
92 Ystaphil
93 Philippine Airlines
97 Pistang Filipino
98 Flea Market

weekly basis. *San Carlos Apartment & Hotel* on San Carlos St also have weekly and even daily rentals. Weekly rates are between P650 and 800 but day rates don't go down below P100.

Mabini Mansions are near the Kangaroo Club and for a two week stay you get down towards US$20 a day — which gets you a one bedroom unit with aircon, fridge, stove and cooking equipment. *Dona Petronila Mall* apartments have bedrooms with two large beds, living area with tables and lounge, kitchen with all facilities and bathroom with shower and toilet. They're air-con and the management is helpful and the monthly cost is about P2500 excluding electricity.

Places to Stay — top end

Hotels in this bracket will all have aircon, bath and other facilities. At the top end you can expect swimming pools, a variety of coffee bars and restaurants, discos, gyms and other home comforts. Good lower priced top end hotels include the *Otani-Manila* and the *Mabuhay Hotel*, both detailed below. Two other hotels in this same $20-30 bracket are the *Tower Hotel* (tel 50 3911) at 1313 Mabini St and the *New Swiss Inn* (tel 59 7080-89 or 6050-59) at 1394 General Luna St.

In the early '70s Manila suffered from a serious shortage of top end hotels — there was the elegant old *Manila Hotel* (a favourite with MacArthur) and the modern *Manila Hilton* but very little else. Then in the mid-70s Manila went in for a crazy boom in hotel construction resulting, in 1976, in a glut of new 'international standard' hotels, most of which suffered several years of low occupancy rates and large losses. Demand seems to have caught up with supply but there's still plenty of choice. Even if you're not staying there some of these new hotels are well worth a visit. There's some extravagant and amusing architecture of the 'lakes in the lobby' variety.

Top end hotels are generally in Ermita-Malate or Makati. A few, like the Hilton, are actually in Ermita but most of the tourist hotels from the mid-70s Manila hotel boom can be found along the bayfront in Malate. The Makati hotels are generally for business users who wish to be close to the business centre of the city. These 'international standard' hotels are generally in the US$70 to 90 price bracket — most people staying there will either be on a package tour or a business trip. Or looking for a discount.

The four main Makati hotels in the international category are the *Inter-Continental*, the *Mandarin*, the *Peninsula* and the *Manila Garden*, all very close together. On the bayfront Manila's best known hotel is undoubtedly the old *Manila Hotel* — an elegant old place in the Raffles (Singapore), Oriental (Bangkok) or Peninsula (Hong Kong) school. It's delightfully tropical in flavour, as romantic as you could ask for and very well kept. Round at the other end of the bayfront hotel strip the *Philippine Plaza* is, by contrast, the very image of a modern hotel with cascading waterfalls in the lobby and various other feats of technological extravagance. If you know how to print money you can book a night in the Imperial Suite, a 10-room rooftop palace at US$1350 which includes your own butler . . . . !

Other central 'international' hotels include the *Hilton*, one of the older big hotels but also the most centrally located if you want to be right in the action in Ermita. *Silahis* (with a Playboy Club), the *Holiday Inn*, the *Sheraton*, the *Hyatt* and the *Regent* can all be found along Roxas Boulevard, the bayfront hotel strip. There's one other major international hotel to consider and that's the *Philippine Village*, complete with casino, out by the airport. Details for the major top end hotels are

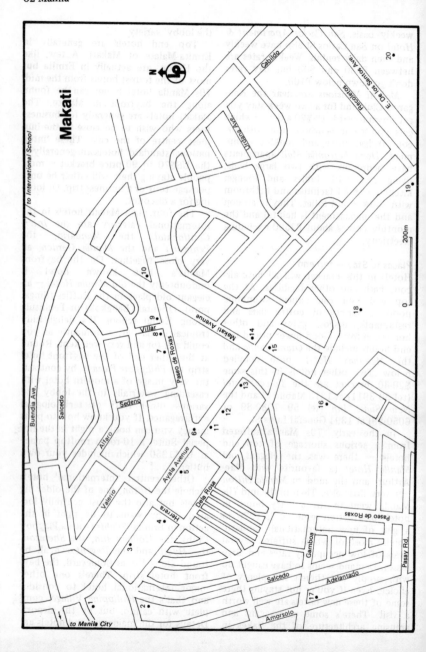

1 Makati Medical Center	10 Mandarin Hotel
2 Indonesian Embassy	11 Japanese Embassy
3 Hongkong & Shanghai Bank, Thai Embassy	12 Austrian Embassy
	13 Lufthansa Office
4 Korean Embassy	14 Manila Peninsula Hotel
5 Canadian Embassy	15 Rizal Theatre
6 Monument	16 Ayala Museum
7 Bank of America	17 Swiss Embassy
8 Australian Embassy	18 Makati Commercial Center
9 German Embassy, City Bank	19 Hotel Inter-Continental
	20 Forbes Park (North)

listed below:

Admiral Hotel (tel 57 2081) 2138 Roxas Boulevard, Malate, overlooking Manila Bay, 110 rooms, singles US$45-55, doubles US$50-60.

Ambassador Hotel 2010 A Mabini St, Malate, faces Manila Bay, 269 rooms, singles US$33-38, doubles US$40-45.

Hotel Aurelio (tel 50 9061) Padre Faura, Ermita, 140 rooms, singles US$24, doubles US$29.

Bayview Plaza Hotel (tel 50 3061), corner Roxas Boulevard & UN Avenue, Ermita, 310 rooms, singles US$35-58, doubles US$40-62.

Century Park Sheraton-Manila (tel 50 6041), corner Vito Cruz & M Adriatico, Malate, 500 rooms, singles US$70-80, doubles US$80-90.

Hotel Enrico (tel 50 8031), 1324 Guinto St, Ermita, 234 rooms, singles US$24, doubles US$32.

Hotel Frederic (tel 80 5611), Buendia, corner F B Harrison, Pasay, 111 rooms, singles P260, doubles P310.

Holiday Inn Manila (tel 59 7961), 3001 Roxas Boulevard, Pasay City, opposite the Cultural Center, 325 rooms, singles P500-600, doubles P550-650.

Hyatt Regency Manila (tel 831 2611) 2701 Roxas Boulevard, Pasay City, beside Manila Bay, 265 rooms, singles US$65-75, doubles US$79-90.

Hotel Inter-Continental Manila (tel 89 4011), Ayala Avenue, Makati, 400 rooms, singles US$70-80, doubles US$80-90.

Hotel Las Palmas Manila (tel 50 6661-9) 1616 A Mabini St, Malate, 105 rooms, singles US$24-30, doubles US$29-34.

Hotel Mabuhay (tel 59 2071), 1430 A Mabini St, Ermita, 103 rooms, singles US$27, doubles US$32.

The Manila Hotel (tel 47 0011) Rizal Park, overlooking Manila Bay, 570 rooms, singles US$72-115, doubles US$90-135.

Manila Hilton International (tel 57 3711), UN Avenue, Ermita, 416 rooms, singles US$66-84, doubles US$80-97.

Manila Garden Hotel (tel 85 7911) 4th Quadrant, MCC, Makati, 525 rooms, singles US$60-70, doubles US$70-80.

The Manila Mandarin (tel 85 7811) Makati Avenue & Paseo de Roxas, MCC, Makati, 504 rooms, singles US$98, doubles US$108.

Manila Midtown Ramada Hotel (tel 57 3911) Pedro Gil corner Adriatico St, Malate, 600 rooms, singles from US$55, doubles from US$65.

The Manila Peninsula (tel 85 7711) corner of Makati & Ayala Avenues, Makati, 537 rooms, singles US$105, doubles US$120.

Manila Royal Hotel Carlos Palanca Sr St, 220 rooms, singles from US$22, doubles from US$24.

Midland Plaza Hotel M Adriatico St, Ermita, 224 rooms, singles US$31, doubles US$35.

Hotel Mirador (tel 57 4911) 1000 San Marcelino, 340 rooms, singles US$33-35, doubles US$37-40.

Hotel Otani-Manila (tel 50 9051) 1000 Roxas Boulevard, Rizal Park, 150 rooms, singles US$23, doubles US$27.

Philippine Plaza Roxas Boulevard, park of Cultural Center Complex, 700 rooms, singles US$72-95, doubles US$90-110.

Philippine Village Hotel at Nayong Pilipino near airport, 520 rooms, singles US$50, doubles US$50-60.

The Regent of Manila (tel 831 0001) 2727 Roxas Boulevard, Pasay, overlooking Manila Bay, near Cultural Center, 464 rooms, singles US$60-70, doubles US$70-80.

Silahis International Hotel (tel 57 3811) 1990 Roxas Boulevard, Rizal Park, overlooking Manila Bay, 600 rooms, singles US$60-70, doubles US$70-80.

Sulo Hotel (tel 98 2411) Matalino St, Civic Center, Quezon City, 60 rooms, singles P265-310, doubles P310-350.

Tradewind Hotel Manila (tel 85 7011) South Superhighway, Makati, 301 rooms, singles P375, doubles P420.

Tropical Palace Resort Hotel (tel 827 1011-40) Phase IV, B F Holmes Paranaque, 352 rooms, singles US$40, doubles US$45.

Places to Eat

Manila has an impressive range of eating places particularly around Ermita.

Filipino Food Ermita is a good place to explore, especially along M H Del Pilar St. On that street *Myrna's* is popular with local people and crowded at meal times. The *Tahanan Restaurant* on the corner of M H Del Pilar and UN Avenue is Filipino again. It used to be known as the Fishnet and has a pleasant beer garden where you can sit outside and watch the passing parade. On the corner of Malvar and J Bocobo St the *Food Fiesta Restaurant* has Filipino and Japanese food and you can eat outside here.

The *Aristocrat*, on the corner of Roxas Boulevard and San Andres St, is a very popular Filipino restaurant and amazingly good value despite its name. It's one of the largest restaurants in Manila. Next door is *Josephine's*, a little more expensive but again the fish soup is superb and the lapu lapu fish is a specialty. The mixed seafood fisherman's basket is also worth trying.

Barrio Fiesta, at 110 Jorge Bocobo St near the Pension Filipinas, is a good place to try real Filipino food although it is somewhat more expensive than ordinary restaurants. The menu is extensive. *Galing-Galing* at 1133 L Guerrero St, behind the Bayview Hotel, is very good but rather more expensive again.

Fast Food There are lots of American-style food places around Manila and international food centres with a whole variety of regional food under one roof. The *Fast Food Center* on M H Del Pilar across from the Casa Pension is another place where you can sit and eat outside. It's a travellers' centre where the beer and food is good value, particularly in the beloved *Inglewood*. *Fast Food* on Padra Faura has international food — self-service and a vast choice of styles. Also on Padre Faura the *Restaurant Center* (Savory) offers a wide variety of international-style restaurants all under one roof.

Shakey's Pizza on Mabini St has quite good pizza (they even offer them in thick and thin varieties!) and rather expensive spaghetti. *Shepard's Inn* on Taft Avenue near the youth hostel has a very friendly proprietor and does excellent scrambled egg with onion and also Filipino food. *Mabini House* on Mabini St has good rice dishes and noodle soup.

Other Asian Food *United House* on Desmaralda St in Binondo is a very good Chinese Restaurant with a very wide choice; you really need at least three people to eat well here. On Adriatico St there's *India House* with Indian food; better value than the *Kashmir* on Padre Faura.

The *Iseya Restaurant* on the corner of M H Del Pilar and Padre Faura has Japanese food and a good value 'Executive Lunch' for P20 between noon and 1.30 pm.

Western Food *Eddie's Steakhouse* on Santa Monica St offers a complete menu for P18; try the coconut pie for dessert. It's closed on Sundays.

Haus Munchen on Mabini St across from the Tower Hotel is for those in need of some solid European food. Wiener schnitzel is the specialty and the serves are substantial. At 1394

General Luna St the *New Swiss Inn* has a similar appeal. They do fondue and even have Swiss wine but they also have a relatively good value menu of the day. Still on the European kick there's *Lili Marleen* on M H Del Pilar St with plain German cooking, very good fried potatoes and even salami bread.

La Taverna on Adriatico on the corner of Pedro Gil has Italian food. It's relatively expensive, particularly the imported red wine! *El Comedor* on the same corner is Spanish and other European. Finally the *Revolving Restaurant* at the Manila Royal Hotel on C Palanca St has good views over Manila. From Monday to Saturday there's an excellent value smorgasbord between 4 and 6.30 pm.

Entertainment

Jai Alai The Jai Alai fronton is on Taft Avenue across from Rizal Park. Games start in the late afternoon (after 5 pm) and they play daily except on Sundays and public holidays. Admission is P2 to 5 and you may have to stand at first. When you see someone get up, to place a bet for example, simply grab his seat — everybody else does. Admission to the Sky Room is P10 but you can use this fee towards drinks or food.

Cockfights There are several cockpits in Manila — the Philippine Cockers Club in Santa Ana; in Caloocan at Grave Park; Libertad St in Pasay; Baclaran in Paranaque. Fights take place on Sundays and public holidays and entry is P1. The Baclaran Cockpit on the boundary of Pasay City and Paranaque is also called the 7-Up Cockpit. Get a jeepney down Taft Avenue or down M H Del Pilar St.

Horse Racing Check the daily paper or phone the Manila Jockey Club on 21 1621. Racing takes place at the Santa Ana Race Track and the San Lazaro Hippodrome.

Casinos The floating casino burnt out but there's a casino at the *Philippine Village Hotel* at the airport. It's open 24 hours and entrance is free although you need your passport and no jeans are allowed. Minimum stake is P10 but there is no obligation to play.

If you get stuck at Manila airport overnight try the lobby of the Village Hotel behind the airport. You can leave luggage at the casino counter and see the unbalanced wealth of the Philippines being recklessly lost and won at the roulette tables. Not many hassles during the night — I just said I had a friend in the casino who kept on winning and I was waiting for him (it's open 24 hours). Mosquitoes are bad though.

Tom Channell

Zoo At the south end of Mabini St, the beginning of Harrison St, the Manila Zoo is open from 8 am to 6 pm. Generally it is dirty and not a good zoo but the monkey-eating eagles and the Tamaraw, a dwarf buffalo from the jungles of Mindoro are particularly worth seeing. The entrance is off Adriatico at the north-east corner and admission is P2.

Cinemas Films are advertised in the daily press. There are cinemas along Rizal Avenue, Santa Cruz and in Robinson's at Adriatico St, Ermita. Beware of pickpockets and bag snatchers in the cinemas.

Theatre Performances are irregular — check the daily press or enquire at the tourist office. Theatres include the *Rajah Sulayman Theatre*, Fort Santiago, Intramuros; *Philippine Folk Arts Theatre*, Roxas Boulevard; *Metropolitan Theatre*, Quezon Bridge and the *Cultural Center*, Roxas Boulevard.

Folk Dances There are Moslem dances on Sundays at 3 pm in the Mindanao section of the Philippine Village at

Nayong Pilipino at Manila International Airport on Airport Avenue, Pasay City.

There are cultural performances and plays daily at 7.30 pm at Pistang Pilipino on the corner of M H Del Pilar and Pedro Gil St. Entrance is free but the special variety show at 9.30 pm has a P30 cover charge. From midnight there's a disco.

Various events take place at the Cultural Center of the Philippines (CCP) on Roxas Boulevard. To find out what's on check the showcases on Roxas Boulevard or call the MOT on 59 9031 for details.

There's Polynesian dancing and food at 8 pm at the two Zamboanga Restaurants at 8739 Makati Avenue, Makati and 1619 Adriatico St, Ermita. Fiesta Pilipina at the Sulo Restaurant and the Plaza Restaurant in the Makati Commericial Center feature traditional Filipino dances and a buffet meal at 7 pm.

Nightlife

All the big hotels have bars and nightclubs, the most exclusive nightlife and live music is found along Roxas Boulevard. A few steps from the bayfront in the Ermita area there is all sorts of entertainment. M H Del Pilar St, between UN Avenue and Pedro Gil, is a non-stop line of bars and cocktail lounges. There are more along the smaller back streets like Alhambra St — where you'll find the *Daktari Club*, complete with Siberian tigers. The real Filipino bars in this district are, unfortunately, stereotyped, careless and cold in their furnishings and atmosphere. The bars run by expatriates are rather better but also rather more expensive.

Ricardo's Espanolas is in that same price category. On the corner of M H Del Pilar and Padre Faura this popular beer garden used to be a petrol station but its utilitarian origins have been quite eradicated. There's live music and after dark it's a very popular scene. It's possible that Ricardo's may be closing, in which case the action will probably shift to the *Casino Espanola* on Roxas Boulevard.

Folk Music *Hobbit House* at 1801 Mabini St in Malate has a very good international atmosphere, P10 cover charge and the dubious attractions of waiters who are all dwarves! *Bodega* on Mabini St in Ermita is also a good 'folkie' place although not as relaxed as Hobbit House. It's a popular Peace Corps hangout and has good submarine sandwiches.

My Father's Moustache on M H Del Pilar St in Malate is a small rustic folk pub — again very relaxed. On Mabini St country and western music is featured at *Club 21*. *Guernica's* at 1826 M H Del Pilar is lively after 10 pm, strolling guitarists, a friendly place. *El Bodegon* at 1537 also has live music in a Spanish cellar atmosphere.

Other Music Good jazz at the *Braukeller* at the Holiday Inn on Roxas Boulevard. Jazz is becoming more and more popular in Manila so watch out for new places.

Discos The big hotels all have discos — they include the *Los Horizon* at the Philippine Plaza; *Apres* at the Manila Hotel; *1571* at the Manila Hilton; *Stargazer* at the Silahis and *Cue* at the Regent of Manila. The disco at the Tower Hotel on Mabini St is also very popular.

Bars Popular bars where you can enjoy a beer without being hassled include the *Kangaroo Club* at 476 UN Avenue, *Lili Marleen's* at 1323B Del Pilar or *Andy Capp's* at 429 Arquiza St. On Padre Faura near the junction with Adriatico in Ermita the *Old English Pub* has a mock-Victorian dark interior with San Mig and draft beer at around P5.50 at the bar, more at the tables. The menu is pricey but the food is pretty good.

Getting Around

City Transport Around Manila city buses announce only their final destination on the sign on front. That can be a large complex like the MIA (Manila International Airport), a street name like Ayala (Ayala Avenue in Makati) or a whole suburb like Santa Cruz (Chinatown). Depending on the distance the trip costs 65c or more. At the end of the Rizal Avenue Extension there is a statue of Andres Bonifacio known as the 'monumento' — this is a very popular stop for jeepneys and buses. A useful jeepney route is from Santa Cruz down M H Del Pilar to Harrison and Taft near the airport to Buendia. That covers most of visitors' Manila.

The air-con Love Buses are very popular in Manila. They are blue, operate on several main routes and cost a flat P4. Non air-con transit buses are P2.50. Have small change to hand as bus drivers usually cannot change large notes. The Escolta-Ayala/Medical Center bus is a useful one for tourists — the Love Bus goes from the Calle Escolta (Binondo/Santa Cruz) through Ermita (M H Del Pilar) to Makati (the embassies) and to the Makati Commercial Center. It returns through Mabini St in Ermita. There are no fixed stops on the way. Don't throw your ticket away — there are frequent inspections.

Airport Transport Manila International Airport, MIA, is only 12 km from the city centre and taxi fares are very low so it's cheap and easy to get into the centre. But ignore the hordes waiting outside the terminal to take you to their taxi, just around the corner. If you fall for this your fare will be outrageously expensive — dollars not pesos! One way to avoid being ripped off by taxi drivers is to approach any of the police at or near the stand — there are always some there — and ask them to call you a cab.

When you're aboard make sure the meter is turned on. Taxis all (or almost all anyway) have meters so there should be no need to bargain, as you must in many Asian countries. Should your driver refuse to turn the meter on get out and into another taxi. There are plenty available. Flagfall is P2.50 and to Rizal Park by Ermita will cost P20 to 25.

If you ask your driver to go via the Roxas Boulevard, past the Cultural Center, towards Rizal Park, you can turn into Santa Monica St and get out at one of the open-air bars on M H Del Pilar — like the Inglewood on the corner. Then you can have your first San Mig before choosing one of the many small hotels close by.

If pesos are very important you can also get into town by bus. Walk out of the international terminal and turn right, walk about 100 metres. The bus stop sign is located under a bridge, should you not find it just ask a cop or one of those blue guards. Ignore the taxi drivers who will tell you there is no bus or that the last one has gone. Every 10 or 15 minutes a silver-with-red-stripe California Bus Company bus will come by — the destination sign will say 'Santa Cruz, Monumento'. The fare is P1.

As you come into town you might travel down Taft Avenue. A metro-rail (LRT) is under construction in Manila and causing considerable disruption to traffic on Taft Avenue and Rizal Avenue. It's expected to be opened around the end of 1984. If you do travel down Taft Avenue the first landmark is La Salle College on your left. Further down on your left you'll see the Hilton Hotel towering over the rest of Ermita — get off shortly before it for the hostels on the right side of Taft Avenue or the Ermita pensions.

Next landmark is the Coca Cola/Jai Alai neon sign on your right and almost immediately you're at the City Hall, this is only about 200 metres beyond the Hilton. Leap off here for the YMCA.

Soon after that you're across the river and you've missed everything!.

For an interesting and cheap (P1.20) way of getting to the airport (domestic or international) take a jeepney from Taft and Padre Faura to Baclaran. At Baclaran grab a jeepney to either airport (you'll have a short walk to get to the international airport). Have one of the traffic cops flag down the appropriate jeepney for you if you're not sure.

Ron Marudi

TRANSPORT FROM LUZON

Most transport from Luzon to other islands operates from Manila but there are also some flights and shipping services from other locations, principally from south Luzon.

To the Batan Islands Twice weekly Philippine Airlines fly from Manila via Tuguegarao and Laoag to Basco.

To Catanduanes There's a daily ferry from Tabaco at noon, the crossing takes about four hours. PAL flies daily from Manila via Naga to Virac.

To Cebu Many ships make the 22 hour voyage from Manila to Cebu. The best of them include the *MV Sweet Roro* of Sweet Lines which departs on Sunday and Thursday at 9 am. The *Dona Virginia* of William Lines goes at 10 am on Sunday and 8 pm on Wednesday.

The *MV Don Enrique* of Sulpicio Lines goes on Sunday at 10 am. The same line's *MV Philippine Princess* goes at 10 am on Tuesday and at 6 pm on Friday.

PAL flies several times daily from Manila and from Legaspi on three days of the week.

To Leyte Several ships go from Manila to Tacloban. The best ones include: *MV Sweet Love* of Sweet Lines which goes on Wednesday at 8 pm and takes 36 hours via Catbalogan. The *MV Tacloban City* of William Lines goes on Monday via Catbalogan at 3 pm and Friday direct at 9 am and takes 22 hours. The *MV Dona Marilyn* of Sulpicio Lines goes on Wednesday at 3 pm via Catbalogan or on Sunday at 11 am direct. The same company's ship *MV Don Alfredo* goes to Maasin on Friday at 10 pm.

PAL flies daily from Manila to Tacloban.

To Lubang Tuesdays and sometimes Thursdays there is a 10 pm departure with the *Mercedes* of Mindoro Navigation Lines from Pier 6 (near Sweet Lines), North Harbour to Tilik. The trip takes nine hours but it's not very reliable. When I woke up the next morning at 7 am we were still in the harbour! So I drove to Pan Bridge at 8.30 am and boarded the *Superstar*, a Mindoro Shipping Lines boat. This departed at 10.30 am and travel time to Tilik was six hours.

To Marinduque A boat departs daily from Lucena City to Balacanan. The departure times are irregular but the trip takes about four hours. From Maila to Lucena City take a BLTB Bus from E de Los Santos Avenue, Pasay.

PAL flies four times weekly from Manila to Boac.

To Masbate The *MV Cagayan de Oro City* of William Lines goes from Manila on Wednesday at 1 pm and takes about 16 hours. The *MV Augustina II* of Escano Lines also goes from Manila on Monday at 9 pm.

The shorter crossing to Masbate is on the daily noon boat from Bulan. The crossing takes four hours.

PAL flies daily except Sunday from Manila to Masbate.

To Mindanao Sweet Lines' *MV Sweet Land* goes to Zamboanga on Sunday at noon. William Lines' *MV Manila City* goes to Zamboanga and Davao, departing at 11 pm on Tuesday. They also have the *MV Misamis Occidental* which goes via Tagbilaran to Ozamis and Iligan. It departs at 10 am on Friday and takes 29 hours to Tagbilaran. Sulpicio Lines' *MV Don Enrique* goes via Cebu to Davao, departing on Sunday at 10 am.

PAL flies from Manila to Cagayan de Oro, Butuan, Davao and Zamboanga.

To Mindoro From Batangas ships go to Calapan and Puerto Galera. The departures to Puerto Galera are frequent. At last check departures were at 12.30 pm and the trip takes two hours. Special trips cost P200 to 250. At 5 pm there's a ship to Calapan, jeepneys to Puerto Galera go the next day.

The *MV Elizabeth* and the *MV Sea Palace* go from Manila to San Jose — see the To Palawan section for more information. PAL flies daily to Mamburao and San Jose.

To Negros Four ships of the Negros Navigation Company (tel 21 2691) go from Manila direct to Bacolod City. The departure times are frequent. The departures are as follows:

MV Claudio	Sun 9 am
MV San Sebastian	Tues noon
MV Don Julio	Tues, Fri 1 pm
MV Santa Maria	Thurs 12.30 pm

There's also the *MV Cebu City* of William Lines which goes from Manila to Dumaguete on Friday at 9 am. The trip takes about 26 hours. The *MV Dona Susana* of Sulpicio Lines goes from Manila to Dumaguete on Thursday at 2 am. The trip takes about 30 hours.

PAL flies from Manila to Bacolod City and via Cebu to Dumaguete.

To Palawan Ships and schedules to Palawan with any company are likely to be changed very often. Check first! Two ships of the Oriental Maritime Service (tel 50 7601) at 1418 San Marcelino St, Ermita go once weekly from Manila. The trip takes three days.

Don't count on departures being on time. When you buy your ticket at the shipping office make sure the ticket is stamped with a number below 400. There are four decks on the ships, the uppermost is first class and the three below are second class. If your ticket number is greater than 400 you'll be quartered below decks!

First and second are not much different — you get the same soup, rice and dried fish to eat three times a day. Take some additional food of your own if that sounds boring. Eating utensils are supplied but there are no hot drinks available so bring a thermos flask.

The ship anchors for four to five hours off Cuyo Island, en route to Palawan, and you can go ashore for sightseeing in one of the small passenger boats. Before landing in Puerto Princesa you must fill out a landing form which is collected before you leave the harbour for the town. After three days on the boat you'll have many useful addresses.

Because of the very long stop-over in San Jose, Mindoro, the following ships are not much faster although you do get coffee with your food on the Elizabeth. The *MV Elizabeth* of William Lines goes from Manila via San Jose on Mindoro. Departure is on Wednesday at 5 pm and it takes 25 hours to San Jose and after a 24 hour stop there another 22 hours to Puerto Princesa. The *MV Sea Palace* of Magasagana Shipping Lines goes from Manila via San Jose and

Coron. Departure is on Wednesday at 7 pm and it takes 26 hours to San Jose, plus a two hour stop in Coron. Magasagana (tel 48 4437 or 47 6964) are at 283-285 Jaboneros St, Binondo, Manila.

PAL flies daily from Manila to Puerto Princesa. There are also charter flights from Manila to Coron.

To Panay From Manila ships go to Iloilo, Roxas, Batan and New Washington.

The MV Don Eusebio of Sulpicio Lines goes to Iloilo, Zamboanga and Dadiangas, departing on Tuesday at 10 am except when it's on a cruise.

The Negros Navigation Company has a number of ships sailing from Manila to Iloilo. The MV Don Claudio leaves on Friday at 1 pm. The MV Dona Florentina sails on Tuesday and Friday at 4 pm. The MV Don Julio departs at 1 pm on Friday.

Aboitiz Lines have the MV Lanao which goes to New Washington/Kalibo via Romblon, departing at noon on Mondays and sometimes on Thursdays too. The same company has the MV Aklan which goes to Dumaguit/Kalibo, leaving at noon on Wednesday and Sunday.

William Lines have the MV Cagayan de Oro City to Batan which leaves at 4 pm on Saturday and takes about 15 hours for the trip. Reportedly William Lines have just started a weekly service direct to Boracay.

PAL has flights daily from Manila to Iloilo and Roxas. The new airport at Kalibo is under construction and will be open for traffic soon. There are charter flights available to Sicogon. For P450 (one-way) you can be flown in a private plane from Manila to Caticlan (near Boracay) in just under two

hours. Contact Mr Yvon Le Seux, tel 59 7838 or 88 5038.

To Romblon From Manila ships go to Romblon on Romblon and Odiongan on Tablas. The Aboitiz Lines ship MV Lanao goes to Romblon, leaving on Monday at noon and sometimes on Thursday too. The MV Grace of William Lines goes to Odiongan, leaving at 1 pm on Tuesday. The same company also has the MV Albert to Odiongan, leaving at 10 am on Friday.

From Lucena City there are also three boats weekly to Romblon.

PAL flies five times weekly from Manila to Tugdon on Tablas.

To Samar There are several ships operating from Manila to Catbalogan. The William Lines ship MV Tacloban City goes on Monday at 3 pm. The Sweet Lines ship MV Sweet Love goes on Wednesday at 8 pm. The Sulpicio Lines ship MV Dona Angelina goes on Saturday at 7 pm while the Dona Marilyn goes on Wednesday at 3 pm.

Three ships daily go from Matnog to Allen. The fare is P12 but there is also a P1 harbour charge on each side. Things can often change here with bad weather conditions. It's possible the ships will leave at 8 am and at noon. If you take a small pump boat to avoid staying overnight in Matnog the crossing can be very rough and wet.

The Cardinal Shipping Company's MV Cardinal Ferry goes at 8.30 am and takes 1¼ hours. The San Pablo Lines have two ships which take two hours to cross — the MV Penefrancia departs at 10.30 am, the MV Maria Christina goes at 1 pm.

PAL flies three times a week from Manila to Calbayog and Catarman.

Around Manila

All the trips described in this section can be done as day outings from Manila. The map shows towns within a few hours drive by bus. Nevertheless, at least an overnight stay should be devoted to Olongapo, Pagsanjan and Matabungkay. Some destinations can be combined — such as Tagaytay for its volcano and Matabungkay for the beach. Other towns make good stops on the way to somewhere else — such as Olongapo on the way to Hundred Islands or Pagsanjan on the way to south Luzon.

There is an expressway from Metro-Manila going north to Dau, a little beyond Angeles, and another goes south to about Calamba. Buses using expressways rather than the ordinary roads advertise this with the sign 'expressway'.

BATAAN PENINSULA

It's not possible to make a round trip of the Bataan Peninsula. The stretch from Bagac to Olongapo is blocked off for military reasons by the Philippines Navy. At Morong about a thousand Vietnamese boat people live in a place known as the 'Procession Center'.

On Mt Samat, a little to the south of Balanga, the provincial capital, you will find Dambana ng Kagitingan, a national monument to the victims of the Bataan Death March. There is a cross over 90 metres high, from which you get a good view over the peninsula and of Manila Bay.

CORREGIDOR

Corregidor was an important fortress island in WW II. Back in 1898 this island, strategically important due to its location at the entrance to Manila Bay, was used by the Americans in the war against Spain. Construction of the Malinta Tunnel began 25 years later and this served as General Douglas MacArthur's headquarters from December 1941 to March 1942. Filipinos and Americans struggled against the Japanese invaders after they had evacuated to the island. Quezon left by submarine and eventually MacArthur was smuggled out on a PT boat. After the island fell the infamous Bataan Death March commenced from here.

Today the Philippines Army runs the place. There is a lot of WW II junk lying around the shattered remains of Arthur's headquarters and a museum of the war with a good three-dimensional map. There are stunning views and sunsets from the summit of the highest hill and a soft drink stand which sells Coke and San Mig beer.

Getting There

Daily, except Mondays, a hovercraft from the Philippine Navy Headquarters, Roxas Boulevard, makes the 50 minute, 45 km trip to 'the rock'. Departures are at 7.30 am and 12.30 pm and the round trip, including a tour during your two hours on the island, costs P280!

There's also a relatively new service being offered between March and May known as the 'summer special'. You catch the *MV Mariveles del Sol*, leaving Rizal Park every Friday, Saturday and Sunday at 8 am and returning at 6 pm. Included in the price of P80 is an island tour. The organiser is Arpan Tourist Industries Corporation (tel 50 1532 or 50 1571).

Naturally there is a more interesting alternative. First take a bus to Mariveles on the Bataan Peninsula — one change on the way. This is where the US forces embarked for Corregidor and where the Bataan Death March commenced. From here hire an outrigger banca for the 13 km trip out to the island — perhaps P100 roundtrip with a bit of bargaining. It's a rather noisy and wet ride over but if you bring your own food and sleep

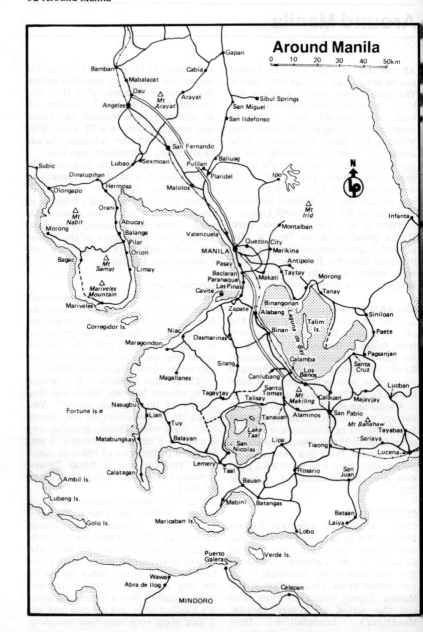

Around Manila

0 10 20 30 40 50km

on the beach the only expense on the island will be a P3 'upkeep charge'. There is also a hotel and youth hostel on Corregidor. Get the banca to come back for your the next day and don't pay until you get back to the mainland.

When the tourists leave the island is quiet and eerie. There's a real sense of history — you can imagine MacArthur stomping around shouting 'I shall return' while the bombs and shells land all around. A friendly Philippines Army officer may be happy to show you some of the less accessible places.

OLONGAPO

The US Navy is stationed here and while this is not a good reason for a visit it is what has sprung up around the base that makes the town interesting. There are countless bars, nightclubs, massage salons, pubs and cinemas. Some of the best rock, country and western and disco music can be heard in the clubs. Olongapo is for entertainment and it's not too expensive although the town's principal industries have been described as 'beer and prostitution'. There are more bars and also beach resorts in nearby Subic but the beaches themselves aren't particularly good. San Miguel, slightly north of Subic Bay, is better than any of the beaches between Olangapo and Subic.

Every year in February on the weekend after Valentine's Day, Olongapo has its Mardi Gras Festival, with live music, beer and dancing in the streets, mainly at Magsaysay Avenue where most of the clubs are.

Places to Stay

The *Bayside Hotel* (tel 5042) at 1695 Rizal Avenue has singles with fan at P25, singles/doubles with fan and bath are P35/45. Those are '24-hour' prices so you can guess what the rooms are generally used for. You must pay daily and in advance but the beds are good and wide so a single is fine for two.

The *MGM Hotel* on Maysaysay Drive has rooms with fan and bath for P45 or with air-con and bath for P70. They're good, clean rooms; there's an 11 am check-out. There are numerous more expensive places here.

There are several resorts along the coast from Olongapo to Subic. You can rent rooms here for P40 to 60 but the beaches themselves aren't particularly good. The *Baloy Beach* is a typical resort along here. Opposite the *Kale Beach Resort* is the slightly rundown *Villa Rovisa* which has a swimming pool although it's no longer in the best condition. You could also try *Gaines Island* in Subic Bay. This resort, really only part of a peninsula, not an island, is run by a retired US Navy man, Ernest J Gaines, who rents out cottages for about P70 or less for longer stays. You can get there for P20-30 with a banca from Barrio Barretto which is between Olongapo and Subic.

Getting There

Coming from Manila there are several buses daily from the Victory Liner Station, Rizal Avenue Extension. The trip takes about three hours.

From Baguio Victory Liner buses depart about hourly from 5.30 am to 5.30 pm. The trip takes six hours.

LAS PINAS

This small town is famous for its unique bamboo organ in the San Jose church. Originally started in 1816 by the Spanish Father Diego Cerra it was made from bamboo to save money and completed in 1824. Standing over five metres high it has 832 bamboo pipes and 122 of metal. In 1973-75 the organ was given a complete overhaul in Germany and now sounds as good as new. A small shop in the church front sells records and cassettes of bamboo-organ music. Note that the church is closed on Sundays until 1 pm.

Las Pinas is also a centre for jeepney

manufacture and the workshops are quite happy to have people looking around although they are closed Sunday mornings. Leaving the church the Sarao jeepney factory is about three km further south at the main street.

Getting There

From Manila a bus going towards Zapote or Cavite on Taft Avenue will get you there in half an hour. You can also take a jeepney at M H Del Pilar St, going to Baclaran and transfer there to a jeepney going to Zapote.

CAVITE

This town on the southern side of Manila Bay has no real attractions to offer and its beaches, like Lido Beach, are not particularly good. It does, however, make a pleasant day trip from the city and the fair and leisure park known as 'Covelandia' is near Cavite. Near the dock in Samonte Park there are a couple of pubs and bars.

Getting There

Plenty of buses make the less than one hour run from Manila, starting along Taft Avenue.

LOS BANOS

The University of the Philippines (UP) has a forestry institute with a botanic garden in Los Banos. Not far from there is the International Rice Research Institute (IRRI). You can also have a healthy bath in the Los Banos hot springs. In Calamba, a little north of Los Banos, the national hero Rizal was born. Rizal House with its garden is now a memorial and museum.

In Tadlac, a small village between Calamba and Los Banos, you can stay with fisher families and go out night fishing on Laguna de Bay. Near the village is the lovely Alligator Lake, a deep volcano lake but without alligators! About a km towards Los Banos you'll see the sign 'Rainbow Falls'. From here

it's a 30 minute walk to the refreshing, 50 metre high falls which are located in a gorge and surrounded by tropical vegetation. Not far from Los Banos is the Philippine Art Center from which you get a good view over the Laguna. There are jeepneys going up there.

From Los Banos a jeepney or tricycle will take you via San Pablo to Alaminos. Hidden Valley in Alaminos is a fascinating private property with interesting vegetation and several springs. Admission is a hefty P70 but this does include a good lunch — bring your swimming gear.

There's a pleasant two km walk up to the Mt Makiling National Park with a good view from the top followed by an easy stroll down.

Places to Stay

The *Lakeview Health Resort Hotel* (tel 5 0101) at 1 Lopez St, Los Banos has rooms at P50/80 with bath. You can rent apartments for P60 to 200 by the Cuyab Hot Springs — complete with hot bath, hotter pool and shower.

Getting There

From Manila take a bus from the Lawton terminal towards Santa Cruz and get off by the crossing in Los Banos. Look for the sign 'UP Los Banos'. Note that the Lawton terminal is due to be relocated. Buses towards south Luzon go through Alaminos and San Pablo City. They go from the Pantranco South Express terminal in E de Los Santos Avenue, Pasay City.

PAGSANJAN

A trip to Pagsanjan (pronounced pagsan-han) is a must on every Filipino tour itinerary. The last section of Francis Ford Coppola's *Apocalypse Now* was filmed here. The Magdapio Waterfalls are only part of Pagsanjan's attractions; it's the river trip through the picturesque tropical gorge which is the real pull. Two 'banqueros' will paddle you upstream against the strong current in a banca or canoe. It's a feat of strength which taxes even two men paddling together. To the last major waterfall you can ride on a bamboo raft for an extra P4 or you can swim — very refreshing.

Shooting the rapids is most exciting in August and September when the river is high. Don't hang too tightly to the side of the boat — keep your hands inside or you'll risk crushed fingers. It's a wet trip downstream so take a plastic bag to protect your camera. The return trip costs P41 per person, plus P5 entry, no more than two to a banca. Extra tips will, of course, be requested. Pagsanjan gets lots of tourists who are ready to throw pesos around. The tourist authority requires notification of entry, the banqueros, who run the hostel and Falls Lodge, mustn't be incited to any sort of rebellion!

Don't go on weekends when the tourists are there in such numbers it's like an anthill. If you stay overnight at Pagsanjan and leave for the falls at dawn you'll be on the river long before the tourist hordes arrive. As the sunlight only reaches the deep valleys late in the day photographers will have quite a bit of difficulty taking pictures in normal light. The tourist office has now placed a sign on the falls stating that it is only the first falls and the main falls are further on.

If you have time take a day trip to the Japanese gardens. The view is splendid. Also worth a visit are two lakes — Sierra and Caliraya — and the exclusive resort Magos Site. You can pick up boats at Agoucillo on the south-west side of the lake. If you are interested in woodcarvings don't miss Paete, the Philippine home of ebony carvings. It's only a short jeepney ride north of Pagsanjan.

Places to Stay

Willy Flores, the postman at 788 Garcia St, behind the post office, has a few rooms at P40. Just ask for Willy Flores, everyone in town knows him. But find your own way there — a guide will want P10 commission and you'll end up paying more.

Miss Estella y Umale's *Riverside Bungalow* on Garcia St has two bungalows with double rooms with fan and bath for P90. It's just two houses from Willy Flores and she's a good cook.

The *Pagsanjan Youth Hostel* on General Luna St has fan-cooled dorm beds at P15 or P2 more if you're not a YHA member. A double with fan in the 'Bamboo House' is P40. The hostel can be a little tricky to find. From the main square go across the bridge over the river and take the first turn right. It's then on your left, a fair way down. Look carefully for the sign. It's run by friendly and helpful people who will help arrange boat trips. An alternative way there from Santa Cruz is to get off the jeepney shortly after you pass the town gate. On the right side is the SHARE-LITE Bake Shop and here you can enquire about the YH. The owner is the husband of the hostel warden and he might take you there in his jeep.

Up market the *Pagsanjan Falls Lodge* has rooms with fan at P100, with fan and bath or with air-con at P135. If you're staying here try to get rooms 10, 11 or 12 in the coconut grove — their verandahs look right out on the river. There is also a very beautiful pool but the hotel is a popular pick-up point for elderly gays looking for young Filipino lovers. Make it clear you're not interested or you'll be continually pestered. The *Tropical Resort Hotel* has a swimming pool, restaurant and clean rooms with air-con and bath for P80.

Places to Eat

The *DURA-Fe Restaurant* in General Jaina St has very good food — try the sweet & sour fish. It shuts at 8.30 pm. Good pancit Canton in the D&C Lun-

cheonette on the National Rd towards the Falls Lodge.

Getting There

Take a Laguna Transport Corporation bus from the Lawton Bus Terminal to Santa Cruz — sometimes even all the way to Pagsanjan. There are several buses daily, the trip takes three hours and costs P12. You can also catch this bus on Taft Avenue. Note that the Lawton terminal is to be relocated, check first.

BLTB buses also go from their terminal in E de Los Santos Avenue in Pasay. From Santa Cruz you take a jeepney to Pagsanjan. Ignore the Santa Cruz tricycle riders! They'll come on the bus and try to convince foreigners that you must take a tricycle from there.

Supreme Lines go from Santa Cruz/ Pagsanjan to Lucena in three hours. The buses from Pagsanjan to Lucena are not quite as frequent as the hostel warden would have you believe. If you don't want to wait take a jeepney to Lucban and from there another to Lucena. If you're continuing from here to south Luzon it's not necessary to first return to Manila. Similarly you can get to Batangas via Lucena but the faster way is to take the bus going to Manila and get off in Calamba. From there jeepneys go direct to Batangas pier. If you prefer to travel by bus take a jeepney from Calamba to Tanauan only and wait there for a bus coming from Manila.

TAGAYTAY (TAAL VOLCANO)

Due to its high altitude (700 metres) and cool climate, Tagaytay was once proposed as an alternative summer resort to Baguio. The very spread-out town offers visitors superb views of the crater lake with its volcanic island but only if the weather is clear. At the viewing place, in front of the hotel, folk dances with native music take place at mid-day — the entrance fee is P10 and is calculated into the bill as part of the general consumption but it's only worth a bottle of beer!

The volcano is the smallest active volcano in the world. If you want to climb it you can make advance arrangements before you leave Manila — contact the Volcanology Commission, Quezon City (tel 60 8303). There's a jeepney from Tagaytay for P10 — taking the whole jeepney would cost P200. It's about 17 km from Tagaytay to the pier and the road is narrow and has little traffic. The boat across to the volcano island and back costs P120 and the boatman will show you the volcano. You can also cross from Talisay; jeepneys travel from Tanauan to Talisay about every half hour.

Places to Stay

The *Taal Vista Lodge* has doubles with bath at P250 but there are several alternatives for cheaper accommodation. You can rent tents in the hotel grounds. They're P75 a double and P15 for mattress and sheets. The P10 entry charge to

Manila

a   Entrance to Fort Santiago
b   Sunday morning on Manila Bay

the hotel is included in the price.

If you ask in the restaurant you should be able to get fairly cheap accommodation in private homes. Alternatively, about three km before the Taal Vista Lodge and just after the roundabout, look for the sign 'room to rent'. A double without bath here is P30, with bath from P70. Another nice place comparable to the Taal Vista Lodge is *Villa Adelaida* with bungalows at P70 per person. Coming from Manila instead of turning right to Tagaytay you have to turn left. It's near the road going down to the lake towards Talisay.

Getting There

From Manila there are several buses daily from the BLTB Bus Company on E de Los Santos Avenue, Pasay. Take the bus to Nasugbu, the trip takes 1½ hours.

If you're going to Tagaytay and Pagsanjan you don't need to return to Manila between the two. Take a bus from Tagaytay to Zapote. From there continue in a jeepney to Alabang and another bus to Santa Cruz. Finally another jeepney will get you to Pagsanjan. It sounds rather complicated but in actual fact it's quite quick and fairly simple.

There's also an interesting back-roads route from Batangas to Lake Taal. Take a jeepney from Batangas to Lemery, the road is bad and very dusty so try to get a seat in the front. It's a 1½ hour ride. From there take a jeepney to San Nicolas on the south-western shore of the lake.

You can stay overnight in the luxury bungalows of the *Playa del Sol*. They cost just P25 except during the summer months of March to May when they cost about P150. You can also ask for a room at the store where you can sit outside at the corner of the plaza. It's near the shore where you can charter a boat for the trip to the volcano island for P100 but you have to get up very early to see the magnificent dawn. Shepherds living at the edge of the crater will act as guides. It's easy to get lost during the descent so a guide is recommended if you want to go to the lake of the old crater. You can climb the new crater, which last erupted in 1965, yourself. There are four craters on the island.

The last jeepney from San Nicolas to Lemery departs at 5 pm to serve the last BLTB bus in Lemery, leaving for Pasay/Manila at 6 pm. If you take the morning ferry from Puerto Galera to Batangas and from there a jeepney to Lemery and San Nicolas there's enough time to climb the new crater and head for Manila with the last bus. From Lemery to Manila it takes three hours and the first part of the road is very dusty. To get to Santa Cruz/Pagsanjan change in Calamba.

MATABUNGKAY

This is the most popular beach in the vicinity of Manila. Although the sand is grey the water is clean and on weekends there are many day-trippers. You can stay overnight in cottages on the beach — they're big enough for two but don't pay more than P60, some ask up to

a   Filipino house and tropical flowers
b   Steam rises near Tiwi, south Luzon

P400! Try the *Sea Lodge* with clean doubles at P60.

The beach at Nasugbu, known as 'white sands', is worth recommending. It's three or four km north and you can get there by tricycle or with an outrigger which will cost P50 to 60 there and back. There is a hotel here, several somewhat expensive cottages, and a restaurant but not too many tourists.

Getting There

Take a bus from the BLTB Company on E de Los Santos Avenue, Pasay towards Nasugbu. The trip takes 2½ hours and from Lian you take a jeepney to Matabungkay. You can also go from Nasugbu to Batangas by jeepney in three stages.

BATANGAS

The only reason for coming here is to continue on to the island of Mindoro but if you do decide to stop off at Batangas be prepared for the porters for Puerto Galera. They're everywhere — at the pier, in town, sometimes even on the buses from Manila. They receive P5 a head or more from their hirer and their leechlike persistence can only be described as obtrusive. The best way to deal with them is to be firm although in the busy season — around Christmas in particular — they can guarantee you accommodation. They will also load your luggage on to the ship and hold a place free for you but anyone who takes them up on this and not the accommodation will have to argue with a very nasty porter.

Should you have any spare time in Batangas you can get something to eat and drink at the small restaurant in town or visit one of the friendly lighthouse keepers — without porters.

Places to Stay

The *Alpa Hotel* (tel 725 2213) has rooms with fan for P25/45, with fan and bath for P50/65 or with air-con and bath for P80/90. There's a swimming pool, an expensive restaurant and a disco on weekends. It's a long way out of town.

The *City Hotel*, on the other hand, is simpler and cheaper and in the centre of town. Or try the *Lodging House*, just five minutes' walk from the centre. It's a lovely place, quiet and fantastically clean although it is a part-time brothel complete with horizontal mirrors by the beds and so on. Rooms with huge fans are P50.

Way up market and on the beach the *Hotel Punta Baluarte Inter-Continental* (tel 89 4011) has 134 rooms from US$40 and up.

Getting There

Always ask for 'Batangas City' when enquiring about transport, otherwise confusion will arise with the Batangas area. Buses from Manila go from the Lawton Terminal or you can stop them on Taft Avenue although the best places will be gone then. The trip is actually only interesting if you're going to Mindoro. Departures from Batangas to Puerto Galera are now at 12.30 pm so you have to get there reasonably early if you don't want to stay overnight. The trip, barring breakdowns, takes 2½ hours and costs around P15. Take a Batangas Pier bus and beware of pickpockets on these buses — they often operate as a team of three.

Air-con buses for Batangas operate from the BLTB Terminal on E de Los Santos Avenue, Pasay City and only cost a few peso more. They don't operate directly to the pier — you terminate in Batangas City and have to take a jeepney to the harbour.

If you arrive in Batangas from Mindoro you can take one of the Manila buses which will be waiting at the pier. You can also travel into town by jeepney and catch a bus there — a BLTB bus to Pasay City. There are also air-con buses there.

There's an interesting back-roads route between Batangas and Taal Lake. See the Tagaytay section for more details. Coming from Tagaytay on this route you first have to take a bus to 'Boundary', the border between the Cavite and Batangas regions, and then a jeepney to Lemery (the last one leaves at 4.30 pm) and another to Batangas City.

SAN PABLO

San Pablo is known as the city of the seven seas. It's good for walks such as to Sampaloc Lake, to Pandin Lake or to Yambo Lake. A specialty of the floating restaurants is freshwater fish.

Places to Stay

You can stay in the *City Inn*, *San Rafael River Resort*, *Bunot Lake Resort*, *Bae-Yiw Resort* or in the *Sampaloc Youth Hostel* on Schetelik Avenue, Efarca Subdivision. The youth hostel has a very friendly owner who accommodates the overflow in her own house and there's also good Filipino food there.

North Luzon

The island of Luzon has an area of over 100,000 square km and some 50% of all Filipinos live here. Luzon takes the top position in the area of culture and economics and also has far more tourist attractions than any other islands. Central Luzon is covered in the Around Manila section. Prime attractions in North Luzon are Mountain Province, with its mountain tribes and rice terraces, and the beautiful islands of the Hundred Islands National Park.

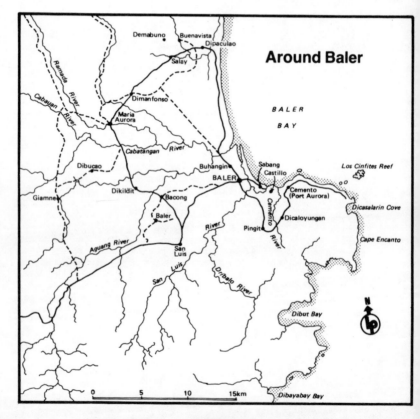

BALER

Baler is in Aurora, the sub-province of Quezon, on the east coast of North Luzon on the Philippine Sea. The main part of Coppola's *Apocalypse Now* was filmed here. Although the town itself is not that interesting from here you can go bushwalking in the surrounding hills, visit one of the Negrito tribes (Dumagats) or spend a few days skindiving or just lazing on the beach at Dibut. The coral at Dibut is very beautiful and you can hire a boat for fishing at P25 an hour, including equipment. There's good surf in Baler Bay in December.

You can walk to Dibut or make other walks into the mountains simply by following the rivers. It's also a beautiful walk to the radar weather station on top of Cape Encanto. Along the way there are several springs such as Digisit Springs. From Dipaculao, north of Baler, it's possible to go into the mountains where some Ilongot tribes live.

Places to Stay

The *Amihan Hotel & Restaurant* in Baler is P15 per person per night or you can rent a cottage from *Cape Encanto Nipa Huts* in Cemento which should be completed — so long as officials have not stopped the owner Lito Jumaquio. A tricycle from Baler to Cemento costs P10. It's cheaper to walk or catch a tricycle to Sabang (just P1) and cross the river (25c) then walk. You have to cross two other rivers but they are not deep. Alternatively you can get in touch with Lito through the Amihan Hotel. The trip takes only 15 to 20 minutes in his boat. He's very knowledgeable about the local country and good places to walk.

Getting There

PNR (Philippine National Railways) and Pantranco North Express at Quezon City have buses to Baler, the trip takes seven hours. You may have to change in Cabanatuan, this is always the case if you are coming from the north. The last trip is at 3 pm. Travel time from Cabanatuan to Baler is three to four hours.

It's a rocky but beautiful trip on the serpentine road through the mountains of the Sierra Madre. Going to Baler you get the best views if you sit on the left side, going to Cabanatuan sit on the right side. Halfway, at the entrance to the Aurora Memorial Park, there are some restaurants and the bus stops for half an hour. Time enough to try the delicious eggcaldo soup in *Lorelyn's Restaurant*.

From Olongapo there are several buses of the Baliwag Trans and E Jose Trans companies going daily via San Fernando to Cabanatuan. Also from San Fernando many Arayat Express buses leave daily for Cabanatuan. The terminal is next to the Philippine National Bank.

BOTOLAN & WEST COAST

There are a number of places to break the journey between Manila and Hundred Islands including Olongapo and Alaminos. Taking the west coast route between these two towns it is worth making a detour to visit the Negrito tribes found there or you can pause at a number of beach resorts.

San Antonio

About an hour's drive from Olongapo you reach San Antonio, a pleasant little town with a clean market where you can eat really cheaply. There is a simple lodging house there. About twice a day a jeepney goes to Pundaquit, five km away, but you can also take a tricycle to the river, about two km away, and walk from there. Pundaquit is a little fishing village in a sheltered bay and for P60 to 80 you can be taken to Camera Island and Capones Island from there. Both islands have white beaches and although they are very rocky a few bushes and palms do grow

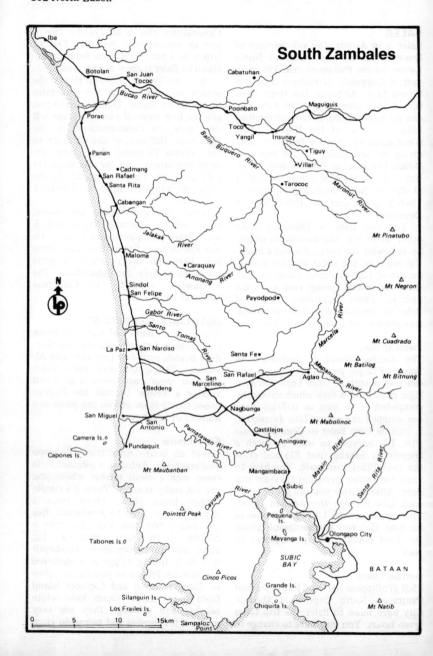

South Zambales

on Capones Island. A lighthouse stands at the western end and the lighthouse keeper is the sole inhabitant of the island which rises like a dome out of the sea. Occasionally a few Americans come here to dive.

From Pundaquit you can walk along wide beaches to San Miguel and even further. The only minor obstacle along the way is not a very deep river. Tricycles go from San Miguel to San Antonio. Note that the jeepneys which commute between San Antonio and San Miguel do not go to the beach. They go to the American military base.

Negrito Tribes

If you want to visit the Negritos in the Zambales Mountains you should interrupt the trip from Olongapo at Botolan, a small town about seven km south of Iba. You can stay overnight with the very hospitable mayor. Alternatively you can find accommodation a little further out, to the south of Porac, in one of the cottages of the *Villa Loreto Beach Resort*, run by Mat (Mateo) Encarnacion and his charming wife, who are very helpful. This costs P25. From Botolan you can travel inland by weapons-carrier (an old truck) to Villar or Maguiguis. The departure time of this overloaded vehicle is 'around noon'. From there you finally reach the Negritos only after hours of interminable walking.

Here you will find the Aitas tribes, none of whom speak English. Their homes in the fields, in the original Negrito style, are worth seeing. Take some tinned or dried food with you — rice is available. As everywhere the children show a strong demand for sweets/candy! Don't forget your sleeping bag.

Once in Villar you are very close to Mount Pinatubo. At 1745 metres it is the highest peak in the south of Zambales Province. If you want to get closer still, or even climb it, you should enquire if Antonio Aquina's Resthouse in Patal Pinto still exists, so that you will have somewhere to stay.

Beach Resorts

Between San Antonio and Iba there are some km long stretches of beach with overnight accommodation possibilities. For example in Iba there is the *Sand Valley Beach Resort & Resthouse*, *General Ordonez Beach Resort* and *Gonzales Beach Resort*. Sand Valley is a very modern place with lovely rooms, good food and service, a sun balcony, very friendly, less than a minute from the beach, very uncrowded and P80 for a single with bath. There are also a few resorts about 80 km north of Iba on Dasol Bay, such as *Tambobong White Beach*.

Getting There

You can travel to Alaminos and Hundred Islands via the west coast instead of taking the direct route. There are several buses daily from the Victory Liner Station, Rizal Avenue Extension in Manila. It's a three hour trip to Olongapo where you must change to another Victory Liner bus via Iba, San Antonio and Botolan to Alaminos. The trip takes six hours.

LUCAP & ALAMINOS

Lucap is the small village which serves as a jumping off point to the Hundred Islands. It's very close to Alaminos from where you can make trips to Bani to see the Nalsoc Caves with its underground river or to Agno for the Sabangan Beach.

Places to Stay

There are lots of places to stay in Lucap and some in Alaminos. The *Ocean View Lodge & Restaurant* in Lucap is a very clean place with a good restaurant and rooms with fan and bath at P30 per person. The *Park View Lodge*, also in Lucap, is similarly priced officially but can be bargained down a little. Food has to be ordered in advance.

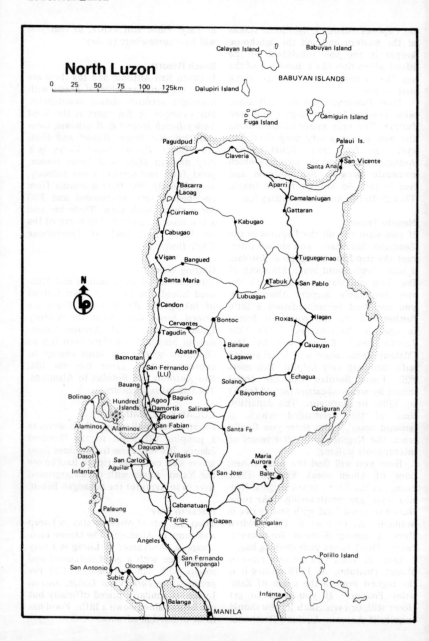

North Luzon

0 25 50 75 100 125km

Calayan Island
Babuyan Island
Dalupiri Island
BABUYAN ISLANDS
Fuga Island
Camiguin Island
Palaui Is.
Santa Ana
San Vicente
Pagudpud
Claveria
Bacarra
Laoag
Aparri
Camalaniugan
Curriamo
Gattaran
Kabugao
Cabugao
Tuguegarnao
Vigan
Bangued
Santa Maria
Tabuk
San Pablo
Candon
Lubuagan
Cervantes
Bontoc
Roxas
Ilagan
Tagudin
Banaue
Cauayan
Abatan
Lagawe
Bacnotan
San Fernando (LU)
Echagua
Bauang
Solano
Baguio
Bayombong
Bolinao
Salinas
Casiguran
Hundred Islands
Agoo
Damortis
Alaminos
Rosario
Santa Fe
San Fabian
Alaminos
Dagupan
Dasol
San Carlos
Villasis
Maria
Aurora
Infanta
Aguilar
San Jose
Baler
Palaung
Iba
Cabanatuan
Tarlac
Gapan
Dingalan
Angeles
Polillo Island
San Antonio
Olongapo
San Fernando (Pampanga)
Subic
Infanta
Balanga
MANILA

The *R&E (Relax & Enjoy)* of Dr Fernandes in Lucap has singles/doubles with fan at P40/55 or a cottage with fan and bath for P150. It's a good, well kept place with a restaurant. *Gloria's Cottages* at Lucap has rooms with fan at P45/70 or with fan and bath at P50/75. It's quite a pleasant, friendly place and prices are definitely negotiable — don't look only at the most expensive rooms.

Still in Lucap there's *Maxine's by the Sea* with rooms with fan and bath from P55/70. There's a restaurant and rooms with air-con are on the way. The *Youth Hostel* at Kilometre One in Lucap is P28/40 for rooms with fan. You should get a discount with a student or youth hostel card.

At Alaminos the *Alaminos Hotel* is a good, clean place with hot water. Rooms cost P25/35 or with fan and bath P45/65.

Places to Eat & Entertainment
Lucap is not a place for active nightlife. By 10 pm the few restaurants have put up their chairs. You can get good value food at the small places by the pier. Or head for Alaminos where the *Plaza Restaurant* usually has a folk singer or there's the *Imperial Restaurant*. Other entertainment possibilities include bowling lanes and a disco.

Getting There
From Manila several buses depart in the morning from Pantranco North Express, 325 Quezon City. The trip to Alaminos takes five hours. From Alaminos tricycles cost P1 per person to Lucap (P1.50 at most). From Alaminos back to Manila they depart half hourly from 3 am to 4 pm.

From Banaue buses depart at 4.30 to 5 am and at 8 am. They go via Baguio to Alaminos. Take the early bus if you want to arrive at a reasonable hour. At Baguio you change buses for Dagupan, Lingayen or Alaminos. With luck the change of bus will waste little time.

HUNDRED ISLANDS
There are actually more than one hundreds islands at Hundred Islands. Officially you are supposed to go to the tourist office at the pier where they have maps of the islands and will show you where to go and provide the boat. There's a 50c entrance fee plus the boat hire which is P60 for an outrigger for up to six people. Four or five hours of island life are enough for most people but if you want to spend one more nights on the islands take plenty of food — buy it in Alaminos Market — plus adequate water.

Most day-trippers go to Quezon Island, particularly on weekends, which is being developed as a tourist resort. On this island there is a house designated as the 'Wild Life Office'. You can spend the night here — pots, pans, a fireplace and two simple beds are provided. The back door is usually unlocked and two simple beds are provided. The back door is usually unlocked but if there is an 'official' there you should ask permission courteously. There are caves with bats on Government Island which is probably nicer. You can swim across to it from Quezon Island.

Don't expect palmy, dream islands in the Hundred Islands. What you will find are large coral reefs with vegetation and small white beaches. The water is not always crystal clear so snorkelling is only moderately good. There are no beaches in Lucap.

BOLINAO
This small, sleepy, virtually untouristed village is north-west of Hundred Islands. A little to the north is a white sand beach, good for snorkelling. If you prefer to be even more secluded you could be left off at one of the nearby islands.

Don't miss the Bolinao Museum — although it shows only a few historical finds the Philippine plant and animals section is worth a look. The old fortress-like church was a defence centre during the attacks of pirates as well as of the English, Japanese and US navies. If you're lucky the priest will guide you and tell you more about it. Ask him to let you have a look into the museum-like kitchen which is still being used.

Places to Stay
The *A&E Garden Hotel* has doubles at P45 and a good information black-board in the restaurant.

Getting There
Jeepneys or minibuses go from Alamin-os Market to Bolinao. Pantranco buses also go from there. The trip takes an hour.

LINGAYEN & DAGUPAN
At the southern tip of the Lingayen Gulf, between Lingayen and Dagupan, there are three famous beaches. Ling-ayen Beach is 15 km from Dagupan, Blue Beach only three km away at Bon-uan and White Beach is 15 km north-east at San Fabian, a lovely little coastal town with very friendly people. San Fabian is a good base for one-day ex-cursions to Hundred Islands and other attractions around here. White Beach is not, however, white — it's more brown-ish-grey and the old name 'Centre Beach' was fairly correct.

Places to Stay
The *Lingayen Resort Hotel* in Lingayen has rooms with fan and bath at P125/150 or with air-con and bath at P150/165. The *Lingayen Gulf Hotel*, near the expensive resort hotel, has rooms with fan and bath from P40 and a restaurant.

In Dagupan the *Youth Hostel Villa Millagrosa*, run by an enthusiastic Catholic lady, is in the Maramba Building on Zamora St. The dorm (with fan) costs P12 while rooms with fan and bath are P28/45. The hostel on the

beach was knocked down by a typhoon but the *Marco Polo Resort* and cottages still stand.

The *Lucky Lodge & Restaurant* on M H Del Pilar St has singles/doubles with fan at P20/25, with fan and bath at P35/50 or air-con doubles with bath for P80. The *Vicar Hotel* on A B Fernandez Avenue has singles with fan at P22, singles/doubles with fan and bath at P44/55 or doubles with air-con and bath at P66. On the same street is the *Victoria Hotel* with rooms with bath and fan for P88/99 and with air-con and bath for P121/143.

More expensive places include the *McAdore International Palace Hotel* on Galvan and Zamore Sts where rooms start from around US$20 and the *Hotel Cadena de Amor* in Calasia which is about five km south of Dagupan. There are plenty of restaurants in Dagupan.

In San Fabian the *White Sand Beach Resort* has cottages from P40 to 80 and a restaurant. The family who run this place also has accommodation in their large, comfortable family home — the *Residenz (Patty) Mejia*. It can accomm-odate eight people, meals are available at reasonable prices and there are cooking and laundry facilities. Singles/doubles are P15/20 but for some reason this lovely place may soon be closed — worth a try. The beach is 15 minutes walk or three minutes tricycle ride away.

Getting There
Pantranco buses and minibuses go from Alaminos to Lingayen and Dagupan where you change buses for San Fern-ando La Union.

Jeepneys go from Dagupan to San Fabian. From there you take a tricycle the 1.5 km to the beach resort. There are more comfortable big Pantranco buses and more frequent minibuses from Alaminos to Lingayen and Dagu-pan. It's about an hour to Dagupan.

From Vigan, Times Transit buses, beautiful green and white (or green-

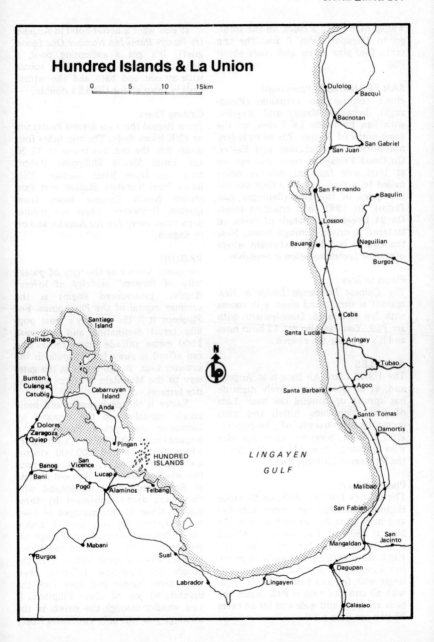

Hundred Islands & La Union

0   5   10   15km

Dulolog
Bacqui

Bacnotan

San Gabriel

San Juan

San Fernando

Bagulin

Lossoo

Bauang

Naguilian

Burgos

Caba

Santa Lucia

Aringay

Tubao

Santa Barbara

Agoo

Santo Tomas

Damortis

LINGAYEN GULF

Malibao

San Fabian

San Jacinto

Mangaldan

Dagupan

Mabani

Sual

Labrador

Lingayen

Calasiao

Santiago Island

Bolinao

Bunton
Culang
Catubig

Cabarruyan Island

Anda

Dolores
Zaragoza
Quiep

Pingan

Banog
Bani

San Vicence

Lucap

HUNDRED ISLANDS

Pogo
Alaminos
Telbang

Burgos

N

white) buses with a clock on the front, go to Dagupan from 6 am. The trip takes four-plus hours and costs about P30.

SAN FERNANDO (Pampanga)

Don't confuse San Fernando (Pampanga), between Manila and Angeles, with San Fernando La Union, on the coast north of Baguio. The town is very noteworthy at Christmas and Easter. On Good Friday, at noon, you can see at least one fanatical believer being nailed to a cross in a rice field outside the gates of the city (Barangay San Pedro). In 1981 they crucified three. On 24 December a parade of oversized lanterns is driven through town. Near the church is a large restaurant where overnight accommodation is available.

Places to Stay

The Chinese *Pampanga Lodge & Restaurant* is simple and clean with rooms with fan at P35/45. Doubles with bath are P50. You can also get 12-hour rates and it's opposite the church.

ANGELES

The USAF Clark Air Base is at Angeles and, as at Olongapo, a lively nightlife has sprung up around the base. Lots of bars, nightclubs, hotels and what seems like thousands of 'hospitality' girls. I don't, however, have any idea who counted them. Near Angeles is the Mt Arayat National Park.

Places to Stay

The *Liberty Inn* (tel 4588) on McArhur Highway, Balibago has singles with fan and bath from P50 or with air-con and bath at P80/100. The beds are good and wide, wide enough for two in fact. The *Far Eastern Hotel* is diagonally opposite the Liberty in a small sidestreet. A single with fan and bath is P30, a single with air-con and bath is P45. Again the beds are good and wide and for an extra P5 you can have a TV.

If you want a better hotel in Angeles try *Randy Rams Inn Number One* (good grief). It's got a swimming pool, a delightful open-air bar, clean rooms with air-con and bath and the widest beds in town all for US$15 a double.

Getting There

From Baguio there are several Pantranco or PNR buses daily. The trip takes four hours but the last bus leaves at 11.20 am. From Manila Philippine Rabbit buses go from Rizal Avenue, PNR buses from Tutuban Station and Pantranco North Express buses from Quezon Boulevard. There are regular departures every day for Angeles and on to Baguio.

BAGUIO

Variously known as the 'city of pines', 'city of flowers' or 'city of lovers', Baguio (pronounced Bagio) is the summer capital of the Philippines. For Filipinos it is the country's most popular travel destination and the cool, 1500 metre altitude draws those who can afford it away from Manila in the summer heat. It also serves as the gateway to the Mountain Province and the rice terraces.

Easter is the peak season and some hotels capitalise on the demand by increasing their prices. Baguio has a population of 100,000 so it's a mystery where the estimated 200,000 visitors are accommodated. Filipinos rave about the winding roads and the cool climate at Baguio and can't understand why Europeans aren't impressed by these things! None of this managed to keep me in Baguio for very long. I missed the Philippines atmosphere. Except for the terrific market this town could have been in any European valley. Even the people are somehow different, their faces seem harder and they lack the uninhibited joy of other Filipinos. If you wander through the streets in the evenings you will only encounter frosty people in thick woollen jackets, not grinning folk with colourful T-shirts emblazoned with cheeky slogans.

Information
Note that the Pantranco bus station is slightly out of town in Baguio, Philippine Rabbit is rather more convenient. Although the exchange rate in Baguio is not as good as in Manila it's better than you'll find in Bontoc, Sagada and, in particular, in Banaue in Mountain Province. Baguio has a tourist office in the Ministry of Tourism Complex where there is also a good, small, new museum. They have a free map of Banaue and the surrounding area. The same map costs P1 at the youth hostel in Banaue.

City Market
Products from Benguet Province, the area around Baguio, are the main items on sale here. Basketware, textiles, vegetables, fruit (particularly strawberries, try the sweet and strong strawberry wine), honey, woodwork and silverwork are all on sale but in the meat section the grinning dog heads are not for sale anymore. After international criticism of the way man's best friend are slaughtered for food this highland delicacy is no longer prominently displayed at markets where westerners go!

Burnham Park
This green area in the middle of the city was named after Baguio's town planner. Boats sail on the small artificial lake and there is a children's playground but it's not a place you simply shouldn't miss. Careful after dark, there have been muggings here at night.

St Louis Filigree
The St Louis University has trade schools where youths are trained to become silversmiths. You can watch as they make the finest filigree by hand. The silverwork is sold at fixed prices in the filigree shop — discounts are available for quantity purchases. As often happens there is no hallmark on the silver, if you particularly want one you should make sure that you get it when you make your purchase. The school is easiest to enter from Assumption Rd.

Easter School
The Easter School of Weaving is to the north-west of the town. Here woven wares like tablecloths, bags and clothing are made. You can watch the weavers at work. Take a jeepney from Kayang St near the market with a sign reading Plaza Guisad/Plaza Pilot Proj.

Lourdes Grotto
If you climb the 200-plus steps to the holy statue of the 'Lady of Lourdes' you'll be rewarded with a beautiful view. Take a jeepney from Kayang St.

Camp John Hay
The camp is a US Army recreation base on the outskirts of Baguio. There are places to stay here and duty free shops — tourists are allowed access to all the facilities. They have a theatre, bowling alley, tennis and golf facilities and several bars and restaurants. In the *Halfway House*, *19th Tee* and the *Main Club* you can get American beer, Californian wine and extraordinary, varied and satisfying meals — all for not many dollars.

From downtown take a jeepney or taxi to the main gate. In the camp military taxis and a shuttle bus operate every 15 minutes. You can send letters to addresses in the US at US domestic postal rates, so long as you have US stamps. Just mail them at the camp post office.

Imelda Park
This used to be a botanic garden but was changed into a sort of open-air museum and named after the Philippines' first lady. You can see the various house styles of the Mountain Province

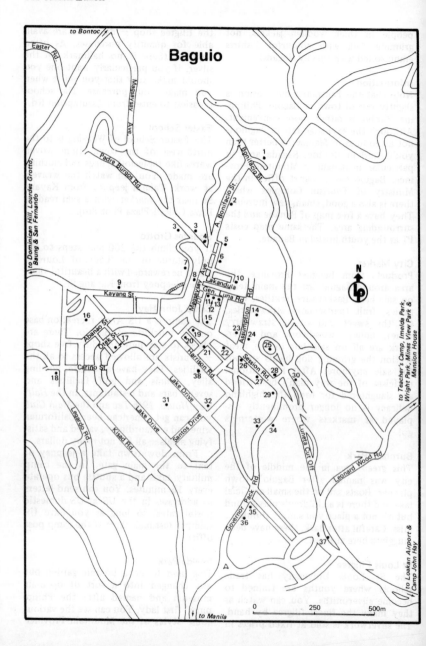

Baguio

to Bontoc

Easter Rd.

Magsaysay Ave.

Padre Burgos Rd.

to Dominican Hill, Lourdes Grotto, Baung & San Fernando

A. Bonifacio St.

A. Bonifacio St.

Magsaysay Ave.

Kayang St.

Abanao St.

Otek St.

Cariño St.

Lake Drive

Lake Drive

Kisad Rd.

Santos Drive

Lesardo Rd.

Lakandula St.

Gen. Luna Rd.

Assumption Rd.

Session Rd.

Harrison Rd.

Governor Pack Rd.

Luneta Cut Off

Leonard Wood Rd.

to Teacher's Camp, Imelda Park,
Wright Park, Mines View Park &
Mansion House

to Loakan Airport &
Camp John Hay

to Manila

N

0   250   500m

1
2
3
3
4
5
6
7
8
9
10
11
12
13
14
15
16
17
18
19
20
21
22
23
24
25
26
27
28
29
30
31
32
33
34
35
36
37
38

1 Gingerbread Man	20 Greenland Hotel
2 Tic Tac Toe	21 Jeepneys to Asin Hot Springs
3 Sweet Cherry Bar	22 456 Restaurant
4 Philippine Rabbit Bus Terminal	23 Plaza Hotel, Cosy Nook
5 Baguio Garden Inn	24 Fire Place
6 Dangwa Tranco Bus & Skyland Motor Express Terminal	25 Baguio Cathedral
7 Silvertone Lodge	26 Shakey's Pizza
8 City Market	27 PAL Office, Ato Book Shop
9 Jeepneys to Dominican Hill, Lourdes Grotto & Bell Church	28 Patria de Baguio
10 Traveller's Lodge	29 Amapola Cafe & Pub
11 Diamond Inn	30 Post Office
12 Emerald Inn	31 Burnham Park
13 Silvertone Branch Inn	32 The Solibao Restaurant
14 St Louis Filigree Shop	33 Pantranco
15 Mido Hotel, Sunshine Restaurant	34 Victory Liner Terminal
16 City Hall	35 Museum
17 Marcita's Liner Terminal	36 Tourist Office
18 Mount Crest Hotel	37 PNR Bus Terminal
19 Colorado Inn	38 Jeepneys to Imelda Park & Mines View Park

here and there is also a Handicraft Centre but the quality of the houses has decreased significantly. The Mines View Park is more interesting than Imelda Park and only a few km further along the same road. From there you will find a lovely panoramic view of the valley and the hills. Take a jeepney from Harrison Rd.

Bell Church
A little north from the downtown area on the way to La Trinidad is a cluster of Chinese temples run by a sect known as the Bell Church. It represents a mixture of the tenets of Buddhism, Taoism, Confucianism and Christianity. You can have your fortune told by priests. Jeepneys depart from Kayang St and pass by on Magsaysay Avenue.

Asin Hot Springs
If you think it's about time you had a swim you should drive out to the Asin Hot Springs where there's a big swimming pool with warm water at 35°C. Entry is P8 and it takes close to an hour to get there by jeepney. The last trip back to Baguio is at 5 pm.

Lion's Club Gorge
Coming from or going to Manila watch out at Lion's Club Gorge, about 10 km out of town alongside the zig-zag road, for an unusual rock shaped like a lion's head.

Miracle Healers
The mass media has reported in detail the practices of Filipino 'faith healers' in Baguio. Using only their fingers they 'open' the skin of the patient and 'operate' with bare hands — a fairly dubious business. Nevertheless the belief in some 'famous' doctors is so strong that people flock to Baguio from all over the world to be cured. The healers have no objection to visitors observing their 'miracles' so long as you are ready to make a donation of at least P100!

Places to Stay — bottom end
St Mary's Pension House on Easter Rd has a dorm at P20 or rooms at P30 per person. It's near the Easter School (out of town in pine woods) and popular with Peace Corps volunteers but food is expensive although good. They also have a library, pool table, darts board and the cellar has been under extensive

renovation to become a new bar complete with fireplace. The *Patria de Baguio* on Session Rd also has a dorm, costing P20. Rooms with bath here are P70/90 for singles/doubles. At 36 General Luna Rd the *Emerald Inn* (tel 6115) has small rooms at P20 but the common toilets are not very clean.

The *Silvertone Branch Inn* is on General Luna Rd, a little up the hill from the Emerald Inn. It's run by pleasant people and has reasonable little rooms at P25/45 or P100 for a double with bath. It's currently undergoing extensions which will provide a lot more rooms off the street, important in Baguio. The neat and clean *Happiness Restaurant* is also here. Behind the big Hilltop Hotel at 17 Hilltop is the *Silvertone Lodge*. Tidy rooms with big beds are P35/45 for singles/doubles.

The *Travellers' Lodge* (tel 5444) at 60 Lakandula St has rooms at P25 per person. It's run by pleasant people and the old rooms were all recently renovated. New rooms are also being added and it looks quite good. There are other simple lodges on the same street — *Lucky Lodge, Baguio's People Lodge* and *Paradise Lodge*.

The *Baguio Garden Inn* near the Philippine Rabbit bus station on Lapu Lapu St has rooms at P35/55 or with bath at P90/130. Some of the rooms are rather small. Also near to the Rabbit station is the *Leisure Lodge* on Magsaysay Avenue with clean doubles and hot running water for P40. Another good place nearly opposite the terminal is *Hotel Linda* with doubles with bath at P50. The same rooms occupied as a single costs P25.

The *Diamond Inn* (tel 2339) on E Jacinto St has regular rooms at P35 for singles, from P60 for doubles. Be careful, the rooms with bath are rather expensive. On Session Rd the *Mido Hotel* (tel 2575) is a good, clean place with rooms at P40/70 or with bath a double is P90. The *Everlasting Hotel* on

the corner of Magsaysay Avenue and Session Rd has clean singles/doubles with fan at P50/60 and with air-con and bath at P90/100.

The *Colorado Inn* (tel 4941) on Perfecta St has rooms at P55 with beds big enough for two but it's a bit dark and gloomy. But there is warm water! The *Greenland Hotel* (tel 4080) on Harrison Rd has regular rooms from P40 to 60, rooms with bath from P100 to 120. It's a good clean place with wide beds but rooms right next to the reception are rather noisy early in the morning. Centrally located at 90 Albanao St the *Attic Inn* (tel 5139) has large rooms with four beds and attached bathroom for P200.

Places to Stay — top end
The *Plaza Hotel* on Assumption Rd at the corner of Session Rd has rooms with bath at P150/190. It's a well cared for and peaceful place; enquire about tourist discounts. The *Diplomat Hotel* (tel 85 4782) on Dominican Hill has rooms for P200/240.

There are something like 50 hotels around Baguio. Some of the best central hotels are the *Mount Crest Hotel* (rooms at P180/210) and the *Pines Resort Hotel* (tel 2020, 2090) (rooms at P295/320). Situated close to the airport, seven km from the city centre, the *Ruff Inn* (tel 2218, 5366 & 5167) has singles/doubles at P100/150.

Highest in standards and price is the *Hyatt Terraces Baguio* (tel 5670, 5780) on South Drive with over 300 rooms priced from US$40 to 60 and everything from a swimming pool and sauna to disco, coffee shops and restaurants.

Places to Eat
The *Kayang Restaurant* on Magsaysay St changes its menu daily. On Session Rd the *Shakey's Pizza Parlour* has an entrance which is easy to miss. At the *Ganza Steak & Chicken House* at The Solibao in Burnham Park you can eat outside.

There are various other restaurants in Session Rd, the main street of Baguio. Everything is pretty good in the *456-Restaurant* although the prices in the tourist 'eating lounge' at the back are higher than the prices for locals at the front. In the *Fili Deli Restaurant*, uphill opposite the PAL office, the sandwiches and cake are good — try the Calamansi-cream cheesecake. At the other end of Session Rd you'll find the rather expensive *Amapola Cafe* where you can also buy the furnishings!

Other good places on Session Rd include *Mario's Restaurant* (try the lentil soup), the *Star Cafeteria* for a good P18 American breakfast, *Canao* for good, big, but rather expensive Filipino meals or the *Sizzling Plate*. *Munchies Paradise* has pizzas, ice cream and cheap beer.

Lucky's Bake House & Restaurant opposite the market, is clean and quite cheap. *Kem's* on General Luna Rd has good food and cheap beer.

Nightlife

The *Ginger Bread Man* and the *Fire Place* are folk music places. The *Cosy Nook Folk House* is opposite the Fire Place and has pleasant management and more folk singing. The *Sweet Cherry Bar* is opposite the Philippine Rabbit station and has a go-go bar.

There are various nightclubs, cocktail lounges and so on in the big hotels and on Marcos Drive.

Getting There

From Manila buses to Baguio go via San Fernando (Pampanga) and Angeles. You can get to Baguio with buses of Philippine Rabbit (Rizal Avenue), PNR (Philippine National Railways, Tutuban Station) and Pantranco North Express (Quezon Boulevard). They depart several times daily and the trip takes five or six hours and costs P33. PNR and Pantranco have air-con buses while Philippine Rabbit has two 1st class buses

daily. They're not much more expensive. Buses are hair-raisingly fast, several travellers have reported that Philippine Rabbit buses are the most terrifying.

Going back to Manila there are departures hourly from 6 am to 5 pm. The trip down takes five hours. At 8 am, noon and 3 pm there are air-con buses from PNR and Pantranco. Philippine Rabbit have two 1st class buses in the early afternoon — faster and not much more expensive than the normal buses. There are also Victory Liner Buses to Olongapo hourly from 5.30 am to 5.30 pm. The trip takes six hours.

You can also get to Baguio by train — the line runs north of Manila to San Fernando La Union, which is not terribly useful since you have to continue by bus whether you're heading for Hundred Islands or Baguio. The 6 am departure from Tutuban Station will get you to Damortis La Union five hours later. A PNR bus departs from there after the train arrives. The bus trip to Baguio takes another 1½ hours.

From San Fernando La Union there are several buses daily from the petrol station near the market. The last bus leaves at 5.30 pm and the trip takes two hours. From Alaminos there are Pantranco buses at 6.30, 8.15 and 10.45 am and at 12.45 pm. The trip takes four hours.

An early morning bus passes through Sagada around 6.30 am and arrives in Baguio about eight hours later.

BONTOC

Bontoc is the main town of the Mountain Province. The Bontocs, who are Igorots, live in and around the town. Further north are the Kalingas while to the south-east are the Ifugaos. There's more information about these tribes in the introductory chapter. The Igorots build their terraces with stone dykes, unlike the earth-walled rice terraces around Banaue.

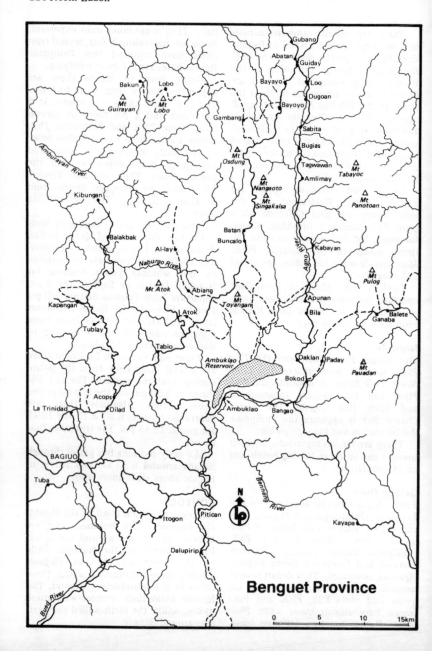

Benguet Province

You can get a general overview of the mountain tribes in the museum in Bontoc. It is run by a Belgian nun and is well worth a visit. She's a local expert on the Mountain Province and is happy to tell interested travellers about the tribes, their relics and their superstitions. The museum includes a typical village of native huts — Bontoc as it was prior to the Americans. There are also many headhunting relics and Chinese vases. Entry to the museum is P5.

The Masferre Studio near the Mountain Hotel is another 'not to be missed'. They sell excellent black and white reprints of photographs from the Eduardo Masferre collection, taken in Mountain Province in the 1930s. If you send them off as postcards they apparently only rarely reach their destination. Have a look at the weavers in Bontoc too.

A swim at dusk in the river is the perfect end to the day, as you watch the children watering the buffaloes and playing around.

Bugnay
This is an interesting day-trip to a Kalinga village. Leave at 7 am on a bus towards Tabuk. The trip takes about two hours and there's a return bus around mid-day. Be prepared to stay overnight just in case the bus doesn't come that day. Emma Poloc, also known as Marsa, of the Pines Kitchenette restaurant, organises trips to the Kalinga village of Bugnay at P250 including the chartered jeep. You can get there by yourself but for the village itself a guide is a necessity/condition and costs P10 plus a charge of P2 if you want to take pictures. It is possible that Bugnay may be temporarily off-limits due to the trouble about the construction of the Chico Valley dam.

Tinglayan & Kalinga Villages
If you have more time you can continue on to Tinglayan by bus — allow at least three days for the round trip, including

stops in villages. Tinglayan to Tulgueo takes three hours. Tulgueo to Dananao takes one to two hours, Dananao to Sumadel takes two hours, Sumadel to Malango takes one hour. From Malango walk along the main road and wait for a bus or jeepney. You can continue on to Lubuagan and Tabuk or back to Bontoc. You could try going into the villages with Kalingas who have been visiting relatives in hospital.

Although the tribespeople are generally friendly it is wise to take a guide from village to village. The chances of anything happening are then very small. In 1978 two Germans were mugged and from time to time travellers have been coerced into handing their money over in more peaceful manners — a fund for the construction of a non-existant local school is one way. Incidentally women are honoured and treated with respect by the Kalingas; mistreating a woman causes loss of face for all time.

Mainit
Between 6 and 6.30 am a jeepney departs from the main street, near the Getty petrol station, for Guinaag. From there it's 45 minutes on foot down to Mainit, a place with a gold-bearing stream. In the afternoon around 2 or 3 pm a jeepney departs for Bontoc. You can go on from Mainit to Guinaag, over the mountain, then walk down through the rice terraces to Maligcong.

Maligcong
It's about a three hour walk from Bontoc and since it can become very hot take some sort of headcovering. You can also catch the 8 am jeepney from outside the Pines Kitchenette and get to within a half-hour walk of Maligcong. Tell the desk clerk the night before and he'll ensure you're picked up. The jeepney returns at 2 pm or you can walk back in about 1½ hours. Don't miss out on going to the village, some of the rice terraces here are superior even to those

at Banaue.

You should carry some provisions, particularly water and gifts for the locals. The forest supervisor is not too keen on lots of matches being indiscriminately handed out as there have been numerous forest fires due to careless use of them. If you're too lazy to use your imagination and just hand out pesos you're really copping out! Whatever you do don't take brandy for some great get-together, it has happened. A small gift is not just recommended, it's compulsory unless you want to be muttered and sworn at by all the villagers.

See if you can find the teacher, he speaks English and can give you additional information. If you don't want to travel under your own steam you can get Emma Poloc to organise an excursion. This costs about P50 for Emma and P150 for the jeep.

Places to Stay

The *Bus Stop Lodge* was just P8 per person until it was burnt out in November '81. The similarly priced *Mountain Hotel* was also burnt out at that time but a traveller reports it is now rebuilt and rooms are P20 per person. *Happy Home*, opposite the bus stop, has good accommodation at P15 to 20 per person and also has good food. It's a stone building, three stories high, with pleasant rooms. The young couple who run it are very knowledgeable and helpful about the local culture.

The *Bontoc Hotel* has rooms at P20 or at P13 per person but it's necessary to bargain. The *Chico River Inn Hotel* has singles/doubles at P25/45 and also has rooms with five beds. There's a restaurant and it's run by helpful people.

The *Pines Kitchenette & Inn* is Bontoc's top notch place. If it's not booked out by tour groups you may be able to bargain a room without bath down to around P30 per person. The normal price is around P100. Simple doubles

cost P50, triples P100. The rsetaurant is also relatively expensive but then you do get a pianist playing European music while you eat!

Some distance outside of Bontoc at km 100 at Mount Data the *Mount Data Lodge* has singles/doubles at P120/200.

While in Bontoc and other towns of the Mountain Province be sure to ask when the water's running. The supply is usually restricted to a limited number of hours in the morning and evening. It is possible too that alcohol is prohibited after 9 pm and the day prior to festivals. There are high penalties for managers or guests who violate this rule so if you fancy a nightly San Miguel make sure you drink it before the prohibited hour.

Getting There

From Baguio there are Dangwa-Tranco buses at 5 to 5.30, 6, 7, 8, 9 and sometimes 10 am. It's a hard 150 km trip taking about eight to 10 hours and costing P30. Student discounts are available. Take a sweater or jacket with you, this trip can be rather cool. The seats by the driver or on the right side are the best for the views.

From Sagada buses go from about 6 am to 12.30 pm — ask about exact departures. If you want to get to Banaue on the same day you must take the first bus. There should be a direct bus from Sagada to Banaue.

From Banaue a bus goes from the market place at around 4.30 to 5 am. It's not very punctual and usually takes two to three hours.

From Lubuagan buses to Bontoc stop by the green house. There are three buses daily and the trip takes 4½ hours on the fairly bumpy road. If possible get a seat near the driver, in order to enjoy the fine views over the rice terraces.

From San Fernando La Union there is a connection to Bontoc from Tagudin, 50 km north of San Fernando, through Cervantes and Abatan to Bontoc and

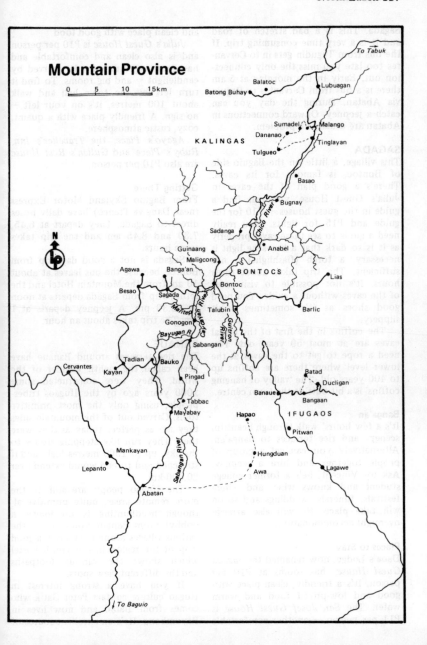

Mountain Province

0   5   10   15km

To Tabuk

Balatoc   Lubuagan
Batong Buhay

Sumadel
Malango
Dananao
Tinglayan
Tulgueo

KALINGAS

Basao

Bugnay

Chico River

Sadanga
Anabel

Guinaang
Maligcong
Banga-an

BONTOCS

Bontoc
Lias

Agawa
Sagada
Bay yugan R.
Gonogon
Sabangan
Bayugan R.
Talubin
Barlic

Besao

Guitron River

Batad
Tadian
Ducligan
Cervantes
Kayan
Banaue
Bangaan
Pingad
Bauko
Hapao

IFUGAOS

Tabbac
Mayabay
Pitwan

Mankayan
Hungduan
Lagawe
Lepanto
Awa
Sabangan River

Abatan

To Baguio

Sagada. This is a bad stretch of road and it is a very time consuming trip. If the bus from Tagudin gets in to Cervantes too late you miss the only connection out. Early in the morning at 5 am there is a bus from Cervantes to Baguio via Abatan. During the day you can catch a jeepney. Onward connections in Abatan are usually no problem.

SAGADA

This village, a little on the Baguio side of Bontoc, is famous for its caves. There's a good plan of the caves in Julia's Guest House. you can find a guide in the guest houses — P10 for the guide and P15 for lights. You really need a guide to see these caves properly as it is so dark that a kerosene light is necessary, a torch (flashlight) is not sufficient. The trip takes about three hours. It's not possible to visit most of the caves without a guide. You need good shoes as it's sometimes a bit slippery.

The coffins in the first of the burial caves are at most 50 years old. You need a rope to get to the caves at the lower level where there are coffins up to 400 years old. The 'valley of hanging coffins' is a bit outside the town centre.

Banga'an

It's a few hours' walk through beautiful scenery and rice terraces to Banga'an. Alternatively you can get a group of people together and hire a jeepney. Ask for Vincent, he's a former college student and knows when and where festivals, funerals, weddings and so on will take place. He will also arrange overnight accommodation.

Places to Stay

Daoa's Lodge, now renamed the *Sagada Guest House*, has rooms at P10 per person. It's a friendly, clean place with good and low-priced food and warm water. The *San Josef Guest House* is P11 per person — another comfortable and clean place with good food.

Julia's Guest House is P10 per person and is also clean and comfortable and has good vegetarian food — served by candlelight — and big rooms. To find it turn left by the town hall and walk about 100 metres, it's on your left — no sign. A friendly place with a quaint, cozy, rustic atmosphere.

Agayo's Place, the *Traveller's Inn*, *Ruby's Place* and *Gulian's Rest House* are also P10 per person.

Getting There

From Baguio Skyland Motor Express (near Dangwa-Tranco) have daily buses direct to Sagada. They depart at 6.45, 7.30 and 8.45 am and the trip takes seven hours.

Sagada is not a good day trip from Bontoc because the bus leaves at about 10 am from the Mountain Hotel and the return trip from Sagada departs at noon or 12.30 pm. A jeepney departs at 1 pm. The trip takes about an hour.

BANAUE

The rice terraces around Banaue have been called the eighth wonder of the world. They were constructed some 2000 years ago by the Ifugaos tribespeople, using only the most primitive tools. Carved out of the mountain sides they are as perfect today as they were then. They run like stepping stones to the sky, up to 1500 metres high, and if stretched end to end would extend over 20,000 km.

The Ifugao people are still, in the more remote areas, quite primitive although headhunting is no longer a hobby! From Banaue you can visit the various villages around — there is a good map of the region in the youth hostel which shows the various footpaths and the different view spots.

If you have a strong interest in Ifugao culture contact Peter Gatik who comes from Batad and now lives in Bayombong. He's an excellent source of information and also leads trekking tours, such as from Batad to Bontoc. Visit Josef Blas in Banaue and see his carved wooden masks, good chess sets too. Banaue is definitely the place to buy tribal crafts from.

If you haven't seen Ifugao dances before, you'll have the opportunity to see them in the evening in and outside the Banaue Hotel. Although the Ifugao culture is being affected by encroaching 'civilisation', the dances are still relatively authentic. Take a light with you if you go to these dances, the path to the hotel is pitch black.

One traveller recommended the 42 km from Banaue to Mayoyao as very scenic with mountains and terraces and numerous other hiking possibilities from there. By walking west from Mayoyao along an abandoned road for one day you can reach a village connected by jeepneys to the lowland.

Note that there is no bank in Banaue and changing money can be difficult. Change money in Bontoc or Baguio although even there the rate is not as good as in Manila. If you're really stuck it's possible to change money at the Banaue Hotel. There's also a shortage of change in Banaue.

Places to Stay

The good old *Wonder Lodge* was burnt out in 1980 but in early '83 it had been rebuilt and was about to have electricity connected. The cost is P15 per person and it's a very helpful and friendly place. The *Adespa Lodge* is simple but good value at P10 per person. At the *Family Hotel* in the Commercial Centre rooms are P12 per person.

The *Friendship Lodge* is similarly priced as is the *Happy Home & Restaurant*. The *Traveller's Inn* is more expensive at P15 per person but it's very pleasant and clean although not on the main road. The brook babbles at night.

The *Val Greg Hotel* is P15 per person or P25 for a double with bathroom.

There's only one bed in the doubles but you can just squeeze two people in. Food is available if you order it. The *Half-Way Inn* is P15 per person and is a well kept orderly place with a good restaurant. It's right in the village and just a few metres away is the very pleasant *Stairway Lodge*. Rooms have balconies with a good view and a double costs P40, but there's no electricity.

The *youth hostel* has dorm beds at P16.50 if you're a YHA member, P33 if you're not. A student card will also do. There are separate dormitories and it is very clean. The food is good but relatively expensive and the portions are small. There's a good local map available here.

In a much higher price bracket the *J&L Lodge* is P55/65 for singles/doubles. The *Sanafee Lodge* has doubles with bath for P110 — you can rent jeeps here. Right at the top of the price scale is the *Banaue Hotel* with rooms with bath for P225/275. It's used mainly by tour groups but it's a good hotel and guests at the youth hostel can use the swimming pool.

Places to Eat

At the *Banaue Hotel* there's a restaurant and you can have breakfast (around P20) while looking out over the rice terraces. Dinner, with several courses, costs P25. Food at the *Terrace Restaurant* at the Trade Center is very good value. Most of the lodges have a restaurant now.

Getting There

From Baguio you should take the 5 to 5.30 am Dangwa-Tranco Bus or a Pantranco Bus via Bayombong direct to Banaue, a seven to eight hour trip.

From Bontoc a bus departs from the Bus Stop Hotel/Mountain Hotel, between 11 am and 12.30 pm. It's the straight through bus which comes up from Baguio and takes a further two to three hours to Banaue. The bus is rather unreliable and also often rather crowded — if it doesn't turn up you can wander around town and recruit other travellers to charter a jeepney which will take 12 to 14. There is also a bus at 8 am. The road between Bontoc and Banaue is narrow and rough and travel is slow but the view is incredible. Take the right side of the bus for the best views of the spectacular countryside.

From Manila there is now a direct Pantranco bus between Manila and Banaue through Bayombong in Nueva Viscaya province. The trip takes about eight hours but is much less spectacular than the Bontoc route from Sagada. The bus leaves from Manila, from the Pantranco terminal in Quezon City, around 7 am. The fare is P45 and student discounts are available. If you wish you can interrupt your journey south of Bayombong and take a trip to Salinas where there are salt springs — the deposits have formed a white, hilly landscape. Travelling from Banaue to Manila the bus leaves at around 7 or 7.30 am from the village plaza and a bit later from the youth hostel. Often it simply rolls out when it's full, early or not, so it's wise to get there very early.

Another way of getting to Manila from Banaue is to take a jeepney from the village square to Lagawe, another jeepney from there to Solano from where you can catch a bus to Quezon City.

BATAD
The rice terraces of Batad are arranged like an amphitheatre, fortunately tin roofs haven't yet appeared on most of the Ifugao houses. Take care when photographing people in Batad, ask permission or be prepared for hassles and demand for payment. A nice long telephoto lens helps.

On the road to Batad from Banaue is a good waterfall with three clear pools to swim in. It's at the 4.5 km point and easy to find as you cross over the bridge there but it's quite a rough track to the waterfall. A walking stick is a good thing to have around here. You can buy one in Banaue or hire one at the youth hostel.

Maurris is a local identity and good guide. He will let you look in his house and will explain when all the pigs, whose bones are stored under the roof, were consumed.

Places to Stay
You can stay with Maurris, or, for only a few pesos, in Mr Loreto Chuccal's *Foreigner's Inn.* You can't miss it as it is the only double-storey house in the village. There's also *Pedro's Hillside Inn* with a fantastic view and a friendly family — P8 a night plus P8 for dinner. Other places include *Rita's* and *Francis' Place.* It's definitely worth staying here rather than just day-tripping from Banaue. Take some food with you, it's cheaper at Banaue market.

Getting There
From Banaue the distance is about 15 km and the first stretch is made in a Banga'an jeepney, heading towards Mayoyao. You then have a 1½ hours walk or you can walk the whole distance in about six hours. The first four hours are easy. Ask when the jeepney or minibus departs — the most recent information is from Banaue at 9 am or from Banga'an at 10.30 am. A jeepney with driver costs P150-180 and will take up to 14 people.

Shortly before Banga'an a signposted path branches off to Batad.

SAN FERNANDO LA UNION
Also known as the city of the seven hills, San Fernando does not have much to offer. From Freedom Park — also called Heroes Hill — there is a good view of the South China Sea. You can see the Chinese influence on the city in the Chinese Pagoda and the Macho Temple where a two-day festival is held at the

end of April.

The potteries in nearby San Juan are worth a visit or you could take a look at the Museum La Union in the Provincial Capitol. If none of these appeal then head for the long beach at Bauang, a few km south.

Places to Stay

The *Hotel Plaza* (tel 2220) on Quezon Avenue has rooms with fan at P30/40 or with fan and bath at P75/100, with air-con and bath at P105/160. The hotel has been significantly improved in part although the rooms in the new building are rather expensive.

There's also the *Casa Blanca Hotel* (tel 3132) on Rizal St which has singles with fan for P30, doubles for P40 and doubles with bath for P50. It's a beautiful, large house with simple rooms and, wait for it, a cocktail lounge! *Mandarin House* has good rooms from P25 plus the advantage of the bus stopping right outside the door.

Places to Eat & Nightlife

You can eat well and for a reasonable price at the *Mandarin Restaurant*. There are lots of cheap snack places around San Fernando. A number of places offer good value special menus at P12 to 15 which include soup, main dish, rice and a banana. Places to try include the *New Society Restaurant* opposite the market and the *Mid-Town Food Palace* on Quezon Avenue. The restaurant at the *Hotel Plaza* is OK but not as good as these places. Smokefish is the speciality of the house at the *Luebben Beach Resort*, about four km north of San Fernando, just before San Juan.

About three km south of San Fernando, opposite the Sun Valley, the *Tobacco Roll Disco* is good but a little expensive. There's also a disco in the *Long Beach Resort*. Between San Fernando and the Bauang beaches at Poro Point is the *International Disco* and some bars as well.

Getting There

From Baguio there are several buses daily from the Marcita's Liner Terminal. The trip takes two hours and costs about P9. Philippine Rabbit departures are similar. Local minibuses load up at a service station behind the plaza, Marcita's Liner buses also operate from here. It's a nice trip on the winding Naguilian road down to Bauang. Try to sit on the left side for the best view.

From Manila there are several daily buses direct from the Philippine Rabbit terminal on Rizal Avenue Extension near the Chinese Cemetery in Caloocan. Philippine Rabbit has two terminals but you can also get on a bus to Tarlac or Baguio at the terminal in Santa Cruz and change later somewhere between Dau and Rosario. The trip takes six hours. You can also travel to San Fernando by train which takes a bit longer than the bus — 'God knows how it stays on the tracks' reported one traveller.

From Alaminos buses go via Lingayen and Dagupan. You can take a big Pantranco bus or a minibus. The minibuses depart more frequently but the Pantranco buses are more convenient. In Dagupan you have to change buses. The whole trip takes three hours, an hour to Dagupan, two hours on to San Fernando La Union.

BAUANG

A little south of San Fernando, Bauang has a long beach with several beach resorts like Nalinac, Bali Hai or Sun Valley. The water is clear but rather shallow — it's OK for a couple of days and Bauang is now one of the most popular swimming resorts in the north. Bauang town proper is a few km south of the Bauang beaches.

A few km south of Bauang are Aringay and Agoo. Opposite the old church in Aringay is the little Don Lorenzo Memorial Museum. A pilgrimage takes place every year, the week before Easter to the Shrine of our Lady of Charity and the little church at Agoo then becomes the most important destination for pilgrims in the whole province of La Union. The high point of the Semana Santa activities is the procession on Good Friday.

Places to Stay

At the *Leo-Mar Beach Resort* you can get a clean double room with bath in a bungalow for P75. Try bargaining in the off-season. At P75 for two bedrooms the *Mark Teresa Apartments* are also recommended. These are situated in the main street, not along the beach front. For P150 and up you can have a non air-con double room with bath in the *Long Beach Resort Hotel* (tel 2 8791 or 2606) or at the *Bali-Hai*. Non air-con rooms are a little bit cheaper. Both hotels offer boat rentals, wind surfing and other entertainment possibilities. The *Crest Ola Hotel* (tel 2983) has rooms at P160/200 and a swimming pool.

The most expensive place would have to be the *Nalinac Beach Resort Hotel* (tel 2402, 2460) where a single room with air-con and bath costs at least P200. There are 104 rooms and 12 bungalows and facilities include a swimming pool, watersport equipment and so on. The *Sun Valley Beach Resort Hotel* (tel 2803) is similarly priced and equipped.

Nearby is the *Lourdes Beach Resort* and next door the cheaper *Fermina's Beach Cottages* with rooms at P50.

Getting There

Jeepneys to the beach go from the Plaza in San Fernando and from Bauang town itself. If you're coming from Baguio on any bus to San Fernando you can get off at Bauang beach. The buses stop near the hotels.

VIGAN

Vigan is, next to Intramuros, the largest architectural remnant of the Spanish occupation. Its planning was doubtless based on Intramuros. After Juan de Salcedo won a sea-battle against the Chinese he was put in charge of the government of the Ilocos Province by Legaspi. Vigan is the best preserved Spanish town in the Philippines. It is also the birthplace of several national heroes and leaders such as Diego Silang and his dauntless wife Gabriela, Father Jose Burgos, Isabelo de los Reyes, Leona Florentina and Elipido Quirino.

The place fairly reeks of history athough it's now a rather noisy city with lots of traffic. Vigan's most splendid moments unfold in the early morning when in the diffused dawn light the calesas and old houses transform the town into something like a 17th century

1 Capitol Building	15 Vigan Plaza Restaurant
2 St Paul's College	16 Victory Restaurant
3 Ayala Museum	17 Philippine National Bank (PNB)
4 Plaza Salcedo	18 Cheryl's Snack Bar
5 Vigan Restaurant	19 Metro Bank
6 Cathedral	20 Venus Inn & Restaurant
7 Vigan Hotel	21 Post Office
8 Municipal Hall	22 Village Inn
9 Unique Cafe, Tower Cafe, Nora's Delight	23 Grandpa's Inn
10 Tower	24 Luzon Inn
11 Plaza Burgos	25 Minibuses to Laoag & Bangued
12 Silver Dollar	26 Philippine Rabbit Terminal
13 Leona Florentina Building	27 Cordillera Inn
14 D'Plaza Inn & Restaurant	28 Times Transit Bus Terminal
	29 Market

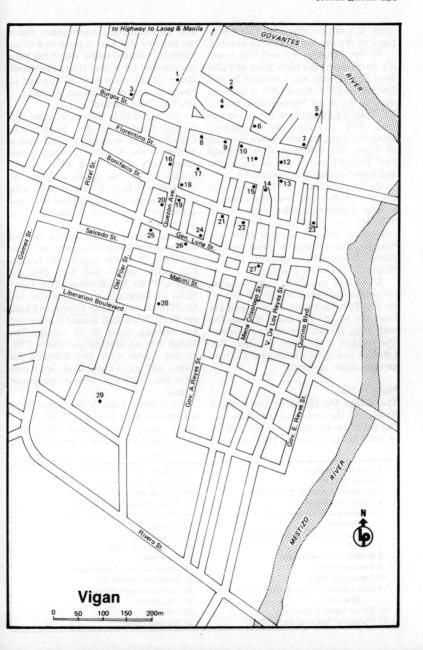

Vigan

0   50   100 150 200m

N

scene. It's surprisingly untouristed compared to the rice terraces or the beaches.

In the partially restored 'old town' it's worth seeing the birth place of Padre Jose Burgos who was executed by the Spanish in 1872. Since 1975 it has been open as the Ayala Museum and entry is P2. There's a library here where you can read. You can also get information about the Tinggian here — they live west of Vigan. The cathedral of St Paul was built in 1641 and is one of the oldest and largest churches in the country.

On the outskirts of the town, past the new market and near the tower, is a little cemetery hidden away in the hills. Mindoro Beach is not particularly noteworthy but on the way there is a tobacco factory and a good pottery place. A traveller reported that at Easayon you can see weaving.

About half way from Vigan to Laoag is Currimao with the Coral Beach Resort. Stop at Port Currimao, about a half km from the resort. The beach is long, the sand grey, the water clear and shallow. The cottages at the resort are about P40 a double and there's a restaurant. There are sand dunes at Pangil.

Places to Stay

The Village Inn (formerly the Redland Hotel), on the corner of Bonifacio and Plaridel St has rooms with fan at P28/45 or with fan and bath at P40/55. It's a well kept and comfortable place. From the balcony you have a good view of an allegedly haunted house which has been uninhabited for a long time. The grandfather of the proprietor is supposed to haunt it and make noises at night — you have been warned!

At the end of Bonifacio St, some 200 metres down from the Village Inn, Grandpa's Inn is more a hotel than a lodging house. It looks new and rooms range from P40 for a bare, fanless double to P100 for double with air con or P150 with bath. It's a nice place with friendly people, good Filipino food and conveniently near the Village Inn for other meals.

Then there's the Cordillera Inn on the corner of Mena Crislogo St and General Luna St where rooms with fan are P35, with air-con and bath P90 for singles, P110 for doubles. The Vigan Hotel on Burgos St has rooms with fan for P50/90, rooms with air-con and bath are P140. It's a well managed place and has running water in all rooms. The Venus Inn on Quezon Avenue is P30/40 for rooms with fan, P90/105 for rooms with air-con and bath. It's a nice clean place with wide beds in the air-con rooms.

On General Luna St the Luzon Hotel has rooms with fan at P20/40. It's a simple place with shared bathrooms. The Plaza Inn is similarly priced but not very clean.

1 Casa Llanes Hotel	14 Discos
2 Buses to Manila	15 Colonial Fast Food
3 Smacky's Kamiviet Restaurant	16 Farinas Bus Lines
4 Fire & Ash Disco	17 Tower Hotel & Restaurant
5 Jeepneys & Minibuses to Bacarra & Pasuquin	18 Jeepneys to Sarrat & Dingras
6 New Laoag Hotel & Beer Garden	19 Market
7 YMCA	20 Post Office
8 Peppermint Restaurant	21 Jeepneys to Paoay
9 Texicano Hotel	22 City Hall
10 Capitol Building	23 Maria de Leon Trans Buses
11 City Lodging House & City Lunch Snack Bar	24 Breaktime Snack Bar
12 Barrio Fiesta Restaurant	25 Golden Dragon Hotel
13 Philippine National Bank (PNB)	26 PAL Office
	27 Cathedral
	28 Modern Hotel

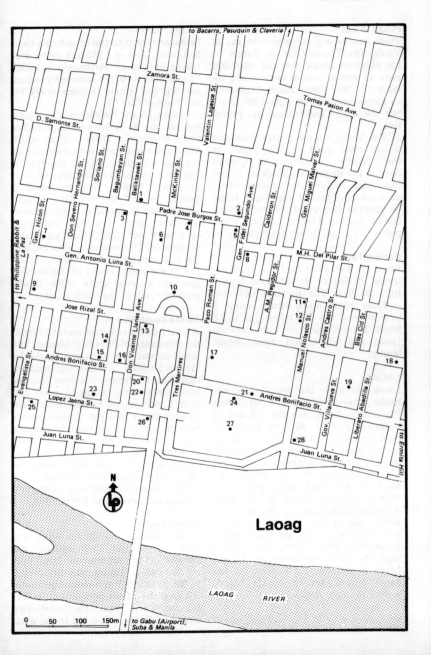

to Bacarra, Pasuquin & Claveria

Zamora St.

D. Samonte St.

Tomas Pasion Ave.

Valentin Lagasca St.

Soriano St.

Bagumbayan St.

Baliktawak St.

McKinley St.

Don Severo Hernando St.

Gen. Hizon St.

Padre Jose Burgos St.

Gen. Fidel Segundo Ave.

Calderon St.

Gen. Miguel Malvar St.

to Philippine Rabbit & La Paz

Gen. Antonio Luna St.

M.H. Del Pilar St.

Jose Rizal St.

Paco Roman St.

A.M. Regidor St.

Manuel Nolasco St.

Andres Castro St.

Blas Cid St.

Don Vicente Llanes Ave.

Evangelista St.

Andres Bonifacio St.

Tres Martires

Lopez Jaena St.

Andres Bonifacio St.

Gov. Villanueva St.

Liberato Abadilla St.

Juan Luna St.

to Ermita Hill

Juan Luna St.

N

Laoag

LAOAG   RIVER

0   50   100   150m

to Gabu (Airport), Suba & Manila

Places to Eat

There are plenty of places to eat in Vigan. The *Tower Cafe* on Burgos St has excellent sandwiches and calamansi juice as well as superb barbecued pork satay. In the *Vigan Plaza Restaurant* in Florentino St there's great ice cream but the coffee and tea are too expensive.

The *Venus Inn* has a large restaurant which serves good chicken niami. At the *Victory Restaurant* on Quezon Avenue the menu changes daily. If you like eating outside there's a lovely open-air restaurant behind the Vigan Hotel on Quirino Boulevard. *Cheryl's Snack Bar* on Quezon Avenue is a large Vigan pub which is still open after 9 pm.

Getting There

From San Fernando La Union there are several Philippine Rabbit buses hourly from the Plaza. The trip takes 2½ hours.

From Aparri buses depart around 5 to 6 am and the trip takes nine to 11 hours. It's less than two hours between Laoag and Vigan and buses depart hourly.

LAOAG

Laoag was made the capital of Ilocos Norte after the partition of Ilocos Province in 1818. See the old sinking belltower and St Williams Cathedral, built between 1650 and 1700 this is one of the many old Spanish churches in this province. From Ermita Hill you get a good view over the city which is on the Laoag River and has a population of 70,000. Although there are not many important attractions in the town it's worth making day trips to the many interesting places in the surrounding countryside. Ilocos Norte is one of the most beautiful provinces in Luzon. Laoag is a jumping off point for the Batan Islands, see the Batan Islands section for more details.

To the North

In Bacarra, next to the church, is a huge bell tower built in 1783 and partly destroyed by a severe earthquake in 1930. The steeple now lies crookedly across the top and is held in place solely by the 'hand of God'!

About 10 km further on is Pasuquin and you can go to Seksi Beach, four km away, by tricycle. There you can watch the women tediously harvesting salt in the late afternoon. When the tide is out they gather the top layer of sand in a light basket. Then sea water is poured in and the resultant densely saline water is caught in a clay pitcher. This is brought to the village and boiled in a large pot until it has practically evaporated. The residue is taken out and put in a hanging basket to drain out the last of the water. Under the basket you can see a long white icicle slowly growing — salt of the finest quality.

To the South-East

A lovely provincial road leads to Sarrat, the birthplace of President Marcos. The house he was born in, which is now the Marcos Museum, is filled with momentoes from his family. It's open Monday to Saturday from 8 am to noon and from 2 to 5 pm, on Sunday from 8 am to noon and 1 to 4 pm. A little further into the centre of the town is a church and a convent, which were both built by Augustinian monks in 1779. The president's wife was instrumental in urging the restoration of the church.

The church of Dingras is completely in ruins following a bad fire in 1838.

To the South

In San Nicolas is a church which was built in the late 17th century and restored in the 19th century. Don't miss the so called 'Malacanang del Norte' in Batac, although you cannot go inside. It's an estate of the presidential family. It's also worth seeing the fortress-like church at Paoay, a few km to the west.

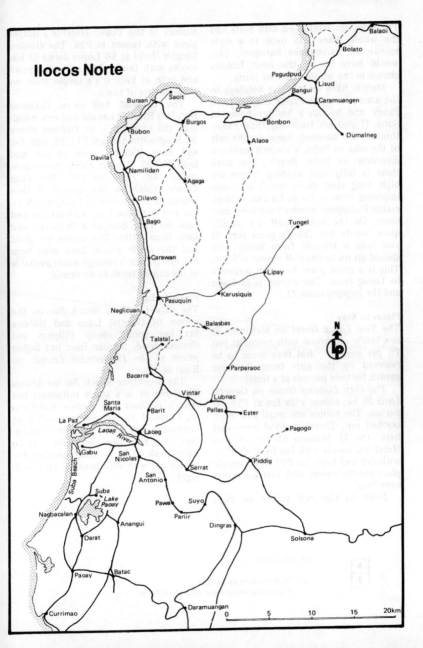

Ilocos Norte

The sides are reinforced with bolts and the whole place was built in a style known as 'earthquake baroque'. This would have to be the most famous church in the whole of Ilocos Norte.

Marcos likes to take his holidays in the attractive countryside around Lake Paoay and he has a holiday home in Suba. If you are travelling from Paoay through the bamboo forest to the left of the lake to Suba, it's worth making a diversion to Suba Beach. The road there is hilly and winding. There are high, long sand dunes which are more imposing than those at La Paz. Innumerable Philippine movies have been shot there. On the beach itself it's usually quite windy but there's good surf. If you take a tricycle from Paoay you should go on to the golf course at Suba. This is a good place to catch jeepneys to Laoag from. The airport is in Gabu and the jeepney costs P1.

Places to Stay

The *New Laoag Hotel* on McKinley St is a lovely old house with rooms at just P5 per person — but they seem to be reserved by the girls from the beer garden for long periods at a time!

The *City Lodging House* on General Luna St has rooms with fan at P15 per person. The rooms are small and often booked out. There's a good restaurant here. On M Nolasco St the *Modern Hotel* has rooms with fan for P30/60 or with fan and bath for P90. It's a simple place but the rooms with bath are rather expensive.

Next to the bell tower on Paco Roman St the *Tower Hotel* is a simple place with rooms at P25. The *Golden Dragon Hotel* at 60 Lopez Jaena St has rooms with fan at P15 or with air-con and bath at P80. It's a simple place on the outskirts of town.

The pleasant and clean *Texicana Hotel* on Rizal St has old and new buildings, the entrance is on General Hizon St. Singles/doubles are P17/28, with fan and bath P35/45, with air-con and bath P80/95. Air-con rooms in the new section are P130 to 160. The *Casa Llanes Hotel* on the corner of Don Llanes St and Burgos St has singles with fan and bath for P66, with air-con and bath for P80, doubles with air-con and bath from P105. The rooms are good and the single rooms have wide beds but ask if there's enough water available as the supply tends to be erratic.

Places to Eat

The *City Lunch & Snack Bar* on the corner of General Luna and Nolasca Sts has good, cheap Filipino and Chinese food. Similar food but higher prices at the *Peppermint Lounge* on Rizal St.

The *Breaktime Snack Bar* on Andres Bonifacio St is a small restaurant but there's no beer. On Andres Bonifacio St, *Colonial Fast Food* is a well kept restaurant with a folk singer in the evenings. *Smacky's Kamiviet Restaurant* on Balintawak St is a small comfortable corner bar with cold beer till after midnight.

North Luzon

a   Rice terraces at Banaue
b   'Earthquake-baroque' church in Paoay

Getting There
Philippine Rabbit buses depart from Vigan via Currimao hourly from 10.30 am. The trip takes two hours. You can also take a minibus from Quezon Avenue, Vigan to Batac, a jeepney from there to Paoay and another from Paoay to Laoag.

From Laoag to Manila there are Philippine Rabbit buses about every hour from 7 am to 11 pm but it's better to catch a Maria de Leon Transportation bus. They leave at 7.30 and 8.30 am and hourly from 5 to 9 pm. Farinas Lines have good buses too but it's a good idea to make a reservation. Quite a few air-con buses leave between 6.30 am and 12.30 pm. The 7 am bus even has a video! A later air-con bus leaves at 9.15 am.

CLAVERIA & TAGGAT
From Claveria you can go on trips to the Babuyan Islands. A passenger boat goes weekly to Calayan Island (five hours, P40) from where boats go to Bubuyan Island (four hours, P25). The people live pretty well here although, or maybe because, they are cut off from modern civilisation. Take some bartering items; the value of money is also recognised! You can sleep and eat at the priest's or the mayor's place and there are now cottages along the beach.

A word of warning: Claveria is sometimes visited by members of the NPA (New People's Army) who conceal themselves in the nearby forests. Weigh up the current situation and decide for yourself whether it's safe to stay here. Otherwise take accommodation in Taggat. It's possible Father Carlos in Claveria, a priest who has been in the Philippines for more than 30 years, can advise you.

Fuga Island would have to be the most beautiful of the Bubuyan Islands — as it is the private property of Mr Lim you must get a visiting permit which you can ask for at his woodyard, near the hotel, although it is hard to find the manager or anyone else authorised to give permits.

A bit to the south of Claveria live the Itas, a Negrito tribe. They still hunt with bow and arrow. If you wish to visit them you'll have to travel about eight km by tricycle and then walk another four km. Ask for Amado (Addo) Antonio. He owns a tricycle and can take you to the Itas. Amado is the top policeman of the whole area . . . . according to Amado! Also ask for Manuel (Totog) Ramos, he knows the Itas and also speaks their language, and will be happy to guide you to the tribe, if you're lucky you will find him in Claveria.

On the way to the Itas you will pass the village of Santa Filomena. If you stay here for a while they will probably slaughter a chicken 'in your honour'. In fact this ceremony is supposed to ward off evil spirits.

If you want to get a tan on Waikiki Beach, you don't need to make an extra trip to Hawaii has Claveria also has its Waikiki, so-called due to its 'resemblance to the world famous beach of

South Luzon

a Lake Buhi
b Cagsawa church ruins and the Mayon volcano
c Pounding rice

Honolulu'. Try the nipa wine (Layaw) which you can get in Claveria and the surrounding area.

Places to Stay

The *Company House* in Taggat is a good clean establishment with rooms with fan at P20 per person, with air-con and bath at P40 per person. The *Public House* is next to the Company House, they are not obviously hotels so you may have to ask directions. Here rooms are P30 per person with fan, P45 with air-con and bath. This place is not many km west of Claveria. From the bus stop you have to go another km to the guest house.

In Claveria there are cottages right on the beach. The *Municipal Beach Cottages* are managed by the town officials, are big enough for two and cost P25. Blankets and pillows cost an extra P15. The *Sun Beach Cottages* are also P20 for two. The cottages are small but there's a disco! You can only get there from the road on foot.

Getting There

From Laoag buses to Claveria depart from the corner of Burgos St and General Fidel Segundo Avenue. The road is bad in parts but the countryside is beautiful. The trip takes 4½ hours.

APARRI

There's nothing to keep you in Aparri. If you wish to continue to the northeast tip of Luzon, go by bus from Aparri to Santa Ana and then continue by triyclce (if there's no bus or jeepney going there) to San Vicente. From here you can go by outboard motorboat to Palaui Island — coral beaches, clear water, and you can stay in the mayor's house.

Places to Stay

The *Victoria Hotel* has rooms at P30 per person. It's simple but relatively clean. They don't like drunks and prostitutes here. *Popo's Hotel* is P20 per person for rooms with fan or P40 with fan and bath. It's also owned by the Victoria Hotel.

Getting There

From Claveria the bus to Aparri leaves from the main street. There are several buses daily and the trip takes four hours. From Laoag a Pantranco bus departs at 2.30 am, you can get on the bus at 10 pm. The trip takes eight hours.

TUGUEGARAO

Tuguegarao is the capital of Cagayan Province and a jumping off point to the Callao Caves which lie about 15 km out of Tuguegarao (towards Penablanca). There is accommodation available in the vicinity of the caves if you want to stay over. With a little bargaining the cottages shouldn't cost more than P25 per person.

From Tuguegarao there is a direct bus to Manila as well as from Aparri. The trip takes nine to 11 hours and you can make some interesting breaks in the journey. At Roxas, Isabela you can experience a truly Filipino way of life — away from rucksack paths or tourist tracks. You can stay at the mayor's rest house, he knows what times the buses go to Manila.

Cauayan is a busy town not far from Roxas with a remarkable number of restaurants and an interesting market. Santa Fe is a small town in the hills noted for its handcrafted products — particularly basket work — and its pleasant climate.

Places to Stay

In Tuguegarao the *Olympia Hotel* has rooms at P25 per person or with bath at P25 per person. The *Mene & Lining Panciteria* in Del Rosario St has relatively good rooms for P12 per person. Other hotels are *LB Lodging House* with singles at P20, *Village Inn* with singles/doubles at P40 and *Georgie's*

Inn with singles with bath at P40. *Pensione Albraham* has singles at P30, with bath at P40 and singles/doubles with air-con and bath at P100. *Hotel Delfino* has rooms from P90.

In Cauayan next to the market is the *Amity Hotel* with singles/doubles with fan at P45/90 and with air-con and bath at P60/110. On top of the hotel is a roof garden restaurant with live folk music, beer and barbecue. In Santa Fe you can stay and eat at *Tony's Restaurant & Hotel* for P12 or opposite at the *Golden Rose Hotel* for P30/50.

At Camalaniugan, the town at the turn-off for San Vicente on the Aparri-Tuguegarao road, there is a hotel/restaurant with rooms for P10 and up. It's simple and clean.

Getting There
From Aparri minibuses start opposite the Victoria Hotel. The first bus starts at 7 am. If you're really on a shoestring you can try checking in the previous evening and sleeping overnight in the bus. Try to sit in the front and enjoy the mild fresh air. The road to Tuguegarao is fairly good as its concrete and the trip takes 2½ hours.

From Claveria it's possible to get a direct Pantranco bus over the new Japanese built bridge. It would save 44 km to take a direct bus from Claveria to Tuguegarao. There are many daily buses direct from Cauayan to Quezon City, Manila with Pantranco and other companies. The trip takes six hours.

TABUK
Places to Stay
The *Tabuk Lodge* is P12 to 18 per person. *Julie's Resthouse & Restaurant* is P8 per person.

Getting There
From Tuguegarao it's a bad road to Tabuk and the bus takes about two hours. From Bontoc via Bugnay the bus services were suspended at the end of 1981 but there are buses via Banaue and Bayombong. They leave Bontoc around 8 am and there's a daily service to Banaue.

LUBUAGAN
In and around Lubuagan the Philippine government has come into head on conflict with the Kalingas due to the Chico Valley dam project. The valleys of the Kalingas will be submerged by the dam which is intended to be the largest in South-East Asia. The Kalingas are fighting against the government's resettlement plans which would be the end of their centuries-long culture, developed due to their isolation from the colonised lowlands and the influences of western 'civilisation'.

Although there were conflicts between the tribes these have been sublimated through a complex set of peace treaties so that a united struggle against the dam plans could be mounted. Resettling the Kalingas would reduce their tribal society to nothing. The Kalingas live in an intensive world of gods and spirits and respect to their dead is intimate and long-lasting. It is out of the question, from the Kalinga's point of view, that they could leave the resting place of their forefathers.

In the last few years the conflict between the Kalingas and the government has escalated, particularly since a Kalinga leader was killed, supposedly by men wearing army uniforms. Since then soldiers and construction workers have been beheaded and Kalingas have been killed. Members of the Communist NPA (New Peoples' Army), which is strong in north Luzon, have supplied the Kalingas with modern arms. Therefore it is wise to be careful in this area. If you go into the mountains you're unlikely to be asked where you're from before the bullets start to fly. Army protection is even more dangerous — in July 1980 at least eight soldiers were overcome and killed.

The project embraces four separate dams with the first under construction at Tumiangan, slightly north-east of Lubuagan. The completed complex should yield about 1000 megawatts of power, enough to reduce the Philippines' energy imports about 10%. To an energy-poor country like the Philippines such potential cannot be ignored but to the Kalingas it is a threat to their very existence.

Places to Stay
There are no hotels in Lubuagan but at

the bus station there is a green house with a small shop where you can stay for P6 per person. There is no electric light in the rooms and the toilet is outside in a wooden shed. The manageress of this house also owns the buses which travel between Lubuagan and Tabuk.

Getting There
It's a bad road from Tabuk and the trip takes about three hours by bus.

South Luzon

The convoluted peninsula stretching south from Manila has an impressive, volcano studded landscape which includes the Mayon Volcano. Mayon's symmetrical cone is said to be the most perfect in the world and it's one of the Philippines' symbols. Here you'll also find the active geothermal area around Tiwi with its hot springs. South Luzon also makes an interesting jumping off point for travels into the islands of the Visayas.

The road to Legaspi, the main town in the south, is long and winding — particularly the stretch to Daet. If you want to you can take one of the large Pantranco buses and go almost non-stop all the way to Matnog right at the southern tip. Between Quezon City and Lamon Bay is the heavily forested Quezon National Park. Forget the famous beach resorts from Atimonan to Gumaca — those at San Miguel Bay are better. Idyllic days at the beach are rare on the Pacific coast due to the harsh climate. March to June is the best time to travel here.

The spurs of Mount Isarog near Naga and Mount Iriga near Iriga are home for several Negrito tribes but the classic cone shape of Mayon is the most imposing feature of South Luzon.

Routes South
Buses south go from Manila through Lucena, Daet, Naga, Iriga and Legaspi. There are several buses daily from the Pantranco South Express terminal on E de Los Santos Avenue, Pasay. Right through to Legaspi takes nine to 11 hours and there are also air-con buses at 8 am, 7 and 8 pm.

You can also take a train south although this is rather slower, about 18 hours to Camalig, just outside Legaspi where the train currently terminates. At Manila station go to the marketing department for a student discount.

LUCENA CITY
Only three to four hours from Manila by bus this is the departure point for boats to Marinduque which go from the river harbour just outside the town. To the north of Lucena, on the road to Pagsanjan, lies the small town of Lucban. Here you can get a good idea of how towns looked in the Spanish era. There is one hotel in Lucban, if you arrive by motorcycle or car note that the only place to stay between Lucena and Daet is at Gumaca.

It's worth making a trip from Lucena by minibus to the Quezon National Park. There are good walks through the jungle-like vegetation with lovely flowers, monkeys and so on but it's not so good if its raining.

Places to Stay
The *Lucena Fresh Air Resort* has singles/doubles at P24/30, with fan at P33/39, with fan and bath at P40/45 or with air-con and bath at P80/105. The rooms have pleasant balconies and there's also a restaurant, swimming pool and other facilities. It's a big, expensive hotel with a neighbouring park. It's probably become even more expensive of late so perhaps you should ask about

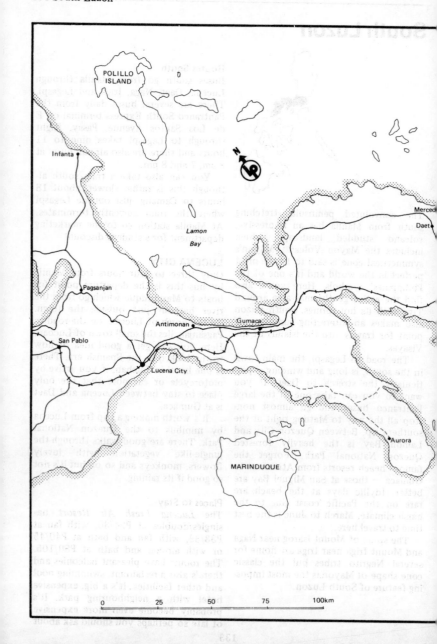

POLILLO
ISLAND

Infanta

Merced

Daet

Lamon
Bay

Pagsanjan

LUCENA CITY

San Pablo

Antimonan

Gumaca

Lucena City

Aurora

MARINDUQUE

0   25   50   75   100km

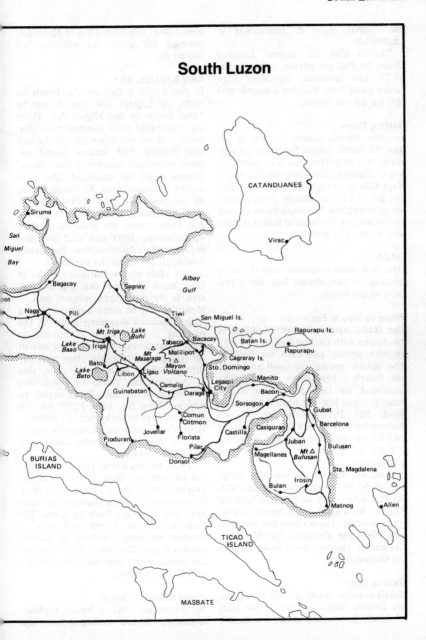

South Luzon

the *Tourist Hotel & Restaurant* in Lucena too.

There's also the *Sunrise Lodging House* for P15 per person, opposite the BLTB bus terminal. *Mar-Mont City Lodge* costs from P50 for a double and also has air-con rooms.

Getting There

See the Routes South section at the start of South Luzon for more information. It's only three to four hours by bus to Lucena City from Manila. On to Naga City is an eight-hour bus trip. You can get to Lucena straight from Pagsanjan although the bus departures are not as frequent as the helpful hostel warden would have you believe.

DAET

Daet is a good overnight stop if you're heading to San Miguel Bay for a few days on the beach.

Places to Stay & Eat

The *Hotel Alegre* on Justo Lukban St has rooms with fan and bath for P33/45 or with air-con and bath for P55/70. The double rooms are good and large but there's a loud disco upstairs. The restaurant on the third floor is not exactly cheap but the food is tasty and good. The *Mines Hotel* on Wincon Avenue has rooms with fan and bath for P42/52 or with air-con and bath for P75/85. It's a simple, clean place with a restaurant.

Also on Wincon Avenue the *Karigalan Hotel* has rooms with fan and bath for P24/50 or with air-con and bath for P72/85. It's a good, clean place and centrally located. There's also the *Sampaguita*. Near the Karigalan the *Mandarin Restaurant* has very good food, as does the *Golden House*.

Getting There

Manila-Legaspi buses go via Daet, see the Routes South section at the start of South Luzon for more details. It's only a short trip from Daet to Mercedes, jumping off point for crossing San Miguel Bay.

SAN MIGUEL BAY

If you'd like a day on the beach en route to Legaspi you can detour to Takal Beach on San Miguel Bay. There are reasonably good beaches near Mercedes and on the other side of the bay near Siruma. Old Siruma Island has some white-sand beaches — the town of Siruma is on the mainland. The river nearby has mangroves. At Tongo Beach, 20 minutes walk from Takal, there is good swimming while between Pinitan and Punta there are good snorkelling opportunities. Deer and wild pigs live in the woods on mountainous Butauanan Island, off the tip of the peninsula.

The staff at the Karigalan Hotel in Daet know all about this trip and the area. In the mornings a jeepney goes to Mercedes. Try to catch a ride to Siruma with fishermen returning home in the morning. It takes about 15 minutes to walk from Siruma to Takal and any of the village children will show you the turn-off which leads to the other side of the peninsula. From the beach veer left to get to the huts. Don't expect to pay anything less than P200 for this trip, you may be lucky but it's unlikely. Early risers ought not to miss the excellent fish market in Mercedes which operates from 6 to 8 am.

From Siruma a boat goes to Bagacay, the harbour for Naga, around 5 pm. If you're coming from Legaspi and want to continue on from Bagacay the same day, you must get there by noon. The boat departs at 1 pm and, after a number of stops, arrives in Siruma around 6 pm. The fare is P10. You can ask about Polly, who runs the cottages at Takal, in Siruma.

Places to Stay — Takal

In November 1981 a heavy typhoon destroyed several cottages here but

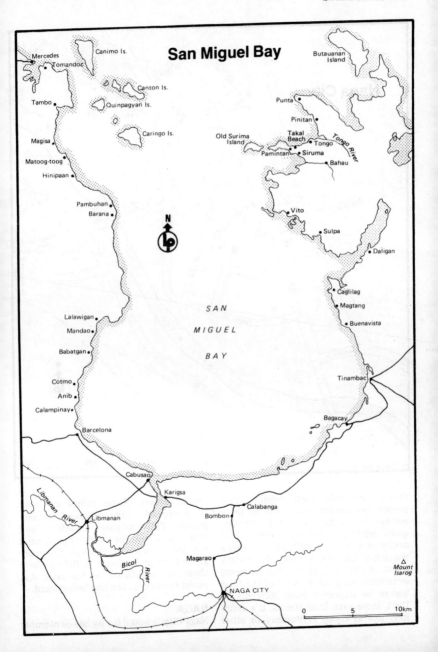

San Miguel Bay

Mercedes
Canimo Is.
Tomandoc
Butauanan Island
Canton Is.
Tambo
Quinpagyan Is.
Punta
Pinitan
Caringo Is.
Old Surima Island
Takal Beach
Tongo
Magisa
Pamintan
Siruma
Tongo River
Bahau
Matoog-toog
Hinipaan
Vito
Sulpa
Pambuhan
Barana
Daligan
N
Caglilag
Magtang
Lalawigan
SAN
Mandao
MIGUEL
Buenavista
Babatgan
BAY
Cotmo
Anib
Calampinay
Tinambac
Barcelona
Bagacay
Cabusao
Karigsa
Libmanan River
Calabanga
Libmanan
Bombon
Bicol River
Magarao
△ Mount Isarog
NAGA CITY

0   5   10km

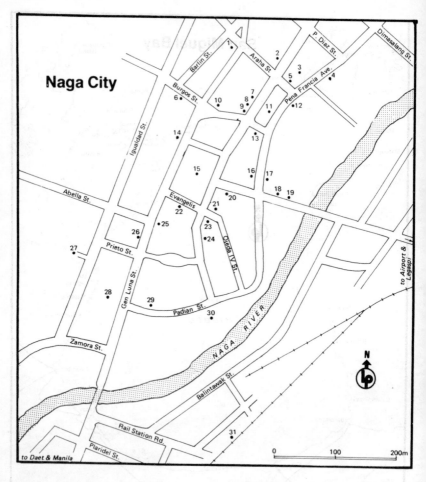

Naga City

they've probably been rebuilt. Two people can occupy one room in these cottages which have wide beds and mosquito netting. They cost P50 or if occupied as a single P30. There is also a restaurant but it's a good idea to ask about the cost of a meal before ordering or to agree on a figure. A lot of the food has to be imported from Mercedes or Daet, some even from Manila. It's definitely not as cheap as Boracay or other similar places. Some things are even more expensive than in Manila. To compensate Polly prepares excellent food and Hanns organises boat trips around the area — such as through the mangrove swamps upstream to Bahau where there are cockfights on Sundays. Ask about the cost of the trip beforehand.

NAGA

Naga City is noted for its late-September

1 Police	15 Plaza Rizal
2 Mama's Snack House	16 The Peppermill Restaurant
3 Pantranco Bus Terminal	17 Country Club
4 Post Office	18 Emerald Rest House & Beer Garden
5 JB Line Bus Terminal, Shell Service Station	19 Fiesta Lodge
6 Lindez Hotel	20 Veulings House of Beer
7 Minibuses to Daet & Lucena	21 Kriss Beer Garden
8 PAL Office, Airport Bus	22 Naga Garden Restaurant
9 Plaza Holiday Hotel, Plazaview Restaurant	23 Shirley Supper Club
	24 Minibuses to Daet
10 Naga Guesthouse, Graceland Fast Food	25 Naga Restaurant
	26 New China Restaurant
11 Plaza Martinez	27 Jeepneys to Bagacay
12 Church	28 Market
13 Crown Hotel & Restaurant	29 Fiesta Hotel
14 Philippine National Bank (PNB)	30 Minibuses to Iriga, Legaspi & Tabaco
	31 Railway Station

Penafrancia festival on the river. You can make day-trips from Naga City to the Inarihan Dam, the Malabsay Falls at Mt Isarog and the Nabontalan Falls. To the east of Naga is Pili, noted for its pili nuts and an access point to Mt Isarog National Park. Stay at the *El Alma Lodging House* there.

Places to Stay

The *Fiesta Lodge* on Paganiban St is a straightforward place with rooms with fan at P14/28 or with fan and bath at P25/40. On the same street the *Emerald Resthouse* is P25/30 for simple rooms. It's also a short time hotel until 10 pm.

On B Burgos St the *Naga Guest House* (tel 2503) has rooms with fan at P22, with fan and bath at P40, with air-con and bath at P80. Again it's a good, simple place. Ditto for the *Fiesta Hotel* (tel 2760) on Padian St which also has a disco on the roof-top. Rooms with fan are P18/30, with fan and bath P45/55, with air-con and bath P60/70.

The *Crown Hotel* (tel 2585) at the Plaza Martinez has singles with fan at P20, with fan and bath at P30 or singles/ doubles with air-con and bath at P70/ 90. It's a good, well kept place but the fan cooled rooms have small beds. Also in the plaza the *Plaza Holiday Hotel* has singles with fan at P25, with fan and bath at P50, singles/doubles with air-con

and bath at P75/120. It's a good place, as is the *Lindez Hotel* (tel 2414) on Burgos St which has rooms with fan at P28/50 or with air-con and bath at P90/ 100.

Places to Eat

Both the *Plaza Holiday Hotel* and the *Crown Hotel* have good restaurants and the *New China Restaurant* has menus which change daily. Another recommended place to eat is the *Peppermill Restaurant* which specialises in seafood and steaks. The spaghetti at *Mama's Steakhouse* is also good value. In the market is a shop which exclusively sells pili nuts — a speciality of the region.

Getting There

Buses and trains from Manila for Legaspi all pass through Naga. If you travel to Naga by train it's probably better to continue by bus — there are more departures, the bus trip is interesting and you can also go via Tiwi and save backtracking there from Legaspi. Naga-Legaspi is about P12, Daet-Naga about the same by minibus.

IRIGA

About mid-way between Naga and Legaspi, Iriga is the jumping off point for visits to Lake Buhi. On this beautiful,

16.5 square km lake they fish for the smallest food-fish in the world. Called sinarapan they are in danger of becoming extinct, like the tabios from Lake Bato. Blame for this lies with the para-sarap — that's what the locals call the fishermen — who fish the lake out with their sakags — the large, fine-mesh, V-form nets. In this process they often destroy the spawn as well. It's to be hoped the BFAR (Bureau of Fisheries & Aquatic Resources) will be successful in preventing such shortsighted catching methods.

Boat trips on Lake Buhi become rather expensive if you charter a boat at the market place, right next to the lake. You can save your money if you take the regular ferry to the other side of the lake and back. The ferry also departs at the market place. The last jeepney back to Iriga departs at 7 pm.

A tribe of Negritos, the Agta, live at Mount Iriga — also called Mount Asog. Every Sunday the staff of the CCF Office in Buhi visits the Agta. This could be a good chance for you to accompany them but ask Professor Isabel Ong for permission first. You can find the CCF Office in the Bridgeschool next to the church, opposite the police station. Lawyer and hotelier Jose C Reyes is an expert on these people and has set up an interesting museum, the Bicol Folklorica Room, in his Ibalon Hotel in Iriga.

Places to Stay
The *Lemar Hotel* (tel 594) on San Nicolas St has singles with fan at P28, with fan and bath at P40, with air-con and bath at P65. It's a good, simple place and the air-con rooms have wide beds. The *Bayanihan Hotel* (tel 556) has singles with fan at P35 or rooms with air-con and bath at P70/90. It's also a good, clean place and the air-con singles are big enough for two. It's on the street where the jeepneys stop, close to the railway line.

The small and elegant *Ibalon Hotel* (tel 352 or 353) on San Francisco St is expensive with air-con singles/doubles from P165/220 but it also has a hostel section at P20 per person. It's the best hotel in town, probably the best in South Luzon after the big Mayon Imperial in Legaspi.

LEGASPI
The main city of the region and capital of Albay Province hugs the waterfront in the shadow of the mighty Mayon Volcano. See the memorial to Filipinos who died here in attempting to repel the American invasion after the Spanish-American War in 1900. There's also a 'headless' monument to the unknown heroes who died at the hands of the Japanese in WW II. It's on the left as you walk out along the pier, neglected and of little interest.

1 Village Garden Nightclub	16 Mayon Hotel
2 Al-Bay Hotel	17 La Trinidad Hotel
3 Shirman Hotel	18 Philippine National Bank (PNB)
4 Small Bars	19 Pantranco Bus Terminal
5 Railway Station	20 Market
6 Ritz Pension House	21 Shangrila Restaurant
7 Shakey's Pizza	22 Legazpi Lodging House
8 Filipino Restaurant	23 JB Lines Bus Terminal
9 Hong Kong Dimsum & Tea House	24 New Legaspi Restaurant
10 Plaza Rizal	25 City Bus Terminal: buses to Tabaco,
11 PAL Office, PLTD	Iriga, Naga & jeepneys to Daraga
12 Rex Hotel	26 Wharf
13 Ideal Hotel	27 Four Seasons Restaurant
14 Xandra Hotel	28 Legazpi Plaza Hotel
15 Peking House Restaurant	

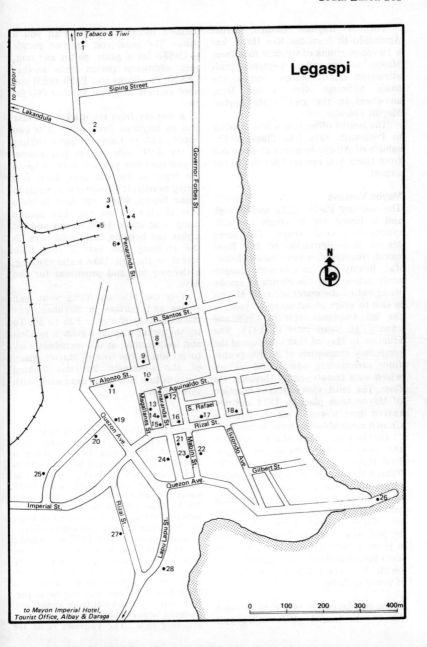

to Tabaco & Tiwi

to Airport

Lakandula

Siping Street

Governor Forbes St.

Penaranda St.

R. Santos St.

T. Alonzo St.

Aguinaldo St.

Magallanes St.

Penaranda St.

S. Rafael

Rizal St.

Mabin St.

Elizondo Ave.

Gilbert St.

Quezon Ave.

Quezon Ave.

Imperial St.

Rizal St.

Lanuza St.

Legaspi

N

to Mayon Imperial Hotel,
Tourist Office, Albay & Daraga

0   100   200   300   400m

The St Raphael Church, across Aguinaldo St from the Rex Hotel, has a 10 tonne chunk of volcanic rock from Mayon as the altar. Legaspi's main attraction is, of course, outside the town although very visible from anywhere in the area — the mighty Mayon Volcano.

The tourist office is in a new building in Penaranda Park (the Plaza) in the suburb of Albay. Jeepneys go there and from there you can get tricycles to the airport.

Mayon Volcano

The volcano stands 2421 metres high and is famed for its nearly perfectly symmetrical cone shape. The name Mayon is a derivation of the Bicol world 'magayon' which means beautiful. Beauty can also become dangerously active — as the clouds of smoke rising out of the crater indicate. Mayon is said to erupt about every 10 years — the last eruptions were in 1968 and exactly 10 years later in 1978. The eruption in May of that year forced the temporary evacuation of 20,000 people from surrounding towns and villages which were threatened by Mayon's lava flow. The most violent recent eruption of Mayon took place in 1814 and destroyed three towns — see the Cagsawa Church paragraphs for more details.

On the north slope of the volcano is the now partially abandoned Mayon Rest House. To get there take a bus to Tabaco then a bus or jeepney to Liagao — get off at the rest house turn-off at about the half-way point. From there you've got an eight km walk up to the rest house — unless somebody comes by and picks you up. You can charter a jeepney from Tabaco. Recently there have been reports of muggings and other incidents at the rest house so take care if you stay there.

Climbing Mayon If you want to climb Mayon the tourist office will supply detailed information and find you a guide. The usual cost for two people is US$50 for a guide, porter and tent, each additional person costs another US$20. Provisions cost P120 and if you need carriers they cost another P60 for two.

A jeepney from the market will take you to Buyuhan from where it is two hours climb to Camp Amparo, starting at the 15th hole on the golf course. If you start late you will have to spend the night at the hut here, there is a spring nearby. It's another four hours to Camp Pepito, where you have to use a tent as there is no hut. This second camp is at about 1500 metres and the nights can become fairly cold here. In the morning you have a four hour ascent to the top. Take warm clothing, a sleeping bag and provisions for two days.

You can also try hiring your own guides and porters in Buyuhan. The standard daily charge is P25 to 30. To try the ascent without a guide is reckless and iresponsible, as it's incredibly easy to get lost at the foot of Mayon. Many of the seemingly harmless looking canyons turn out to be dead ends, with sheer drops.

Mayoneering

They call her beautiful, from 'magayon' in the local dialect, but she's a treacherous and threatening beauty. Since a Dutch ship first spotted her erupting in 1816, the mighty Mayon volcano has shown her strength something like forty times — most recently in 1968 and 1978. That 10 yearly schedule was a sobering thought as I struggled through the loose lava towards the top in 1977.

Many visitors to the Philippines make a trip south from Manila to see Mayon, reputed to be the world's most perfectly shaped volcano cone, but far fewer admire the view from up top as well as from below. Mayon may not be as perfect as it's claimed but from almost any position around her base she's an awe inspiring sight. The Cagsawa ruins are probably the best known viewpoint and one of the most eloquent reminders of 'beautiful's' darker side. In February 1814, Mayon erupted violently and without warning. The town of Budiao was swept away by the flood of hot volcanic mud that coursed down the mountain side and at nearby Cagsawa the terrified villagers took shelter in the church. The wall of mud swept over the church and the final death toll from Cagsawa and other villages around Mayon reached 1200. Today the crumbling church tower and fragments of the walls stand as a mute reminder of that terrible day.

Since a Spanish priest first climbed to the crater in 1592, many have made the climb and a few have died in the attempt. Mayon is not a difficult mountain to climb, no particular expertise is required, but towards the top it is perilously steep and you must climb over loose, crumbling stones and volcanic ash. Every step sends showers of rocks down on your fellow climbers and an unwary step could send you following.

There are a number of guides from the surrounding towns for making a Mayon ascent, but doyen of these Mayoneers is undoubtedly Ricardo Dey. Since his first ascent in 1951, Ricardo has been to the top so many times he seems to know every boulder and lava flow along the way; although every year a few of them take up new positions! For a party of up to three people he charges US$50 including his services, all the necessary equipment and food, and the hire of a porter to carry it. Larger groups cost slightly more as additional porters and tents may be needed. By the time we had returned to the provincial capital of Legaspi after our Mayon assault I felt Ricardo had earned every penny!

I was sitting outside my hotel at 6 am when the jeepney with Ricardo and the porter pulled up. My hotel manager's cheerful parting words rang in my ears: 'You cannot climb Mayon, you will die!' Mayon offers two possible routes to the top — the south route which we were to take and the northern route from the Mayon Rest House.

Since the northern route starts at about 800 metres while the southern route starts much closer to sea level, at about 300 metres, the climb is somewhat shorter. But getting to the starting point at the rest house is rather more complicated and the climb is said to be less interesting. For some climbers the southern route will also be more popular because it brings you out on the higher edge of the irregular cone. It was only 10 km from Legaspi to our starting point so we were soon out of the jeepney and heading along a dried-up river bed towards Mayon.

At first we walked through coconut plantations and then through dense undergrowth. At times deep canyons dropped off beside our path. During eruptions the lava cuts these steep channels and, perhaps surprisingly, they are now one of the volcano's greatest dangers. During heavy rainstorms, or the typhoons that periodically batter this area of the Philippines, flash floods can roar down these channels, sweeping tons of volcanic mud before them and carrying bridges and houses away. In 1976 just such a flood swept away the Manila-Legaspi rail line.

The gradual climb to Camp 1 at 800 metres takes less than three hours and we stopped for a rest and an early lunch. Unless you make a very late start Camp 1 is not an overnight stop — the second camp, higher up the mountain at about 1400 metres, is the usual overnight halt and from there one makes the final ascent in the early morning, then descends right back to Legaspi during the rest of the day.

Above Camp 1 the climb takes on a different aspect; the trail steepened, the vegetation became sparser and from here to Camp 2 we followed the lava trail of an old eruption. The smooth lava leapt and bucked down the mountain like a frozen river of stone and made interesting climbing. At times we had to divert into the surrounding undergrowth when the trail dropped in a spectacular lava flow. Once we had to use our ropes to climb a particularly steep section but in general it posed no difficulty and our small party made it to Camp 2 in another three hours' climb. Here the terrain changed again; the vegetation was now very sparse indeed, just the occasional tuft pushing through the jumble of rocks and stones. The smooth lava flows of the lower slopes were now superseded by an angry tangle of boulders. Our small tent sheltered in a gully; the dangers of avalanches are not to be taken lightly.

Next morning at 5.30 we were set to go but the weather certainly was not. Down below we caught occasional glimpses of the plains and coast but above the clouds were solid. Still, we had not come this far not to at least make an attempt so, leaving Francisco, the porter, to pack up camp, Ricardo and I started off, hoping that the clouds would clear or that we would find the top was above them. Visibility was poor and the clouds damp and cold; twice we were forced to bivouac under large rocks as the rain swept across us. Like Rome, Mayon has seven hills from Camp 2 to the top, but when we reached the last hill our task seemed hopeless. From here to the summit was the hardest part of the climb and as we looked up visibility was almost nil. The wind whipped across the unprotected slope so fast that any attempt to continue would have been foolhardy.

Soaked from the clouds and perspiration we waited, shivering, for the weather to improve, but half an hour later it looked even worse. My hotel manager was right — I could not climb Mayon.

In half an hour we had descended almost to Camp 2, a distance which had taken two hours to climb, when suddenly, amost as if a curtain had been whipped back, the clouds disappeared. Below the green flanks of Mayon swept smoothly down to the sea. The tower of Cagsawa church could be seen as a tiny needle, far away across the plains. Above us the cruel grey summit of Mayon beckoned. Well, what would you do? We turned round and started back up. Ricardo seemed strangely reluctant, but for me the top was tantalisingly close and I seemed to virtually fly back to our previous high point. As soon as we started to scramble through the loose top section I realised just how

foolish it would have been to climb in the clouds. Each step sent showers of sand and rocks bouncing down the side and at times the slope was so steep that progress could be made only by crawling on all fours. Worse still, many of the tiny stones were razor sharp and, despite the clear sunny sky, the wind still howled across the mountain side and plucked away at you as you inched your way up.

Finally, shortly before noon — six hours after our daybreak start, we reached the top. The effort was worth it. Mayon may only be 2450 metres but never have I had such an impression of sheer height. The view below stretched for ever in any direction and the smooth slopes of Mayon's 'perfect' cone allowed nothing else to impinge on the view. The crater itself was only about 300 metres wide and 50 deep and there was no spectacular bubbling lava to see — just ominous clouds of white sulphur gas drifting up from numerous vents. At the bottom of the crater a mass of tightly packed boulders act as the volcano's plug. When the internal pressure is stronger than the plug Mayon will again blow her top — perhaps as a huge fireworks display as in 1968, or just as smoke and dust as in 1978.

After a quick lunch, a long look around and the customary hero photos, we started back down. Almost immediately I realised the reason for Ricardo's reluctance to start back up. I was exhausted. Climbing up I'd never noticed the energy I was burning; going down there was none left. By the time we'd got to the bottom of the loose section my legs were already like rubber and as we descended further my rest stops became more and more frequent. Finally we reached the last rise above Camp 2 and I persuaded Ricardo to go ahead and get some tea on the boil. As soon as he disappeared I seemed to fall apart. If I stood up my legs folded underneath me and if I tried to walk my feet wouldn't go where I aimed them. It feels ridiculous to take an hour to walk what you know is just a stroll to the end of the street, but that's what I did. Even visions of a cold San Miguel beer hardly helped, and in the Philippines that's a bad sign!

I finally crawled, literally, into the camp and gulped down four cups of tea so fast that next day my scalded throat wouldn't allow me to swallow. If at that point you'd told me I could walk for another five hours I'd have laughed, but the recuperative effects of tea and calamansi (the tiny lemons which are a Filipino cure-all) work wonders and at 4.30 we headed down. By the time we reached Camp 1 it was raining heavily again, night had fallen and I was moving like a zombie, but we were too wet to consider stopping for the night. Finally, at 9.30, we got down to our starting point, walked down to the main road and a passing jeepney took us into Legaspi. Ricardo thought it was the hardest Mayon climb he'd ever made as it was the first time he'd had to do it twice! I could only agree. When I finally staggered up the stairs to the hotel the cold beer was long forgotten — I only had the energy to toss my shoes in the bin and myself into bed.

Tony Wheeler

Cagsawa Church

The catastrophic eruption of Mayon on 1 February 1814 totally destroyed the villages of Camalig, Cagsawa and Budiao on the southern side of Mayon. About 1200 people perished and ash fell as far away as the China coast. Many local residents took shelter in the church at Cagsawa, only to be smothered by falling ash. Today only the church steeple stands as a mute reminder of 'beautiful's' terrible powers. The rest of the village was buried under ash and lava.

There are some other ruins at Budiao, about two km away, but not so interesting. Cockfights take place in Daraga on Sundays and holidays. The Daraga church was built to replace the one at Cagsawa. Sensibly it was built on a hilltop.

Getting There To get to Cagsawa take a jeepney from the public market to Daraga or towards Camalig. Or take a Guinobatan Polangui, Das or Ligao

jeepney from Penaranda St — they go straight there. The Cagsawa ruins are a short distance beyond Daraga, off the road to the right.

Camalig

The town of Camalig is famous for the Hoyop-Hoyopan limestone caves which are in Cotmon, 11 km out of Camalig. The name means 'blow-blow', from the sound of the wind rushing through. Bones have been found in the caves and potshards which are over 2000 years old. They are now on display in a small museum in the Camalig Catholic church but unfortunately the museum is no longer open due to the dangerous state of the building.

Ask for Alfredo Nieva who will guide you to the Calabidogan Caves about two or three km (a 45 minute walk) away from the Hoyop-Hoyopan Caves. You can go a few hundred metres into the caves, which are chest-deep in water in parts. There are large caverns with bats and beautiful stalactites. It's up to you how much you pay the guide. Take swimming gear, sandshoes, torch or flashlight, camera and lots of plastic bags to keep everything dry. It's best to arrange a time with Alfredo the day before, he also has a coconut wine distillery which he is very happy to show off.

Getting There Camalig is about 14 km from Legaspi, jeepneys go there from the public market or from the bus terminal. From Camalig you have to take a tricycle to the cave. Occasionally it's possible to catch a jeepney which will be cheaper. Look for a jeepney with a Cotmon sign near the market, fare is P1. After 6 pm the only possible way to return to Camalig is to arrange a special ride.

Places to Stay — bottom end

The *Ideal Hotel* on Magallanes St has rooms with fan at P25/40 or with air-con and bath at P65/85. It's a simple, rather disorganised hotel. The *Legazpi Lodging House* on Mabini St is just P18 per person in fan-cooled rooms but not all rooms are so clean, despite renovations, and the entrance is hard to find.

The *Ritz Pension House* on Penaranda St has rooms with fan at P22/30, with fan and bath at P28/40, with air-con and bath at P70/80. It's a simple, well kept place. The small bathrooms with the fan-cooled rooms are shared with the room next door. The singles are small and cramped but the doubles are good and the people who run it are very friendly. There are also illuminated Jesus dioramas, sacred hearts and a full length mirror (horizontally!) beside at least one of the double beds in the 'short-time' rooms. Rooms on the main street are rather noisy.

Also on Penaranda St the *Olympus Hotel* (it was the Shirman) has rooms with fan at P40/50 or with air-con and bath at P60/75. It's a good, clean place and has a nightclub in the penthouse. On Aguinaldo St the *Rex Hotel* (tel 2743) is another good place and has rooms with fan and bath from P40/55 or with air-con and bath for P95/125.

Back on Penaranda St the *Hotel Xandra* has rooms with fan and bath at P50/75, with air-con and bath at P85/110. Ask for a room with concrete walls which is more likely to be rat-proof. There's also a restaurant which is good value and has live entertainment. The *Mayon Hotel* on the corner of Penaranda St and Rizal St has rooms with air-con at P80/100, with air-con and bath at P115/145. The *Albay Hotel*, back on Penarandra St, is fully air-con and bridges the gap to Legaspi's top end places. It's good value with fan, shower, toilets, hot water, balcony and a view of Mayon! Singles are P60 to 90, doubles P70 to 130 and it's only a 60c tricycle ride from Plaza Rizal.

Places to Stay – top end

On Lapu Lapu St the *Legazpi Plaza Hotel* is a good new place where rooms with air-con and bath cost P110/140. *La Trinidad* (tel 2951-55) has air-con rooms with bath at P175/220. It's the best hotel in the downtown area, centrally located with swimming pool, coffee shop, restaurant and even a cinema in the complex.

Legaspi's top of the top end hotel is actually several km out of the city, on a hillside looking across to Mayon. Due to lack of custom it's also (temporarily?) closed. The *Mayon Imperial Hotel* (tel 4941) is a large, international class hotel with singles at US$40 to 44, doubles US$45 to 52. There's a bar, restaurants, disco, swimming pools, tennis courts and all the usual mod cons. A free shuttle bus service operates between the hotel and the public market in the city – or would if the hotel was operating.

Places to Eat

The *Shangrila Restaurant* on Penaranda St has Chinese and Filipino food and the upstairs area is a favourite meeting place. On the same street the *Hongkong Dimsum & Tea House* has a very extensive menu – there's even eight sorts of coffee and seven sorts of beer!

Chinese and Filipino food are also found at the *Peking House Restaurant* and the *New Legaspi Restaurant*, both on Penaranda St, and at the *Four Seasons Restaurant* on Rizal St. These places are all clean looking and offer all-inclusive breakfasts, lunches and dinners which are good value. Try the *New Legaspi's* pineapple pie for a special treat.

The *Golden Dragon* is another good place to try while the *Great Wall Palace* on Magallanes St is an interesting ice cream parlour.

The *Filipino Restaurant* on Penaranda St is a Filipino restaurant with a special reputation locally. If you really want to try 'native' food then arrive early in the evening when it's all on view. This may be your chance to sample the local specialty known as the 'Bicol express' — a red hot pepper which is likely to have you running for relief at express speed.

Nightlife
The nightclub at the top of the *Olympus Hotel* has a cover charge but excellent views from the roof garden. The *Mayon Imperial* has Legaspi's best nightclub and disco — if it's open. There's also a big disco at the *Kagayunan Resort Hotel*.

Getting There
See the Routes South section at the start of South Luzon for information on buses to Legaspi from Manila. There are regular and air-con buses on the nine to 11 hour run from the Pantranco South Express terminal. The bus fare ranges from about P100 to 150.

Trains from Manila take much longer, at least 18 hours, and terminate at Camalig from where connecting buses operate to Legaspi. You can still buy tickets for the train from the old Legaspi station. The railway line between Camalig and Legaspi was cut by a flood down Mayon a few years back and has never been repaired.

From Legaspi back to Manila there are numerous Pantranco buses daily from 5.30 am to 9 pm. The trip takes nine to 11 hours. Air-con Pantranco buses go at 8 am, 6 and 8.30 pm. At 8 pm the resort air-con bus departs from the Mayon Imperial Hotel for Makati.

LEGASPI TO TIWI
There are several resorts and the small town of Tabaco along the coast road from Legaspi to Tiwi. For the Kagayunan Beach Resort take a jeepney towards Santo Domingo and say you want to go to the Mayon Riviera. There's a long lava-sand beach here and sometimes there are big waves. About three km

beyond Santo Domingo you find the Reyes Beach Resort. It's a well kept, pretty resort with black sand. Sirawgan Beach is of a similar standard.

Tabaco is not of great interest, just a jumping off point for the boat to Virac on Catanduanes Island. Probably the only thing worth seeing in Tabaco is the two-storey market.

Places to Stay & Eat
The *Kagayunan Resort Hotel* costs from around US$20. The *Reyes Beach Resort* has cottages with fan and bath from P50 to 90 and a good restaurant. At *Sirawgan Beach* doubles are P40.

In Tabaco *Tony's Hotel* on Riosa St near the market has rooms with fan at P28, with fan and bath at P33 and an apartment with air-con and bath for P90. There's a disco and the *EF-Palace* restaurant in the same building. Opposite the Municipal Hall is the *Royal Crown* canteen, a very clean restaurant.

Getting There
To the beaches take a bus or jeepney from Legaspi towards Tabaco. Ask if there's a direct bus to Santo Domingo — some of them take the circular route around the outskirts. From Santo Domingo take a tricycle to the beach.

Buses and jeepneys operate from Legaspi to Tabaco and on to Tiwi or Ligao. There are direct Pantranco buses between Tabaco and Manila from 9 am to 7.15 pm. An air-con bus leaves at 4.50 pm. The 5.15 and 7.15 pm buses go via Legaspi. The trip takes eight to 11 hours.

TIWI
North of Legaspi, Tiwi is famed for its hot springs which, unfortunately, have been commercialised in appallingly bad taste. Since the pilot geothermal plant (a second plant is under construction) started running at full power most of the springs have dried up in any case. The youth hostel is, however, a pleas-

ant place to stay while you explore the area — beaches, steam issuing from the ground and some interesting old church ruins in the town of Tiwi. The bubbling springs of Lake Naglagbong have already been developed for tourists.

Sogod Beach and Putsan Beach are two famous, but not particularly good, black sand beaches. Swimming has become dangerous since the geothermal plant runs its hot water containing sulphuric acid into the ocean. Be careful! If you walk to Putsan take a look at the primitive pottery. There are better swimming opportunities on the Coral Island, ask at the hostel for the best way to get there.

Places to Stay

The *Bano Youth Hostel* has doubles with fan and bath for P80, a little more if you're not a member. The double cottages in the garden are P30 including fan. Some cheaper rooms are being added on to the back of the main building but the whole place is getting a bit run down. There's an outside swimming pool and in the basement there are thermal baths at this very relaxed place. Expat workers from the geothermal plant often drop in for a few drinks here. There's a casually run restaurant too but the food is fairly uninspiring.

The *Tiwi Hot Spring Resort* has cottages with fan and bath at P80, with air-con and bath at P110. It's near the youth hostel — both places can get crowded out by workers and technicians on the geothermal and tourist projects.

Getting There

From Legaspi buses to Tabaco go from the City Bus Terminal and from Tabaco you continue by jeepney. Or from Penaranda St in Legaspi regular jeepneys go direct to Tiwi. From Tiwi to the Tiwi Hot Springs Resort, a distance of about three km, take a tricycle. The whole trip takes about an hour. The fares are Legaspi-Tabaco P3.50, Tabaco-

Tiwi P1.65 and Tiwi to the youth hostel less than P1.

Leaving Tiwi, if you want to continue on from Legaspi to Matnog on the same day, you must depart early in the morning or you'll face connection problems in Irosin. Twice daily there's a direct Pantranco bus between Pasay in Manila and Tiwi. From the Tiwi market departures are at 9 am and 3 pm and the trip takes seven to nine hours.

BULAN

Bulan is simply a departure point for boats to Masbate.

Places to Stay

The *Mari-El Lodging House* is a straightforward place with rooms at P18 per person. There are several other places by the pier.

Getting There

From Legaspi to Bulan there are direct buses hourly from 4.30 am to 3 pm. Take a Pantranco or JB Liner bus, the trip takes 3½ hours. Take a bus by 8 am if you want to get to Bulan in time for the boat to Masbate. There's a ferry once a week on from Masbate to Cebu.

SORSOGON

There are no boats from Sorsogon to Masbate but this is a place to visit volcanic Lake Bulusan from. The spectacular centre of the triangle Juban-Bulusan-Irosin, Mt Bulusan with its long spurs, is 1560 metres high. Next to it, at a height of 600 metres, is a small crater-lake of the same name. Surrounded by lush vegetation the mountainous landscape is stunning — they call it the Switzerland of the Orient. Take a picnic with you, there are tables here. A few cottages are under construction and should be finished in 1984.

You can also reach Gubat, near Rizal Beach, from Sorsogon or Legaspi but this highly-praised beach is definitely

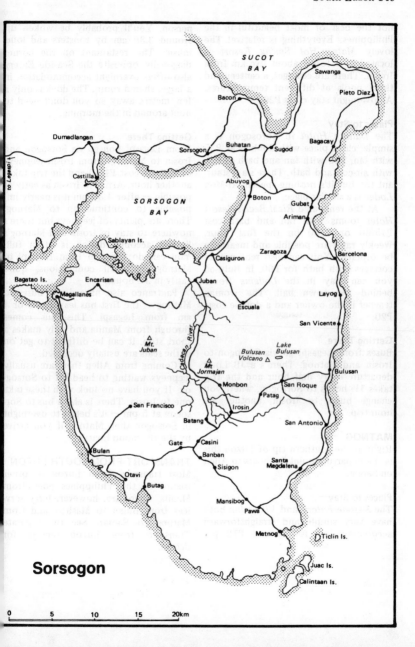

Sorsogon

0   5   10   15   20km

not the best or most beautiful in the Philippines. Everything is relative! The lovely *Mateo Hot Spring Resort* is located in a forest about five km from Irosin. There are cottages, a canteen and three pools at different temperatures. An overnight stay costs P20.

Places to Stay

The *Dalisay Hotel* in Sorosogon is a simple, clean place with doubles at P35 with fan, P45 with fan and bath or P95 with air-con and bath. There's a restaurant too but it's nothing special. *Al-Mon Lodge* is a similar place.

At the renovated *Rizal Beach Resort Hotel* rooms with fan and bath cost P45/60 or P100 on the first floor. Weekly rates are possible and meals can be ordered. You can also rent private cottages with bath for P60. In Bulusan you can stay in the *Lodging House* behind the town hall. The woman teacher is the owner and a double costs P20.

Getting There

Buses from Legaspi go via Sorosogon to Irosin and Matnog. There's a JB Liner departure every half hour and the trip takes 1½ hours to Sorosogon, where you change buses to Irosin, another 2½ hour trip.

MATNOG

Right at the southern tip of Luzon this is the departure point for boats to Allen on Samar.

Places to Stay

The *Seaside Eatery* and *Villa's Inn* both have very simple and straightforward accommodation for around P12 per person. You'll probably be woken up around 3.30 am by roosters and loud music. The restaurant on the corner diagonally opposite the Seaside Eatery also offers overnight accommodation in a large, shared room. The dock is only a few metres away so you don't need to hunt around in the morning.

Getting There

From Legaspi you go via Sorosogon and Irosin to Matnog. From Irosin jeepneys to Matnog cost P1.50 and the trip takes another hour. Arrive in Irosin as early as possible — after 4.30 pm it is nearly impossible to continue on to Matnog. There are plenty of jeepneys but there's nowhere to stay in Irosin and Matnog's limited accommodation is often full. You can do the trip from Legaspi to Matnog, with all connections, quite easily in 3½ hours.

Pantranco also have direct buses to Matnog — the first bus leaves at 3 or 4 am from Legaspi. This bus comes through from Manila and only makes a short stop. It can be difficult to get on as the seats are usually occupied.

Coming from Allen there are usually jeepneys waiting to head off to Sorosogon. If you have no luck with these take one to Irosin. There is also a bus to Sorsogon at 5 pm — it's better to overnight in Sorsogon than Matnog if you arrive by the afternoon boat.

TRANSPORT FROM SOUTH LUZON

Most transport from Luzon to other islands in the Philippines goes from Manila. There are, however, ferry services from Bulan to Masbate and from Matnog to Samar. See the separate Transport from Luzon section for details.

Around Luzon

A number of islands around the main island of Luzon are also generally included with Luzon. They include the Batan Islands scattered off the far north of Luzon, Catanduanes off the southeast coast near Legaspi and off the west coast the smaller islands of Lubang, Marinduque and Masbate and the larger island of Mindoro.

1 Batan Islands
2 Lubang
3 Mindoro
4 Marinduque
5 Masbate
6 Catanduanes

Batan Islands

The Batan Islands are the northern-most islands of the Philippines. Y'ami is only about 150 km from Taiwan. The largest and economically the most important islands are Batan, Ibayat and Sabtang. Basco is the capital, named after the Spanish governore Jose Basco.

The climate on the Batan Islands is rough in comparison to other parts of the Philippines. All 10 islands are relatively frequently hit by typhoons from June to September. It is often rainy and stormy from October to February/March. The best months for a visit are April and May.

Products which aren't produced on the Batan Islands are twice as expensive as on Luzon, they have to be flown in. Rice, maize and camotes (sweet potatoes) are grown here and fishing is the most important occupation.

BATAN ISLAND
Don't expect very much in the way of sights, about the only excitement is the Sunday cockfights. There are a couple of quite good beaches and you can

151

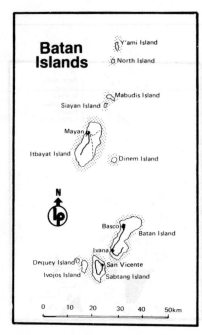

also visit various villages but there are no primitive tribes. Until a few years ago there were Americans stationed on Batan Island but the defence post has been taken over by the Filipinos.

Basco

Places to Stay & Eat Well there are no hotels but you can get accommodation in the *Casa de Tolentino* — nice people and good rooms for P10 per person. You can eat with Mr Elcano, who owns a bakery near the Casa. Meals should be ordered in advance, the food is good but not exactly cheap.

There is a small hotel (six rooms) being constructed at the moment. It may finished by the time you arrive there so ask around.

SABTANG ISLAND

In contrast to Batan Island there are no cars on Sabtang Island. It's quite pleas-

ant to go around the island on foot and to visit the four villages — there are no tribes. The mayor of Sabtang will place a guide at your disposal, free of charge, who will show you all the short cuts. Through him you will find it much easier to get to know the villagers, who are really nice people, with a definite addiction to alcohol. If you offer your guide a couple of bottles of beer, he won't say no.

There are no hotels on Sabtang Island but you can stay with the mayor or with Mr Louis, the principal of the Fishery School. You can also get something to eat there, no-one will charge you money or accept it, so it is rather nice if you 'happen' to have a small gift on hand.

Getting There

A boat goes once weekly from Basco to Sabtang Island. If you don't want to wait for it you have to go to Ivana, but the bus to Ivana only goes when a plane lands — enquire about departure times or ask the supervisor if a jeep is going to meet the plane. The jeep trip is free and much more comfortable than the bus trip. In good weather a boat goes daily from Ivana to San Vicente (Sabtang). Departure time is approximately 8.30 am and the travel time is 30 minutes. It comes back the next day at 8 am and the trip is free.

ITBAYAT ISLAND

There are no beaches here, only rocky coastline, You can stay and eat with the mayor. Coconut crabs are a speciality of the island. These crabs have a penchant for coconuts and will even climb the palm trees for them. Consequently they taste very strongly of coconut.

Getting There

Boats go from Basco to Itbayat — irregularly. Travel time is four hours and the trip is free. The boats only go in good weather and are fairly unpredictable — not too good for travellers on a fixed schedule.

TRANSPORT TO & FROM BATAN

From Manila As ships go from Manila to Basco only about five times per year (irregularly) and there are no boat connections from North Luzon, you must fly. The plane from Manila goes via Laoag and you can catch the flight there.

The weather is a decisive factor in arrival and departure schedules. On rainy days when the grass landing strip is wet, planes neither take off nor land so you should be prepared for disruptions to your travel plans.

From Laoag Flights with PAL operate three times weekly and departure time is 10 am. The flight takes one hour. Buy your ticket as early as possible in San Fernando and remember the student discount. The trip by jeepney to the airport is six km and costs less than a peso. They leave from near the Modern Hotel and the City Hotel.

Catanduanes

Also known as the 'land of the howling winds', this kidney shaped island lies in the Pacific Ocean, separated from south Luzon by the Maqueda Channel and the Gulf of Lagonoy. The main island and a few smaller islands form the province. The most important of these are Panay in the north-east and the Palumbanes Islands in the north-west, which comprise Palumbanes, Porongpong and Calabagio.

Catanduanes is mostly hilly, the only flat land is found east of the capital, Virac, and around Bato and Viga. The shape of the landscape is a result of the climate. Along the coast the hills are nearly always barely covered with grass, many palms are uprooted and broken off and the numerous cliffs and gouged-out bays are typical of the east and north-east coast. The powerfull typhoons are responsible for this. They blast into this section of the Philippines, straight off the Pacific. In Catanduanes you have to reckon with rain throughout the year, particularly from November to January, not so much from April to June.

The main industries are fishing, farming and forest-husbandry. The Gulf of Lagonoy and the Maqueda Channel are the most prolific fishing grounds. The major agricultural crops are abaca palms and coconuts. Then there is rice, sweet potatoes and kassava as well as fruits such as avocado, jackfruit, papaya and oranges. The timber yields are mainly hardwood and mahogany. Mining has not been developed much although yields of coal, gold, silver, zinc and copper are possible.

Many islanders have left in search of work and settled mainly in Manila. The greatest emigrations take place after the most severe typhoons when homes and crops have been destroyed. Returns to to the islands are then only for serious reasons like family reunions and fiestas. The people are friendly and extremely religious. They are Bikolanos and speak Bikolano, a language of south Luzon. Visitors are nearly always invited into their homes — you are dependent on this hospitality because, apart from in Virac, there are no hotels around the island.

VIRAC
Favourite day trips from Virac are to Igang Beach (10 km west), the Belongbong Falls in Bato and the Binanuahan Falls in Cabugao, a little south of Bato.

Places to Stay
The *Cherry Don Resthouse* on the Town Plaza has rooms at P15 per person. The *Catanduanes Hotel* on San Jose St has rooms with fan and bath at P50/70. There's also a restaurant here and PAL have their office in the hotel.

GETTING AROUND
A jeepney travels daily from Virac to Gigmoto. The bumpy road follows the east coast and winds around one bay after another. This is just as enchanting for travellers as the more comfortable road which leads from Bato through jungle, undergrow and tiny villages, across the island to Viga.

TRANSPORT TO & FROM CATANDUANES
Daily at 12 noon there's a boat from

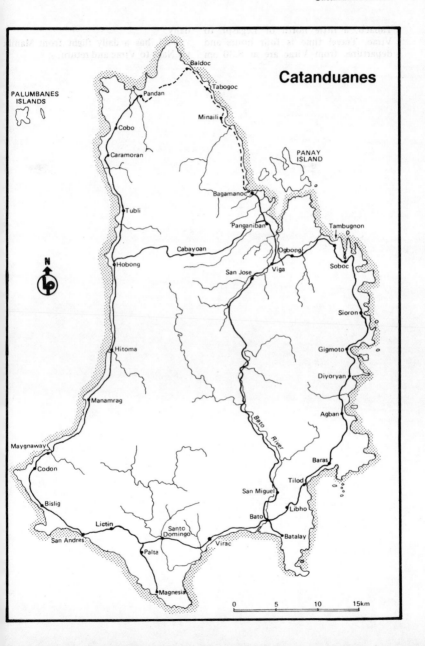

Tabaco, a little north of Legaspi, to Virac. Travel time is four hours and departures from Virac are at 8.30 am daily.

PAL has a daily flight from Manila via Naga to Virac and return.

Lubang

The Lubang Islands are part of the province of Mindoro Occidental. They hit world headlines in 1974 when, after hiding in the mountains on Lubang Island for 30 years, the Japanese soldier Hiroo Onoda finally decided it was time to give himself up as a WW II prisoner of war! Fumio Nakahura, a captain in the Japanese Imperial Army, held out for another six years before being discovered in April 1980 on Mount Halcon on Mindoro.

Today Lubang is still a favourite hunting spot for Japanese rifle-club members. They arrive by the planeful from Manila and stay at the World Safari Club on Lubang Beach. They spend their time shooting at targets, clay pigeons and so called wild pigs, bought in the villages shortly before the hunting party arrives, then driven out to be hunted and shot. The wilder the appearance of the pig, the higher the price. Filipino beaters risk their lives for a few pesos a day in these hunts, but even for people not involved it's risky. After massive public protest the World Safari Club may be forced to move its operations to the mountains of Mindoro Island. Lubang's income will then, once again, be restricted to the sale of garlic.

The people of Lubang want to take advantage of the tourist trade, but will need to change their attitude drastically to make a go of it. I couldn't wait to head off to Mindoro or Manila when I

was there. In Tilik and further east, the people were distant to the point of being unfriendly. It is particularly noticeable here as Tilik is the port of arrival. However, if you leave Tilik going to Lubang town, the people are different and become more and more friendly.

AROUND LUBANG

Tilik is the port of arrival. Cono Beach at Vigo is no dream beach but it does have good surf. There's a beautiful sandy beach at Tagbac, but the seabed is muddy.

For the short boat trip from Balaquilas to Ambil Island and back you'll be up for P100, even after hard bargaining. It's not worth it, particularly if you're intending to search for jade, which Filipino geological technical literature might lead you to believe could be found here.

If you travel by paddle boat from Tilik to the other side of the bay, check that there are at least two hand-breadths of space above the water. The centre of the bay is unprotected and even a light breeze can blow water into the boat. I was drenched when I tried this trip.

Places to Stay
In Tilik the family Demotrio Tezalona has rooms at P25 to 28 per person. It's the modern stone house with the glass-front, directly across from the church. You can also eat there.

Getting Around
From Tilik there is a jeepney service to Lubang and, also from Tilik, a truck will take you to Looc. It only operates when a ship arrives and it costs P20 per person. By carretela (calesa) the regular journey from Tilik to Lubang costs P7. Daily rentals for a carretela are P50 and for a jeepney P400! Walking is free of charge and it's probably the best way of getting around.

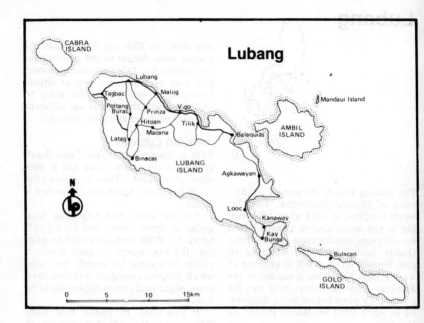

TRANSPORT FROM LUBANG

To Luzon From Tilik the Mindoro Shipping Lines *MV Superstar* goes to Manila on Thursdays and Saturdays at 10 am. The trip takes six hours. Mindoro Navigation Lines have the old *MV Mercedes* to Manila on Saturday at 8 am. The trip takes nine hours but it's unreliable.

To Mindoro The *MV Mercedes* from Tilik goes on from Manila to Mamburao and Sablayan.

Marinduque

Marinduque is the almost circular island between South Luzon and Mindoro. The capital is Boac on the Boac River but Santa Cruz has the largest population. The people of Marinduque are Tagalogs and most of them come from Batangas and Quezon provinces.

Coconuts and rice are the most important agricultural products. Two large mining companies mine iron ore and copper — there are large copper deposits in Labo at Santa Cruz which you can visit.

The annual Moriones Festival at Easter is Marinduque's main tourist attraction and one of the most colourful religious ceremonies in the Philippines. Dressed as Roman centurions wearing large carved masks, the participants capture Longinus, the centurion who was converted after he had stabbed Christ in the side with his spear. The festival ends with a mock beheading or 'pugutan' of the hapless Longinus. The celebration is preceded on Good Friday by groups of 'antipos' flagellating themselves with bamboo sticks. There are more foreigners on the island during the Moriones Festival than at any other time of the year.

SANTA CRUZ

The Bathala Caves, about 10 km northwest of Santa Cruz, are worth a visit. They're on private property owned by the Mendoza family and you should introduce yourseld and ask for permission before going to see the caves. After that feel free to take a dip in the natural swimming pool behind the Mendoza's house but be prepared — the caves are full of bats.

Places to Stay

The new *Joville's Resort Hotel* opened recently but better value is *Rico's Inn Boarding House*, opposite the school, with doubles at P20.

GASAN

Places to Stay

You can get good accommodation here at *Amigo's Lodge*.

BOAC

Places to Stay

The three main travellers' hotels are all on Neponuceno St. The *Boac Hotel* has singles with fan for P20, doubles with fan and bath for P70. The *Ruby Lodging House* has singles/doubles for P25 per person, it has a good restaurant. *Lagio's Resting House* is a large house diagonally opposite the Ruby and charges P60 for full board. There are two hotels outside the city, the *Seaview* and the *Sunraft*, both in Cawit. In Balanacan you can stay in the *Lodging House* for P15 per person.

AROUND THE ISLAND

Salomague Island

Marinduque has only recently begun to be opened up for tourism but if you're interested in diving the Salomague Island Resort on the east coast is a must.

Maniuayan Island

The still very peaceful Maniuayan Island is a good place for swimming with its km-long beaches and good snorkelling and diving on the coral reefs off-shore. To get there you can travel to Bitik by tricycle from where a boat leaves at 8 am and makes the crossing in about 45 minutes. There are still no cottages on the island but if you can get hold of a small tent it would be ideal here. There's a store close by where you can buy drinks and confectionery.

Torrijos

A typhoon destroyed all the cottages on White Beach, just outside of Torrijos, so a tent would also be useful here until rebuilding is complete. You can get private accommodation with the Rivilla Modesto family right next to the market. If you have no luck there ask the mayor. For a few pesos you can hire paddle-bancas for fun or to explore the steeply sloping coral reefs about 200 to 300 metres from the beach.

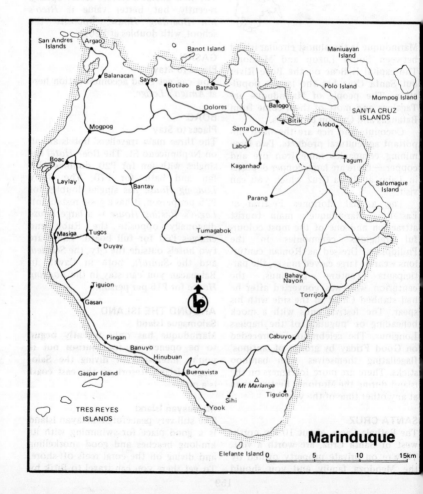

Marinduque

Tres Reyes Islands

Gaspar Island is the only one in this group to the south-west with a beach. Take along drinking water if you want to spend a few days with the fishermen here. It will cost you P40 by boat to get to this island. Recently an old Chinese merchant ship was found here at a depth of 40 metres. It was loaded with porcelain and is supposed to be over 500 years old.

TRANSPORT FROM MARINDUQUE

Ships travelling to and from Lucena City in Luzon dock at Balanacan, north of the Boac-Santa Cruz road. If you want to enter or leave Marinduque by air the airport is at Masiga, about 12 km south of Boac.

To Luzon There are one or two boats daily from Balanacan to Lucena City, early in the morning. PAL flies four times weekly from Masiga Airport to Manila. There are extra flights at the Easter festival time.

To Mindoro Boats go from Balanacan and Gasan to Pinamalayan on Tuesdays, and Fridays and sometimes on Wednesdays. Departures from Balanacan are at 7 am with a short stop in Gasan, from where they continue the trip at 9 or 10 am, the fare is around P20.

Masbate

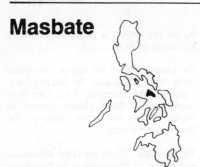

The province of Masbate includes Masbate Island, Ticao Island and Burias Island. Before WW II Masbate was a leading goldfield. Today it is noted for its meat production, with herds of up to 4000 head of cattle. You can reach Masbate from Cebu, Luzon or Romblon.

Places to Stay & Eat
Hotel Dalisay and *Hotel La Cabana* both have doubles for P20. A double at the *St Anthony Hotel* costs P40 or you can have a room with air-con and bath for P90.

For a good meal try *Peking House* in the port area or the *Petit Restaurant* opposite the St Anthony Hotel. If you like tuba you should try the white tuba which is a speciality of Masbate.

TRANSPORT FROM MASBATE
To Cebu The *MV Augustina II*, Escano Lines, comes each Tuesday from Manila and goes on to Cebu. The trip takes 13 hours. The *MV Malitbog* departs on Saturdays at 5.30 pm or at least it may do.

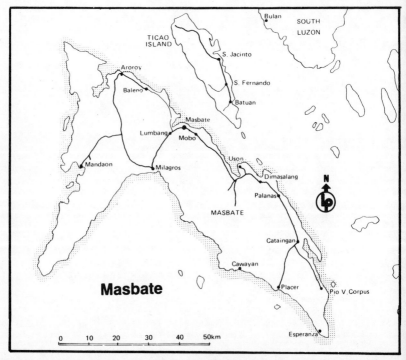

From Cataingan, in the south of the island, there's a daily, except Saturday, ferry to Cebu. It's supposed to depart at 6 pm but may leave earlier. P48 for a fairly comfortable bunk. The trip takes 14 hours. A jeepney from Masbate Town to Cataingan is P10 and departs from the market. It's a very dusty ride and the last jeepney of the day leaves at 1.30 pm.

To Luzon There is a daily boat from Masbate to Bulan on South Luzon. The boat departs at 5 pm and the trip takes four hours. Each Friday the *MV Augustina II* arrives in Masbate from Cebu and departs for Manila. PAL flies daily from Masbate to Manila.

Mindoro

Directly south of Manila the large island of Mindoro is divided into two halves — the western province of Occidental Mindoro with Mamburao as its capital and the eastern province of Oriental Mindoro with Calapan as its capital. Only along the coastal strip is there a dense population. In the jungles and mountains of the inland there are various groups of the Mangyan tribes.

Fishing, rice cultivation and coconut plantations are the main economic activities. There is also some cattle herding around San Jose. Although the name Mindoro is a contraction of the Spanish description 'Mina de Oro' (goldmine) no major gold discovery has yet been made although there are panners and Mangyans finding gold in small quantities. The difficult terrain has also slowed development of Mindoro's copper and iron potential and the only mining activity has been the quarrying of marble. There has, however, been some success in oil prospecting in south-west Mindoro.

The usual travel route on Mindoro is from Puerto Galera, with its superb beaches and coral reefs, to Calapan, Roxas and Mansalay. From Mansalay you can get to the villages of the Mangyans. You can tour the more isolated Occidental Mindoro coast overland but in the rainy season most parts are impassable so you have to go by boat.

PUERTO GALERA

The fine beaches and excellent diving at Puerto Galera have been attracting knowledgeable budget travellers for some time. By bus and ferry Puerto Galera is only five hours from Manila. Recently the town has been going through some major development and there are now many more places to stay. You can reach the beaches around the town by jeepney or outrigger boat from the docks. Come to an understanding with other 'beachcombers' and share the costs.

The sudden wealth of Puerto Galera has attracted foreign interest and investment. It has also split the town into two opposing camps: the developers and the environmentalists. The developers advocate expansion at any price while the environmentalists are concerned about the detrimental effects development is having on the town and the local population. Comparisons with Kuta beach in Bali, Hikkaduwa in Sri Lanka and Pattaya in Thailand have some basis but Puerto Galera has something of all three. Some foreigners don't care about the feelings of the locals and sunbathe and swim topless or even nude. There's fine weed and magic mushrooms and a diverse and transient multi-national influx of visitors, both Filipinos and from overseas. The gays and girls from Ermita come here to enjoy the company of their boyfriends.

It's a trendy place which tourism, unless carefully supervised, could easily destroy. The fact that tourism is like fire should be heeded more in Puerto Galera — you can cook your food with it but it can also burn your house down. Anybody who is in a position to watch the changes over the last five years will probably agree with me that what we have here is a forest fire. The spark has well and truly caught

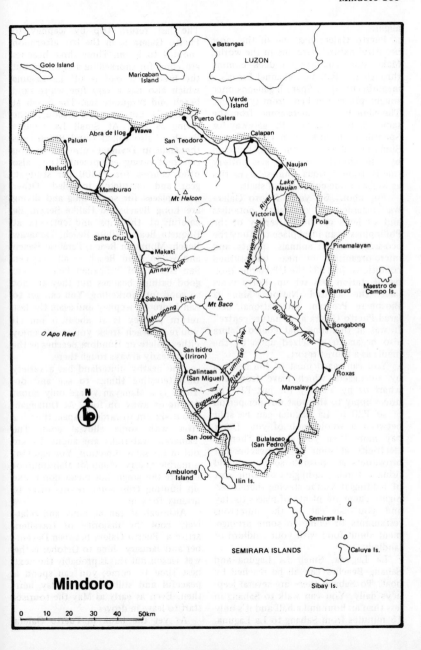

Mindoro

0   10   20   30   40   50km

alight.

Puerto Galera has one of the most beautiful natural harbours in the world. Make sure you are on deck coming through the Batangas channel for it's a magnificent sight. Spanish galleons once sought protection here from typhoons. The name Puerto Galera comes from the same era as it was once the gateway for Spanish trade links with China, India, Sumatra and Java. In the small museum by the church you can see pottery shards from various Chinese dynasties as well as a fine collection of shells.

For about 50 years Puerto Galera was regarded by zoologists, botanists and students of the University of the Philippines as an ideal place to study the eco-structure of animals, plants and micro-organisms in near undisturbed conditions. In 1934 the UP Marine Biological station was set up. Forty years later the United Nations Man & Biosphere Program International declared Puerto Galera as a 'nature centre'. It was at this time that Puerto Galera also began to be seized upon by the media as a tourist resort.

You can reach most of the beaches by outriggers which leave from the wharf or by jeepney for just P1. The prices apply to the boat not per person — so P20 to La Laguna can be split between a whole mob of you. Don't pay more than you should! There is electricity at some of the beaches but brownouts are possible so you should bring a torch (flashlight) or some sort of lighting if you're staying there overnight. There are plenty of places to stay and you can eat in the numerous restaurants or come to some arrangement about food with your landlord or landlady.

La Laguna, Small La Laguna and Sabang Beaches can all be reached by boat. To Sabang there are several jeepneys daily. You can walk to Sabang in less than an hour and a half and it's only 15 minutes from Sabang to La Laguna.

The last return trip by jeepney to Puerto Galera is in the late afternoon about 4 to 5 pm. These three beaches are good for snorkelling and diving but the best coral reef is off La Laguna which also has a very fine white sand beach and turquoise sea. The beach at Sabang is not so good although the diving is fine. At Small La Laguna Beach — also called Coral Beach — is the Galleon Diving Centre where you can rent diving equipment. They also offer courses for P1300 per student, gear and instructor included. Other good places for snorkelling and diving are Long Beach and Halike Beach. Be careful of the rips and currents at Boquete Beach. White Beach, Tamaraw Beach, Mountain Beach, Paradise Beach and White Sand Beach — all between San Isidro and Talipanan Point — are good bathing beaches but they are not so good for snorkelling. You can get to San Isidro by jeepney and again the last return journey is at about 5 pm. If you're a beach freak you won't enjoy either Balete or Hundora Beaches as the sea is nearly always rough there.

The nearby hinterland has a variety of interesting things to see and do. There is a Mangyan village only about 1½ hours away on foot. At Dulangan, about six km towards Calapan, there's a river with some alluvial gold. The Tamaraw waterfalls are about 15 km out in the same direction. You can visit a marble quarry, climb Mt Malisimbo or explore the jungle but please don't take up hunting trips some resorts offer to arrange for you.

Although it can be rainy and relatively cool the majority of travellers arrive at Puerto Galera between December and January. June to October is the wet season but this is probably the next best time to come; you can spend a peaceful and still sunny holiday here then. Even as early as May the tourists start to leave in droves.

As yet the bank in Puerto Galera

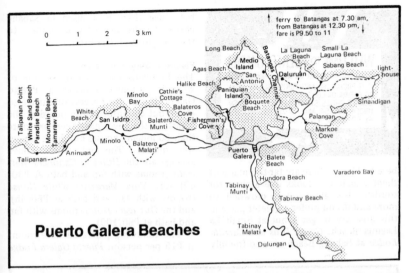

Puerto Galera Beaches

does not change travellers' cheques. Try the post office or Meg's Hotel if you have to but the rate will not be good.

Places to Stay — at the beaches

The wharf at Batangas is crowded with touts trying to hustle you into booking accommodation through them. A few of them go as far as travelling on the buses from Manila in order to win your custom. They earn P5 a head so, if you want to be left in peace, be firm. They do, however, have several advantages to offer — they'll reserve you a place on the boat, carry your luggage and at the height of the tourist season you're at least guaranteed a roof over your head which can be a good thing. You can always ask around for better accommodation the next day.

There are cottages for hire along almost every bay around Puerto Galera. When one bay is built out — as at La Laguna Beach — they simply develop the next — Sabang. There's also a small village at Sabang and this is about the only beach with electricity — sometimes.

You can easily walk from one beach to the next. They've even built cottages at the tiny beach between, known as Small La Laguna. These cottages extend to Tabinay Beach in the south and as far as Talipanan Point on White Sand Beach to the west. Prices start at a minimum of P30 per room or P15 per person and can go as high as P100, depending on the location of the cottages and how they're fitted out. Check with the large board at the landing point. If you want to stay longer and are willing to pay in advance you can get reasonable rates. So don't forget to bargain but keep quiet about the price you get!

Paradise Beach Lodge at Talipanan is one slightly more expensive place that gets recommendations — it's not so crowded and there is more space between the cottages than at nearby White Beach. Rates for singles/doubles are P25/40. *Santo Nino Beach Resort*, about 20 minutes from the town at Little Balateros Cove, is also popular. At La Laguna Beach pulling down all the cottages and starting again wouldn't

WELCOME TO PUERTO GALERA
Please help us preserve our beautiful marine reserve.
IT IS PROHIBITED AND PUNISHABLE BY LAW
TO GATHER OR COLLECT MARINE ORGANISMS:
CORALS, SHELLS, STARFISH etc. & TO SPEARFISH
UNDER P.D. 354 AND P.D.1219 AS AMENDED
BY P.D. 1698 IN THIS MARINE RESERVE.

be a bad idea. There are far too many of them and it just looks like a slum for tourists. It's almost too crowded to more and if you prefer a quieter place in this area try to get a hut at Small La Laguna Beach. *Green Hills* and *Cartillo Lodge* at Sabang Beach are also friendly

but since there is a disco in Sabang check the distance of your cottage to the very noisy 'Little Ermita'.

Places to Stay — in town

The following list is a cross-section of what is currently available in Puerto Galera. It's in the process of change so check out the information board at the wharf. In the town itself there are more than 20 lodging houses but don't expect star quality. The only three above average are the *Hotel El Canonera Marivelis* (rooms with fan and bath at P30/40), the *Villa Margarita White House* (rooms with fan and bath at P50/65), and the *Outrigger Hotel* (rooms with fan and bath at P60/100).

The following places all have rooms at P15 per person: *Puerto Galera Lodge*

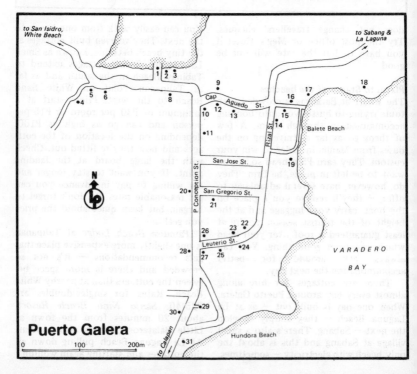

Puerto Galera

to San Isidro, White Beach

to Sabang & La Laguna

Cap Aguedo St.

Rizal St.

Balete Beach

San Jose St.

P. Conception St.

San Gregorio St.

Leuterio St.

VARADERO BAY

to Calapan

Hundora Beach

0 100 200m

---

at Balete Beach is quiet and here you have a refreshing breeze. *Melxa's Nipa Hut* is a typical place with small rooms, as is *Montiel's Nipa Hut* where you have to be lucky to find a room free. *Malou's Hilltop Inn* has a friendly atmosphere and is near the beach. *Apple's Huts* are 'freaky' cottages, nicely situated on the hillside. *Fishermen's Cove* is also peaceful although a little far out. The owners are good information sources and they also have cottages at Mountain Beach.

Places to Eat

Almost every inn has a restaurant attached so you've got plenty of choice. For a cosy atmosphere there's *Montiel's Nipa Hut* or for western food (Filipino style) you could try *Malou's Hilltop Inn* — old Father Thiel taught them German cooking. The *Palabok Restaurant, Susanna's Restaurant* and *El Canonero* also dish out western-style food. Try the *Fisherman's Cove Beach House* for tasty Filipino food.

At *Marissa's Restaurant* in the market you have a choice of great curries or Filipino food. In *Rejah's Inn*, opposite the *Mairitch Bakery*, you can get vegetarian food. Other restaurants here include the *China Moon* and *The Outrigger*, both cater for international dishes. Some of these seem to have spent far too much money in the

process of setting themselves up and consequently they're over-priced. Then they're surprised when people prefer to forgo their comforts and spend their money at the rustic restaurants run by the locals.

Getting There

From Manila take a bus at the Lawton Terminal going to Batangas Pier. The trip takes 2½ hours. Watch out, this bus is a favourite for pickpockets! BLTB buses leave from E de Los Santos Avenue in Pasay but only for Batangas City, from where you have to take a jeepney to the pier. This company has air-con buses too.

The ferry from Puerto Galera departs at 12.30 pm and the trip takes two hours. At 5 pm a ship leaves Batangas for Calapan where you have to stay overnight since jeepneys only operate in the daytime. It's complicated and expensive to fly from Manila to Mindoro since the airport is at Mamburao from where you have to take a jeepney to Abra de Ilog and then charter a boat, which costs at least P150, to Puerto Galera.

CALAPAN

This is the alternative to Puerto Galera for the boat crossing from Batangas in Luzon. The Sanduguan Festival was

1 Wharf
2 El Canonero Marivelis Hotel & Restaurant
3 Susanna's Restaurant
4 Villa Margarita Bayview House
5 Villa Margarita Bamboo House
6 Villa Margarita White House
8 Palabok Restaurant
9 Church, Museum
10 Clinic
11 School
12 Bank
13 Post Office, Basketball Court
14 Melxa's Greenhill Nipa Hut
15 Malou's Hilltop Inn
16 China Moon Restaurant
17 Varadero Bamboo House
18 Apple's Huts
19 Puerto Galera Lodge
20 Joy Milewski's Restaurant
21 Sharon's Inn
22 Sharon's Inn
23 Suzara's Pharmacy
24 Alfred Hotel
25 Montiel's Nipa Hut & Restaurant
26 Traveller's Lodge & Restaurant
27 Rejah's Inn & Restaurant, Bookstore
28 Mairitch Bakery
29 Market, Marissa's Restaurant
30 Sanz Shine Lodge

held here for the first time in May 1981 — sanduguan means 'friendship' in the Mangyan language. At the festival they re-enacted the first encounter between the seafaring Chinese traders and the indigenous Mangyans at Aroma Beach. It was such a great success it is likely to be repeated every year.

Places to Stay

The *Travellers' Inn* costs P25/40 for singles/doubles with fan or P80 for a double with air-con. The *Casa Blanca Annexe* is just P20 per person for a room with fan. At the *Eric Hotel* singles/doubles with fan are P30/40 — in the annexe rooms are P10 cheaper. At the market the *Hotel Riceland* offers singles for P35 or with fan and bath for P65. Double rooms here run as high as P120. This place has quite a reasonable restaurant.

Getting There

From Puerto Galera jeepneys depart from near Meg's Hotel and the docks in the morning. The trip takes two hours. Roxas-Calapan is a five or six hour bus trip and costs P20.

BONGABONG & ROXAS

Boats cross to Tablas on Romblon from both of these ports. This would probably be the only reason for staying here. During the daytime you can spend some time waiting in Roxas on Melco Beach. Roxas has an old cinema for evening entertainment, with a bit of luck it won't have been renovated yet. If the antique projector is still being used the whole thing becomes hilarious in a grim sort of way. There's also a new cinema.

Places to Stay

In Bongabong the *Mabuhay Lodging House*, near the market place, has rooms for P10 per person. In Roxas the *Santo Nino Restaurant & Lodging House* has rooms at P10. A new hotel has opened

near the Santa Nino and also some new restaurants. Avoid *Serospes Hotel* reported one traveller.

A good alternative to staying in town in Roxas is to head out to the beaches. *Catalina's Beach Resort* is walking distance from the town and has bungalows at P15 per person. Melco Beach is a P1 tricycle ride from town and there are some lovely cottages at P15 per person and a restaurant. Although the beaches are not that special it's a good place to stay while you wait for boats for Tablas or Boracay.

Getting There

From Calapan large buses leave the market place or dock at 4.30 and 11 am and 3 pm but they're often less than punctual. The trip takes seven hours through Bongabong to Roxas. The road now is not bad at all and a good bus can make the trip in under five hours — including lunch and a breakdown or two. The fare is P25.

You can break the Calapan-Roxas trip at Bongabong. Several minibuses also make the daily trip from the marketplace to Bongabong. Until 6 pm buses or jeepneys also go from Bongabong to Roxas. Ask the drivers at the market place — other sources of information are fairly useless.

The building of the road from Calapan to Roxas is being financed by the World Bank. Prior to this road improvement project's completion this was a very rough stretch, especially in the south. If possible catch a large bus.

MANSALAY

This is a good starting point for visits to the Mangyan tribes but be warned, Father Postma, who has published a number of books and articles on this tribe in the past few years, does not appreciate rubber-necks or camera-happy tourists. So anyone going here as a casual tourist should think twice. If, however, you are genuinely interested in the problems of these minority groups you will find him an informative and co-operative person to deal with.

Places to Stay

Restaurant Clicks, near the market, no longer takes guests. It's purely a restaurant. The house close by occasionally takes guests but overall it's not easy to find accommodation here. As a last resort check the *Municipal Beach Resort.*

Getting There

There are several jeepneys daily from Roxas but if you wish to visit a Mangyan tribe go early. Otherwise you will have to walk in the mid-day heat. There is a new road from Mansalay to San Jose.

SAN JOSE

Besides Sablayan this is the starting point for diving excursions to the Apo Reef. Lying at the southern tip of Mindoro Occidental this city is also handy for people planning a trip to Palawan. There are swimming and snorkelling opportunities on the nearby islands such as Ilin Island or Ambulong Island where you can stay in the *Ambulang Rest House* at P80 for a double room. You can get there on boats from the river mouth next to the market.

There is a beautiful beach at Calintaan where you can rent a three bedroom, furnished house for P100 a week as one traveller reported. The journey by jeepney takes about four hours and is only possible in the dry season as two rivers must be crossed.

Queen's Ranch is a good place for a day trip. It's a two hour trip by jeepney and you can also stay overnight there. It takes about eight hours on foot to get from Queen's Ranch to the Mount Iglit Tamaraw reservation.

In Occidental Mindoro there are many tribes, the most remote of which have little contact with civilisation.

With luck you may meet a Mangyan in San Jose who will guide you to his village. Getting there takes an hour by jeepney to Bato Ili from where it is several hours' walk. Footwear is important because there can be snakes on the paths. You can stay overnight in the village but bring small gifts such as canned fish, biscuits (cookies) or matches.

You can get good information in San Jose from Hugo Kayser, the manager of the *Red Baron Restaurant.* Tricycle drivers will know where it is.

Places to Stay

The *Kapit Bahay Mini Hotel* has singles at P20 or doubles with bath for P35. The colourfully painted doors and windows are lovely. At *Mosquera's Hotel* the equivalent prices are P20/25 while at the *Executive Inn* rooms are just P15. The *A J Inn* is P12.50 per person.

More expensive places include *Roda's Hotel* where rooms with fan are P35/55 for singles/doubles or P95/135 for air-con rooms with bath. It's a hotel which has seen better days. At the airport the *Red Baron Restaurant & Lodge* is P55 to 65 for rooms with bath. It's a clean, small hotel opposite Aroma Beach. The one plane daily doesn't bother anybody. Nearby there is the large *Inihaw Natin Restaurant* with rooms with bath at P75. They have a speed boat and offer trips to the Apo Reef. Ask here for accommodation on Ambulong Island.

Getting There

From Mansalay to Bulalacao is a two hour jeepney trip — leave early if you don't want to spend the night in Bulalacao. From there to San Jose a boat leaves in the morning, before noon. Actual departure times depend on the tides and the trip takes 2½ hours. The route on up the west coast from San Jose to Mamburao is very rugged

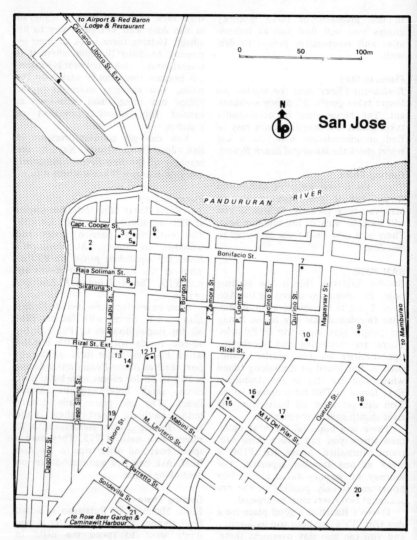

to Airport & Red Baron
Lodge & Restaurant

Cipriano Liboro St. Ext

0   50   100m

N

San Jose

PANDURURAN RIVER

Capt. Cooper St.

2   3 4
            5   6

Bonifacio St.

7

Raja Soliman St.

8

Sikatuna St.

P. Burgos St.

P. Zamora St.

P. Gomez St.

E. Jacinto St.

Quirino St.

Magsaysay St.

to Mamburao

Rizal St. Ext.

10

13 14   12 11

Rizal St.

Diego Silang St.

Dagohoy St.

16

15

17

M.H. Del Pilar St.

Quezon St.

18

19

M. Leuterio St.

Mabini St.

C. Liboro St.

20

F. Barretto St.

Soldevilla St.

21

to Rose Beer Garden &
Caminawit Harbour

and in the rainy season you have to travel part way by boat as the road is impassable.

From December to May during the dry season there is also a bus right around from San Jose to Calapan and Puerto Galera. RCG Liner and Ramadel Express buses leave at 8.30 am and 5.30 pm and the trip takes nine to 12 hours. The first part of the journey is fairly rough, but it gets better from Mansalay on. The evening bus will only go if there

1 Ferry to Sablayan
2 Market
3 Loreto Shipping Lines
4 Golden Hotel
5 Cora's Restaurant
6 Msagana Shipping Lines
7 William Lines
8 Mosquera's Hotel
9 Pilot School
10 High School
11 Buses to Mamburao, Bulalacao & Calapan
12 Kapit Bahay Mini Hotel & Restaurant
13 A J Inn, Hong Kong Restaurant
14 PAL Office
15 Bachelor's Inn
16 Philippines National Bank
17 Market
18 Church
19 Ramadel Bus Terminal
20 Divine World College
21 Roda's Hotel

are enough passengers but it's better to travel in the day in any case because the countryside is so beautiful. The last jeepney leaves Calapan at 4 pm for Puerto Galera. Because the morning bus arrives later than this you will need to spend the night. Don't get off at the pier, get off in the town. The first jeepney from Puerto Galera leaves from the market at 7 am and the trip takes two to three hours.

MAMBURAO
From this town at the north of the south-west coast you can visit Paluan by jeepney. Here there is a village with many horses and a black sand beach but no accommodation for visitors.

Places to Stay
At the *Travellers' Inn* rooms are P20 per person or rooms with fan and bath are P30 per person. At the *Shell House Hotel* rooms are available at P20 per person.

Getting There
From San Jose the boat leaves at 8 am and pauses at Sablayan. If you want to stop there stay at the *Elisas Hotel*. Arrival time in Mamburao is 5 pm. Note that there are two piers in San Jose. The south pier is at Caminavit Port, four km out, and boats go from here to Bulalacao. The north pier is the one for Sablayan and Mamburao. In the dry season there are also jeepneys and

minibuses from the *Kapit Bahay Mini Hotel* in San Jose at 7.30 am.

You can continue from Mamburao to Abra de Ilog and then Puerto Galera. To Abra de Ilog take the 6 am jeepney to connect with the boat for Puerto Galera or Batangas. The trip takes two or three hours and costs P10. The pumpboat departs Abra de Ilog at 8 to 9 am (or 10 am to noon?) — or when it's full. It takes 1½ or more hours to Puerto Galera and the fare is P25 but it's possible it may go directly to Batangas! Be prepared for there seems to be no direct boat to Puerto Galera. In that case you will have to charter one which will cost at least P150. There is no hotel in Abra de Ilog.

TRANSPORT FROM MINDORO
To Lubang The *MV Mercedes* of Mindoro Navigation Lines goes once weekly from Sablayan to Mamburao and on to Tilik.

To Luzon The best connections are between Calapan and Batangas. Departures are at 7.30 am and then between 9 and 10 am. There also might be a boat in the afternoon. Evening departures are at 7.45, 9 and 9.30 pm. In Batangas big buses for Manila meet the boats and depart immediately.

At 7.30 am a ship goes from Puerto Galera to Batangas. There are possibly odd departures from time to time. The regular fare is around P10 but special trips cost from P200 to 250.

If you want to take an air-con bus from Batangas to Manila you have to take a jeepney from the harbour to the terminal in the city. Watch out for pickpockets in all the buses!

Three times weekly there's a ship from San Jose to Manila. The best and fastest ship is the *MV Elizabeth* of William Lines. This trip takes 12 to 17 hours.

PAL flies daily from San Jose and Mamburao to Manila.

To Marinduque The best ship service is between Pinamalayan and Gasan with one or two departures weekly.

To Palawan On Wednesdays at 10 pm, according to the schedule, the *MV Elizabeth* of William Lines goes from San Jose to Puerto Princesa. Travel time is 24 hours but you must be prepared for possible delays of 24 hours.

On Thursday, also according to schedule, the *MV Sea Palace* of Magasagana Shipping Lines goes from San Jose to Coron and on to Puerto Princesa. It can also run late. More exact departure times and reservation details can be found at Caminavit Port.

To Panay Once weekly there's a large outriggerboat from San Jose to Buruanga on the north-west tip of Panay. Once each week on Monday at 10 am there's also a boat from Roxas via Looc on Tablas (Romblon) to Bor-

acay, Malay and Buruanga. It's a long trip to Boracay, you don't arrive at White Beach until around 7 pm so beware of sunburn, hunger, cold and other discomforts. Some people have hired the regular outrigger from Roxas to Tablas for a sidetrip to Boracay. If there are at least 10 passengers the *MB Catalina* leaves Roxas every two days or even daily direct to Boracay. The trip takes six to seven hours and costs P75. Enquire at *Catalina's Aqua Farm & Beach Resort.*

To Romblon Sunday, Wednesday and Friday at 9 am there's a boat from Bongabong to Carmen on Tablas and on to Romblon on Romblon. The trip takes about six hours.

Twice weekly a boat goes from Roxas to Looc on Tablas for P35. From there it continues to Kalibo on Panay for another P37. On Sunday, Tuesday and Friday morning at 10 am a large outriggerboat goes from Melco Beach near Roxas to Odiongan on Tablas. The trip lasts four hours (if there are no breakdowns) and costs P30. Watch for flying fish during the crossing and beware of sunburn and (even worse!) a sore bottom! For P3 you can travel steerage but it's no great advantage as you are bound to get wet later anyway — the sea in the Tablas Strait is not at all calm. See the Transport from Romblon section for information on transport from Tablas to Boracay and Panay.

The Visayas

South of the island of Luzon is the main island group of the Philippines, the Visayas. The main islands in this group are Bohol, Cebu, Leyte, Negros, Panay, Romblon, Samar and Siquijor. The Visayas are the central island group, bordered to the south by Mindanao and to the west by long, narrow Palawan.

Bohol

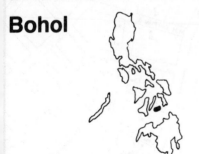

Situated between Leyte and Cebu, Bohol is the 10th largest island of the Philippines. It is of great historical importance as the site of the 'blood compact' between Legaspi and Chief Sikatuna. Today most foreigners go to Bohol in order to see the 'Chocolate Hills'. Erik Von Daniken certainly had a great time writing about this unique landscape.

The souvenir shops in Manila are well stocked with the weaving, basketry and other handicrafts for which Bohol is famous. The prices, however, are much lower in Tagbilaran City.

TAGBILARAN
There are no special sights to see in Tagbilaran, the capital of Bohol, but it's easy to get to Panglao Island and you can make various excursions to places around the coast. Note that the post office is upstairs in the market building.

Panglao Island
It is worth making a day trip by jeepney to Panglao Island's Bikini Beach (P25 by tricycle if you bargain) and Alona Beach. Both are very good and Doljo Beach is also beautiful but has rather shallow water. You can also go to one of the three islands off Doljo Beach. To Bontod Island it costs between P20 and 40 depending on how well you bargain. There are no cottages on Doljo Beach but ask Roberta Hora if her guest room is free. It's a double room at P5

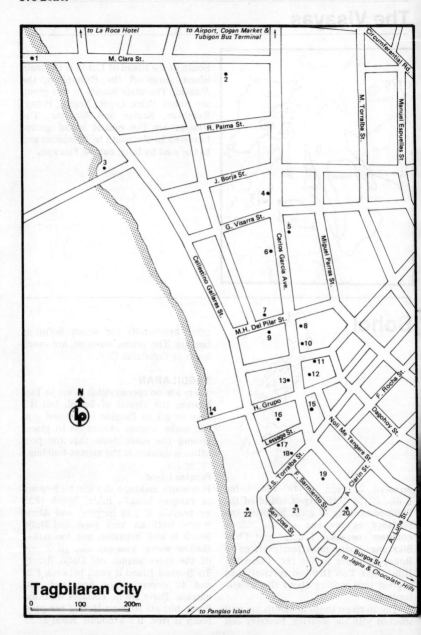

to La Roca Hotel

to Airport, Cogan Market &
Tubigon Bus Terminal

M. Clara St.

●1

●2

R. Palma St.

●3

J. Borja St.

●4

G. Visarra St.

●5

Carlos Garcia Ave.

●6

Celiestino Gallares St.

Miguel Parras St.

M. Torralba St.

Manuel Espuelias St.

Circumferential Rd.

●7

M.H. Del Pilar St.

●8

●9

●10

●11

●13 ●12

N

●14

H. Grupo

●16

●15

Lessage St.

Noli Me Tangere St.

F. Rocha St.

Dagohoy St.

●17

●18

●19

J.S. Torralba St.

F. Sarmiento St.

A. Clarin St.

●21

●22

San Jose St.

●20

Burgos St.

to Jagna & Chocolate Hills

Tagbilaran City

0   100   200m

to Panglao Island

1 Wharf	12 Agora Market, Post Office (2nd floor)
2 University of Bohol	13 Elena's Carenteria
3 Dagohoy Hotel	14 Clifftop Hotel
4 Trans Asia Shipping Line	15 New Life Hotel
5 PAL Office	16 Divine World College
6 Rosmage's Folkhouse	17 Vista Lodge
7 Vista Lodge Annex	18 Bistro de Paris
8 LTS Lodge	19 Plaza
9 Gie Garden Hotel	20 Philippine National Bank (PNB)
10 Sweet Lines	21 Church
11 Bus Terminal	22 City Hall

per person and she also cooks for you. One traveller wrote that Mormbo Beach is also good for snorkelling.

The south-west coast of Panglao is a good spot for snorkelling and diving; hundreds of starfish. If you want to take a look at the extensive coral reefs here you can borrow diving equipment from the Gie Garden Hotel or from Jacques Trotin at Bistro de Paris (both in Tagbilaran) or from the shell dealer in Panglao on Panglao Island.

You can swim in the cave lake of Hinagdanan Cave (in Bingag at Davis) — the water is refreshingly cool but there are plenty of bats inside so the water is not really the cleanest. The limestone cave is about 20 by 25 metres and is off a side track about a km from the unpaved road to Bingag, some 14 km from Tagbilaran. Catch a JG Express jeepney for Panglao or hire a tricycle, about P15 round trip. Entrance is free.

Places to Stay
The *New Life Hotel* on Carlos P Garcia Avenue is simple, singles/doubles with fan cost P16 per person and there's a reasonable restaurant. The *Vista Lodge* on Lesage St is good value and has a new restaurant downstairs. Singles/doubles with fan cost P20/35, rooms with bath cost P35/50 and with bath and air-con P55/85.

The *Executive Inn*, behind the market, is P15 for a bathless single — friendly but loads of cockroaches. If Boy Loma is staying here ask him to

arrange to take you out to Panglao and the Hinagdanan Cave. There's also the *Sea Breeze Inn* with similar prices. Opposite the Gie Garden Hotel the *Vista Lodge Annex* has doubles with fan at P30, with bath too at P55. Or there's the simple *Clifftop Hotel* with rooms from P20 and a garden by the sea.

The *Gie Garden Hotel*, where an air-con single/double with bath costs P98/140, is one of the best hotels in town. The lady doctor who runs this neat and clean hotel conducts tour groups. She has also had a couple of cottages built on Pamilacan Island. The brand new *LTS Lodge* is at 27 Carlos P Garcia Avenue. It's very clean, the staff helpful and there's even hot water. Air-con rooms with bath are P100/120.

Places to Eat
The *Gie Garden* has good food — try their calamari with cucumber salad. The small *Majestique Restaurant*, just five tables, is opposite the community hospital and does excellent hamburgers. At the *Bistro de Paris*, next to the Plaza, you can get French hamburgers (!) and, if ordered in advance, seafood. Jacques, the French guy, is a good information source, especially about diving. You'll also find a good range of food at the *Horizon Restaurant* near the bus station.

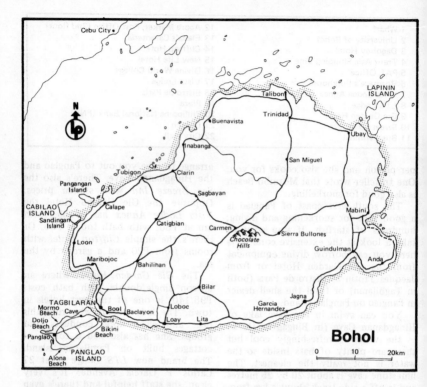

Bohol

0   10   20km

Nightlife

There's live music at *Rosemages Folkhouse* and at the *Clifftop Hotel*. The *New Life Channel Five Disco* and *Adam's Apple Disco* are also popular. For a late beer try *Elena's Carenderia*, opposite the Agora Market. The two cinemas on Garcia Avenue are good value, a fine way to fill in time while you wait for that late ferry departure.

Getting Around

Tricycles around town cost 75c but you can expect to pay double to or from the ferry pier.

AROUND THE ISLAND

Although the Chocolate Hills are Bohol's major attraction there are a number of other places of interest around the coast.

Close to Tagbilaran

There are various places of historical interest to the north and east of Tagbilaran City along the coast. The old Punta Cruz Watchtower dating from 1796, during the Spanish period, is north at Maribojoc. Just outside Tagbilaran to the east there's a memorial to the bloody conflict between Legaspi and Datu Sikatuna in Bool.

Baclayon & Pamilacan Island

One of the oldest church in the Philippines, it was built in 1595, stands in Baclayon, just beyond Bool. There's a small museum adjoining the church.

From Baclayon outrigger boats travel to beautiful Pamilacan Island. The crossing takes about 45 minutes. On Wednesdays, market day, and Sundays, church day, you can travel with the returning fishermen for just a few pesos. For a special trip it will cost you P150 or slightly less if you bargain. Mostly the people return to their island in the afternoon (about 3 pm). They always anchor their boats on the right side of the pier, if you look toward Pamilacan, so if you can wait you don't need a special ride.

Places to Stay There's accommodation available on Pamilacan Island. The few cottages cost P15 per head and the Gie Garden Hotel in Tagbilaran is the owner. Bring food at least for the first day because the caretakers might not be prepared for visitors. From the second day on there's no problem.

Loay to Jagna
In Maambong at Garcia Hernandez, just before Jagna, is Roxas Park with two natural freshwater swimming pools. On the way is Loay which is about 15 minutes from the beach. Also worth a visit is the huge old church with attached monastery at Loboc, just inland from Loay.

One traveller wrote that Bohol has several waterfalls including the Tontonlac falls about two km north of Loboc. They're reached through the associated hydro-electric plant (the guard requests that all firearms are deposited before entry!). Catch a local JG Express jeepney, they're the most beaten up red wrecks ever seen, or walk from Loboc past rice fields, palm jungles and traditional nipa huts covered with bougainvillea up to the top of the hill. There the turn off is to the left from the Carmen Rd, by the hydro-electric bus shelter. The falls drop about 15 metres in two stages at the base of a steep jungle valley. A neatly laid out garden/viewing area has been built for visitors.

Places to Stay In Loay you can get full board accommodation at *Paradise Unlimited* for about P150. It's run by Bill and Bruna Yost — Bill's an American, Bruna a Boholano — who also arrange tours.

Ubay
Places to Stay Right at the opposite end of the island from Tagbilaran you can stay at the *Saguise Hotel & Restaurant* in Ubay. It's clean but a little pricey at P20 per head.

CHOCOLATE HILLS
There are two legends about the origins of the chocolate hills, and also a couple of geological explanations. The first legend tells of a battle between two giants who pelted one another with stones and sand until they tired of this, sealed a friendship and left the island; but neglected to clean up the battlefield after them — otherwise there wouldn't be any chocolate hills.

The other legend is far more romantic: Arogo, a young and unusually strong giant, was in love with Aloya, an ordinary mortal. After she died Arogo wept bitterly and the proof of his deep grief is the chocolate hills, because they are his tears turned into hills.

The geological explanations are much more prosaic. Some geologists hold that Bohol was entirely submerged in prehistoric times and that the hills were formed on the sea-floor through volcanic eruptions and subsequently shaped and rounded by submarine currents. Other geologists hold that this is utter nonsense and the most popular theory now is that the hills are caused simply by special weathering of a marine limestone formation over impermeable claystone. Comparisons have also been made with Hundred Islands. Whatever the case they stand about 50

the Chocolate Hills

metres high and in the dry season, when the grass dries out and turns chocolate brown, they look just like a collection of collosal chocolate drops.

Places to Stay

At the *Chocolate Hills Complex* there's a hostel with dorm beds at P18, doubles at P70 and a restaurant. The views from the top of the hill are superb. The restaurant is expensive but there is no other place to eat. If you're lucky there may even be water in the swimming pool.

Getting There

Buses to Carmen and the Chocolate Hills Complex leave regularly (every 30 minutes to one hour) from the market in Tagbilaran. The last departure is at

5.30 pm, the trip takes two hours and the fare is P12. Big buses run to Carmen, the smaller ones continue to Ubay. Tell the driver you want to get off for the complex, from where you're dropped off you have a half km walk, uphill of course, to the top of the highest 'chocolate hill'.

Don't worry about missing the place — the complex is just past the 53 km marker from Tagbilaran but the other passengers who have apparently been ignoring you so far will all hiss at the driver to put you off — even if you're just passing by! Don't be confused by some smaller hills around the 38 km marker. An alternative route is to take a jeepney to Loboc for P2.50 and then connect with the local Jagna-Carmen route.

If you want to take the 11 am ship to Cebu from Tubigon you have to first get from the Chocolate Hills Complex to Carmen. You can try walking or hitching from the hills complex to Carmen if a bus or jeepney doesn't turn up. Try to be on the main road to Carmen around 7.30 am. The bus should leave from the Carmen market at about 8.30 am and takes two hours to Tubigon. The last bus leaves at 5 pm.

From Carmen to Jagna you have to first take a bus to Loay and change there. There are several buses daily to Ubay, the trip takes 3½ hours. From here boats operate to Maasin on Leyte.

TUBIGON

This port on the north-west coast is principally an alternative departure point for ferries to Cebu.

Places to Stay

The *Alexandra Reserva*, near the pier, has rooms at P10 per person but it's pretty basic. Rooms are usually rented here by the hour!

Getting There

Several buses daily make the 1½ hour trip from Tagbilaran to Tubigon. See the Chocolate Hills section for transport details from there to Tubigon. The main route between Tagbilaran and Tubigon is along the coast road, not through Carmen.

TRANSPORT FROM BOHOL

To Cebu PAL flies four times weekly between Tagbilaran and Cebu City. The Sweet Lines ship *MV Sweet Heart* goes from Tagbilaran daily at 11 pm or 12 midnight for Cebu City. The crossing takes three to four hours. The reason for this late departure is so that visitors in a hurry can catch morning flights back to Manila. It's wise to board at least an hour early to ensure a place. There are sleeping cots for all passengers and bedding can be hired for P5. You

can sleep on board until it gets light in Cebu. Bridge deck is about P30, lower deck a few peso cheaper. You cannot buy tickets before the day of departure and the Sweet Lines Office in Tagbilaran closes at 5 pm so don't get caught out.

There's also the daily *MV Asia China* of Trans Asia Shipping which leaves Tagbilaran at 8.30 am and takes 2½ hours.

From Tubigon there are ships daily to Cebu City at 9, 10 and 11 am, 4 pm and 12 midnight. The crossing takes two to three hours and costs P16.

To Leyte There are boats making the 3½ hour trip from Ubay to Maasin or Bato, at least every other day, supposedly for P25 per person. There are no longer boats from Jagna to Leyte.

To Mindanao William Lines have the *MV Cebu City* which departs Tagbilaran at 11 pm on Sunday for Ozamiz. The trip takes about six hours. A ship should go to Cagayan de Oro on Fridays or Saturdays from Jagna. There are ships at 1 pm on Tuesdays and Fridays from Tagbilaran to Cagayan de Oro. The *MV Asia Philippines* of Trans Asia Shipping Lines goes from Tagbilaran to Cagayan de Oro every Monday at 11 pm, the trip takes eight hours.

Almost every day boats go to Mindanao and Manila from Jagna. There are several buses daily from Tagbilaran to Jagna. A ship leaves Jagna for Butuan on Thursdays at approximately 8 pm, the trip takes 10 hours.

To Negros The William Lines ship *MV Cebu City* leaves Tagbilaran on Tuesday at 10 to 11 pm for Dumaguete. The trip takes about five hours.

To Siquijor The *MV Sweet Sound* of Sweet Lines goes from Tagbilaran to Larena every Tuesday and Friday at 1 am.

Cebu

This island, over 200 km long and just 40 km across at its widest point, with Cebu City as its capital, is the centre of the Visayas. It lies locked between Negros, Leyte and Bohol. Apart from the main island of Cebu, numerous small islands belong to this province, the most significant of which are Mactan, Bantayan and Camotes. Cebu is hilly for the most part, only the coast and a section of the north is a little flat.

Even before the Spaniards came, when Cebu was still called Sugbo, trade relations with China had been established. At present many different developments are bringing profit to the area. Near Toledo copper is being mined while coal, iron-ore, gold and silver are also starting to be produced by the mining companies. Cement has been manufactured for several years but hopes for future trading rest with the discovery of oil. Cebu also provides the west with fashionable shell and coral decorations and rattan furniture.

Maize growing dominates agriculture and there are sugarcane fields in the north of the island, more are being planted. The mangoes of Cebu are famous throughout the country and during the harvest — March, April and May — they cost only a peso each.

The people are very friendly; they speak the main dialect of the Visayas which is Cebuano. Many Chinese live in Cebu and they speak their own language, English is also widely understood.

There are many expensive beach resorts on Cebu, to which you will be referred again and again during the tourist season. If you can forgo luxury you may feel more content on the beaches yet to be discovered by the tourist hordes. It's worth seeing the coral gardens at Moalboal and the guitar factories on Mactan Island. Lovely stoney treks lead through the island's interior and there are numerous refreshing waterfalls.

CEBU CITY

Cebu City is the second largest city in the Philippines with a population of half a million. The 'Queen City of the South' is probably rather more interesting than most big cities in the Philippines. Colon St, in the centre, is the oldest street in the Philippines. Life in the suburbs and neighbouring barrios of Cebu is much friendlier than in Manila.

Information

Cebu has plenty of hotels, restaurants and cinemas but practically everything closes at 11 pm. Cockfights take place on Sundays in the Century Game Club near the Capitol. Note that travellers' cheques can only be changed at the Bank of the Philippine Islands and the Chartered Bank. The banks are located around the city hall, next to Magellan's Cross. Try also the moneychanger opposite the Bank of the Philippine Islands and the black market near the post office.

Cebu is the centre for making guitars in the Philippines — see the introductory section on things to buy. Shop for shellcraft at the St Theresa Orphanage Shop called Jewel of the Sea — excellent quality, good prices, good cause.

Fort San Pedro

Legaspi himself turned the first sod of

earth in the construction of the fort on 8 May, 1565. He gave it the name of the ship in which he crossed the Pacific. It was originally constructed to counter marauding pirates but at the end of the Spanish era, in 1898, it was taken over by Filipino revolutionary fighters. Later it served the Americans as a defence post and barracks and from 1937 to 1941 it was used for training purposes.

In WW II the fort was taken by the Japanese who used it as a prison camp. The bitter struggles of the war years have left their traces. Restoration work was begun in the late '60s and a beautiful court was laid inside the fort. If you're after information from the MOT you don't need to pay the entry fee. The main entrance to the fort is very impressive.

Magellan's Cross

The first Catholic mass was held in Cebu on 14 April, 1521. Rajah Humabon, his wife, sons and daughters let themselves and 800 islanders be baptised by Father Pedro de Valderrama. Magellan commemorated the beginning of the Christianisation of the Philippines with the erection of a cross. Fragments of this original cross are said to be inside the cross you can see today in a pavilion near the City Hall.

Basilica Minore del Santo Nino

The building of the current basilica is earlier but San Augustin Church was completed in 1740 and the undoubted focus of the stone church is Santo Nino, a small Jesus-child statue. If you want to see it, it stands to the left of the altar, you must either use a telescope or wait in a long queue. In 1565 the treasure, with its jewelled crown and jewel-set clothes, was rediscovered by Juan de Camus, one of Legaspi's soldiers, in a hut near the basilica. Since that time Santo Nino has been the patron saint of the Cebuanos.

Taoist Temple & Cebu Zoo

Some six km from the city centre lies Beverley Hills, the millionaire quarter of Cebu City. Also here is the temple of the Taoist religious community. The size and architecture show that a substantial part of the Cebu population is of Chinese origin. There is a beautiful view of the city from this decidedly Fu Manchu temple.

If you walk another two km from the temple you will come to the Cebu Zoo. It has relatively few animals but is attractively laid out. Opposite the zoo entrance is a little 'museum' with a bizarre collection of freak animals, some live, some stuffed and all grotesquely amusing!

Getting There The trip by PU from the city to the temple costs P8 to 10, establish the fare first. From the city you can get fairly close to the temple on a Lahug jeepney. Get on at Palaez St at the Cathay Hotel or at Our Place. Get off in Lahug, cross the small bridge, turn right and you then have a 1½ km uphill walk.

Cebu Heavenly Temple of Charity

Halfway up to the Taoist Temple you can see on the left hand side the Cebu Heavenly Temple of Charity. The pleasant temple complex is built on top of a hill and beneath is a natural spring. The middle altar within the temple houses the image of the supreme god and Milagrosa Rosa, the patron saint of the temple.

Getting There Take a Lahug jeepney, as for the Taoist Temple, but after crossing the small bridge don't turn right but go straight ahead. After 100 metres there is an iron gate with two guardian lions on the left side. Walk through this gate and follow the trail until you hit a road after about 400 metres. Turn right and after 200 metres you will see the gate of the temple complex. If it is closed go

1 Tung Yan Restaurant	24 House of Men, Mutya
2 Magellan Hotel, St Moritz Bar & Apartments	25 Tagalog Hotel
	26 Pete's Kitchen
3 Jumalon Museum	27 Jercy's Kitchenette
4 Binamira's Antiques	28 Mercedes Hotel
5 Casa Vasca	29 Cathay Hotel
6 Club 68	30 Snow Sheen Restaurant
7 Iglesia Ni Cristo (Church)	31 Snow Sheen Restaurant
8 Great American, Tuxedo Junction	32 Consulate Hotel
9 Shakey's Pizza	33 Queen's Inn
10 Lawiswis Kawayan	34 Rajah Humabon Hotel
11 Kan Irag Hotel, Bachelors Too Bar	35 Lovena's Inn
12 PAL Office, Airport Bus, Rajah Hotel, Avis Office	36 Ruftan Pensione & Cafe
	37 Ngo Hiong House (Angela's)
13 Barbecue Stalls, Beer Garden	38 Sky Vue Hotel
14 Playgirl, Pow Disco	39 PAL Office
15 Andy's Folkhouse, Before & After Six	40 Patria de Cebu
	41 Carbon Market
16 Town & Country Hotel	42 Basilica Minore Del Santo Nino
17 Arbel's Pension House	43 Magellan's Cross
18 YMCA, American Consulate	44 Eddie's Log Cabin
19 Royal Pension House	45 Plaza Independenzia
20 Elicon House	46 Eddie's Log Cabin
21 Triton Hotel	47 Fort San Pedro, Tourist Office
22 San Carlos University	48 Post Office
23 Our Place	

around the temple to the open main gate.

Caretta Cemetery
This is only important if you are in Cebu on 1 November (All Saints Day) — see also holidays. Opposite is the Chinese cemetery, go by jeepney from Colon St towards Mabolo St.

Carbon Market
The various handicrafts and agricultural products of Cebu are offered for sale at this colourful public market. There are also products of other Visayan Islands, for example basketware from Bohol.

Jumalon Museum
Julian Jumalon is a biology professor who collects butterflies and forms unique mosaic pictures from their wings — OK if you're into killing butterflies. The so-called art form created by him is called Lepido Mosaic

Art, admission P1, closed noon to 3 pm daily. You can see lots of butterfly wings for free, and what's more they are still on the butterflies, all over the Philippines. The museum can be rather difficult to find.

Binamira's Collection of Antiques
In the antique collection of Dr Leocardia Binamira are handcarved furniture, ornaments and much more. If you are into antiques you should see this display although the private house is rather hard to find and the old lady is not always there. One traveller reported that the collection is now closed — check first.

University of San Carlos Museum
The museum of the university, founded in 1595, was opened in 1967 by First Lady Imelda Marcos. It has an anthropological and a biological section. Philippines objects from different

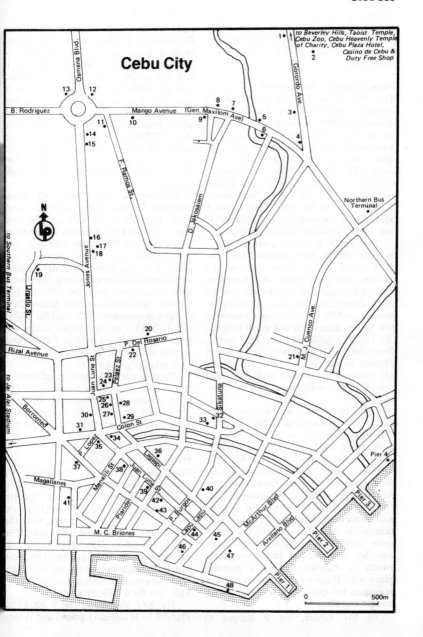

Cebu City

to Beverley Hills, Taoist Temple,
Cebu Zoo, Cebu Heavenly Temple
of Charity, Cebu Plaza Hotel,
Casino de Cebu &
Duty Free Shop

Osmeña Blvd

B. Rodriguez

Mango Avenue (Gen. Maxilom Ave)

Gorordo Ave

F. Ramos St.

D. Jakosalem

Northern Bus
Terminal

to Southern Bus Terminal

N

Jones Avenue

Urgello St.

to Abi Stadium

Rizal Avenue

Borromeo

Juan Luna St.

Pelaez St.

P. Del Rosario

M. J. Cuenco Ave

Sikatuna

Colon St.

Pier 4

P. Lopez

Manalili St.

Magallanes

Juan Luna St.

P. Larde

Leon(sp).

P. Burgos

Lapu Lapu

McArthur Blvd

Arellano Blvd

Pier 3

Pier 2

M. C. Briones

Pier 1

0   500m

epochs are shown, items from other Asian nations are also displayed. The museum is closed during lecture times. Entry is P1.

Places to Stay — bottom end

The *YMCA* (tel 9 2013) is at 61 Jones Avenue, about halfway from Fuenta Osmenta (where the airport bus stops) to the city centre. There is a variety of accommodation available from comfortable dorm beds at P28 to singles/doubles with fan for P30/56. Couples are also accepted and YMCA members pay P5 less. Temporary membership costs P10. The YMCA also has a swimming pool and table tennis, billiards and bowling facilities.

The *Town & Country* (tel 7 8190) is only about 100 metres from the YMCA and also on Jones Avenue. It's modern and quite plush with a reasonable restaurant and the rooms on the upper floors are good value with singles/doubles at P30/40. Sometimes known as the Town House this is a good bargain. At 165 J Urgello St, just 500 metres from the Town & Country, is the *Royal Pension House* (tel 9 3890). The rooms are nice and clean with wide beds and priced at P45 with fan or P75 with air-con.

In the same Jones Avenue area, down a side street between the YMCA and the Town & Country, is *Arbel's Pension Hotel* (tel 6 2393) at 57E Jones Avenue. It has singles/doubles with fan for P30/40 and is clean and pleasantly run by nice people but some rooms have no windows. The *Ruftan Pensione & Cafe* (tel 7 9138), at the corner of Legaspi and Manalili Sts near the Ding How Restaurant, is related to Arbel's but much more central. It's a good clean place run by nice people and has simple rooms at P20/40. This is a popular place with Peace Corps workers and the managers are quite used to dealing with budget travellers.

In the centre, on P Burgos St

opposite the Cebu Cathedral, is the Catholic run *Patria de Cebu* with rooms ranging from singles for P25 up to doubles with bath for P50 but it's rather run down. The *Cebu Mayflower Hotel* (tel 9 1939) has singles/doubles with fan for P35/55 and air-con rooms with bath for P70/95. It's a peaceful place near the Capitol. *Lovena's Inn* (tel 9 9212) on Juan Luna St is nicely central and has rooms with fan and bath for P39/52, with air-con and bath for P53/75. Some rooms are better than others.

The *Consulate Hotel* (tel 9 6753) on Sikatuna St has rooms with fan and bath for P50/70 or with air-con and bath for P90/105. A single is good for two but check the rooms first and bargain if necessary. *Elicon House* (tel 7 3653) is on the corner of P del Rosario and General Junquera Sts and has rooms with air-con and bath for P70/95. It's a good, clean place and the Elicon Cafe is right downstairs. The *Tagalog Hotel* (tel 7 2531) is on Sanciangko St and has rooms with fan and bath at P70/80 and air-con and bath at P80/105 but it's only relatively clean.

Right down at the bottom of the low price range in Cebu is the *Queens' Inn* at 7 Colon with rooms at P15 per person. Or the extremely simple *Lamplighter's House of Man* where you can get a bed for just P7.

Places to Stay — middle

The *Cathay Hotel* (tel 9 7621) is on Pelaez St and has rooms with air-con and bath for P90/125 and up. The 4th floor singles have big beds and are good for two. The 5th floor rooms, near the disco, are probably the best value. The *Rajah Humabon Hotel* (tel 7 7671-5) on Juan Luna St is a relatively good hotel although not all rooms are clean. With air-con and bath rooms are P100/120. Ask for a 10% discount.

The *Sky Vue Hotel* (tel 7 3051) on Plaridel St is similarly priced and is very

pavilion with Magellan's Cross

clean but rooms with windows are more expensive. There's a massage parlour on the 1st floor — room service available! The *Kan Irag Hotel* on F Ramos St is also in this same price bracket and is very clean and comfortable.

The *Triton Hotel* (tel 7 3750, 59) on M J Cuenco Avenue is more expensive at P135/185 for rooms with air-con and bath. It's very clean, run by friendly people and has good service and a pool. The newly opened *Raja Soliman Hotel* on Manalili St is very clean and has good service. Rooms with fan are P60/70, with air-con and bath P88/115. Ask for a 10% discount.

Places to Stay — top end

In the inner city area the *Mercedes Hotel* has the best accommodation available — a single with air-con and bath costs from P200. The *Rajah Hotel* (tel 9 6231) on Fuente Osmena St has 106 rooms. Rooms start from P115/140. On Gorondo Avenue the 200 room

Magellan International Hotel (tel 7 4611) has everything from a pelota court to a swimming pool. Singles/doubles with air-con and bath cost from P180/230. Directly in front of the Magellan are the relatively good value *St Moritz Apartments*.

The expensive *Montebello Villa Hotel* (tel 8 5021-31), on the edge of the city at Banilad, has 140 rooms from US$35. On the slopes just outside of the city is the magnificent new *Cebu Plaza Hotel* (tel 5 03061) in Lahug. It's a multi-storey hotel with 400 rooms, all mod cons from swimming pool and tennis courts to restaurants and a casino. Rooms start from around US$30.

Places to Eat

There are lots of places to eat along Colon St although you can eat much more cheaply off this beaten track. The *Snow Sheen Restaurant* on Juan Luna St and Colon St has very good and low-priced Chinese and Filipino food. Try torta congrejo although it's not on the menu. *Pete's Kitchen* on Pelaez St also has keenly priced Chinese and Filipino food.

The *Ruftan Cafe* on Legaspi St is good for breakfast. The *YMCA Restaurant* on Jones Avenue has good scrambled eggs with onions and tomatoes. It's also low priced. *Eddie's Log Cabin* on M C Briones St is a good place with a complete fixed price meal for P22. There's a real log cabin in there.

Shakey's Pizza on General Maxilom St (used to be Mango Avenue) has live music in the evenings. There are lots of places to eat along this street including *Dairy Farm* and *Kalilili Chicken*, also the *Lighthouse* where you eat Filipino food with your fingers and the slightly expensive *Casa Vasca* where they serve excellent Spanish dishes. *La Pampanguena*, off F Ramos St, has Filipino food — eat your fill for less than P20 but get there before 8 pm if possible. *Ngo Hiong House* (Angela's) on the corner of Lopez and Borromeo St has Filipino food which you eat in the traditional manner with your fingers.

The Sky Vue Hotel's *Revolving Restaurant* has a smorgasbord with coffee and cake for around P20 on Tuesdays and Thursdays. In the evening the revolving restaurant starts revolving at 7.30 pm. On Gorordo Avenue the *Tung Yan Restaurant* is probably the best Chinese restaurant in town. It's relatively expensive and is found in an old villa near the Magellan Hotel. *Gardenia's* at the Cebu Capitol Commercial Complex in North Escario St North, has good food at reasonable prices and a stunning setting. *Fastfoods*, a collection of fast food places under one roof on Jones Avenue just before the Colon area, is a good place to eat.

Nightlife

Cebu has plenty of nightclubs which continue to proliferate to the detriment of some good pubs. The comfortable *Tinyland Beer Garden* has been converted to a third class go-go joint. *Carl's Pub* has become the *Playgirl* but *Our Place* will hopefully remain *Our Place*. Here you can drink cheap beer, and eat good European food. The barbecue stalls and beer gardens at the Osmena Circle are also good value.

Andy's Folkhouse is a real misnomer as it's an expensive pizzeria not a folk club at all. The Sky Vue Hotel, on Plaridel St, has the *Elbow Room* with TV, pianist and female singer. A lot of clubs are on Mango Avenue, like the *Slabadu* next to the *Beehive Theatre*, where you can enjoy jazz. In *Tuxedo Junction* there is rock and folk, the *Lawiswis Kawayan* has a combo playing sweet and disco music for dancers up to 1 am while the *Great American* kicks on late at night.

Before & After Six on Jones Avenue is dark and relatively expensive although it does have live music. *Inner Circle* and *Lover City* are popular discos. Or for something completely different you can learn to dance in one of the two or three individual dancing schools. You can't miss their blaring music. If you fancy something a little sleazy try the port area when a ship is in harbour, *Slapsy Maxie's* is popular and not too expensive — it's at the Plaza Independencia towards Pier 1. The casino is now near the Cebu Plaza Hotel. And there's jai alai in the evenings (but not on Sundays) and cockfights at the Century Game Club near the Capitol.

If you want to have cheap food and good fun try to find the 'sing-restaurant', *Adventure Galley*, Anihan St, Gentle Breeze Subdivision, Mandanue City (tel 8 1432). It's not far from Cebu City and the owner Bebut Suazo and his staff are very friendly. Every night from 9 pm to at least 1 am there is live organ music and the customers are invited to sing. It's great

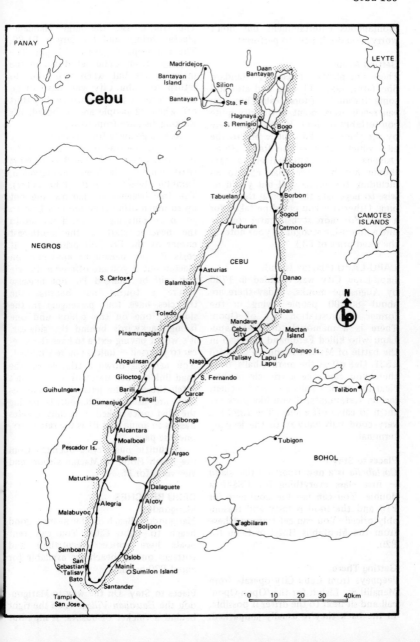

spontaneous entertainment but don't worry, you don't have to perform!

Getting Around

There are plenty of jeeneys (standard 65c fare), taxis, PU-cabs and also still some tartanillas (horse cabs) but you can reach every point in the city quite comfortably on foot. If you arrive here by air there's a P5 shuttle bus to the city which stops at the Rajah Hotel, Osmena Circle. Alternatively a taxi should not be more than P25 to 30 including the bridge toll but you'd be wise to negotiate the price at the beginning. Otherwise you could be taken for a ride! For more stylish travel you can hire a limousine straight to your hotel at the fixed price of P32.

LAPU-LAPU (Mactan Island)

Lapu-Lapu City was founded in 1730 by Augustine monks. Today there are about 80,000 people living in the former administration city of Opon. There is a memorial to Chief Lapu-Lapu who killed Ferdinand Magellan in the battle of Mactan Island on 27 April 1521. Get off at the market halls, from there you can take a tricycle further. Near the market halls are two excellent lechon restaurants; if you like pork get them to carve off a slice. The *1890* is a very good pub halfway to the jeepney terminal.

Places to Stay

Cortabella is a new resort on the island — first class everything for US$40 a double. You can use the pool here for P16 and the food is tasty and reasonably priced. You can get transport here from the Mentablis Hotel in Cebu for P20.

Getting There

Jeepneys from Cebu City operate from Manalili St. Listen for the 'Opon-Opon' call and sit next to the driver if possible. In the back they're usually jampacked.

The trip crosses the large Mandaue-Mactan bridge and the fare is P1.80. The last jeepney goes at 11 pm. The jeepneys from Cebu set down in the main square but when you want to return to Cebu City you have to go to the jeepney terminal where they start off when 22 people are on board. It's walking distance from town.

As you go away from Lapu-Lapu city by tricycle the resorts are passed in the following order — Hadson Beach Resort (P10 entry), Maribago, Marigondon, Tambuli Beach Resort (P30 entry). The free beaches are narrow and not up to much other than hiring a boat to go to an outlying island. Tricycles to the beaches start at the south-east corner by the FG Enterprises store. It costs P1 per person to anywhere on Mactan but if you are offered a tricycle you will be charged P6, not because you're a tourist but because the tricycles have four passengers in the side-car, one on the pillion and one facing backwards behind the side-car. It's worth paying extra to have the side-car to yourself — unless you're a midget. You can flag down a tricycle on the road linking each beach or resort. Don't catch those at the jetties or beaches as they are used to rich tourists paying the first price asked — it only creates hassles to argue that P1 is the rate everyone else pays.

A shuttle bus service operates from the Rajah Hotel to Mactan airport and vice versa for P5.

CEBU BEACHES
Marigondon

Marigondon Beach is the nearest good beach to Cebu City. You can rent boats here (prices negotiable) and cottages on the beach are available for about P30 per day.

Places to Stay On the way to Marigondon the *Hawaiian Village* is on the right behind a thicket of bushes. A nipa hut

Lapu-Lapu (Mactan Island)

with a wide bed and running water costs P40 per day. The *Tambuli Beach Resort* at Tambuli Beach is exquisite, expensive and exclusive. It costs P30 just to enter, which is deducted from your bill if you have a meal. There are said to be some nipa huts here at P40, however. It costs P10 to enter the Hadson Beach Resort.

Getting There A tricycle to Marigondon Beach costs around P15 to 20 depending on whether you want to visit Lilang's Guitar Factory. Try to bargain and arrange a time to be picked up for your return trip.

Maribago

On your way to Maribago from Lapu-Lapu you can see the guitar factories —

Lilang's Guitar Factory is the largest and best. If you want to buy one pay the extra peso and get an 'export guitar' — a good one will cost US$200 to 300! The others may be ridiculously cheap but they don't last long in a non-tropical climate. Don't buy guitars with turtle shell backs as the turtles are protected and in Australia, in particular, the guitar will be confiscated on arrival. PAL do not allow guitars as hand baggage but you can buy a not-very-attractive suitcase or flight bag for a few peso in the Mactan airport supermarket.

Getting There A tricycle from the Lapu-Lapu market to Maribago should be about P1.50 per person.

Olango Island

Olango Island is the long island visible from Maribago or Marigondon. There are small white beaches and beautiful palm trees. The water is very shallow. An outrigger to an island near Olango might cost around P50 to 100 for a half-day trip.

Places to Stay There are often Japanese staying on the island at the *Santa Rosa by the Sea* bungalow-hotel. It's expensive and, like the resorts on Mactan Island, they charge admission to the property!

Getting There From Maribago boats go to Olango Island for P1 or 1.50. They depart when there are seven passengers therefore a 'special ride', ie the boat to yourself or for less than seven passengers, shouldn't be more than P7 to 10. Say Santa Rosa Island rather than Olango Island — everyone will know where you mean.

TALISAY

It's a nice day trip from Cebu City to Talisay but nothing more. The beaches, like Tanggue Beach, are nothing special.

Places to Stay & Eat
The *Tourist Seaside Resort* has a swimming pool — try to bargain the price for accommodation. A single with fan and bath is P50, with air-con and bath P85. At *Canezares Beach*, only about 100 metres from the resort, you can rent a cottage for P40 and there's good food here too.

Seafood is available at *Lutran's Eatery*. In the evening travellers and residents meet at the sari-sari store by the police station. You can get cold beer at the *Beachcomber Bar* directly in front of the Tourist Seaside Resort.

Getting There
Talisay is due south of Cebu City. Jeepneys operate there directly, travel time is about 30 minutes.

SOGOD

North of Cebu City, the MOT recommends the *Club Pacific Resort* but it's only really for groups. Cottages cost P150.

Getting There
There are several buses daily from the Northern Bus Terminal in Cebu City and the trip takes two hours.

TOLEDO

Directly west of Cebu City on the west coast this is the jumping off point for boats to San Carlos on Negros Island. South of Toledo, about halfway to Moalboal, the Mantayupa Falls are at Barili.

Places to Stay
If you have to stay overnight go to the *Vizcayno Restaurant* and ask for the *Lodging House* which costs about P10 per person.

Getting There
Several buses daily make the 1½ hour trip from the Southern Bus Terminal in

a   Panning for gold in Negros
b   Approaching the summit of the Mayon volcano
c   River crossing in south Luzon

Cebu City. Buses to Barili go from the same terminal and the trip takes two hours. From Barili to the Mantayupa Falls costs P10 round trip by tricycle. Don't bother bargaining.

MOALBOAL

Moalboal is on the west coast, south of Toledo. Panagsama Beach, three km from the main road at Moalboal, has a beautiful beach and good diving. This area is rapidly becoming more and more popular and deservedly so. There's cheap yet comfortable accommodation, the properly tropical white sand beaches and turquoise-coral-filled waters and superb sunsets. Diving equipment is available from the Reef Club Diving Lodge. From Panagsama Beach you can catch a boat to the nearby Pescador Island.

Places to Stay & Eat

If you want to stay in town enquire in the *People's Bakery*, they rent rooms. You can rent cottages from P15 per person on Panagsama Beach. There is *Pacita's Nipa Hut*, further along to the left, which is more private and has good accommodation and nice meals too. *Evie's Mabuhay Lodge & Cold Inn* is also a good place to stay. There's also good food available at *Eve's Kiosk*.

Oscar Regner's *Reef Club Dining Lodge* is on Bas Diot Beach which is an extension of the Panagsama Beach. One night's accommodation with full board will cost P150. Snorkels and diving masks can be rented for P10 a day. A diving session costs P125.

Getting There

Several buses daily make the three hour, 90 km trip from Cebu City's Southern Bus Terminal. A friendly bus driver may even drive you right down to the beach, it's worth a try so ask. Otherwise take a tricycle from the main street, look for Moalboal' buses as they often take you right to Panagsama. This is not so of buses which just pass through Moalboal.

The connection from Toledo to Moalboal and vice versa is tricky. Plan on having to change buses three times.

MATUTINAO

In the luxurious tropical vegetation of the mountains near Matutinao there are the refreshingly cool Kawasan Falls, probably the best waterfalls on Cebu Island. The two natural pools are good for swimming and they are so deep that you can jump in even from a high level. This area is also a good starting point for mountain treks.

Places to Stay & Eat

There are a few cottages for P15 per person. In the small restaurant you can get regular meals and cold drinks. Since there are only a few cottages there might be no vacancy for you to stay overnight, so better do a daytrip first and check it out.

Getting There

Take a bus from Moalboal going south and get off at the church in Matutinao. Follow the trail uphill next to the river.

A
B

a   A steam age dinosaur brings in the sugarcane in Negros
b   Black Nazarene procession in Quiapo, Manila

It's a 20-minute walk.

SAN SEBASTIAN, TALISAY & BATO
Right at the south of Cebu these are the ports from where ships operate across to Tampi or Hilecon near San Jose on Negros.

Places to Stay
The *Contessa Restaurant*, near the pier in San Sebastian, is just a few peso per person.

Getting There
From Moalboal there are several buses daily for the one hour trip to San Sebastian. They stop at the high school. Unless you like being a curiousity take a bus which goes direct to San Sebastian. If your bus stops at Samboan you'll have a big crowd of onlookers.

ARGAO & SANTANDER
It's possible to ferry across from Santander to Tampi on Negros Island.

Places to Stay
In Argao it's possible to stay with 'Charly the German' but expensive at US$20 per person including meals. He has a boat and motorcycle available. The very exclusive *Argao Beach Club* opened in 1980 — information from the Bayview Plaza in Manila, the Cebu Plaza in Cebu City or the Tambul Resort on Mactan Island.

Getting There
There are several ABC buses every day from the Southern Bus Terminal on the 140 km run Cebu City-Argao-Santander. If you only want to go to Argao you can take a minibus to the Argao bus terminal.

SUMILON ISLAND
This small island off the south-east coast of Cebu is a favourite for divers. Along the west coast the Sumilon Marine Park is a protected area where any kind of fishing is prohibited. The Silliman University in Dumaguete on Negros have a guard on Sumilon who is in charge to take care that nobody contravenes the law. The water here is only two to five metres deep and it's excellent for snorkelling. Bring your equipment.

Places to Stay
There are two cottages and a big nipa hut which is used as the research centre. It costs P10 per person to stay overnight.

Getting There
From Cebu City take an ABC bus from the Southern Bus Terminal going to Santander. Get off at Mainit. From Moalboal go by bus and/or jeepney via Samboan and Bato to Mainit. In Mainit you can rent a paddle-banca for about P50 for a roundtrip. If you want to stay overnight on Sulimon they will pick you up the next day. A roundtrip with a motor-banca from Liloan (near Bato) costs P150. You can also go from Dumaguete, see the Negros chapter.

TRANSPORT FROM CEBU
If you're planning to leave Cebu City by boat it will pay you to check the shipping schedule carefully. Ships are cancelled and rescheduled without warning and staff at the ticket stands don't bother to check the alterations. There are ads in the daily newspapers *The Freeman* and *The Republic News* but for more accurate information you should ring the companies themselves. You'll find their numbers in the telephone yellow pages. Tell them you're a tourist.

The main shipping line offices in Cebu are.

Aboitiz Lines, Juan Luna St
Escano Lines, Pier 4
George & Peter Lines, D Jakosalem St

Sweet Lines, Arellano Boulevard
Sulpicio Lines, Pier 4, Gothong Building
William Lines, Gotiaco Building

Unless you want to get your student discount there is no need to go through the companies since along Colon St there are plenty of booking agencies who will issue you a ticket within five minutes — they're very efficient.

Cebu City is the shipping centre of the Visayas and the port is a continuous hive of activity. There are plenty of pickpockets operating there and in the general jostle of boarding and leaving ships it's very easy to get ripped off — take great care.

The airport shuttle bus leaves on the hour every hour from 2 am from outside the PAL office at the Rajah Hotel, Osmena Circle. This is important to know for night flights to Manila. During the day the service is more frequent.

To Bohol PAL flies Cebu City-Tagbilaran four times weekly.

There are quite a few ships between Cebu and Bohol. Sweet Lines have the *MV Sweet Heart* daily to Tagbilaran at noon, the trip takes four hours. They also have the *MV Sweet Sound*, *Sweet Name* or *Sweet Ride* also daily at 10 pm. Bohol tickets from Sweet Lines must be bought at their Arellano Boulevard office opposite pier 2, they are not sold in town. The *MV Asia China* of Trans Asia Shipping Lines departs daily at 6.30 am for Tagbilaran, the crossing takes 2½ hours.

Anco Shipping Lines operate the *MV Tubigon* to Tubigon daily at noon, 6 pm and 10 pm. The crossing takes three to four hours on this shorter route. Aboitiz Lines on Juan Luna St also operate a ship daily at 10 pm to Tubigon. Their ship makes it in about two hours. The fare to Tagbilaran is about P20, to Tubigon P16. Note that transport out of

Tagbilaran is much easier than Tubigon. There's a bus from Tubigon to Carmen departing soon after the boat arrives. You have to rush to catch it and it's crowded. The fare is P5 and the trip takes about 1½ hours.

To Camiguin Bisaya Shipping on M J Cuenco Avenue operate the *MV Dona Filomena* to Binone on Saturdays at 7 pm. The trip takes about 12 hours. It's probably easier to get to Camiguin on the regular six times a week ship to Cagayan de Oro in Mindanao. The 10 hour trip costs P41. From there buses run to Balingoan for P11 in 1½ hours. Three times daily at 8 am, 11.30 am and 3 pm ferries cross to Binone. The fare is P4 and the trip takes two hours. Boats depart Cebu at 6 pm and you can arrive in Camiguin by 1.30 pm the next day.

To Leyte PAL flies daily to Tacloban from Cebu City.

Almost all ships to Leyte go by night. Gothong Lines have one on Wednesdays at noon to Palompon.

Aboitiz Lines have the *MV Ormoc* to Baybay on Monday, Wednesday and Saturday at 10 pm. The trip takes five hours. Kasamahan Shipping Lines operate the *MV City of Ozamis* to Maasin on the same days and at the same time. The crossing takes six to seven hours. They also operate the *MV Kasamahan* to Bato on Monday and Friday.

George & Peter Lines have the *MV Georich* to Maasin on Tuesday and Sunday at 7 pm. K&T Shipping Lines have the *MV Guiuan* to Liloan on Monday and Friday at 8 pm. Aboitiz Lines operate the *MV Ormoc* or the *MV Ramon Aboitiz* to Ormoc daily at 10 pm. The crossing takes five to six hours. Their ship the *MV Picket* goes to Bato daily at 9 pm, a five to six hour trip.

There are several ships making the 12 hour Cebu City-Tacloban trip. Sulpicio Lines have the *MV Dona*

Vicenta which goes on Tuesday at 4 pm. Western Samar Shipping have the *MV Evelyn* which departs Monday, Wednesday and Friday at 5 pm. K&T Shipping Lines have the *MV Samar Queen* which goes on Tuesday, Thursday and Saturday at 6 pm. This ship can be booked at their office at 38 Palma St or on the ship.

To Luzon PAL have several flights daily to Manila and also cheaper night-flights. Three times weekly they fly to Legaspi.

There are many ships operating between Cebu City and Manila. The trip takes about 22 hours. Some of the best include the William Lines ship *MV Dona Virginia* which goes on Monday at 8 pm, Friday at 10 am. Sulpicio Lines' *MV Philippine Princess* goes on Wednesday at 7 pm, Sunday at 10 am while the *Don Enrique* goes on Friday at 10 am. Sweet Lines operate the *MV Sweet Roro* on Friday at 7 pm and Tuesday at 9 am.

To Masbate Ships to Masbate operate irregularly and schedules should not be depended upon. The Escano Lines ship *MV Augustina II* goes on Thursdays at 10 pm and the trip takes about 13 hours. The Grace Shipping Lines ship *MV Young Lady* goes on Wednesday.

To Mindanao There are a lot of flights between Cebu City and various Mindanao centres. And even more shipping services. PAL flies to Alah Valley, Bislig, Butuan, General Santos City, Cagayan de Oro, Cotabato, Davao, Dipolog, Iligan, Malagang, Ozamiz, Pagadian, Surigao, Tandag and Zamboanga. Shipping services include:

Butuan — Gothong Lines' *MV Dona Casandra* goes on Monday, Wednesday and Saturday at 6 pm, the trip via Nasipit takes 12 hours. Bisaya Shipping have the *MV Don Mariano* on Monday at 6 pm, Wednesday and Friday at 7

pm. They also have the *MV Dona Filomena* on Tuesday, Thursday and Saturday at 7 pm.

Cagayan de Oro — This trip takes 12 hours also. Escala Lines have the MV *Fatima* on Monday at 5 pm but it's not totally regular. Sulpicio Lines have the *MV Cagayan Princess* on Monday, Wednesday and Friday at 7 pm. They also operate the *MV Dona Paulina* on Tuesday, Thursday and Saturday at 7 pm. The William Lines ship *MV Ozamiz City* goes on Monday and Friday at 8 pm.

Davao — Sulpicio Lines operate the *MV Don Enrique* on Mondays at 11 pm, the trip takes 24 hours.

Dipolog — This crossing takes 10 hours. George & Peter Lines have the *MV Jhufel* on Monday and Friday at 10 pm. They also have the *MV Don Victoriano* on Tuesday and Saturday at 9 pm, the *MV Geopeter* on Wednesday at 10 pm and the *MV Don Joaquin* on Thursday at 9 pm.

Iligan — It's a 12 hour crossing to Iligan. Escano Lines operate the *MV Fernando Escano II* somewhat irregularly on Saturdays at 7 pm. Carlos Gothong Lines have the *MV Dona Conchita* on Monday, Thursday and Saturday at 7 pm. Sweet Lines have the *MV Sweet Name* on Friday at 8 pm.

Ozamiz — Several ships operate this route, it takes nine to 12 hours. The William Lines' *MV Ozamiz City* goes on Wednesday at 7 pm. They also operate the *MV Cebu City* on Monday at 8 pm, this ship is faster. Also on Monday they have the *MV Misamis Occidental* at 7 pm. Carlos Gothong Lines have the *MV Don Bonifacio* on Tuesday, Thursday and Saturday at 7 pm.

Surigao — Cebu City to Surigao takes about 12 hours. Sweet Lines have the *MV Sweet Time* on Monday, Wednesday and Friday at 8 pm. George & Peter Lines have the *MV Georich* on Tuesday and Sunday at 7 pm and on Thursday at 9 pm.

Zamboanga — George & Peter Lines

operate the *MV Geopeter* or *MV Jhufel* to Zamboanga via Dumaguete. Departures are on Monday, Wednesday and Friday at noon and the trip takes 23 hours. They also operate the *MV Jhufel* directly to Zamboanga on Wednesday at noon, a 16-hour trip.

To Negros There is a ship weekdays at 7 and 11.30 am and 4 pm from Toledo to San Carlos. On Sundays there are only departures at 8 am and 1.30 pm. Other departure times are possible on holidays. There is only one service on Maundy Thursday and Good Friday is a rest day. The trip takes two to three hours and the last bus from San Carlos to Bacolod leaves when the last ship arrives from Toledo.

There is a daily ship from Tangil to Guihulngan. There are several ships daily from San Sebastian to Tampi or Hilecon. They're not very punctual but the last departure should be at 4.30 pm. The trip takes one hour. There are also several ships daily from Santander, Bato and Talisay to Tampi.

You can also take the George & Peter Lines ship which goes daily except on Sundays from Cebu City to Dumaguete. The trip takes six hours. Gothong Lines has ships on Monday, Wednesday and Friday at 10 pm from Cebu City to Dumaguete. Negros Navigation have a ship each Wednesday from Cebu City to Bacolod City.

PAL flies daily from Mactan Airport to Bacolod City and Dumaguete.

To Panay The route between Cebu and Panay by ship from Cebu City to Iloilo is irregular but you can also travel via Negros and at similar cost and less time if you're in a hurry. Catch a 6.30 am bus from Cebu City to Toledo (P4), get the ferry to San Carlos (P12), a bus to Bacolod (P17.50) and the 3 pm boat to Iloilo (P15).

William Lines operate ships on the 15 hour Cebu-Iloilo service. Gothong Lines have the *Dona Josefina* to New Washington (probably via Leyte) on Friday at 8 pm. The trip takes about 18 hours. They also have the *Don Calvino* to Roxas on Wednesday at noon. This trip takes about 16 hours.

PAL fly Cebu-Iloilo daily.

To Samar The *MV Helen* of Western Samar Shipping goes to Catbalogan on Saturday at 6 pm. The trip takes about 14 hours.

To Siquijor From Cebu City George & Peter Lines have the *Dona Magna* to Larena on Monday at 9 pm and the *Dona Rosario* on Friday at 9 pm. The *Dona Rosario* also operates to Lazi on Monday at 9 pm while the *Dona Magna* goes to Lazi on Friday at 9 pm.

Sweet Lines have the *MV Sweet Sound* to Larena via Tagbilaran on Tuesday and Friday at midnight.

ISLAND HOPPING

It's in the Visayas where possibilities for island hopping in the Philippines are at heir best. A possible island hopping :ircuit of the Visayas could take you to nost of the places of interest with ninimal backtracking. Starting from Vlanila you could travel down to the Bicol region and from Matnog at the southern tip of the island there are ferries every day across to Allen at the northern end of Samar. The new road down the west coast of Samar means it is now a quick and relatively easy trip through Calbayog and Catbalogan then across the bridge to Tacloban on the island of Leyte. This was where Mac-Arthur 'returned' towards the end of WW II. From Tacloban or Ormoc there are regular ships to Cebu City or less regularly from Maasin to Bohol.

Cebu was where Magellan arrived in the Philippines and there are a number of reminders of the Spanish period. From Cebu there are daily ferries to the neighbouring island of Bohol, famed for its 'Chocolate Hills'. Ferries also cross daily between Cebu and Negros, either in the south of the island to Dumaguete or closer to Cebu City from Toledo to San Carlos. You can then continue by bus to Bacolod from where ferries cross to Iloilo on Panay.

Panay has the usual assortment of bus and jeepney routes plus the only railway line outside of Luzon. At the north-west tip you can make the short crossing by outrigger to the beautiful and laid back island of Boracay. After a spell of lazing on the beach there you can find another boat to cross to Tablas in the Romblon group, usually to Looc in the south. Take a jeepney to Odiongan and a boat from there to Roxas in Mindoro. Another bus ride will take you to Puerto Galera, a popular travellers' beach centre. Finally there are daily ferries to Batangas, only a few hours by bus from Manila. Quite an interesting and adventurous trip.

Visayas

0   50   100 km

Lucena
Boac
Marinduque
SIBUYAN SEA
Naga
Iriga
Daraga
Legazpi
Sorsogon
Burias Is.
Ticao Is.
Bulan
Bulusan
Allen
Catarman
San Bernardino Strait
Roxas
Romblon Is.
Tablas Is.
Sibuyan Is.
Odiongan
Looc
Masbate
Masbate Is.
Calbayog
SAMAR
Boracay Is.
Atiklan
Kalibo
Roxas City
VISAYAN SEA
Biliran Is.
Catbalogan
Borongan
Bantayan Is.
Basey
PANAY
Tacloban
LEYTE
Ormoc
Abuyog
Leyte Gulf
San Jose de Buenavista
Iloilo City
Guimaras Is.
Bacolod
San Carlos
CEBU
Toledo
Mandaue
Cebu City
Mactan Is.
Baybay
Homonhon Is
Dinagat Is.
Sogod
Liloan
Moalboal
Tubigon
BOHOL
Carmen
Tagbilaran
Maasin
Surigao Strait
Surigao
NEGROS
San Sebastian
Tampi
Santander
Dumaguete
Siquijor
MINDANAO SEA
Mambajao
Camiguin
Butuan City
Dapitan
Dipolog
Oroquita
Gingoog
MINDANAO
Ozamiz
Iligan
Malaybalay
Marawi

Leyte

Leyte is one of the Visayan Islands and lies between Samar and Mindanao. The over two km long Marcos Bridge, the longest and probably most attractive bridge in South-East Asia, links the islands of Samar and Leyte over the San Juanico Strait. Central and south Leyte are slightly mountainous while there are plains in the north and west. Europeans are very rare on Leyte (and Samar), expect to get stared at a lot.

Copra is Leyte's most important export product. More than 30% of the agriculturally usable surface is devoted to coconuts and forestry is also of increasing importance. Leyte's capital, Tacloban, has an excellent port with facilities for handling large ships and overseas trade. The main dialect in Tacloban and district is Waray-Waray; while in the north-west and the south Cebuano is spoken. You will be able to get on quite well with only English.

Leyte is particularly remembered as the place where General MacArthur fulfilled his 'I shall return' pledge. In October 1944 US troops landed at Red Beach near Tacloban and commenced to push the Japanese out of the Philippines. A little further south Talosa is noted, in the Philippines, for being the hometown of Mrs Marcos.

TACLOBAN

The capital of Leyte is a port town with about 100,000 inhabitants. MacArthur's historic return to the Philippines is depicted in a large relief at the Provincial Capital Building. It is also celebrated on 19 and 20 October annually with parades, cockfights and other events. History buffs will probably want to make a trip to Red Beach, near Palo, about seven km out of town to see the spot where MacArthur landed.

A day trip to Sohoton National Park, at Basey on nearby Samar Island, is also worth doing. In the town itself make sure you go to the market at the west end of the port. It's bursting with life and colour. The museum in the Tacloban Divine World University is a repository for relics and artefacts from Leyte and Samar and houses pre-historic finds from the Sohoton cave diggings.

Red Beach

On the beach at Palo a memorial recalls the return of MacArthur. There are no wrecks, or parts of wrecked ships, on the beach on in the surf and you need a lot of imagination to recognise any rusty-red colouration on Red Beach.

Jeepneys depart regularly from Tacloban; before coming into Palo a road branches off to the left. From the main road it is about two km to the park. If you overshoot the road to the park there is a Caltex service station about a hundred metres beyond it on the left. Some jeepneys go direct from Tacloban to Imelda Park, ask the drivers. When you return to Tacloban catch a jeepney going in the same direction. It loops back in a different direction.

Sohoton National Park

There are waterfalls, subterranean waterways and a true cave labyrinth in this national park. Because of the glittering stone formations, the caves are often called 'wonder caves'. The largest and most beautiful are Panhulugan I, Bugasan III and Sohoton. Two guides live at the park and they will take

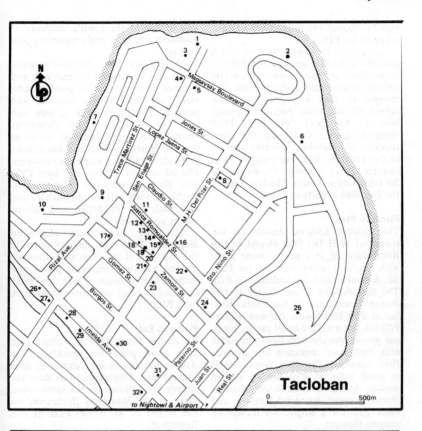

Tacloban

0   500m

to Nightowl & Airport

1 Tourist Office (MOT)
2 Leyte Park Hotel
3 Children's Park
4 Plaza Libertad
5 Provincial Capitol Building
6 Botanical Gardens
7 Wharf
8 Benedicto Pensione & Disco
9 Buses & Jeepneys
10 Market
11 Felisa's Cafe & Food Supply
12 Imperial Hotel
13 San Juanico Lodging House
14 San Juanico Fast Food & Snacks
15 Central Lodging House
16 El Tranco Bus Terminal
17 Primerose Hotel
18 Asiatic Restaurant
19 Savory Steak House
20 Moongold Restaurant
21 La Azotea
22 Mandarin
23 Geisha House
24 City Hall
25 Minibuses to Samar
26 Rodie-oh-Disco & Folkhouse
27 Hotel Village Inn
28 PAL Office
29 Sergeant Pepper's Pizza Parlour
30 Cecilia's Lodging House
31 Divine World University & Museum

you by dugout canoe into the narrowest caves for P15.

To get to the park you can rent a motorboat from Tacloban for P180 — if possible get one with a powerful enough engine and bargain hard. It's cheaper to take a jeepney to Basey (about P3) and from there get a pumpboat to the park for about P100 (bargain again!). Going up the river, reported one traveller, is better than actually arriving. Real *Apocalypse Now* country. Basey is known for its colourful tapestries and mats. The last jeepney for Tacloban departs at 4 pm!

Places to Stay

The *Central Lodging House* on the corner of M H Del Pilar St and Justice Romualdez St is a pretty basic place with singles/doubles with fan for P20/35. A double with fan and bath is P45. The *San Juanico Travel Lodge* at 104 Justice Romualdez St has rooms with fan at P30/35 or with fan and bath at P40/50. It's a simple hotel run by pleasant people but the beds have 'chocolate hills mattresses' reported one discomfited traveller. The new *Grand Hotel* is good value at P70 for an air-con double. At 119 Zamora St the *Christian Hostel* is clean, has good facilities and costs P25 for a single. No unmarried couples though!

Cecilia's Lodging House at 178 Paterno St is a clean, good place but badly signposted. With fan rooms are P30/45, with air-con and bath they're P100/135. The *Allee Lodge* on the corner of Burgos St and M H Del Pilar St has rooms with fan at P30/45. There's also the *Strand Hotel* with air-con doubles at P80.

On Justice Romualdez St the *Imperial Lodging House* is a simple hotel with rooms at P25 for a single with fan, P50 for a double with fan and bath or P95 for a double with air-con and bath. After a few minutes to settle in one of the staff is likely to introduce you to one of the town's 'students' — assuming you're a male travelling solo that is.

Moving up a price notch the *Primerose Hotel* on the corner of Zamora St and Senator Enage St is a good middle class hotel with rooms with fan and bath at P50/70 or with air-con and bath at P90/110. The *Benedicto Pensione* on Lopez Jaena St is one of the best hotels in town and has a disco and video. With fan and bath rooms are P50/90 or with air-con and bath P95/105. Finally there's the *Village Inn* on Imelda Avenue with rooms with air-con and bath for P115/165 and special rooms up towards P200.

The new *Leyte Park Hotel* on Magsaysay Boulevard, directly opposite the end of M H Del Pilar, looks impressive and has two swimming pools, one shaped like a heart. There are great views of the bay and room rates start from P300.

Places to Eat

On Justice Romualdez St, *Felisa's Cafe* is a good place for breakfast. The *Asiatic Restaurant* on Zamora St does Chinese and Filipino food as does the *Savory Steak House* on the same street. Ditto at the *Moongold Restaurant* on the corner of M H Del Pilar St and Zamora St.

Angelica's Restaurant does good Filipino food. On Imelda Avenue you can try *Sergeant Pepper's Pizzeria*. It's a friendly student place, good for darts and a beer.

Nightlife

There's jazz at the *Village Inn* and disco at the *Stone Age*. You'll find simple nightlife along Del Pilar St or you can try the *Nightowl*, a better nightclub but ask about cover charges here. The *Kuratsa Cafe* is the nightclub at the Grand Hotel and has relatively cheap beer.

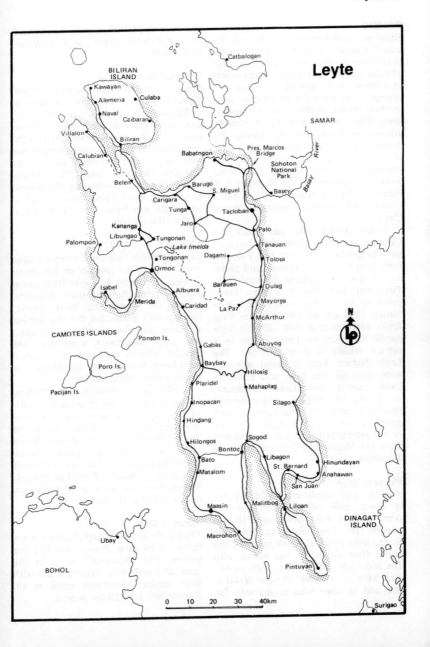

Leyte

BILIRAN ISLAND

Kawayan
Alemeria
Culaba
Naval
Caibaran
Villalon
Biliran
Calubian
Belen
Babatngon
Pres. Marcos Bridge
Sohoton National Park
Barugo
S. Miguel
Basey
Carigara
Tunga
Tacloban
Jaro
Palo
Kananga
Tungonan
Tanauan
Libungao
Lake Imelda
Dagami
Tolosa
Palompon
Tongonan
Ormoc
Barauen
Dulag
Isabel
Albuera
Mayorga
Merida
Caridad
La Paz
McArthur
CAMOTES ISLANDS
Ponson Is.
Abuyog
Poro Is.
Gabas
Baybay
Pacijan Is.
Hilosig
Plaridel
Mahaplag
Inopacan
Silago
Hindang
Hilongos
Sogod
Bontoc
Libagon
St. Bernard
Hinundayan
Bato
Matalom
San Juan
Anahawan
Maasin
Malitbog
Liloan
DINAGAT ISLAND
Macrohon
Ubay
BOHOL
Pintuyan
Surigao

SAMAR

Basay River

N

0 10 20 30 40km

ORMOC

Ships go from Ormoc to Cebu and the wharf is always busy. It's a good atmosphere here in the evenings with a glass of tuba on the quay wall. A little north of Ormoc, in Tungonan, there are hot springs. It is intended to produce geothermal power to make Leyte independent from energy imports. A ghostly atmosphere hangs over the damage the fumes have brought to the vegetation. If you want to visit the geothermal project you must apply, about two weeks in advance, to the Engineer E B Patanaeo, Project Manager, PNOC EDC, Geothermal Project, Tungonan, Ormoc City.

From Ormoc you can reach the Camotes Islands in about three hours in an outriggerboat. Tudela and Poro on Poro Island are two tranquil and pleasant villages. Lake Imelda National Park, Tungonan Hot Springs and an entry point to the newly established Leyte Nature Trail are all within Ormoc City limits and worth a visit. There's little public transport to these places so a private vehicle is your best bet. The Leyte Nature Trail is about a metre wide and 50 km long and connects Lake Imelda and Lake Mahagnao. It crosses the rugged, virgin-forested mountain range dividing Leyte in half geographically. Information on the newly established trail can be obtained from the Ministry of Tourism Office in Tacloban.

Places to Stay

A clean and simple place, *Eddie's Inn* is about 250 metres from the bus terminal and has rooms at P16 per person. The *Dors Hotel* on Bonifacio St has been renovated and renamed the *Hotel Don Felipe*. It has rooms with fan and bath at P35/55 or with air-con and bath at P70/80. *Pongos Hotel* is the best in town with rooms with fan

and bath at P40/60 or with air-con and bath at P75/95. There's also the *Rajah* on Rizal St.

Getting There

From 4 am to early afternoon (around 3 pm) buses go hourly from the harbour in Tacloban. It's a good road all the way and travel time is about two to three hours. The fare ranges from P10 to 25 depending on the bus company and the bus; more expensive buses are air-con. The first bus from Ormoc to Tacloban leaves at 5.30 am following the arrival of the ship from Cebu. You can get a bus all the way from Allen on Samar for P31, a 10 hour trip.

BAYBAY

You can reach this small town by ship from Cebu or by jeepney or bus from Ormoc. If coming to Leyte from Cebu this is a great place to arrive if you're looking for something more exotic. Baybay isn't much but the ship arrives at dawn and the backdrop of rugged lush green mountains, a centuries old Spanish church and tower, coconut palm-lined beaches and the rising sun makes a very exotic picture.

VISCA, the Viscayan State College of Agriculture, is about seven km north of Baybay. It's a surprisingly modernistic complex funded by the World Bank. There's a fairly decent beach here and limited guest house accommodation by the sea for about P25 a night. South of Baybay towards Maasin there are some good guest huts on the beach at Hilongos.

Places to Stay

Ellen's Hotel is a straightforward place in the dock area. Rooms are P12 per person. The *Travellers' Inn* is in the same area and has a restaurant but with little choice, sometimes none at all. Rooms here are P18 per person.

Getting There
Several buses daily go from the harbour in Tacloban. The last bus goes sometime between 11 am and 6 pm — ask! The trip to Baybay takes 2½ hours. There are several buses daily on the 50 km run from Ormoc to Baybay.

BATO
This small port town is between Baybay and Maasin and from here there are shipping connections to Cebu and to Bohol.

Places to Stay
The *Portview Lodging House* is clean and has rooms with fan at just P12 per person. For the same rate you can stay at the *Green House* or at *Rolly's Zodiac Lodge & Restaurant*.

MAASIN
Places to Stay
Hotels are pretty basic and equally basic in price in Maasin. The *Eureka Hotel* is P20/28 for singles/doubles while the *Sky View Lodging House* (formerly the Maasin Hotel) is P22/28. The Sky View is better value than the ageing Eureka although neither are very special. The best place in town is the *Ampil Pensione* on the main road for P20 to 35 per person. You can eat here for P10.

A few km further south is Ibarra where the *Esfa Beach Resort* has a cottage with two beds at P30 per day; there's a beach here and deep water. Very unfriendly staff, however, reported two travellers.

Getting There
The Tacloban-Baybay buses continue to Maasin, another couple of hours' trip. The road between Baybay and Hilosig is very rough — a new one is under construction but it could take years to complete. So it might be better to take a bus from Tacloban to Sogod and go by jeepney from there to Maasin. In the rainy season some bridges south of Baybay are impassable for a few days. From Maasin there are no regular boats crossing to Ubay but outriggers do make the journey when they have sufficient passengers. The 3½ hour trip costs P30 per person.

LILOAN
A bridge now connects Leyte to Panaon Island near Liloan where a 'safe from storms' ferry terminal is being constructed for ferries to Mindanao.

Places to Stay
At Bitoon Beach near Liloan a Swiss couple rent out cottages for about P40 including meals. It's a good area for snorkelling and diving. Equipment is available and it costs about P50 to 100 for a dive. It's possible that these cottages have not yet been rebuilt, following a bad typhoon. Enquire at the pharmacy by the city offices for private accommodation.

Getting There
From Tacloban the road past Abuyog and Sogod is a part of the Pan-Philippine Highway. Although the road has been built on a grand scale the Mahapalag-Sogod section can sometimes be blocked by landslides and is then only passable in four-wheel drive vehicles. Enquire about the current situation in Tacloban.

TRANSPORT FROM LEYTE
To Bohol Every Thursday at about 10 am an Aboitiz Lines ship goes from Bay-Bay to Jagna. The trip takes seven to eight hours. An Escano lines ship goes on Sunday at mid-day from Maasin to Jagna.

At around 4 or 5 am an outrigger-boat leaves Maasin for Ubay. The trip takes 3½ hours. The departure can be delayed well into the morning. There are small shops around the harbour which are open all night. You can browse there to while away the waiting time. There is also a boat every morning at 10 am from Bato via Lapinin Island to Ubay.

To Cebu PAL flies daily from Tacloban to Cebu (Mactan Airport). There are numerous ships operating on the 12 hour trip from Tacloban to Cebu City. The *MV Dona Angelina* of Sulpicio Lines goes on Monday at 10.30 am. The *MV Eduard* of William Lines goes on Wednesday at 8 pm. The *MV Sweet Grace* of Sweet Lines goes on Friday at 7 pm. The *MV Evelyn* of Western Samar Lines goes on Tuesday, Thursday and Saturday at 6 pm. The *MV Samar Queen* of K&T Shipping Lines goes on Monday, Friday and Sunday at 6 pm.

From Ormoc there's the *MV Ormoc* or the *MV Ramos Aboitiz* of Aboitiz Lines which goes on Tuesday at 10 am and 10 pm, Wednesday at 10 pm, Thursday at 10 pm, Friday at 10 pm, Saturday at 10 am and Sunday at 10 pm. This is a five to six hour trip costing around P30. The *Ormoc* also goes from Baybay on Tuesday at 10 pm, Thursday at midnight and Sunday at 10 pm. It's a five hour trip to Cebu City.

From Bato the *MV Picket* of Aboitiz Lines probably goes daily at 9 pm. This is also a five to six hour trip. The *MV Georich* of George & Peter Lines goes from Maasin on Monday, Wednesday and Friday at 11 pm. Again it's a five to six hour crossing. The Masmatan Line ferry now operates Cebu City to Maasin and Liloan in the south of Leyte. The *MV Guiuan* of K&T Shipping Lines goes from Liloan every Thursday and Sunday at 6 pm. From Naval on Biliran Island there's a daily boat to Cebu Island. This is of particular interest if you're travelling on a motorcycle as this connection is a less expensive alternative to the departure from Ormoc.

To Luzon The *MV Tacloban* of William Lines goes from Tacloban to Manila on Wednesday at 1 pm and Saturday at 7 pm. PAL flies Tacloban-Manila daily. Pantranco buses now operate Maasin-Ormoc-Tacloban and right through Samar and Luzon to Manila.

To Mindanao The *Cardinal Ferry* of the Cardinal Shipping Company operates from Maasin to Surigao daily at 11 pm. It's a five hour trip. It's possible that this service will leave from Liloan instead of Maasin. If you are travelling south from Luzon you can enquire in Matnog on the way. From here you can also catch a Cardinal Ferry Company boat to Samar. The Tacloban tourist office may be able to provide more up-to-date information. It's quite possible that if the ferries are not running boats are available from Liloan to Surigao.

A George & Peter Lines ship goes on Monday and Wednesday from Maasin to Surigao. An Archipelago Lines ship operates on the same route on Sunday morning. An Escano Lines ship goes on Thursday evening from Maasin to Butuan. On Tuesday at 6 pm a ship goes from Maasin to Butuan and at 8 pm there's another to Surigao.

To Samar The *MV Helen* of Western Samar Lines goes from Tacloban to Catbalogan every second day. Departure is around 10 to 11 pm and the trip takes four to five hours. Every second day the *MV Stacey* of K&T Shipping Lines goes from Tacloban to Guinan on south Samar. The trip takes six to seven hours.

Four buses of the EV Tranco Company go daily from 4 to 8.30 am from Tacloban via Catbalogan, Calbayog and Allen to Manila. Buses at 2.45, 4.15 and 9.30 am go only to Allen. The trip that far takes five hours.

Negros

Negros lies between Cebu and Panay in the south-western part of the Visayas. Mountain chains in the centre of the island divide Negros into the provinces of Occidental, with its capital Bacolod, and Oriental, with its capital of Dumaguete. The extensive Tablas Plateau sticks out in the south while there are wide plains to the west of a line drawn from Illog to Cadiz.

Negros is the sugar island of the Philippines with about 75% of the Philippines' total production. There are large sugar cane plantations and refineries in Victorias and Binalbagan.

One of the great attractions of Negros is the old steam engines which operate, side-by-side with modern diesels, on the sugar cane fields. Colin Carraf describes them in in detail in his book *Iron Dinosaurs* and you can see black and white photographs of them at the tourist office in Bacolod. During the milling season from October to April it is possible to travel short distances on these magnificent museum pieces. Check it out at the mill office if you're interested. The best of them belong to the Hawaiian Philippine Sugar Company in Silay; Vicmico in Victorias; Ma-ao Sugar Central in Bago; La Carlota Sugar Central in La Carlota and the Insular Lumber Company in Hinobaan, which has a rare, small steam engine. Worth seeing also are those owned by Biscom in Binalbagan; Sagay Sugar Central and Lopez Sugar Central in Sagay; Danao Sugar Central in Toledo and San Carlos Million Company in San Carlos.

The native inhabitants of Negros are the Negritos from whom the name of the island comes. Several tribes still exist in the mountain regions. The main dialect in Negros Occidental is Illongo but in Negros Oriental they speak Cebuano.

'Sugarland' is also involved in Filipino tourism with vacation spots like the Mambucal Mountain Resort, Santa Fe Resort and the Taytay Beach Resort. It is hoped that the Canloan Volcano will become a similar attraction to the Mayon Volcano of Luzon. Danjugan

Island, off the south-west coast, has extremely good swimming and diving possibilities.

BACOLOD

With a population of 260,000, Bacolod City is the 'sugar capital' of the Philippines. The appearance of this friendly Filipino metropolis was improved by some new streets built in the centre of 1981. Next to the San Sebastian Cathedral there is the Bacolod City Plaza with its benches under shady trees. Cultural programmes are held here on Sunday afternoons and on special occasions. The name Bacolod comes from the hill, a 'buklod', on which the first church was built.

The city is a leading producer of ceramics in the Philippines but most of the workshops, such as NLS Ceramics and Bilbao Ceramics, are in the suburbs. Only MDS Ceramics, at 26 Rosario St, is certainly located.

Out of Bacolod quite a few great day trips are possible. If you are a train buff you will find a number of trips right up your alley.

Places to Stay — bottom end

There's a very wide variety of accommodation in Bacolod. The *YMCA* (tel 2 6919) on Burgos St is a good clean place with dorm beds at P18 (P16 if you're a member) or singles with fan at P25, with fan and bath at P35. Check the doors though, some don't lock. Ted Canada has pleasant private accommodation at P20 per person at 30 Libertad St across from the school.

On Lacson St the *Gabina Yanson Lodge* has very simple rooms at P22. The *New Pacific Lodging House* (tel 2 4142) on North Drive has rooms with fan and bath at P28 or with air-con and bath at P50. It's a simple hotel and has some cheaper rooms with common bath.

The *Standard Lodging House* (tel 2 8351), on the corner of San Sebastian and Gatuslao St, is a simple clean place with a variety of good rooms. Rooms with fan are P25, with a fan and bath P40, with air-con and bath P80. The *Friendship Inn* (tel 2 3312) on Bonifacio St is not for late-risers — the Filipinos and Chinese have little respect for other guests' hearing! Bathrooms are shared between two rooms and costs are P40 for a single with fan, P45 for a

1 Negros Navigation Company	21 Coney Island Ice Cream
2 New Pacific Lodging House	22 Shopping Center, Fantasy Food
3 Northern Bus Terminal	23 Shakey's Pizza
4 Majestic Go Go Disco	24 Market
5 Satellite Go Go Disco	25 Friendship Inn, Batchoy Restaurants
6 Stardust Go Go Disco	26 Sulamban Restaurant
7 Bascon I Hotel, Royal Pub House	27 Tourist Office
8 YMCA	28 City Hall
9 Las Rocas Hotel, Rocking Galleon Disco	29 Barrio Fiesta Restaurant
10 Jumbo's Food Centre	30 Mardi Gras Restaurant
12 San Sebastian Cathedral	31 Mandarin Hotel & Bar
13 Food Park	32 Post Office
14 William Lines	33 Standard Lodging House
15 City Plaza	34 Halili Inn
16 Manakon Country Beer Gardens & BBQ	35 Ang Sinugba Restaurant
17 International Restaurant	36 Ted Canada
18 Bascon II Hotel	37 Sports Complex
19 Sea Breeze Hotel	38 Southern Bus Terminal
20 PAL Office	39 Jeepneys to Mambucal

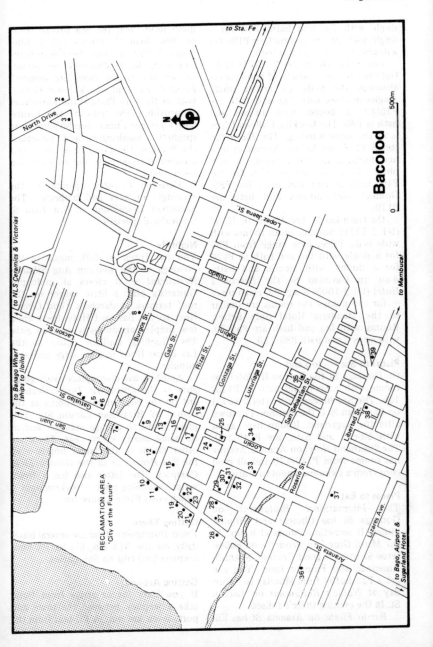

Bacolod

single with fan and bath, P60 for a single with air-con and bath or P100 for a double with air-con and bath.

Las Rocas Hotel (tel 2 1373) at 13 Gatuslao St has a variety of good rooms although the beds are rather small. Singles/doubles with fan and bath are P35/42. A double with air-con and bath is P80. The Rocking Galleon Disco is in the same building. The *Halili Inn* (tel 8 1548) on Locsin Avenue is in a new building and has a pleasant atmosphere. There are singles with fan for P40, with air-con and bath for P80. Doubles with air-con and bath are P110.

On Gatuslao St the *Mandarin Hotel* (tel 2 1721) has nice clean rooms with wide beds. Prices here range from P55 for a single with fan and bath to P120 for a double with air-con and bath. Also on Gatuslao St the *Bascon I Hotel* (tel 2 1005) is a good, clean place — for the money the rooms are similar to the Mandarin Hotel only better. Rooms with fan and bath are P55/70, with air-con and bath P85/110.

Places to Stay - top end

On Gonzaga St the *Bascon II Hotel* has rooms with air-con and bath at P125/155. The *Sea Breeze Hotel* (tel 2 4571) on San Juan St is the best hotel in town after the Sugarland. Rooms here, again with air-con and bath, are P145/180. The *Sugarland Hotel* on Araneta Avenue has rooms from P140/170 and all mod cons from a swimming pool to a disco.

Places to Eat

The *International Restaurant* on Gonzaga St has Chinese and Filipino dishes. It sometimes shuts at 8 pm. At the *Mardi Gras Luncheonette* on Ballesteros St there is good Chinese, Spanish, American and Filipino food. You can get a P25 buffet from Monday to Saturday at *Noble's Restaurant* on Lacson St. In the evening there's a disco.

Barrio Fiesta on Araneta St has Fil-

ipino food. Near the Sea Breeze Hotel on San Juan St there's yet another *Shakey's Pizza Parlour*. Next door is the *Sandwich House*. Two good restaurants to see the sunset from are *Jumbo's Food Circus* and *Tita's Food Center*, both at the City Plaza at the waterfront — providing the 'city of the future' hasn't yet been built. Jumbo's has good spaghetti, hamburgers and pancakes. On Rizal St the *Food Park* contains a number of restaurants, one of which has good steaks.

Manakon Country operates in the evenings for beer and barbecue. The *Sulamban Restaurant* on San Juan St is a seafood specialist.

Nightlife

You can listen to folk music in the evenings in the well-run *Ang Sibugba Restaurant* — it closes at midnight. Guitarists play a little longer on the roof terraces at *Jumbo's Food Circus*. Next to the Bascon I Hotel there are a few simple bars/discos with go-go girls. The *Rocking Galleon Disco* in the Las Rocas Hotel is quite large and very popular.

Another bar/disco place with go-go girls is the *Open Air Disco Restaurant* on the roof of the building at the corner of Rizal and Lacson Sts. This place seems to change manager and/or its name nearly every year. There are other discos in the larger hotels — eg the *Sea Breeze* or in the *Golden Field Complex*. The latter also has a freshwater swimming pool — 'rocking pool — which costs P10 entrance fee.

Getting There

From Dumaguete there are several buses daily on the 313 km, 6½ to 7½ hour (express bus) trip via San Carlos.

Getting Around

If you leave for or arrive from Iloilo take a jeepney between the town and port, seven km out. A PU-taxi from the

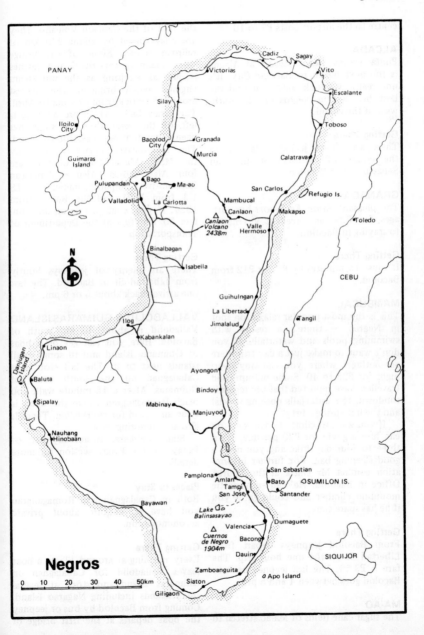

Negros

0 10 20 30 40 50km

centre to the airport costs P7 to 10.

ALCADA
Punta Taytay Beach Resort at Alcada is the next beach to Bacolod City. It's not really a knock out. You find the best beaches on Negros in the south-west of the island.

Getting There
There are several jeepneys daily from the corner of Gatuslao St and San Sebastian St in Bacolod.

GRANADA
The pleasant *Santa Fe Resort* has cottages for P28, an excellent alternative to staying in Bacolod.

Getting There
It's just 15 minutes by PU for P12 from Bacolod.

MAMBUCAL
This is the most popular relaxation spot in Negros — there's a resort with swimming pools and waterfalls. If you don't want to make just a day trip there are cottages where you can stay overnight for P25 to 40. Some unimpressed travellers have reported that the resort is rundown, the waterfalls nothing special and the hot springs dirty.

If you want to climb the volcano you can hire a guide for P20 per day. It's a three to four day hike and you need a good sleeping bag. For further information contact Mr Gatia at the Tourist Office in Bacolod. He's an enthusiastic mountain climber and could guide you if he has spare time.

Getting There
From Bacolod jeepneys depart from Libertad St on the one hour trip. The fare is P3.50. The last jeepney back to Bacolod goes between 4 and 5 pm.

MA-AO
The sugar cane fields of Ma-ao stretch to the foot of the Canlaon Volcano. They are criss-crossed by about 280 km of railroad tracks. Some of the bridge work spanning the rivers and ravines is just as exciting as the old steam engines which bring in the harvest around the clock from October to April. The straw bails, which are all that is left of the cane after the sugar has been extracted, are used for firewood. The locomotives currently used by the MSC (Ma-ao Sugar Central) are four Alco 2-6-0s (Alco = American Locomotive Company), namely the TS 1-3 from 1921 and the BM 5 from 1924. If you want to ride on one contact Mr Dreyfuss at the Department of Transportation.

Getting There
There are plenty of jeepneys hourly from Libertad St in Bacolod. The last one arrives back about 5 or 6 pm.

VALLADOLID & GUIMARAS ISLAND
Valladolid is about 30 km south of Bacolod. Here you can get on a boat to Guimaras Island and to some small islands next to it. The last stop is at Cabalagnan on the south coast of Guimaras. After a 15 minute walk you reach Romagangran where the water is clear and good for snorkelling. There is also an interesting cave.

Since Guimaras is actually part of Panay see the Panay section for more details.

Places to Stay
Both in Cabalagnan and Romagangran you have to enquire about private accommodation.

Getting There
Every morning at around 11 am a boat leaves Valladolid for Cabalagnan on Guimaras Island and stops at several small islands including Nagarao Island. Coming from Bacolod by bus or jeepney the boat departs at the first bridge of

Valladolid, so ask the driver to drop you there. In Cabalagnan the departure time for Valladolid is between 3 and 4 am. The fare is P10.

SILAY

A little out of Silay is the Hawaiian-Philippine Sugar Company, one of the largest plantations on the island. It has a web of railway tracks totalling about 180 km in length. The steam engines used here are in an excellent state of preservation and are nicknamed 'Red Dragons' because of their colour. Most of them were successfully kept secret from the Japanese during the war by being hidden in the densely wooded hills. They include a 1920 Henschel 0-6-0 and six Baldwin 0-6-0s built in 1919, 1920 and 1928.

Getting There

Minibuses and jeepneys from Bacolod for Victorias go via Silay.

VICTORIAS

Just outside of Victorias is a large factory complex where cane is processed into packaged consumer products — it's a jeepney trip from town. Vicmico is an acronym for Victorias Milling Company.

The Victorias Milling Company owns the largest train track network in Negros, incorporating about 365 km of line. It is two foot gauge and is probably the longest of its type in the world. As with the Hawaiian-Philippine Sugar Company, the diesel and steam engines are all controlled by radio transmission from a central point. The dark green Oldtimer is only used in the peak season from January to February. Since petrol prices have increased wood is being used for fuel again. Amongst the engines used here are eight Henschel 0-8-OTs from 1926-28, as well as two Bagnall 0-4-4Ts which were built in 1924 for the line from Kowloon (Hong Kong) to Canton in China. If you want to see any

of them or have a ride on one ask for Mr Calsa at the entrance gate.

Also in Victorias see the 'St Joseph the Worker Chapel' with an unusual wallpainting showing an angry Filipino Jesus. The 'Angry Christ' has even received international attention through an article in *Life* magazine.

Getting There

It's a one hour trip from Bacolod through Silay to Victorias. There are numerous minibuses from the Northern Bus Terminal every day but the Ford Fiera jeepneys are more comfortable and they probably leave straight from Libertad St if you ask.

SAN CARLOS

Ships go to Toledo on Cebu from here. Otherwise the town has nothing to recommend it although, a traveller reports, there is a quiet island off the coast called Sipaway. People eke out a living growing corn on salty, rocky land. There are a couple of pleasant, quiet beaches and good paths for wandering. Bring your own food and water, although there are some sari-sari stores. There are little boats zipping back and forth to Sipaway all day for 75c each way.

Places to Stay & Eat

Van's Lodging House has rooms at P12 per person — a simple place near the pier. Near the park is *Papal's Lodge* with rooms at P18 per person. The rooms are large, have showers and are good value. Otherwise there's the *Excelsior* at P20 per person. *La Suerte Pension* is run by an old woman who charges P40 per person for bed, breakfast and dinner — excellent value. The *San Carlos Lodging House* is P15 per person.

The *Coco Grove Hotel & Restaurant* is the best place in town. Rooms with fan and bath are P60/80 and with air-con and bath they cost P90/130.

You can eat at *Cisis Food Service*

next to Papal's Lodge or at the cheap places in the market just down the road.

Getting There

Bacolod-Dumaguete buses go via San Carlos. It's three to four hours from Bacolod to San Carlos. Buses marked 'boat service' go as far as the camp site. Other buses stop in the main street where trishaws wait for boat passengers.

From Dumaguete there are several buses daily from the Ceres San Carlos terminal at the Northern Bus Terminal. 'Shopping' jeepneys go to the terminal. It's a three to four hour trip from Dumaguete to San Carlos.

DUMAGUETE

The generously laid out Silliman University Campus is in the suburbs of Dumaguete and is the only protestant university in the Philippines. Named after its founder, Dr Horace B Silliman, it has a small anthropological museum and a cafeteria where you can eat for a reasonable price. Other information about the university is available from the Administration Building — the Public Relations Department no longer exists.

Silliman Beach isn't a good swimming beach but near the beach there is a Marine Laboratory where diving courses are run twice a year. The lab also has a trimaran which you can charter for trips to Sumilon Island — a

divers' paradise off the coast of Cebu. It can also be reached from Mainit or Santander. The trip takes an hour from Dumaguete and the boat costs about P150. Apo Island, which has a camp site, is also a favourite with divers.

Places to Stay

Opena's Hotel & Restaurant on Katada St has singles with fan at P35, doubles with fan and bath at P80, rooms with air-con and bath at P85/95. It's a pleasant, clean hotel in a new building. On Real St the *Hotel El Oriente* is another nice, clean place — rooms here cost from P50/90 for singles/doubles with fan and bath. With air-con and bath rooms start at P90. They also own a beach resort hotel a little further out. The *Al Mar Hotel* on the corner of Rizal Avenue and San Juan St has rooms with fan and bath from P50/55 and with air-con and bath from P120.

On Silliman Avenue the *Insular Hotel* is a good hotel near the university. Rooms with fan and bath are P90/100 or with air-con P110/135. On the same street the *Lodging Inn*, across from the main entrance of the university, is P15 a single or you can try *Jo's Lodging* at P15 per person. The rather run-down *Victory Lodge* is even cheaper. These Silliman Avenue places are all within walking distance of the wharf. Another cheap place is *William Lodge*, a block

1 Province Hospital	16 Jo's Bake House & Restaurant
2 Bamboo Grove Beer Garden	17 Garland Restaurant
3 Silliman University Campus	18 Insular Hotel
4 Northern Bus Terminal	19 Philippine National Bank (PNB)
5 Pier 1	20 Hotel Oriente
6 Pier 2	21 Al Mar Hotel, Sinueba Bar & Restaurant
7 William Lines, George & Peter Lines	22 Kamagong Restaurant
8 Opena's Hotel & Restaurant	23 Jeepneys & Minibuses to San Jose &
9 Provincial Capitol Building	Tampi
10 University Cafeteria	24 Market
11 Silliman Co-operative Store	25 Church
12 Administration Building, Museum	26 City Hall
13 Barbecue Stalls	27 Jeepneys to Valencia
14 Carlos A Gothong Lines	28 Southern Bus Terminal
15 Jo's Lodging Inn	

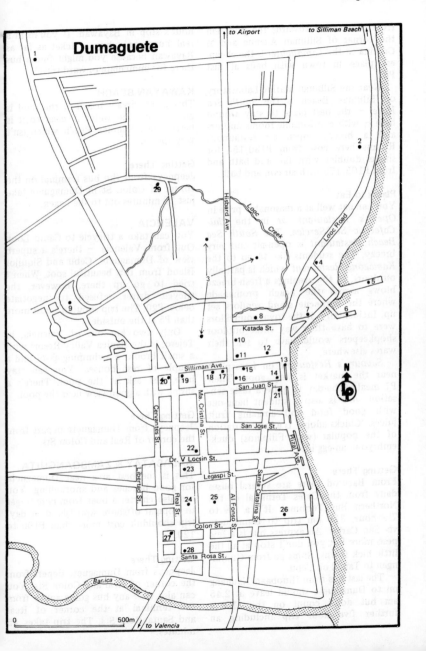

from the market towards the port. On the corner of Silliman Avenue and M Cristina St the *Lamplighter* is the cheapest place in town with beds at just P5.

Near the Silliman Marine Laboratory on Silliman Beach is the *South Sea Hotel* — the best place to stay around here — with comfortable rooms upstairs and a breezy, open air restaurant. Rooms here cost from P130/154 for singles/doubles with fan and bath and from P165/175 with air-con and bath.

Places to Eat

You can eat well at a reasonable price in *Opena's Restaurant* or in the *Uni-Cafeteria Self-Service*. The *South Sea Beach Restaurant* is open-air and very breezy. The students like to go to the *Kamagong Restaurant* which is partially outdoors. In the evenings a fresh breeze blows across the beach promenade where the barbecue stand vendors set up. Incidentally, if the town councillors were to have their way these outdoor shopkeepers would have to sell their wares elsewhere.

Savoury's Restaurant on Legaspi St near the market is very good. Their P7 meal-of-the-day is quite a taste sensation. *Jo's* is also a student hang-out with good food and amazing fruit juices. 'Chicks adobo' is a local variation of the popular (with Filipinos) duck-embryo-in-an-egg idea.

Getting There

From Bacolod there are several buses daily from the Ceres Terminal or the Northern Bus Terminal. It's a 6½ to 7½ hour, 313 km trip to Dumaguete via San Carlos. An express bus is a few peso more but you don't stop at all the little hick towns. Ships go from Guihulngan to Tangil on Cebu.

The last bus from Hinobaan/Nauhang on to Dumaguete should leave at 2.45 am but don't count on this. It's a further five hour trip including an

hour's stop in Bayawan. If you're in a real hurry only buy a ticket as far as Bayawan because you might find a bus there for immediate onward travel.

KAWAYAN BEACH

This is no dream beach — the sand is grey — but the water is clear so it is better then Silliman Beach which isn't very special.

Getting There

Jeepneys from the bus terminal on the corner of Colon St in Dumaguete take just 10 minutes out to the beach.

VALENCIA

You can take a tricycle to Camp Look Out from Valencia — there's a superb view of Dumaguete, Cebu and Siquijor Island from this beautiful spot. When I tried to go up there, however, the tricycle driver refused to negotiate below P20. The trip shouldn't cost more than P5 at the outside.

Only two km out of Valencia, in Tejero, is the Banica Valley Resort with a small brook, a swimming pool and a couple of rest houses. You can stay here, just ask at the pool. There's a shrine with a good view near the pool.

Getting There

Jeepneys from Dumaguete depart from the corner of Real and Colon Sts.

MALABATAY & ZAMBOANGUITA

This is the best area near Dumaguete for good beaches and snorkelling. You can also charter a boat from here to get to popular offshore Apo Island. A day-trip shouldn't cost more than P100 to 120.

Getting There

Jeepneys from Dumaguete depart from the corner of Real and Colon Sts. You can also take any bus going south from the terminal at the corner of Real and Santa Rosa Sts. The trip takes 45 minutes.

TWIN LAKE

About 15 km inland, north-west of Dumaguete, is the romantic hidden crater of Lake Balinsasayanao and the smaller Lake Danao right next to it. These are volcanic lakes surrounded by dense rainforest. Conservationists and ecologists have demanded that this so-called twin lake and the surrounding countryside be declared a national park, thereby hopefully preventing the building of a hydro-electric power station in this area. There is a small nipa hut where you can stay overnight but bring facilities and supplies.

Getting There

Since there is no transportation you have to hike. The trail starts about two km south of San Jose. Take any bus from Dumaguete going north and watch out for the small sign on the left where you have to get off.

SAN JOSE

Ships for San Sebastian, Bato and Talisay in Cebu depart from Hilecon/ Tampi near San Jose.

Getting There

Jeepneys from Dumaguete for San Jose depart from Real St on the corner of Jones St.

BINALBAGAN

The Biscom in Binalbagan is the biggest sugar mill and sugar plantation in the world. Biscom is an acronym for Binalbagan Sugarmill Company.

Getting There

Buses go from the Southern Bus Terminal in Bacolod. The trip takes two hours.

KABANKALAN

This small town, about 40 km south of Binalbagan, celebrates the Sinulog Festival on the third weekend of January each year. There are parades, tribal shows and horsefights. The Kabankalanons say its older and more original than the popular one in Cebu City.

Getting There

Buses go from the Southern Bus Terminal in Bacolod. The trip takes three hours.

HINOBAAN

In early '82 a veritable gold rush took place here. National and international press reports of new finds lured innumerable opportunists and adventurers to this spot but the real gold fever only set in when it was revealed that one Filipino supposedly panned P23,000 worth of gold in one day. Shortly after this a promising 17 km section of the Bacuyongan River was invaded by an estimated 20,000 people trying their luck. A lot of them found it too — the average daily booty was said to have stood at around a gram per person at that time and buyers were paying about P80 a gram.

After about eight weeks of gold frenzy one digger had been buried alive in a landslide, another killed by a falling tree while panning and three had died as a result of fights over claims. In two months this latter figure was to rise to 17. When all was said and done the most lucrative activities turned out to have been those of the buyers, merchants and traders who transformed the sleepy village of Nauhang into a lively new town complete with its own wild west character. From here an uninterrupted stream of jeepneys leaves the Crossing Gold Southbend for Spa III, about seven km inland to Sitio Sangke, where the trodden path towards the promising river begins.

Places to Stay & Eat

Established in 1977 Jean and Graham Johnson's *Paradise Beach Resort* has a tennis court, Hobie Cat to sail, windsurfing equipment and a swimming pool. It's a brick house, the best place to stay in Hinobaan and singles/doubles are P60/80 per night although more expensive rooms go up to US$30. All prices include breakfast and the food here is very good. The resort is closed from mid-July to mid-November.

While in town try binacol (chicken with onions and lemon grass, cooked in a young coconut). It's a specialty of south-west Negros and tastes fantastic. You can get it at the Beach Resort where wine lovers may also be tempted to sample the huge wine celler.

Getting There
It's a five or more hour bus trip from the Southern Bus Terminal in Bacolod to Hinobaan. Quite a few Ceres Liner Company buses leaves from the early morning until at least 8 am. They follow the south-west route to Dumaguete via Hinobaan and Bayawan. The road is good as far as Kabankalan but it gets worse after that. To compensate the countryside becomes much more interesting.

Buses which only go as far as Hinobaan leave every hour from 11.30 am onwards till the late afternoon. Occasionally the trip will end in Nauhang but don't pay more than P5 for the tricycle from there to Hinobaan.

TRANSPORT FROM NEGROS
To Bohol The William Lines ship *MV Cebu City* goes from Dumaguete to Tagbilaran on Saturday at 3 pm. The trip takes about three hours.

To Cebu On Wednesday at 11 pm the *MV Dona Maria* of William Lines departs from Bacolod directly for Cebu City. On Monday at 7 am the *MV Santo Nino* of Negros Navigation Company departs from Bacolod to Cebu City. The trip takes 15 hours. The harbour is at Pulupandan, 31 km south of Bacolod and buses go there from the Southern Bus Terminal.

From San Carlos there are departures at 5.30 and 9 am and 1.30 pm each weekday for Toledo. On Sunday departures are at 5 and 10.30 am. Maundy Thursday and Good Friday are rest days. The trip takes two hours. When the weather is bad the trishaw drivers like to tell you that there are no ships sailing. They just want to take you to a boarding house and pick up a few pesos in commission.

From Guihulngan there's a daily boat to Tangil. If you want to go to Moalboal take this boat, the schedule from Toledo to Moalboal is not very good.

From San Jose and Tampi there are several boats daily to San Sebastian, Talisay and Bato. The last departure daily is around 3.30 but it's unpunctual. The trip takes one hour.

There are almost daily ships between Dumaguete and Cebu City — ask at the George & Peter Lines, William Lines or Carlos A Gothong Lines offices.

PAL flies daily from Bacolod and Dumaguete to Mactan Airport at Cebu City.

To Luzon Five ships of the Negros Navigation Company go from Bacolod to Manila. Sailing times are frequently different — the *MV Don Claudio* departs on Monday at 7 pm for the 19 hour trip to Manila. The *MV San Sebastian* goes on Tuesday at midnight. The *MV Don Julio* goes on Wednesday at 4 pm. The *MV Santa Maria* goes on Friday at 7 pm. The *MV Connie II* goes on Saturday at midnight.

The William Lines ship *MV Cebu City* goes from Dumaguete to Manila on Wednesdays at 8 am. The trip takes 28 hours. The *MV Dona Susana* of Sulpicio Lines departs on Monday at 5 pm from Dumaguete for Manila.

PAL flies two or three times daily from Bacolod to Manila.

To Mindanao About three times weekly (usually Monday, Wednesday and

Friday) a George & Peter Lines ship goes from Dumaguete to Zamboanga. The trip takes 16 hours and departure time is about 7 pm. George & Peter Lines also have a ship from Dumaguete daily at 8 am for Dipolog. The trip takes four to five hours. On Monday a ship from the same company goes from Dumaguete to Oroquieta and Cagayan de Oro.

To Panay The *Don Vicente* and the *Princess of Negros* of the Negros Navigation Company go from Bacolod to Iloilo. The trip takes 2½ hours and there are departures twice daily at 7 am and 3 pm except on Fridays and Sundays. The Friday departures are at 7 am and 4 pm and on Sundays at 8 am and 4 pm. The trip costs P20 1st class or P14 2nd. Banago wharf is out of town so allow 30 minutes for a jeepney (P2) or 15 minutes for a taxi (P7 to 10).

To Siquijor Every day at 2 pm the *MB Saint Christopher* departs from Dumaguete for Larena. The trip takes three hours and costs P10.

Panay

Panay is the large triangular shaped island in the western part of the Visayas. It consists of the provinces of Iloilo, Capiz, Aklan and Antique. The largest city is Iloilo City with a population of about 250,000. Agriculture is the dominant branch of the economy although textile industries are also found in Iloilo City. Fabrics are made from the fibres of the pineapple leaf — the Filipino barong tagalog shirt is tailored from this fabric.

Main tourist attractions in Panay are three festivals — the Ati-Atihan festival in Kalibo, the Binirayan festival in San Jose de Buenavista and the Dinagyang Festival in Iloilo. The island has a number of decaying forts and watchtowers — relics from the days of the Moro pirates. The island of Sicogon has been open to foreign traffic for some years but there is another 'dream island', Boracay, off the north-western tip of Panay. Some people may be unhappy that word on this little secret paradise is beginning to slip out but word-of-mouth has already been spreading the news. Before and after the Ati-Atihan festival Boracay can actually get fairly full.

ILOILO

The capital city of Panay is one of the larger towns in the Philippines, but it's just another big town even though it was important during the Spanish era. One of the most striking sights in the town today is the jeepneys, some of which are styled like '50s American road cruisers. The small Museo Iloilo, also called the 'Window of the Past', is worth seeing. It has a notable collection of art and culture from the pre-Spanish era. There's also the interesting Gothic-Rennaissance church in Molo, near the city proper.

1 River Queen Hotel	22 Centercon Hotel, Summer House Restaurant
2 The Key	23 Mansion House Restaurant, D'Wheels Pub House
3 Museum	
4 Capitol of Iloilo	24 Iloilo Lodging House
5 PAL Office	25 Ferry to Jordan, Guimaras Island
6 St Paul's Hospital	26 Abada Restaurant
7 Family Pension House, Tree House Snack Bar	27 Swan Restaurant
8 Iloilo Motorcycle Club	28 Kong Kee Restaurant
9 Del Rio Hotel	29 International House
10 Tourist Office	30 Magnet Bar & Restaurant
11 Sarabia Manor Hotel, Casino, Madule Disco	31 Shakey's Pizza Parlour
12 Universidad de San Augustin	32 Post Office, Immigration, Customs House
13 Casa Plaza Hotel	33 Plaza
14 YMCA	34 Railway Station
15 Shoemart, Jeepneys to Pavia	35 Central Market
16 Oak Barrel Restaurant	36 Bodega Pub
17 Kings Head Pub	37 Plaza Libertad
18 Buses to Roxas	38 Negros Navigation Lines, Ferries to Bohol
19 Buses to Kalibo & Estancia	39 Rotary Park, Lighthouse
20 Buses to San Jose de Buenavista	40 Ferries to Buenavista & Guimaras Island
21 Market	41 Wharf

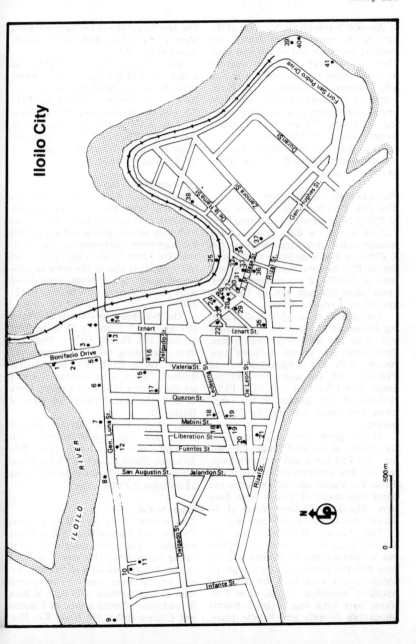

Iloilo City

ILOILO RIVER

Fort San Pedro Drive

Durant St.

Zamora St.

De la Rama St.

Gen. Hughes St.

Rizal St.

Bonifacio Drive

Gen. Luna St.

Iznart St.

Delgado St.

Valeria St.

Ledesma St.

De Leon St.

Quezon St.

Mabini St.

Liberation St.

Fuentes St.

San Augustin St.

Jalandon St.

Rizal St.

Delgado St.

Infante St.

N

0   500 m

Arevalo, a suburb six km west of the city, is the centre where fabrics and clothing are made out of jusi and pina. There are actually only two weaver's looms in Arevalo and these are at Sinamay Dealer in Osmena St. In Pavia, a little to the north of Iloilo, they hold buffalo races every year on 3 May starting at 8 am. To get there catch a jeepney outside the Shoemart.

Iloilo has a tourist office but it's inconveniently situated for the wharf or the hotel area.

Places to Stay — bottom end

The YMCA on Iznart St has dorm beds at P23 (P18 to members) or rooms from P23/45 but it's a dirty hole and not recommended. *International House* (tel 7 4786) on J M Basa St has singles with fan at P25 or rooms with air-con and bath at P65/75. It's a straightforward, clean place although not all travellers are very enthusiastic about it.

Across from there is the *Iloilo Lodging House* on Aldeguer St. It is simple and clean but with very small rooms. Bathrooms are shared between two rooms. With fan singles/doubles are P40/50, with fan and bath P60/85. Large rooms for four cost from P110. *D'House* at 127 Quezon St has large, clean, airy rooms with fan for P30 per person.

There's good dorm accommodation for women at the *Girl Guide Association* for P12 for a bed with mosquito net. It's past the museum, off Bonifacio Drive. For a small amount extra you can enjoy huge meals of 'garden fresh' food here. The *E&E Lodging House* at 40 Mabini St is P12 for a very basic single.

The *Family Pension House* on General Luna St is a clean, good place run by pleasant people. Rooms with fan cost P35 per person or you can get an air-con room with bath for P90. An excellent breakfast is less than P10. There have been lots of good reports about this friendly and helpful place.

The tree house snack bar here is a good place to sip a beer and has live entertainment at night.

The *Centercon Hotel* (tel 7 3431), on a lane off J M Basa St where it meets Iznart St, is clean, quiet and very central. Rooms with air-con and bath are P70/90. With air-con doubles at P90 the *New Century Hotel* on the same street is also good value. The rates are similar at the clean and quiet *Hotel Madias-as* (tel 7 2756) on Aldeguer St.

Places to Stay — top end

The *River Queen Hotel* (tel 7 6667) on Bonifacio Drive has rooms with air-con and bath at P100/130. It's a better hotel with only air-con rooms and a beautiful but expensive restaurant on the riverside. On Iznart St the *Casa Plaza Hotel* (tel 7 6964) is also in the more expensive category. It's a clean, good hotel with air-con rooms with bath at P115/160.

The best place in town is the *Hotel Del Rio* (tel 7 5585) in M H Del Pilar St, near the Tourist Office. There's a disco, swimming pool, restaurants and rooms from P135/160 for singles/doubles. Other more expensive hotels are the *Sarabia Manor* on General Luna St and the *Royal Palms* on General Hughes St.

In Oton, a little distance out of town, are two beach resorts with cottages from around P100. The *Anhawan Beach Resort* (tel 7 4668) has a pool and other facilities as well as its 11 cottages at P120.

Places to Eat

The *Summer House* on J M Basa St has Chinese and Filipino food but is rather expensive. You'll find most of the best eating places along this street. More of the same at the *Mansion House Restaurant* on the same street — try pancit lomi here is possible. Still on J M Basa St and still offering a mix of Filipino and Chinese dishes the *Kong Kee Res-*

taurant is also very good and has a very long menu.

You can also find one of the Philippine's many *Shakey's Pizza Parlour*, on J M Basa St. It's a meeting place for local young people and has live music. There's another pizza place in the market. On Aldeguer St, *Abada's Theatre Restaurant* is open 24 hours a day. It has Filipino food Turo-Turo style and live music. The *Oak Barrel* on Valeria St is one of a number of Batchoy-restaurants on this block. The nearby *Iloilo Supermart*, on the corner of Delgado St and Valeria St, is also a good place for cheap food.

Back on J M Basa, *Ganeco Fast Foods* is both modern and clean — look out for the waiter, Nelson, he's fantastic. The owner, Mrs Maria Victoria Gan, is very helpful and can give you good information.

Nightlife

Good atmosphere, folk music and draft beer in the *Bodega Pub* in the evenings. It's open all weekend. You can also hear folk music at the *Swan Restaurant* or sit outside at the *Open Air Restaurant* on Fort San Pedro Drive and listen to the lap of the water. The comfortable *Kings Head Pub* opens at 4 pm. Like the Bodega it's a peace corps hangout and a good place for information.

The *Sarabia Madule Disco* in the casino on General Luna St is a favourite of the moment. The *Del Rio Disco* and the *Bayani Super Nightclub* on Delgabo St are also popular. For a simple night out try the *Magnet Bar* or any of the pubs nearby or head for the *D'Wheels Pub House*, a friendly and relaxing place to go. The *Iloilo Kitchenette* has live music in the evenings but it's not much to write home about.

Getting There

From Roxas there are several Skylark Liner Company buses daily to Iloilo. The last bus departs on the 4½ hour trip

at 11.30 am. The Roxas-Iloilo trains depart at 4.30, 8 and 10 am and at 3 pm. Ditto in the other direction.

GUIMARAS ISLAND

This island is an interesting day trip from Iloilo City. At Bundulan Point, Jordan, there is a huge cross which many believers make pilgrimages to during the Easter week. From here you can also get a good view of the city and Iloilo Strait. Here also on Good Friday the re-enactment of the crucifixion of Christ has become a major tourist attraction. Outside Buenavista, on the island, is the Daliran Cave but the walk there is better than the cave itself.

Nueva Valencia has a small Trappist monastery, built only a few years ago. The monks here have devoted themselves to the cultivation of calamansis, an important facet of the economy of Guimaras Island. This monastery is definitely not a tourist attraction so don't go unless you are really interested.

About 45 minutes walking distance south of Nueva Valencia you can find a good swimming beach at a bay where two fishing families live. Further south Calabagnan and Romagangran are places foreigners very seldom go. The water here is very clear and it's excellent for snorkelling. In Romagangran there is also an interesting cave. Offshore there are some idyllic islands as well as the Taclon diving site off the south-west tip of Guimaras.

Places to Stay

There is still no commercial accommodation on Guimaras Island and your only hope of finding somewhere to stay is with one of the local people. Try to find a nice way to give them a reasonable amount for board and lodging.

From Jordan you can take a regular jeepney (but only once or twice a day) to San Isidro for P5 and from there cross to Nagarao Island off the south of Guimaras where there is a resort with

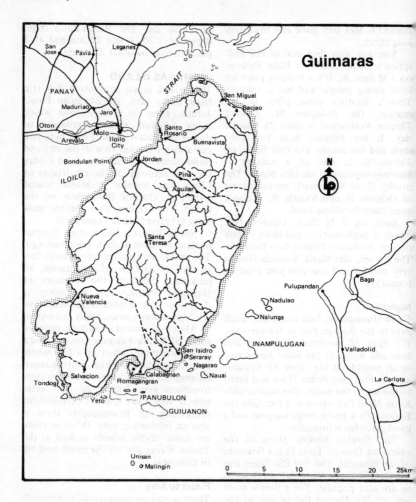

Guimaras

STRAIT

San Jose · Pavia · Leganes

PANAY

Madriao · Jaro

Oton · Molo · Iloilo City · Arevalo

Bondulan Point

ILOILO

San Miguel
Bacjao

Santo Rosario

Buenavista

Jordan

Pina

Aguilar

Santa Teresa

Pulupandan · Bago

Nadulao

Nalunga

INAMPULUGAN

Valladolid

La Carlota

Nueva Valencia

San Isidro
Seraray
Nagarao
Nauai

Salvacion
Tondog · Romagangnan

Calabagnan

PANUBULON

Yeto

GUIUANON

Unisan
Malingin

0 5 10 15 20 25km

a	Children clown for the camera
b	Gold site in southern Negros
c	Laundry day on Lubang Island

expensive overnight accommodation at P120 per person as well as a few cheaper rooms at P30 per person. Coming from Iloilo it's wise to book at Pacito or Bebot Mosquera, Pototan (tel Pototan 313) since the resort only has bunks for eight travellers. Make sure to ask about vacant low budget accommodation if you don't want to stay in the expensive cottages. It costs P20 (for the whole boat) to cross over in the hotel's pumpboat.

If the prices for meals in the restaurant are more than you are willing to spend (breakfast P30, lunch or dinner P70) ask the local fishermen to fix food for you. There are some other interesting islands around Nagarao.

Getting There

Boats for Guimaras Island go from Iloilo hourly from 5 am to 5 pm and cost P2.25. They also go to Jordan from near the railway station and to Santo Rosario/Buenavista from Rotary Park. Jeepneys go from Jordan to Nueva Valencia, some as far as Romagangran and Calabagnan but there are no jeepneys in the afternoon returning to Jordan from the latter two villages. From Jordan to San Isidro jeepneys go only once or twice a day so you might have to wait for a long time. The trip takes about an hour. Between Jordan and Buenavista there are only tricycles which cost P15 to 20. The last boat leaves for Iloilo around 5 to 6 pm.

You can continue on from Nagarao Island to Valladolid in Negros on a daily pumpboat, the crossing takes about two hours and costs P10. This boat leaves Calabagnan early in the morning around 3 or 4 am and picks up passengers on some other islands between Guimaras and Negros.

SICOGON & GIGANTE ISLANDS

These islands are off the north-east tip of Panay. Sicogon Island is very beautiful but also, for budget travellers, very expensive. Gigante Norte and Gigante Sur are both very precipitous. There are lots of caves in the rocky crags, the 'enchanted rocks', and innumerable mysterious stories are told about them. It is rumoured that the islands, with their tangled mass of caves and passageways, used to serve as hideouts for pirates.

It is also said that Gigante Sur has 10 caves, only three of which have been discovered to date. Most islanders are too fearful and superstitious to explore them. Others are simply disinterested. Turtle Cave, also known as Pawikan, has a gigantic entrance hall in the top opening and white monkeys can be seen swinging on the roots which hang down. Tiniphagan Cave and Elephante Cave have been even less explored than Turtle Cave and it's quite possible that connections to other caves start here.

A good point of departure for the caves is Barrio Lantangan. You can ask about private overnight accommodation here too — it's up to you how much you pay for it. It's recommended that you hire a guide and take stout shoes, a torch, candles and drinking water. In

a   Sabang Beach, Puerto Galera, Mindoro
b   Inter-island ship

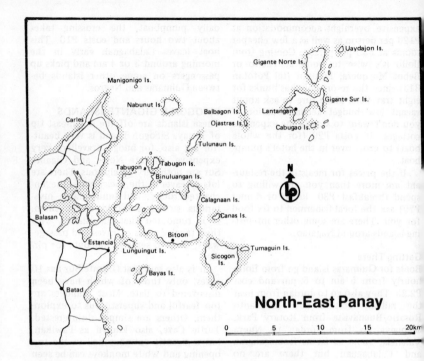

North-East Panay

the vicinity of the caves is a natural swimming hole. On Gigante Norte you can easily reach Langub Cave from Barrio Piaoa. There is a beautiful shore with crystal clear water all along the Barrio.

Just a little to the south of the two Gigante Islands are the small islands of Cabugao Norte and Cabugao Sur. As well as a few huts there is another small cave and a pretty good swimming bay on Cabugao Norte. The settlement on Cabugao Sur is slightly larger. There's a very fine sandy beach and good swimming here.

Estancia, a dirty little town, is the jumping off point for the islands and a stopping point if you take the east coast route from Iloilo to Roxas.

Places to Stay

In Estancia the small *Family Pension House* is about all there is for accommodation. Otherwise you'll have to eat at a sari-sari store.

The *Sicogon Island Club* is not for budget travellers — a cottage for two at this beach resort is over US$40. There is no chance for private accommodation on the island! Enquire at the Sicogon Development Corporation, 2nd floor, Omega I Office, Salcedo St, Legaspi Village, Makati, Manila.

Getting There

Getting to Roxas from Iloilo via the east coast takes two days. First catch an early morning or mid-morning bus to Estancia from the corner of Mabini and Ledesma Sts. The connection to Roxas is on the following day.

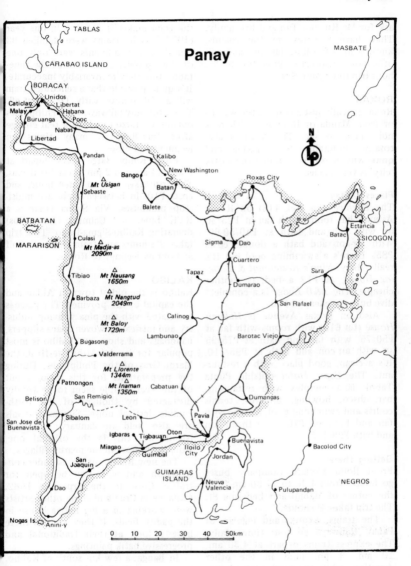

From Estancia boats cross to the Sicogon and Gigante Islands and other destinations. As strangers are usually thought to be here in order to go to Sicogon — and are also thought to be very rich — the special rides on offer are generally very expensive. If you want to go across to the Gigante Islands ask for Mr Rustum Tan and his family. They have relatives on the islands, know a lot of fishing families and can offer you a reasonable price for the 2½ hour trip to Gigante Sur.

ROXAS

Roxas is really just a stop on the way to or from Manila or Romblon — there is not much to see. The town is also totally unsuitable for relaxing and quite why Roxas is awarded the suffix 'city' is very unclear.

Places to Stay

The *Beehive Inn* (tel 418) on Roxas Avenue has rooms with fan at P25/30 or with fan and bath at P40/50-60. With air-con and bath a double costs P85. There's a swimming pool but it's really dirty. *Nino's Restaurant & Lodging House*, at P12 a bed, is another cheapie. The *A&B Lodge* is a complete dive but very cheap at P10.

Also on Roxas Avenue is *Halaran House* (tel 615) with rooms with fan at P50/75, with fan and bath at P75/95 or with air-con and bath at P95/110. It's a clean, good place with a restaurant. The *Capiz Hotel* outside Punta Tabok is a complex with restaurant, bar, disco, bowling, billiards, tennis courts and swimming pool. Rooms with fan and bath are P70/95, with air-con and bath P98/135.

Getting There

From Iloilo Skylark Company buses go hourly from 4.30 to 11.30 am from the corner of Mabini and Ledesma St. The trip takes 4½ hours.

The trains, express and regular, of Panay Railways go four times daily. The express trains depart at 4.30 am, 10 am, 3 pm (and in the other direction) while the regular train leaves at 5.30 am, 8 am and 12.30 pm (and in the other direction). The trip is supposed to take three to 4½ hours but five is usually more like it. That is if the train makes it at all — in one year (1976/77) the trains were derailed 93 times! And derailments were only one of their problems! Beware of the time-tables too, they're invariably inaccurate. It's quite possible that a scheduled train will go 10 minutes early. Or not at all. This is the only railway in the Philippines outside of Luzon and it's a real change after travelling so many times on jeepneys and buses.

From Kalibo large buses depart at 8 and 11 am and 2 pm direct for Roxas. The trip takes two to three hours and costs P10. In between there are multi-stop minibuses. Via Sigma there is a R&K Liner and Calmark (Love Bus) operating Kalibo-Sigma-Iloilo. This trip takes 2½ hours and from Sigma it's half an hour by jeepney to Roxas.

KALIBO

Kalibo is the oldest town in Aklan and the capital of the province. The place is associated with the pina weaving industry and intricately woven abaca slippers, handbags and shoes but Kalibo is most popular for its Ati-Atihan festival, the Mardi Gras of the Philippines. During the preparations for this major event of the year people seem to be totally distracted by thought of the forth-coming festival noise. Similar festivals are also held in January on other islands but this is the original one, along with those in the nearby villages.

The new Kalibo airport is under construction and will soon be open for traffic. Close to the airport in 1982, Chita de la Cruz and some other artists were working in a big native house in the paddy fields. If they are still there have a look at their traditional and progressive batik paintings.

In Banga, a few km south of Kalibo, you can visit the Aklan Agricultural College with its well-equipped experimental station. There are some very interesting experimental plant projects here.

Kalibo

0   100m

1 Buses & Jeepneys to Nabas, Pandan,
   Malay & Caticlan
2 Jeepney Terminal
3 PAL Office
4 Market
5 Moonglow Hotel & Restaurant
6 Philippine National Bank (PNB)
7 Museum
8 Church
9 R&K Liner to Iloilo
10 Aboitiz Lines
11 Kalibo Lodge
12 Calmark Bus to Iloilo
13 High Chapparal Restaurant & Hotel
14 Iris Lodge
15 Everlasting Hotel
16 Little Moonglow Pension
17 Gothong Lines
18 William Lines
19 Casa Felicidad

Places to Stay

The *High Chapparal Restaurant & Hotel*
has rooms at P15 per person. It's a
good, clean place and for the money
about the best value in town. On R
Pastrana St the *Everlasting Hotel* is
another clean, good hotel with rooms
with bath at P20 per person. Or at least
it was before it was burnt out. It could
be more expensive after some renov-

ations have taken place. On the same
street the very simple *Iris Lodge* is just
P14 per person. The *Kalibo Lodge* on
C Laserna St is a simple place in the P15
per person price bracket. In the *Kalibo
Youth Hostel* on Bankaya Avenue dorm
beds are P20.

The *Glowmoon Hotel* on S Martelino
St has singles/doubles with fan and bath at P25/
50 with fan and bath at P55/90, with
air-con and bath at P90/135. It's
another clean, excellent value place and
it has a restaurant where the food,
though not cheap, can be excellent. The
Hotel Ati-Atihan on Old Busuang has
rooms with fan and bath at P35/70,
with air-con and bath at P100/135. It's
got a cocktail lounge, restaurant and
swimming pool (with water?) but it's
difficult to get there in the evenings
without transport. It's also becoming
rather expensive.

Be prepare for an astronomical es-
calation of prices at the time of the Ati-
Atihan festival. An overnight stay can
then cost up to P300. Hotels are mostly
booked out long in advance but you can
try your luck in private houses — where
a piece of floor may cost P20. Special
ships run here from Cebu and Manila
at the time of the festival. You can stay
on board if you booked a roundtrip.

Getting There

From Iloilo R&K Liner and Calmark
(Love Bus) buses go hourly. The last
departure is at 12.30 pm and then again
at 10 pm. The trip takes five hours and
the fare is P22. From Roxas several
buses go from 5 am to 12.30 pm. The
trip takes three hours.

BORACAY

This is a wonderful little island for
lazing around on. It's seven km long and
only one km wide at its narrowest
point. The three larger villagers or Barangays are Yapak, Balabag and Manoc
Manoc, and the numerous smaller ones
(Sitios) are connected by a never

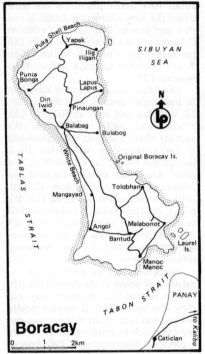

Boracay

0   1   2km

also knows where you can change dollars or travellers' cheques in an emergency, although at a poor rate of exchange. It's better to bring pesos with you, but P100 notes cannot always be changed everywhere.

It seems to have become obligatory when in Boracay to roast one of the flying dogs from the caves at Yapak. Although the islanders understand that this practice is hastening the extinction of this unusual four-legged animal they do not want to go against the peculiar wishes of the foreigners. Along the same lines, they seldom protest openly about what to them is the offensive behavior of the topless tourists on the beaches and even in the villages. Occasionally, when idly conversing with local people, they air their feelings. Then you discover that tourists were allowed on the island at a time when serious poverty and want threatened, due to a drastic fall in the price of copra. Now, however, the people of Boracay are earning money again, and it is good to discover that the money earned does stay with the islanders and doesn't disappear into the coffers of foreign companies.

There are lots of possibilities for leisure and diversion on this holiday island. For P25 you can hire a small sail boat for the whole day. For a third of this you can rent a canoe. An hour's windsurfing costs P30. It remains to be seen how much an hour's horse-riding will cost. A couple of fairly run down old nags are going to be dusted down and trotted out for this. On the other hand diving facilities have been available for ages, and you can get rides to the coral reefs off the neighbouring island for some snorkelling.

After sunset, tuba and dinner a lot of travellers are drawn to the local pubs by the sound of the stereo. Some people like the *Beachcomber* which is popular for dancing if you're in the right mood at a late hour. Others prefer the scene at *Ralf's Place* in Angol, where you can

ending mesh of paths and trails. Because of this complexity the Boracay map only gives a broad overview of the walking routes.

On the west coast the shore is as white as sugar, and the top section near Balabag has particularly fine sand although the water here is very flat. It's deeper in the lower section, where you can even see the coral near the shore occasionally. There are better snorkelling possibilities on the east coast, but you do have to be careful of rips. For years on the beach at Yapak shells were dug out of the sand and sold. It's said that Boracay puka shells are the best, for whiteness and lustre, in the world. Calito, the post master at Balabag still seems to know a good source for these now very rare shells. He lounge around on plush cushions sipping your pina colada, and whiling away the tropical night playing a little chess or backgammon.

Boracay is a lovely dream island but what sandflies! They even beat the north Queensland ones! Their bite is not so annoying (or noticeable) but they just hang on until the blood drips out of you. Some areas of the body are worse than others but if you are at all affected by sandflies be certain to take some repellent with you.

Piers & Jill Beagley

Boracay is a great place but it's really simply another 'international travellers' centre', not the real Philippines at all. Unhappily there's a large population of the 'let's get stoned under a palm tree' mentality who, incredibly, have been pushing dope to the islanders. The first immigration sweep has already occurred — a Batu Ferringhi action replay on the horizon I'm afraid.

Rob Mitchell

Places to Stay

In the last couple of years the accommodation possibilities offered by the original places (like *Williams Place, Happy Home, White Beach Guesthouse*) have been greatly added to by building lots of lovely new cottages. Most of them are located on White Beach between Balabag and Angol. Each cottage has either two single or one double bed, nearly always its own terrace and hardly ever its own bath. Showers and toilets are usually shared by the inhabitants of several cottages. The cost P30 for two people. For single accommodation you can usually get the price down by bargaining, during the off-season. There are only a few guest houses and you pay P15 a single room, eg at *Yap's Rest House* and *Ome's Beach House*, both in Balabag. There is another guest house a little further away in Diniwid.

The Ministry of Tourism has ordered that the cottages can only be built from natural materials. In order to avoid unrestrained construction and uncontrolled deforestation, to make room for the cottages a lot of palm trees need to be felled, future building permits are very difficult to obtain. As well as this it was ruled, after an inspection of the island in 1982, that all houses outside of the 30 metres limit from the beach would have to go. The distance is calculated when the tide is in. A lesson seems to have been learned from the mistakes made in Puerto Galera.

Places to Eat

You can only eat in the guest houses by ordering in advance. If you would rather opt for a spontaneous decision you will find, apart from one or two restaurants in the nearby villages, quite a few good eating places with a large selection of food in Mangayad. The *Villacelo* is famous for its great salads and it also does good spaghetti. You can buy fresh bread at the bakery next door, baked in the evenings in the wood-fuelled stoves.

Happy Home does fantastic pancakes and *Aqua Blue* has first rate squid as well as good Chinese-style food. At the *Starfire* there is a standard menu as well as numerous specials which are changed daily. Then there is the *Travellers Place* where most people prefer to drink after a little eating. Thanks to gas and kerosene fridges most restaurants are now able to offer cold drinks.

Getting There

There is now a direct boat, the large outrigger *MB Jem*, that goes from Kalibo to Boracay. It usually departs after 10 am Saturday from Camanci, the river mouth four km from Kalibo. The trip takes three hours to reach Boracay's White Beach and costs P30. On Sunday it leaves Boracay at 8.30 am for Looc for P25. Monday it returns to Boracay and on Tuesday continues to Kalibo in the morning. On Wednesday it's back to Boracay again and Thursdays it goes nowhere. On Friday it returns to Kalibo about 8.30 am.

It's 1½ hours by jeepney from Kalibo to Nabas and in good weather a boat crosses to Boracay between 10 am and noon. The trip takes two hours. Possibly you'll land on the east coast and have a half hour walk to the white beaches and overnight possibilities on the west coast.

From Kalibo onward travel along the new coast road via Nabas to Caticlan is simpler and from there you can go, usually with very little waiting, in a small boat across to Boracay. Travelling time, including the inevitable flat tyres, is about three hours plus 15 minutes in the boat. The fare is P12 by bus or jeepney then P5 by boat to White Beach. They tend to overload the boats across to Boracay so take care, more than one traveller has lost his gear from a capsized boat. There are always boats travelling past White Beach and if you want to go to Caticlan just wave one down, the fare is the standard P5 and the early morning is the most reliable time.

Check at Roger's about the boat service to Looc on Romblon and the Boracay Air flights to Manila from Malay for P600. That is the pilot that skims over the palm trees of Boracay coming or going from Malay airport. A last minute report from a traveller indicated that William Lines have just started a direct ship between Manila and Boracay.

THE SOUTH COAST

The south coast from Iloilo to Anini-y on the southern tip of Panay and around to San Jose on the opposite coast is full of interest. All along the coast between Arevalo and San Joaquin there are beach resorts with cottages you can rent but the beach and the sea here are not so good. That doesn't stop them being highly recommended, particularly Anhawan at Oton which is nothing special and costs P100/200 for

singles/doubles. You can get a big room for P50/60 at the beach resort in Tigbauan. It's a pleasant place for trips to the spots along the coast and to the Nadsadan Falls in Igbaras, a few km inland.

Guimbal

At the 'home of the sweetest mangoes in Iloilo province' there is a yellowish sandstone church of Spanish-Filipino times and three 16th century watchtowers. From these cone-shaped buildings, now moss-covered, smoke signals were once sent up to warn of pirate attacks.

Miagao

Eleven km further and about 40 km south-west of Iloilo there is an impressive fortress-like church in Miagao. It was built in 1787 in an earthquake-baroque architectural style with two sandstone towers. Its unusual facade is worth seeing, it combines European elements — St Christopher — with Philippine plants — coconut palms, papaya trees.

San Joaquin

The Church of San Joaquin, 15 km further again, was built of white coral in 1869 and its facade is carved as a sculpture of the Spanish victory over the Moors at the battle of Tetuan in Morocco, 10 years earlier. Water buffalo fights take place in San Joaquin on the second Saturday in January each year.

Anini-y

From Anini-y you can easily reach Nogas Island with its white, sandy beaches and its excellent sites for snorkelling and diving. So don't forget to bring your own equipment. Since there is no regular transportation ask the fishermen in Anini-y to bring you there. If you like they can also arrange accommodation for you. While in Anini-y see the old church, a massive building of white coral rock. It was built by Spanish

Augustinian fathers during the Spanish colonial era.

SAN JOSE DE BUENAVISTA

San Jose de Buenavista is a jumping off point for ship services to Palawan. The Binirayan Festival has been changed from the end of December to 28 April-1 May. Some travellers break their journey at Culasi and spend a couple of days on Mararison Island. Getting there takes about 25 minutes on the daily outrigger. Ask at the restaurant about accommodation in Culasi.

Places to Stay

You can get good accommodation here at the *Rizalitos Hotel* — a double with air-con and bath is P135. The *Fatima Lodging House* next door is also good value with basic singles or doubles at P18 per person. You can also try the *G&G Restaurant & Grocery* with rooms at P20 per person but closing time is 9 pm.

Getting There

The Seventy Six Bus Company offers a regular service from Iloilo via Miagao to San Jose de Buenavista, starting at 4 am. Buses leave approximately every 1½ hours or when they are full. The last trip is at 4.30 pm. Travel time can vary greatly depending on the driver. It should only take 2½ hours from Iloilo to San Jose de Buenavista but as a result of four flat tyres this bus ride took me more than six hours.

Travelling north from San Jose de Buenavista you can either take a jeepney to Pandan or a bus to Kalibo. At Pandan there is also a connection to Malay, Nabas and Kalibo. Some jeepneys from San Jose de Buenavista only go as far as Culasi. If you're travelling south from Boracay to San Jose de Buenavista the best way is to go to the road crossing just behind Nabas (from Caticlan) and wait there for a bus or jeepney. Don't go via Malay and Buruanga.

TRANSPORT FROM PANAY

To Cebu Two ships of the William Lines operate direct service between Iloilo and Cebu City. Departure times depend on cruise schedules and the trip takes about 15 hours. Carlos A Gothong Lines operates two ships each week from Roxas and New Washington/Kalibo to Cebu City.

The usual alternative way to Cebu is a boat to Bacolod from Iloilo (P15), bus from Bacolod to San Carlos (P17.50),, the ferry to Toledo (P12) and then a bus to Cebu City (P3). If you are in a hurry take the boat at 7 am from Iloilo to Bacolod and head straight to the San Carlos Bus Terminal to get the bus serving the ferry leaving San Carlos for Toledo at 1.30 pm. If everything works well you will be in Cebu City around 5 pm.

PAL flies daily from Iloilo to Cebu City.

To Luzon Aboitiz Lines operate the *MV Lanao* from Roxas to Manila. It departs on Thursday at midnight and sometimes on Sunday at 6 pm and the trip takes 18 hours. The same company has the *MV Aklan* from Dumaguit/Kalibo to Manila. Departure is on Tuesday at 8 am and the trip takes 16 hours. Services from Iloilo tend to get booked up 10 to 14 days ahead in late May.

The William Lines ship *MV Cagayan de Oro City* goes from Dumaguit or Batan either on Tuesday or Thursday at 3 pm and the trip to Manila takes about 14 hours and costs P65. Some say this is the best ship. You can also get tickets for this boat in Boracay. The *MV Dona Josefina* of Gothong Shipping Lines goes from New Washington/Kalibo on Sunday at 11 am. The trip to Manila takes about 16 hours.

All other services are from Iloilo to Manila. The Sulpicio Lines *MV Don Eusebio* operates on Sunday at 2 pm except when it is engaged on cruises. This is the fastest ship, taking 21 hours.

The other services all take 25 hours and are all operated by Negros Navigation. The *MV Don Claudio* departs on Friday at 1 pm; the *MV Dona Florentina* on Monday and Thursday at 1 pm; the *MV Don Julio* on Sunday at 1 pm; the *MV Santa Maria* on Tuesday at 12.30 pm.

PAL flies daily from Iloilo and Roxas to Manila. Kalibo will be on schedule again after they finish construction of the new airport. For P66 per person you can charter a small aircraft from Malay near Caticlan to Manila – contact Rogers Place on Boracay.

A last minute report from a traveller indicated that William Lines now have a direct service between Boracay and Manila. The ship leaves Boracay on Sunday at about 2 pm and the trip takes 20 hours. The fare is P65 in economy class, P80 in 2nd class.

To Mindanao The *MV Panay* and the *MV Guimares* of the Compania Maritima go from Iloilo to Zamboanga athough cruise schedules may interrupt. Saturdays at 6 pm the *Dona Florentina* of the Negros Navigation Company go from Iloilo to Cagayan de Oro. On Wednesdays at 5 pm the Sulpicio Lines ship *MV Don Eusebio* sails from Iloilo for Zamboanga — again unless cruise schedules intervene. The *MV Davao City* of William Lines leaves Iloilo on Thursday at 6 pm for Zamboanga and Cotabato. The trip to Zamboanga takes 21 hours.

To Mindoro Once weekly, usually on Sunday, a large outrigger-boat sails from Buruanga to Roxas. Special rides from Boracay to Roxas can be arranged as well. On Sundays at 10 am a boat goes from Culasi, Antique to San Jose.

To Negros The *Don Vicente* and the *Princess of Negros* of the Negros Navigation Company go alternately from Iloilo to Bacolod. The trip takes two to 2½ hours. Departure times are often changed but in general they are from Monday to Saturday at 7 am and 3 pm, on Friday at 7 am and 4 pm, on Sunday at 8 am and 4 pm. See the section on Guimaras Island for another possible route to Negros.

To Palawan From Culasi there should be a fast 40 person boat every day to Cuyo, Araceli, Roxas and Puerto Princesa. Ask about when it goes. The *Cardinal Ferry* goes once weekly from San Jose de Buenavista via Cuyo, Araceli and Roxas to Puerto Princesa. The following schedule is not totally reliable:

San Jose	dep Wed 10 am
Cuyo	arr Wed 4 pm
Cuyo	dep Wed midnight
Araceli*	arr Thur 6 am
Araceli*	dep Thur 9 am
Roxas	arr Thur noon
Roxas	dep Thur 3 pm
Puerto Princesa	arr Thur 9 pm
*Dumaran Island	

To Romblon The Aboitiz Lines ship *MV Lanao* leaves Roxas for Romblon on Thursdays at midnight and sometimes on Sundays at 6 pm. The trip takes six hours and the ship continues to Manila.

There is now a regular service from Boracay to Romblon. On Mondays, Wednesdays and Fridays at 7 am a boat gos to Looc on Tablas. The fare is P35 per person. Other possibilities between Boracay and Romblon or Tablas also exist.

Romblon

Romblon is practically in the middle of the Philippine archipelago. The province of Romblon, whose capital is also Romblon, is made up of about 20 islands and islets, the largest of which are Romblon, Sibuyan and Tablas. All three are hilly and Sibuyan is, in addition, still thickly forested.

Due to its large marble deposits Romblon is also known as 'marble country'. According to experts Romblon's marble is at least equivalent to Italy's. It generally comes in large slabs. When tourist ships visit Romblon sales booths are set up on the dockside and marble souvenirs — vases, figures, ashtrays and so on — are offered for sale. Cruise ships generally only stay for a few hours in Romblon and, needless to say, prices then escalate. The trip to Bonbon Beach by tricycle can cost P100 when normally it is only P1! Don't buy anything while there's a cruise ship in port although the local people do differentiate between the tourists and the travellers.

ROMBLON ISLAND
ROMBLON

Romblon is a small port town with one of the best natural harbours in the Philippines. During the typhoon season it is often used as a shelter for endangered shipping.

The two forts in Romblon were built by the Spanish in 1640, and it is said that they have underground tunnels leading to the coast. Today Fort San Andres is used as a weather station. From both forts you can get a grand view of the city with its Spanish-style architecture and the notable St Joseph's Cathedral. This church, built in 1726, has a fine collection of antiquities which can be seen on request.

A trip to one of the island's two lighthouses, Sabang or Apunan, is a good way to spend some time. If you don't suffer from giddiness, and have enough faith in the building, climb up and enjoy the view of palm trees, rocky cliffs and marble quarries.

If you fancy a game of football contact Nelson Lim. He is a football expert and is only too willing to have in-depth discussions on the subject. He will also quickly arrange a game between visitors and his team mates!

Romblon's market is also worth a visit and it has two good beaches, Bonbon and Tree House.

Places to Stay

The *Sea Side Hotel* at the harbour is run by pleasant people and has rooms at P18 per person.

Agnay is a few km south-west of Romblon and here you can stay overnight in the superb *Selangga Tree House* for P20 per person. It's right on the beach and for this price you have use of the cooking facilities and a shower. Full board accommodation costs P75 per person. Check it out with Reylando 'Babette' Festin in Romblon.

A little further south is Mapula. Ask at the port for Jun Tumanon, he has some simple, clean cottages right on the beach for P35 — including three meals — per person, less if you bargain. The beach is not very good but the atmosphere here is friendly and relaxed. It costs P2 by tricycle from Romblon to Mapula.

Beach bungalows at Chamban cost P25 per person and an additional P10

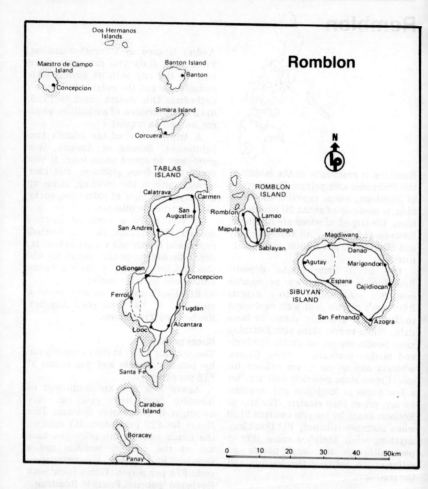

Romblon

Dos Hermanos Islands

Maestro de Campo Island
Concepcion

Banton Island
Banton

Simara Island

Corcuera

TABLAS ISLAND

Calatrava
Carmen

San Augustin

ROMBLON ISLAND
Romblon
Lamao
Mapula
Calabago
Sablayan

San Andres

Magdiwang
Danao
Marigondon

Odiongan
Concepcion

Agutay
Espana
Cajidiocan

SIBUYAN ISLAND

Ferrol

Tugdan
Alcantara

Looc

San Fernando
Azogra

Santa Fe

Carabao Island

Boracay

Panay

0 10 20 30 40 50km

N

to 15 per meal. A sailing boat is available free of charge. For more information see Franzisco Benedicto in Romblon.

TABLAS ISLAND
SAN AUGUSTIN
On the island of Tablas you can use San Augustin as a base to visit the Bitu Falls at Dabdaban and the Cajbo-aya ruins.

Places to Stay
The *S&L Lodge* has rooms at P20 per person but be sure to bargain. There are a couple of other small lodges.

Getting There
From Romblon on Romblon to San Augustin on Tablas there are ferries in the morning from the harbour. There's no exact departure time, just ask. The trip takes 45 minutes. From Looc there

are several jeepneys daily, two hours, P12. They connect with the boat from Romblon.

ODIONGAN

Pronounced 'Odyongan' this is only a way-station to somewhere else. There is nothing worth seeing. Travelling from San Augustin to Odiongan via Calatrava and San Andres you can see the Tinagong Dagat, the hidden lake, in Kabibitan alongside Calatrava. The two lakes have diametres of 100 and 80 metres. From San Andres, Despujols, there is a path leading straight up the Mablaran Falls.

Places to Stay

At the *Anita Fernandez Lodge* rooms are available at P28 per person, food must be ordered in advance. You can also eat in a small restaurant at the market. The *Summer Restaurant* is, supposedly, Odiongan's best place but don't even bother going. All that's being offered are empty shelves and vacant faces. I got the impression they just couldn't cope with guests. Incidentally the sign reading 'Lodge' on the building's facade has not meant anything since 1970.

Getting There

From San Augustin jeepneys depart from the harbour and the trip takes two hours and costs P12. The Odiongan harbour is a bit out of town — tricycles operate a shuttle service there for less than a peso.

LOOC

Looc has a PAL office, buy your ticket here if you plan to fly from Tugdan to Manila.

Places to Stay

You can stay in *Pador's Guesthouse* (the green house) at the Plaza for P12 per person. Very good meals here cost about the same — crab, calamari, chicken, salad, rice, fish and vegetables

all included reported one happy traveller. The very clean *Tablas Pension* costs P18 per person. There are restaurants in the market halls but the food isn't much good.

Getting There

From San Augustin you can get a jeepney direct to Looc. The 45 km trip costs P12. Several jeepneys daily make the one hour trip from Odiongan for P10. Some boats go from Looc to Boracay Island off Panay — ask. Or you can continue further to Santa Fe — there are several jeepneys daily from the park in Looc. The 45-minute trip costs P6.

You can get from Looc or Santa Fe to Boracay — see Transport from Romblon below. Although there are no regular boats from Santa Fe to Boracay it's possible to charter one. You can arrange to stay overnight in Santa Fe with the mayor for P12.

TUGDAN
Places to Stay

Gutierrez Cool Spot is a simple place by the airport. Run by some nice people it costs P12 per person and meals are also available for P12.

Getting There

Several jeepneys daily make the 45 minute trip from the park in Looc. The fare is P6.

SIBUYAN ISLAND

Sibuyan is more mountainous, wilder and less explored than the other two main islands. There are good waterfalls here — the Cataga Falls, Lambingan Falls at Magdiwang and the Kawe-Kawe Falls in Lumbang Este at Cajidiocan, the most heavily populated city on the island. In one of the many sagas and myths about 2050 metre high Mt Guiting-Guiting the many waterfalls are explained like this:

The souls of wealthy land-owners and corrupt politicians are gathered on the mountains where they wait fruitlessly for the day when the proverb about the camel passing through the eye of a needle will come true. According to the scriptures it is easier for a camel to perform that feat than for a rich man to enter the kingdom of heaven. These souls undergo much pain and suffering as they wait and their tears are the source of the great waterfalls. An additional source of frustration for these souls in limbo is their inability to leave the mountain. Their evil deeds in life have created ideal conditions for a thick, impenetrable slime and moss to flourish, making descent impossible.

Another myth claims that a giant magnet in the mountain draws climbers to the moss where they die of hunger. It also affects aircraft instruments, causing them to crash into the mossy mountain.

South of Sibuyan the coral reefs of the small, white-sand Cresta de Gallo Island are well known as a good diving place.

Getting There

There's a daily boat from Romblon to Magdiwang on Sibuyan. It departs between 11 am and 1 pm and the trip takes about two hours.

TRANSPORT FROM ROMBLON

To Luzon The *MV Transmar* and the *MV Kalayaan* go about weekly (usually mid-week) from Romblon on Romblon via San Augustin on Tablas to Lucena City. On Friday (or Sunday) at 6 am the *MV Lanao* of Aboitiz Lines comes from Panay and leaves at mid-day for Manila. The trip takes 14 hours.

Monday morning at 3 am the *MV Santa Catalina*, Visayas Lines comes from San Carlos to Romblon and leaves for Manila after a four-hour stop. The trip takes 15 hours. The Donus Dei Bookstore at the harbour has information.

Each Sunday at midnight the *MV*

Albert of William Lines goes from Odiongan to Manila. The trip takes 15 hours.

PAL flies from Tugdan on Tablas to Manila every day except Saturdays.

To Masbate From Sibuyan Island there's a once weekly ship to Masbate.

To Mindoro The *MB Jan Jan Liner* goes on Thursday at 7 am from Romblon on Romblon via Carmen on Tablas to Bongabong. The fare costs P35. The *MB Joel* goes on Tuesday and Saturday at 8 am on the same route for the same fare. The *MB Joanne* leaves from Looc on Tablas for Roxas at 10.30 am on Saturday. It's a three hour trip for P30. The *MB Jem* from Boracay connects with the Joanne so you can go straight through from Boracay to Mindoro.

Every second day, possibly daily, an outrigger boat goes from Odiongan to Roxas. The trip takes four hours.

To Panay On Friday the Aboitiz Lines ship *MV Juan* comes from Manila at 6 am and an hour later departs for Roxas City. There's a twice weekly boat from Roxas on Mindoro to Looc on Tablas and then on to Kalibo for P37. So if you have no direct connection from Looc to Boracay you can still get there quite easily via Kalibo.

There is now a regular service between Looc on Tablas and Boracay Island. Departures are on Tuesdays, Thursdays and Saturdays and the fare is P35. On Monday at 3 pm the *MB Jem* goes directly to Boracay from Looc. The boat waits for jeepneys from the airport and the trip costs P30. Looc to Boracay takes about two to three hours by motor launch. Sometimes you can get a boat from Santa Fe, also on Tablas, to Boracay.

To Samar The *MV Odeon* goes irregularly from Romblon on Romblon to Catbalogon and on to Cebu.

Samar

The second largest island of the Visayas, Samar lies between Luzon and Leyte. The over two km long Marcos Bridge over the San Juanico Strait connects Samar with Leyte. There are about 180 small islands in the three provinces of Eastern, Northern and Western Samar. Amongst them is Homonhon, where Ferdinand Magellan first set foot on Filipino soil on 16 March, 1521.

The landscape of Samar is hilly and steep with most of the island thickly forested. Only along the coast and in the north around Catarman are there plains. The main crops are rice, maize and sweet potatoes but Samar is not self-sufficient. On the other hand there are good harvests of abacas and coconuts and Borongan in East Samar is a leading centre for copra production.

The inhabitants of Samar are Visayans who call themselves Warays and speak the Waray-Waray dialect. Samar has an unusual climate for the Philippines. Apart from a May-June dry period rain can fall at any time of year although November to February is the wettest period. Typhoons occur from October to November.

The Sohoton National Park is Samar's outstanding natural attraction but it is most easily reached from Tacloban on Leyte. There is also the Blanca Aurora Waterfall at Gandara.

Samar is a trouble zone. There is very often heavy fighting between the New Peoples' Army (NPA) and government troops. Check the situation before you venture inland although the west coast is OK.

ALLEN
Allen is simply the port for the ferry service from Matnog, it has nothing else of interest.

Getting There
Buses and jeepneys from Catarman go in the morning but if possible take a big bus — they're more comfortable. Philippine Eagle Bus Lines and Salvacruz Lines are the operators on this route and the trip takes three to four hours.

CATBALOGAN
Catbalogan hasn't all that much to offer travellers so most people head straight on to Tacloban. It is the jumping off point for trips to the east coast, however. You can change dollars and travellers' cheques at the Philippine National Bank.

Places to Stay & Eat
If you do pause overnight *Tony's Kitchenette* has nice rooms with fan for P15 and good — if expensive — food. The name of the *De Luxe Hotel*, on De Rosario St, must be a joke — make a large detour around this place! The *Town Hotel* on San Bartolome St is a simple place with rooms at P10 per person, P2 more with fan. The *Fortune Hotel*, on De Rosario St, has singles/doubles with fan for P20/40. It's simple but clean and has a good restaurant. *Kikay's Hotel* on Curry Avenue has rooms ranging from P18 for a single with fan to P76 for an air-con double with bath. It's relatively clean and quite good and has a restaurant. Catbalogan's water supply is not the best — you often have to shower Indonesian 'mandi' style with a dipper of water.

You can eat well at the *Fortune*

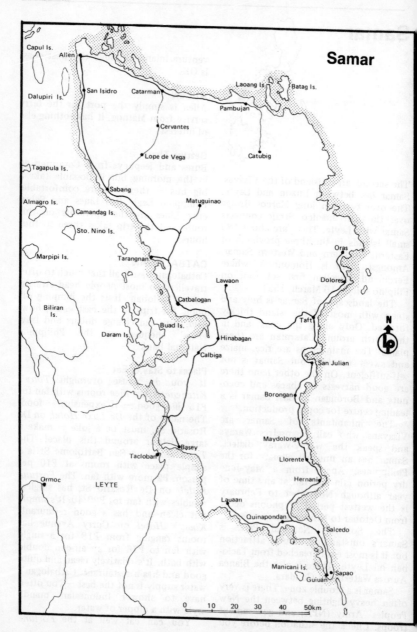

Samar

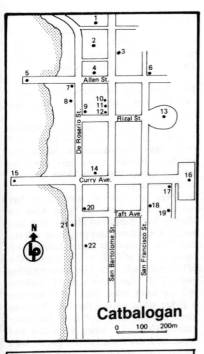

Catbalogan

0   100   200m

1 Church
2 Plaza
3 Pantranco & EV Tranco Buses
4 Buses to Calbayog
5 Pier 2
6 Buses to Tacloban
7 William Lines
8 Fortune Hotel & Restaurant
9 De Luxe Hotel
10 Town Hotel
11 Sweet Lines
12 D'Swing Beer Inn
13 Statue
13 Kikay's Hotel
15 Pier I
16 Samar Capitol Building
17 Court House
18 Samar National School
19 Philippine National Bank (PNB)
20 Lee's Kitchenette
21 Buses to Tacloban
22 Western Samar Shipping Lines

Hotel or the *Kitchenette Inn. D'Swing Beer Inn* is responsible for most of Catbalogan's simple nightlife.

GETTING AROUND
Allen-Calbayog-Catbalogan-Tacloban
The new coastal road from Allen through San Isidro to Calbayog is now open so you no longer need to take the bumpy road through Catarman. The docks in Allen are very close to the Pantranco or EV Tranco bus terminals. Buses from here go right through Calbayog and Catbalogan to Tacloban on Leyte. Travel time Allen-Catbalogan can be as little as three hours and Catbalogan-Tacloban can be just two hours but you should count on six to seven hours total for Allen-Tacloban.

Catbalogan-Catarman If you want to take this route you must be prepared to get up early. The Philippine Eagle bus starts at 4 am, the Salvacruz Lines bus goes at 5.30 am — possibly from the Petron petrol station. The trip takes seven hours.

Catbalogan-Calbayog There are several buses daily and the new EV Tranco ones are best. The trip takes 1½ hours and costs P7 by minibus.

Catbalogan-Borongan-Guiuan A SBL Lines bus departs at 9 am from Pier One to Borongan, travel time is five hours. You should be able to get a jeepney from Borongan to Guiuan on the southern tip of Samar. There is a boat service between Guiuan and Tacloban on Leyte. You can overnight in Guiuan at *Arsenio's Boarding House.*

Catbalogan-Tacloban A large boat operates on this route but if the weather is good it's more interesting to sail through the islands in a pumpboat. Better still would be this boat trip with a quieter engine! Ask at Pier One. There are also several buses daily and the trip takes two hours. There's also a non-stop very fast minibus service which costs P10.

TRANSPORT FROM SAMAR

To Cebu The Escano Lines ship *MV Rajah Suliman* goes from Calbayog to Cebu City every Thursday. Once weekly the *MV Odeon* comes from Romblon to Catbalogan and continues on to Cebu City.

To Leyte Weather permitting there's an outrigger boat from pier one in Catbalogan to Tacloban daily at 9 am. Western Samar Shipping's ship *Helen* goes on the same route on Monday, Wednesday and Thursday at 10 or 11 pm. The crossing takes five hours. Note that only 1st class tickets are numbered, otherwise get there early. Also operating on this route is the *Sweet Rose* or *Sweet Love* of Sweet Lines each Friday and the *Tacloban City* of William Lines on Tuesday.

From the Petron petrol station in Catbalogan there are two buses daily to Tacloban. Departures are at 4 and 11 am and the trip takes four to five hours. The best buses are those of the EV Tranco/Pantranco Company — they're also faster.

Every second day a boat goes from Guiuan on south Samar to Tacloban, usually the *Rey Jamar* or the *Stacey*. The trip takes six to seven hours.

To Luzon PAL flies three or four times weekly from Calbayog and Catarman to Manila.

There are quite a number of shipping services. Sweet Lines have the *Sweet Rose* from Catbalogan to Manila on Sundays. William Lines have the *Tacloban City* on the same route at 6 pm on Wednesdays.

There are several services in the morning and afternoon from Allen to Matnog but things can change with bad weather. Cardinal Shipping have a ferry and there is also San Pablo Lines which operates the *MV Maria Christina* or the *MV Penefrancia*. The two hour crossing costs P12 plus there's a P1 harbour toll on both sides. Make sure you get a ticket when paying the fare. You can sleep on the ferry for free. The ferry carries about 10 buses each trip and buses now run from Leyte right through Samar, cross to Luzon on this ferry and continue to Manila.

Siquijor

The island of Siquijor is 20 km east of the southern end of Negros and is the smallest province in the Philippines. The main towns are Siquijor, Larena, Maria and Lazi. Siquijor is the capital, Larena and Lazi have harbours with services to other islands. There is a surfaced road round this hilly island which connects the well kept villages and small towns. Jeepneys and tricycles are the main form of transport. The people of the island are friendly and unintrusive. The population is about 70,000.

The main industries include agriculture and fishing. Manganese mining in the area north-west of Maria reached its peak before WW II. To date minerals like copper and quartz have not been mined.

When the Spaniards discovered the island they called it 'Isla de Fuega' which means island of fire. From this it would seem that they might have seen a large fire as they sailed by. It is thought that what they really saw may have been the light of countless glowworms. There is a legend that Siquijor used to be entirely underwater for millions of years. Crashing earthquakes, storms and flashing lightning accompanied its emergence from the sea. In fact there is some evidence for this phenomenon in the fossilised mussels, snails and other underwater creatures which can still be found in the central highlands today.

You know for certain that there is something mysterious about Siquijor when you tell a Filipino that you have been there. They'll start relating stories about witches and magicians and healers with wondrous powers. There are many mysterious events on this singular island, which are further enhanced by the practice of voodoo and black magic. It's best to avoid these . . . .

LARENA

This picturesque little place has a few lovely houses but it really only comes to life when a boat docks or sets sail. Or when the locals get together for one of the regular festivals, usually at least twice a week, when they dance uninhibitedly in the streets! Near the market is a large restaurant and jeepneys wait for passengers here.

If you walk from Congbagsa, near Larena, and follow the path which leads right shortly after the National Food Authority, a large white building, you'll come to a beautiful bay with white beaches. If it weren't for the very sharpedged stones which are found in the water the place would be perfect. There is even a freshwater spring in the rocks here.

Places to Stay

The *Tourist Guest House* is near the wharf but only a few minutes on foot from the centre. It's very clean and quiet and costs P15 per person. Smaller, simple inns are located around the boat landing.

SIQUIJOR

The main town (village?) boasts a Provincial Capitol Building, hospital and post office. A little to the west, near Cangalwang, there is a little country road. I don't recommend the beach there.

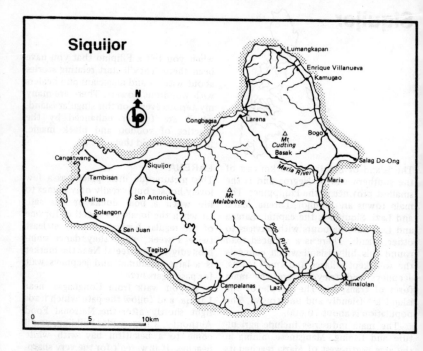

SAN ANTONIO

In the island's hilly interior this is the centre for healers, also known as Man-anambals. The road leading here is bad and if you are travelling by tricycle you will need a lot of effort to make the journey. Don't expect to find a witches' brew in San Antonio, the work of these healers actually has little to do with witchcraft. It's much more an original attempt to effect cures through herbs and other natural ingredients.

A visit to this district during the Easter celebrations would be interesting. The quacks from the southern Philippines come here for a big 'information exchange' and create dubious plant mixtures after performing various obscure rituals.

LAZI

This port has a small landing and is comparable to Larena. On Sundays the rustic cockpit stages well-attended cockfights. The Minalolan coral reefs, a little to the east, are not suited to either swimming or snorkelling.

SALANG DO-ONG

In the northernmost corner of Maria Bay this is a favourite weekend holiday resort of the Siquijodnons. Jeepneys do not go there regularly and you have to walk two km from the road to the small swimming beach. The last trip back to Larena is around 4 pm.

TRANSPORT FROM SIQUIJOR

To Bohol The *MV Sweet Sound* of Sweet Lines goes from Larena to Tagbilaran on Thursday and Sunday at midnight. The trip takes three hours. George & Peter Lines have the *MV Dona Magna* on the same route, departing at noon on Sunday and taking four hours.

To Cebu The *MV Dona Rosario* of George & Peter Lines goes from Larena to Cebu City on Sunday at 9 pm. The trip takes nine hours. The same ship goes from Lazi to Cebu City on Thursday at 8 pm. The trip takes 10 hours.

To Mindanao The *MV Sweet Sound* of Sweet Lines goes from Larena to Plaridel on Saturday and Tuesday at midnight. It's a six hour trip.

To Negros The *MV St Christopher* goes daily at 7 am from Larena to Dumaguete, a three hour trip.

Mindanao & Palawan

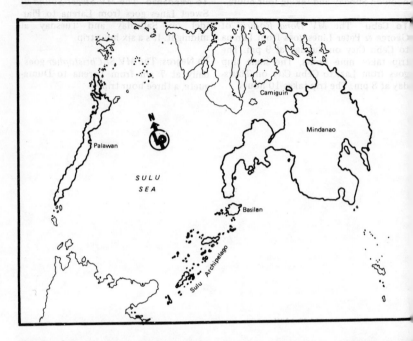

South of the Visayas is the large island of Mindanao, second in size only to Luzon, while to the west is the long narrow island of Palawan. Smaller islands associated with Mindanao include the tiny island of Camiguin off the north coast, the island of Basilan off Zamboanga and the archipelago pointing down to Borneo, the Sulu Islands.

Basilan

The southern end of Basilan meets the north-eastern end of the Sulu Islands and is separated from the south-western tip of Mindanao by the Basilan strait. Since 1973 Basilan has been an independent province comprising numerous small islands as well as the main island. Roughly 200,000 people live here, about a third of them Yakans, an ethnic minority group found only in Basilan. They are peace-loving Moslem farmers and shepherds, who are as well-known

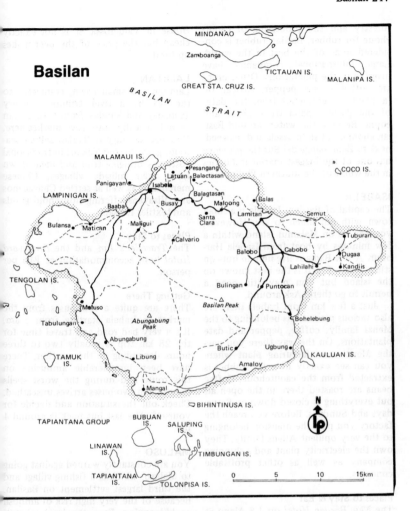

Basilan

MINDANAO

Zamboanga

TICTAUAN IS.

GREAT STA. CRUZ IS.

MALANIPA IS.

BASILAN STRAIT

MALAMAUI IS.

Pesangang

COCO IS.

Latuan Balactasan

Panigayan Isabela

LAMPINIGAN IS.

Balagtasan

Busay Maloong Balas

Baaba Santa Lamitan Semut

Bulansa Matican Maligui Clara

Tuburan

Calvario Balobo Cabobo

Dugaa

Kandiis

Lahilahi

TENGOLAN IS.

Bulingan Puntocan

Basilan Peak

Maluso

Abungabung Peak

Bohelebung

Tabulungan

Abungabung

Libung Butic Ugbung KAULUAN IS.

TAMUK IS.

Amaloy

Mangal

BIHINTINUSA IS.

TAPIANTANA GROUP

BUBUAN IS.

SALUPING IS.

LINAWAN IS.

TIMBUNGAN IS.

TAPIANTANA IS.

TOLONPISA IS.

0   5   10   15km

N

for their hospitality towards visitors as for their colourful, elaborate and detailed ceremonies, festivals and weddings. Apart from the Yakans, Basilan is also inhabited by Chavacanos, Visayans, Samal, Tausug and a few Badjao.

Basilan is very hilly and rugged and relatively unexplored in the centre. It is

said that numerous anti-government rebels have their hide-outs here. In the north of the island the climate is fairly constant, that is there is no obvious dry or rainy period. Rainfall is possible at any time of the year. On the other hand the south has a dry season from November to April.

The main industry of the area is

forestry and the processing of caoutchouc for rubber. Basilan rubber is considered some of the best in the world. Large international companies have invested in the plantations. Other crops are coffee, cocoa, pepper, African oil (a plant oil extracted from the dates of the African palm tree), abaca and copra. Because the waters around Basilan abound in fish, mussels and seaweed, next to Zamboanga del Sur the province has one of the biggest marine industries in the whole of the southern Philippines.

ISABELA

The capital of Basilan, Isabela is a small town with not much to see. However, you can be on Malamui Island within a few minutes by boat from Isabela Harbour. A few Badjaos live here in huts on stilts. White Beach is the best known on the island but you may still need a permit to go there. Ask around.

Just a few km from Isabela there are also various plantations belonging to the Menzi family; coffee, pepper and date plantations. On the way there you pass the Menzi manufacturing plant where you can see exactly how the rubber is extracted from the caoutchouc. Coffee beans are roasted there in the open air but everything is closed down on Saturdays and Sundays. Before you reach the factory you pass the mansion belonging to the very opulent Allens family. They own the electricity plant and a shipping company as well as other profitable concerns.

Places to Stay & Eat

The *New Basilan Hotel* on J S Alano St has singles from P15 to 25 or rooms with fan and bath from P30. The New Basilan is better than the nearby *Selecta Hotel.*

The restaurant in the New Basilan is very well run but you can eat better and more economically in the *New International Restaurant* (general merchant). The food in *Awin's Ice-cream*

House in Valderossa St is not exactly cheap but the price of the beer makes up for it.

LAMITAN

Lamitan is a small town, connected to the sea by a river tributary. Every Thursday and Sunday from 6 to 11 am there is a really impressive market here. You can see ragged Badjao selling seafood, gaily dressed Yakans in traditional costumes bringing fruit and meat down from their hillside villages, Chinese merchants, as well as settled Chavacanos and Visayans offering household goods and textiles for sale.

Places to Stay

The *Traveller's Inn* and the *Boulevard Hotel* have accommodation at P16 per person.

Getting There

There are quite a few buses from the market in Isabela starting from 5 am. It's a very bad road and travel time for the 28 km trip is usually two to three hours depending on the weather. There have been innumerable ambushes on this route and during the worst spells only one in two buses arrives unscathed. Check out the situation and decide for yourself. The last bus back is around 4 pm.

MALUSO

You are constantly warned against going to Maluso, which is a fishing village and the third largest settlement on Basilan, because of the very high risk of ambush or kidnapping. Even the local inhabitants, not just the usual collection of scare-mongers, will warn you against this trip and they are to be taken seriously. So if you want to go anyway make absolutely certain you know exactly what is involved.

TRANSPORT FROM BASILAN

Five times a day one of the Basilan

Shipping Lines' large ships leaves Isabela for Zamboanga. Departures are at 6.30 and 9.30 am, 12.30, 2 and 3.30 pm and the trip takes 1½ hours. Every morning there is a ship leaving Lamitan for Zamboanga, the wharf is outside of Lamitan. Connections to the islands of the Sulu Archipelago are irregular. It's better to go to Zamboanga first and travel from there.

Camiguin

Camiguin is located off the north coast of Mindanao — it's quite an idyllic, get-away-from-it-all sort of place. There are many springs and falls and seven volcanoes on this relatively small island, the most famous is the Hibok-Hibok Volcano which last erupted in 1951. Lanzones orchards on its slopes are the best in the Philippines. The colourful Lanzones festival takes place in Mambajoa at the end of October (usually 24 and 25 October) each year.

The hospitality of the Camiguenos is famous and it's certainly one reason why visitors like to come back to Camiguin — the word Camiguin is pronounced like 'come again'. Instead of 'hi Joe' the people usually greet you with 'hi friends'! It is possible to travel around the island by tricycle and jeepney from Mambajao, the capital city (or village?). There are, however, scarcely any vehicles between Yumbing and Catarman.

Camiguin has been an autonomous province since 1966. It still gets relatively few visitors. Note that this is a volcanic island and there are no white sandy beaches around the coastline — it's volcanic rock or odd patches of coarse, black sand. Also the volcanoes tend to catch the clouds in the wet season and there can be a lot of rain. The rainest months are from December to mid-March and fine weather can only be guaranteed from April to June.

MAMBAJAO

The capital of Camiguin is the main accommodation and travel centre. It also has a branch of the Philippine National Bank where you can change travellers' cheques, but the rate of exchange in Cebu is better and it's better still in Manila. In the Capitol Building here there is a section for tourists which could be of use. You may laugh but 'anyone for tennis?' is not such an odd question to ask in Mambajao — there are two good courts. If you're interested you can get more information about them from Mrs Tia's son.

Places to Stay & Eat

The *Tia Lodging House*, next to the Municipal Hall, and the *Caves Lodging House* both have rooms for P15 per person. Slightly more expensive, the *Camiguin Travel Lodge* costs P20 per person and is run by a dropped-out Filipino ad man who is a fund of knowledge on local attractions and events. It's very noisy in the early morning because the location is just across from the market. The Travel Lodge also has a restaurant. For a good cheap meal in Mambajao try grilled fish in the market.

Out of town there are several beach bungalows, some with kitchens, for less than P20 per person or up to P100 with full board. They're good value. Just a five minute walk from the town proper at Cabua-an Beach there is *Gue Cottage*. It's clean and quiet and costs P25 for two people. Contact Mrs Gue in Mambajao, her house is across from the Caltex station.

HIBOK-HIBOK VOLCANO

Standing 1320 metres high, Hibok-Hibok is the most active of the seven volcanoes of Camiguin. In December 1951 it erupted without warning killing over 2000 people. A small collection of photographs and news

250

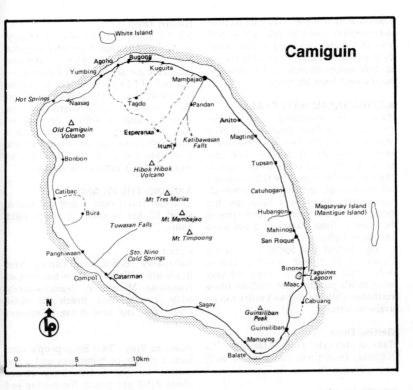

Camiguin

White Island
Bugong
Agoho
Yumbing
Kuguita
Mambajao
Hot Springs
Naasag
Tagdo
Pandan
Old Camiguin
Volcano
Esperanza
Anito
Magting
Katibawasan
Falls
Itum
Bonbon
Hibok Hibok
Volcano
Tupsan
Catibac
Catuhogan
Mt Tres Marias
Bura
Hubangon
Magsaysay Island
(Mantigue Island)
Tuwasan Falls
Mt Mambajao
Mahinog
Mt Timpoong
San Roque
Panghiwaan
Sto. Nino
Cold Springs
Binone
Taguines
Lagoon
Compol
Catarman
Maac
Sagay
Cabuang
Guinsiliban
Peak
Guinsiliban
Manuyog
Balate

N

0   5   10km

paper cutting can be seen at Comvol Station, the seismographic organisation which monitors volcanic activity. The team at the station will quite happily show you over the place and explain to you the uses of the seismographic instruments. They appreciate small gifts from the outside world.

Also for a small fee someone will guide you up to the volcano and arrange a night's lodging at the station. The Provincial Tourism Office used to arrange guides but one traveller wrote that they no longer do, better check this first. Their guides charge P50 and go over Esperanza, a shorter but steeper route. Alternatively, you can ask to be directed to Artemisio Salvo who lives at the edge of the town of Itum. He and

his son Enrico will act as guides for P30 to P40. If you want to start in Naasag ask for Dory Lagunay, he's a guide too.

It is not practical to make the trip without a guide as there is no specific path. There are times when you walk through metre-high grass and the whole area looks much the same. Also the weather is very changeable around the volcano; clouds can roll in quickly and it's easy to become completely disorientated. If you make an early start you'll have no worries about accommodation. Once at the top you can climb down to a moss-encircled crater lake, it takes about 45 minutes. If you do decide to visit the lake it would be wise to spend the nights before and after the trek at Comvol

Station as it will save you a lot of time. Alternatively you can take a tent with you and spend the night in the mossy field beside the lake. Comvol Station is at 400 metres altitude and is about an hour's walk from Mambajao.

KATIBAWASAN WATERFALL

There's good swimming at this waterfall, three km from Pandan. A tricycle will take you the two km from Mambajao to Pandan, from where you have to walk. The trail turns to the right at the end of the town. The falls are about 50 metres high and the water is refreshingly cold. There is a resthouse but bring your own food, the best time to be there is from 10 am to 2 pm when the sun is high.

The Ardent Hot Spring is a natural swimming pool with water at almost 40°C. This area will be improved very soon so it's possible that facilities like a resthouse with shower and toilet will be available already.

Getting There

Take a tricycle from Mambajao to Kuguita, from there you have to walk about 2½ km.

WHITE ISLAND

White Island is a small island about three km north of Agoho. It's a simple sand spar so there's only sand and coral — no shade, but good diving. Since most of the fishermen who fish in this area visit the island you are seldom alone. In the mornings you can buy any quantity of fresh fish and, if you are lucky, you can catch the crabs which live in the sand and are good to eat. There is not much else on the island so take firewood, food, sun protection and a sleeping bag — particularly if you intend to stay overnight. A tarpaulin or tent is definitely needed as shelter from the constant winds — you will find most equipment you need in Mambajao.

Getting There

It's 15 minutes by tricycle or jeepney to Agoho. Although there are no regular boat connections to White Island you can easily get across with a fisherman — at a cost of P25 per boat. You then have to stay all day on the island and, if you don't want to stay overnight, you should arrange a definite time to be picked up. Getting out and back will double the price but you should be able to bargain it down to P40. You can also rent boats in Yumbing and Naasag.

AROUND THE ISLAND

You can travel right round the island, about 65 km in total, in about eight hours.

Kuguita

Mahayahay Beach and Turtles Nest Beach are at Kuguita, three km west of Mambajao. Mahayahay Beach is sandy while Turtles Nest Beach has some coral. You can hire diving equipment here.

Places to Stay Two Swiss people have built a couple of bungalows and a restaurant on the beach. They charge about P100 per person for lodging and three meals. Four km further west in Agoho there is the *Agohay Beach Resort.* The cottages have western-style baths and are equipped with cooking facilities. They cost P75 for two. It's a quiet place with a sandy beach and good sunsets.

Hot Springs & Bonbon

About an hour's walk outside of Naasag, three km south-west of Yumbing, you find the Tangub Hot Springs where you can sit on a stone in the sea and bathe. At mid-tide the springs are a mixture of seawater and freshwater at bathtub temperature. There's also good coral in this area.

Bonbon has some interesting church ruins and a cemetery which is submerged in the sea. Some years ago grave stones could be seen at low tide but now you need imagination to conjure up the cemetery. Snorkelling is very good in this area.

Getting There   Go by tricycle from Mambajao to Naasag, from where you can walk to the hot springs. The connection from there to Bonbon is very bad, it may be better to walk.

Tuwasan Falls
Just outside of Catarman is a track which goes to the Tuwasan Falls. The local people compare the two most significant falls of Camiguin with two different women; one, Katibawasan, who wears lots of make-up; the other, Tuwasan, a natural, untouched beauty. It is said that a hydroplant will be built here in 1983.

The nearby Santo Nino Cold Springs are refreshingly cool and you can swim in a nice large pool which is 1½ to two metres deep. There is a small store, a picnic shelter and toilets. The place is also known as the Kiyab Pool.

South of the Island
Guinsiliban, a village in the south of the island, has a 300 year old Moro watchtower which you may like to visit. Between Binone and Maac is the exquisite artificial lake, Tanguine Lagoon. It's a 10 minute walk from Binone, about two km from the wharf. Boats travel from Binone to Magsaysay Island, a popular diving area nearby.

Places to Stay   At the lagoon you can stay at the *Travel Lodge Lagoon* which is associated with the Camiguin Travel Lodge. It's a quiet place right on the lagoon and costs P25 per person or with private bath it's P30 per person. There's a good restaurant built on the water and they have their own generator so there is electricity from 6 to 10 pm.

Opposite   Magsaysay   Island   in

Mahinog is the *Mychellin Beach Resort*, a western-style resort with doubles for P50. Coffee is free of charge and there is electricity from 6 to 9 pm.

Magting
If you have time, visit the million year old caves at Magting. Here you can see the skeletons of the primitive tribes and the tools, weapons and utensils they used. There's only a pebble beach here but you can rent outrigger canoes and snorkels from the cottages. Magting is about seven km from Mambajao, P2 by jeepney.

Places to Stay   At Magting you can stay at *Sancho Padilla Cottages* for P35 per person. The cottages have a kitchen, bathroom, sittingroom and spacious verandah.

Getting Around
For the best connections on a circuit of the island it's best to start early but be prepared to get stuck and if necessary to walk a few km. Between Mambajao and Binone several jeepneys and buses travel all day long, Binone is the port for Camiguin. There is also regular transport between Binone and Catarman, the second largest town. Along the west coast from Mambajao to Catarman and vice-versa there is only one jeepney every day. It leaves Mambajao at about 4.30 am and Catarman at 6 am.

For short distances you may use tricycles but the service is only good in Mambajao. You are more independent if you rent a motorcycle, there is no commercial rental in Mambajao but some owners will rent their bikes for P55 a day — bargain.

TRANSPORT FROM CAMIGUIN
To Cebu   The *MV Dona Filomena* of Bisaya Shipping leaves Binone Sunday lunchtimes and sails first to Butuan and doesn't arrive at Cebu City until Tuesday lunchtime.

To Mindanao There are three ships daily from Binone to Balingoan. They depart at 5.30 am, 8 am and at 12 noon. On Tuesday and Saturday at 12 midnight there's a ship from Binone to Cagayan de Oro, travel time is five to six hours. The *MV Dona Filomena* to Cebu City sails via Butuan, departing on Sunday at lunchtime.

Sulu Islands

The Sulu Islands are at the extreme southernmost tip of the Philippines. They stretch for about 300 km from Basilan to Borneo and divide the Sulu Sea from the Celebes Sea.

A well-known pirate hangout these waters are avoided by knowledgeable sailors wherever possible. Sailing vessels and trading ships have been boarded by pirates and raided. In August 1981 the 134-tonne *Nuria 767* was attacked by pirates and 10 people murdered. There are also often bloody battles between pirates and smugglers.

The Sulus comprise about 2600 islands clustered together in one large group, divided into the sub-groups Jolo (pronounced Holo), Samales, Pangut-aran, Tapul, Tawi-tawi, Sibutu and Cagayan de Tawi-tawi (Cagayan Sulu). There are two provinces, Sulu with Jolo as its capital and Tawi-tawi with Bongao as its capital. Basilan Island is a separate province from the Sulus.

Attempts by the Spanish to gain a foothold on these islands failed and the Americans had little more success. Presently the government troops are trying to prevent the MNLF (Moro National Liberation Front) from realising its aim of political autonomy.

People of the Islands

Among the most significant minority groups on the archipelago are the Samal and the Badjao. Both groups seem very gentle and peaceful. The main islands of the Samal are Siasi, Tawi-tawi and Sibutu. These people are Moslem and make their living predominantly from fishing, agriculture, and small time trading. Their houses are always close to the water's edge, often even standing in the water on pylons.

The Badjao live on boats scattered throughout the entire archipelago, but concentrated around Tawi-tawi and Sibutu. They are sea-gypsies, and are generally held to be animists. A lot of them, especially those who have given up the nomadic way of life and, like the Samal, are settled in stilt villages, have adapted to the new environment and converted to Islam. Of all the inhabitants of the Sulu Islands, Badjao are on the lowest rung of the social ladder. Like the Samal, they feel oppressed by the Tausug, the largest, and economically and politically most dominant tribe.

The Tausug are Moslem and are considered to be powerful, full of fighting spirit, and freedom loving. Quite a few generations have made their living from booty, the slave trade, and smuggling. The native inhabitants of the Sulu Islands, are the Buranun, and are said to have been the forefathers of the Tausug. They were originally converted to Islam, as most of the inhabitants of the archipelago up to the present day have been. Apart from the sea-gypsies, there is also a small community of catholics and Buddhists on the islands.

Visiting the Sulu Islands

To the end of 1981 the Sulu Islands were totally out of bounds to visitors. You could sail on any boat leaving Zamboanga, but without a permit you were not allowed to disembark. Permits were issued at the military camp in Manila

255

(Ministry of Defence, Camp Aguinaldo).

Sometimes you could apply to the division stationed in Zamboanga, the south western command (SOWESCOM), but generally you would be redirected to the head office in Manila. If you did not have an acceptable reason, such as an officially recognised study proposal on the Badjao or Tausug, you could give up any hope of ever getting a permit.

That has now been changed (temporarily?). Foreigners are allowed in without a visa and are allowed unrestricted movement and unlimited stay. This sounds great, but in reality the situation is a little different. A lot of islands and sections of islands are still inaccessible because of continuing tension (eg Jolo and Tawi-tawi). Other exotic islands are so nearly within reach but no one will sail to them because of fears of pirate activity or because the inhabitants are feared or hated (eg Laa near Simunul and Sipangkot near Tumindao).

It is absolutely imperative to take warnings seriously. When I wanted to cross from Bongao to Bilatan the boatsman responded with a cheerless 'maybe tomorrow'. That evening there was quite a shoot-out on Bilatan. Just a few days earlier I was refused a ride from Bongao to Laa for fear of ambush. The

following night you could not miss hearing a long exchange of shots from across the sea. The marine escort given our ship on the trip from Sitangkai to Bongao was probably there for a reason too.

Added to this are various quite severe accommodation and water shortages. In Jolo and Bongao there is only one simple commercial accommodation possibility. Apart from this you must seek private accommodation where, understandably, you can expect to pay the market price. On the southern islands, like Bongao, Sibutu, Tumindao, and Sitangkai, there is apparently quite a severe water shortage. You get a guilty conscience just brushing your teeth. Cutlery is washed in sea-water polluted with sewage and rubbish. You can practically hear the hepatitis knocking on your liver.

Nevertheless I must say that a trip to the Sulu Islands offers an entirely new kind of Filipino experience. The impressions gained are manifold and memorable and more than make up for the effort.

Getting Around

You usually get to the Sulu Islands from Mindanao or Basilan. For getting

facing this page — Sulu Islands

a Sitangkai, the 'Venice of the Far East'
b Sea gypsies in the Sulu Sea

facing the next page — On the water

a Basligs anchor off Zamboanga City
b Children on an outriggerboat

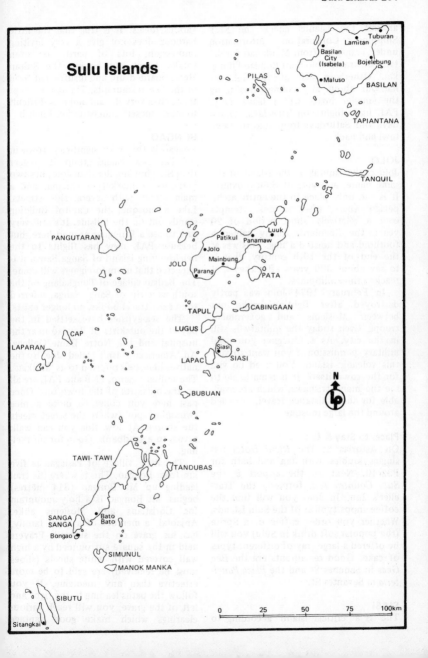

Sulu Islands

Tuburan
Lamitan
Basilan
City
(Isabela)
Bojelebung
Maluso
BASILAN

PILAS

TAPIANTANA

TANQUIL

PANGUTARAN

Patikul
Luuk
Panamaw
Jolo
Mainbung
JOLO
Parang
PATA

CABINGAAN

TAPUL

CAP
LUGUS

LAPARAN
Siasi
SIASI
LAPAC

BUBUAN

TAWI-TAWI
TANDUBAS

SANGA
SANGA
Bato
Bato
Bongao
SIMUNUL
MANOK MANKA

SIBUTU

Sitangkai

N

0   25   50   75   100km

around the islands check the SKT Shipping Corporation information under Transport from Mindanao for details of travel Jolo-Siasi-Bongao-Sitangkai. Otherwise ask at the relevant harbour about any connections using the smaller boats which leave daily. PAL have flights on Tuesdays, Thursdays and Saturdays from Jolo to Tawitawi and back.

JOLO

Jolo is the capital of the island of the same name, and also of Sulu province. It is the only place in the entire archipelago where, after various attempts over a relatively short period of 20 years, the Spaniards finally gained a foothold and hoisted a flag. This was at the end of the 19th century, that is to say about 300 years after they first reached the Philippines.

In February 1974 Jolo was partly destroyed after fighting broke out between Moslems and government troops. Even today the military is still in the city. As a foreigner you need military permission if you want to visit this volcanic island. You need no visa for the town itself. It is remarkable to see the many trishaws, which are available for short distance travel, crowded around the large mosque.

Places to Stay & Eat

On Astorias St the *Ricni Hotel* has singles/doubles with fan and bath for P22/40. Next to the airport is the *Sulu Country Inn*, formerly the Traveller's Inn. In Jolo you will find the coffee shops typical of the Sulu Islands. Whether you order coffee or a Sprite (the popular soft drink in Sulu) you will be offered a large tray of different types of cake. Good restaurants are the *Bee Gees* in Sanches St and the *Plaza Panciteria* in Sevantes St.

SIASI

This is a 'critical island' according to various locals. It is true that the little harbour does not give a very inviting impression; lots of partly or even totally burnt out houses, the Sultan Hotel boarded up, and insufficient food in the few restaurants. The people kept themselves very distant and it is difficult to make oneself understood in English.

BONGAO

Bongao is the most significant town in the Tawi-tawi island group. It's bigger than Siasi but smaller than Jolo, has two harbours, a market, a cinema, and a main street with several side streets. Like a mosque, the Capitol Building stands out on the hillside. It's still very rare to see a foreigner around here, but because PAL now has flights to the neighbouring island of Sanga Sanga it is expected that more foreigners will come. The Badjao village of Tungkalang on the south-west tip of Sanga Sanga, referred to in early travel books, no longer exists.

The sea-gypsies have settled in the bay at the outskirts of Bongao near the hospital and the Notre Dame College. An 'Americano' isn't called 'Joe' by the natives here, he's referred to as 'Milikan'. The military camp, PNB and PAL are all on the outskirts of the town too. Once past here you come to quite a nice swimming spot (where the street meets the shore). At low tide you can walk across to a sandbank. Good for snorkelling.

The little village of Pasiagan is five km from Bongao. This is where the trail leading up Mt Bongao (314 metres) begins. Mt Bongao is a holy mountain for Christians and Moslems alike. Anjaotal, a member of a royal family, has his grave on the summit. Prayers held in the square surrounded by a high wall covered with white sheets (shoes must be removed) are said to be more effective than any medicine. If you follow the paths leading to the right and left of the grave, you will reach various clearings which make good vantage

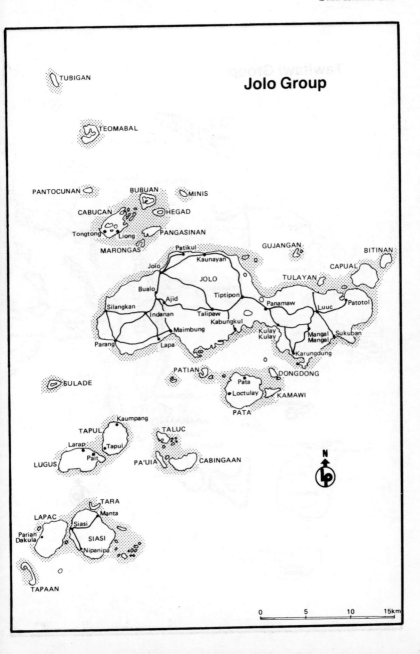

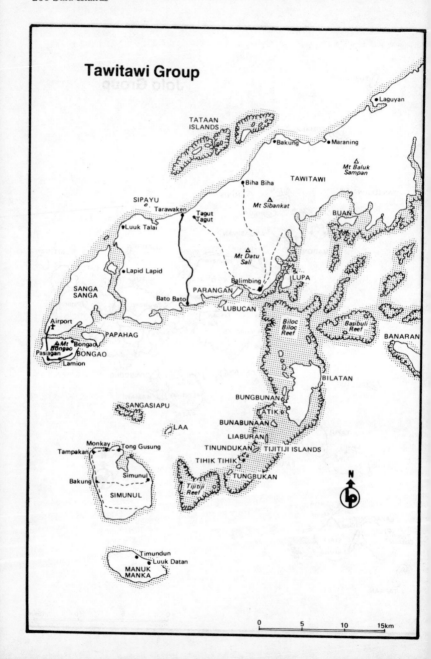

Tawitawi Group

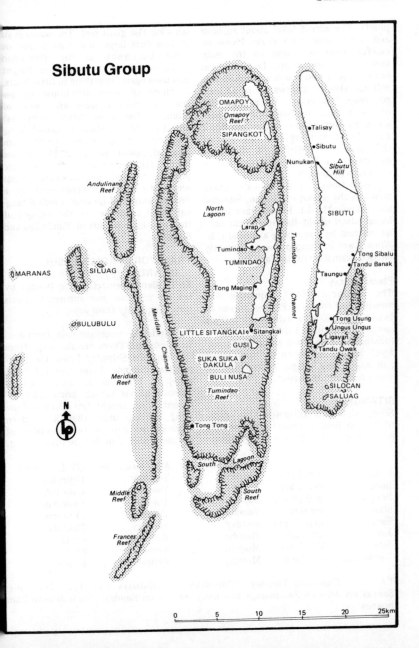

points. The ascent takes about an hour and is tiresome and tedious. Please be careful, your behaviour on this holy mountain is important. Local custom has it that if you touch a monkey you will die shortly afterwards, or at least go completely insane. It's a good idea to take bananas for the monkeys. There are numerous unseen snakes, so don't grab blindly at every tree and vine. At the start of October a fiesta is celebrated in Bongao and the hill is overrun with people.

From Bongao you can catch small boats to the island of Bilatan, Simunul and Manuk Manka. Bunabunaan is the burial island of the Badjao and can only be reached by organising a special ride. When I was in Bongao I was constantly advised against a visit to Tawi-tawi.

Places to Stay

The *Southern Hotel*, opposite the mosque, has rooms at P20 per person or better doubles with bath at P90. It's a simple hotel with a lovely balcony overlooking the main street and a restaurant. *Lyn's Snacks* is also on the main street and has a very simple cottage by the water for P10 per person.

SITANGKAI

Sitangkai is also known as the Venice of the Far East. It's said that more than 6000 people live in the houses built on

stilts on the giant reef. The water is so shallow that large ships have to anchor three km away in the Tumindao Channel and must ferry their freight and passengers from there in little boats.

There are more stilt-house villages scattered over a large area west of Sitangkai. The largest village (50 houses) and the most distant is called Tong Tong, and is not far from the Meridian Channel, which is 50 to 100 metres deep. Like elsewhere the Badjao have planted seaweed and seawrack forests under the water. Sea-cucumber are a further source of income. From Sitangkai small boats sail to the villages of the two larger islands of Tumindao and Sibutu.

TRANSPORT FROM THE SULU ISLANDS

To Basilan Connections to Basilan by sea are irregular but apparently boats leave frequently from Jolo.

To Mindanao Ships sail daily from Jolo to Mindanao. There are also ships from the Magnolia Shipping Lines, the Sampaguita Shipping Lines and the SKT Shipping Corporation which sail to Zamboanga via various ports. The *MV Queen Helen* caught fire at sea in June 1982 but has more than likely been replaced, so here is the timetable of the three SKT ships before the accident.

		MV Queen Helen	MV Dona Isabel	MV Lady Ruth
Sitangkai	dep 1 pm	Sunday	Tuesday	Thursday
Bongao	dep 5 am	Sunday	Tuesday	Thursday
Bongao	dep 10 am	Sunday	Tuesday	Thursday
Siasi	arr 6 pm	Sunday	Tuesday	Thursday
Siasi	dep 10 pm	Sunday	Tuesday	Thursday
Jolo	arr 2 am	Monday	Wednesday	Friday
Jolo	dep 5 am	Monday	Wednesday	Friday
Zamboanga	arr 2 pm	Monday	Wednesday	Friday

PAL have flights on Tuesdays, Thursdays and Saturdays from Tawi-tawi (Sanga Sanga) via Jolo to Zamboanga and daily, except on Sundays, from Jolo to Zamboanga.

Mindanao

Mindanao is the second largest island of the Philippines. Its landscape is dominated by mountain chains running north-south. Close to Davao is Mt Apo, the highest mountain in the Philippines. Mindanao is one of the richer islands of the Philippines even though little of its mineral wealth has yet been tapped. At present agriculture is the main source of income — there are large pineapple plantations at Cagayan de Oro, banana plantations at Davao and forestry projects are rapidly expanding.

It is not, of course, true that only Moslems live in Mindanao but it is true that the majority of the Philippines' Moslems live there and on the nearby Sulu Islands. The area around Lake Lanao in central Mindanao is a highly Moslem area.

There has been an on-going struggle for an autonomous Moslem state on the island for some years. The battle between the MNLF (Moro National Liberation Front) and the government troops can present some dangers to travellers although, as usual, these situations are often portrayed as being worse than they are. Nevertheless you should enquire about possible disturbances before making overland trips in western Mindanao. Avoid buses carrying soldiers — these are especially likely to be shot at.

SURIGAO

There are a number of beautiful small islands near Surigao which can be reached from General Luna on the island of Siargao. They include the islands of Guyam, Daco La Janoza, Anahawan and Mam-on. On La Janoza Island visitors are splashed with water by locals just before they want to leave — to ensure they'll stay longer at least until their clothes are dry! Note that in December and January it can still rain very heavily in north-east Mindanao but 'waterproof' travellers will be recompensed by a great untouched landscape along the east coast.

Places to Stay

The *Fredden Hotel* on Borromeo St is a simple hotel but with big beds. Rooms with fan are P30. On the same street the *Litang Hotel* costs P20 for a single, rooms are small. On San Nicolas St the *Garcia Hotel* has singles/doubles with fan at P25/50 or with fan and bath at P80/90. With air-con and bath they're P100/110. It's a clean, good hotel but don't bother with their P10 breakfast.

Back on Borromeo St the *Tavern Hotel* costs P60/70 for rooms with fan and bath, P90/100 with air-con and bath. It's another pleasant hotel and has a seaside restaurant.

SIARGAO ISLAND

It's a beautiful trip through superb island scenery (many Boracays!) from Surigao to Siargao Island where you arrive at Dapa. Bring enough pesos with you, the bank in Dapa doesn't change travellers' cheques or cash dollars. A jeepney runs from Dapa to the small town of General Luna where you should try poot-poot, an excellent, if a little pricey, local fish dish.

There are said to be crocodiles at Numcia, 24 km from General Luna. Around Pilar and Del Carmen you can find mangrove swamps with 'water-

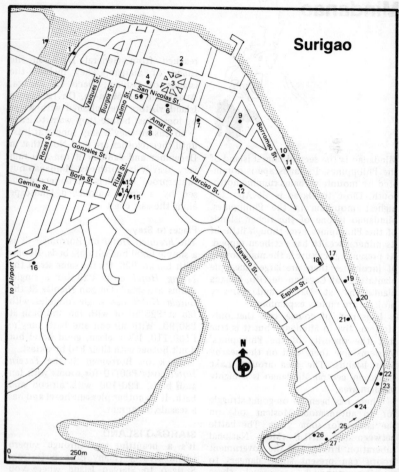

Surigao

streets'. It's worth doing a daytrip by outrigger but don't forget your mosquito repellent. Between Dapa and General Luna there is a beautiful long, white, sandy beach at Union. On the east side of the bay there are two empty huts, you can cross the bay by a small paddle banca. Bring your own food.

A road along the coast connects Dapa and Union but the jeepneys go on the main road, parallel but a little

further north towards General Luna. At about the half-way point you can see a hill on the left side and a lone house on the right side. Get off here and follow the steep path down to the beach. This path will continue along the coast to General Luna.

Places to Stay

In Dapa you can stay at the guest house of the Health Station. Ask the mayor first. It's P40 per person and includes three meals. In General Luna accommodation is available with Father Oscar Fabroa at the church rectory but ask politely. If you can't get a room here ask the mayor.

1 Ferries to Liloan & Leyte
2 City Hall
3 Plaza
4 Lodge & Restaurant
5 Perlas Restaurant
6 Church
7 Garcia Hotel
8 Northeastern Mindanao College
9 Market
10 Litang Hotel
11 Superlines Bus Terminal
12 PAL Office
13 Philippines National Bank
14 Post Office
15 Grandstand
16 Provincial Hospital
17 Long Distance Telephone Company
18 Superstar Bus Terminal
19 Fredden Hotel
20 Tavern Hotel & Restaurant
21 Church
22 Sweet Lines
23 Small Bars
24 George & Peter Lines
25 Wharf
26 Philippine Port Authority (PPA)
27 Ferries to Dapa, Siargao Island

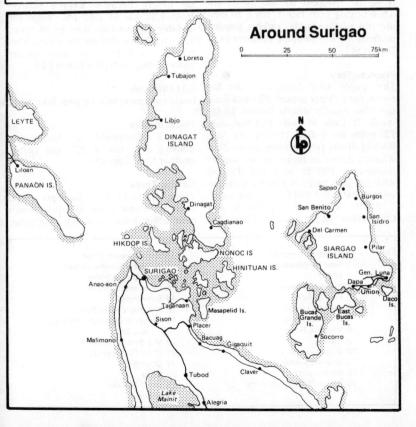

Around Surigao

Getting There

Boats depart Suriago between 10 am and noon (depending on the load) for the five to six hour trip to Dapa on Siargao Island. At 7 am daily a goes Surigao to Loreto on Dinagat Island. It arrives late afternoon after many stops on the way.

BUTUAN

Butuan is located on the Agusan River and has a port with many connections to the Visayan Islands. If you want to travel with Trans Asia Shipping Lines to Jagna on Bohol you will depart from the seaport at Lumbacan. Sometimes ships to other islands also do not depart from the riverport so ask for details when buying your ticket. It's a 30 minute trip to Lumbucan, catch a jeepney in front of the shipping agencies in R D Calo St.

Places to Stay

The simple *A&Z Lowcost Lodge* has rooms for P15 per person, P5 extra for a fan. The equally simple *Canton Lodge* on R D Calo St costs P18 but only P2 extra for a fan. The *Butuan New Society Hotel* (also known as the New Winston Hotel) on Burgos St has singles/doubles at P25/35 with fan, P35/50 with fan and bath or P50/60 with air-con and bath. Not bad for just one night.

At the corner of San Jose St and Conception St the *Elite Hotel* has singles/doubles with fan at P50/60, with fan and bath at P60/85, with air-con and bath at P75/105 — less with a little bargaining. It's a clean and good hotel. On Villanueva St the *Silagen Hotel* has rooms with air-con, wide beds and bath at P110/140. Finally there's the *Imperial Hotel* on San Francisco St which has rooms (again with wide beds) with fan and bath at P55/65 or with air-con and bath at P75/100.

Getting There

Several jeepneys and minibuses daily make the two to three hour trip from Surigao to Butuan. From Davao there are hourly Bachelor Express services from 4.30 am to 1.30 pm except the mid-day bus actually does go at noon. The trip takes five to six hours. Mintranco and Ceres Liner also operate buses on this route, the fare is P40.

BALINGOAN

Boats cross over to Camiguin from here.

Places to Stay

Ligaya's Restaurant & Lodge has doubles with fan at P25 and there's another hotel opposite.

Getting There

From 4.30 to 11.30 am there are several Bachelor Express Bus Company buses each other from Butuan to Balingoan

1 Shipping Agencies	14 New Winston Hotel
2 Seba Shipbroker	(New Society Hotel)
3 Wharf	15 Philippine Airlines
4 Bisaya Shipping	16 Urios High School
5 Post Office	17 Elite Hotel
6 Canton Lodge	18 D'Cellar Coffee Shop
7 Emerald Hotel	19 Crown & Empress Cinemas,
8 Imperial Hotel	Bus Stop
9 Market	20 M J Santos Hospital
10 Siligan Hotel	21 Urios High School
11 Milanies Restaurant	22 Church
12 Restaurants	23 Plaza
13 Butuan City Restaurant	24 Small Market
	25 Police

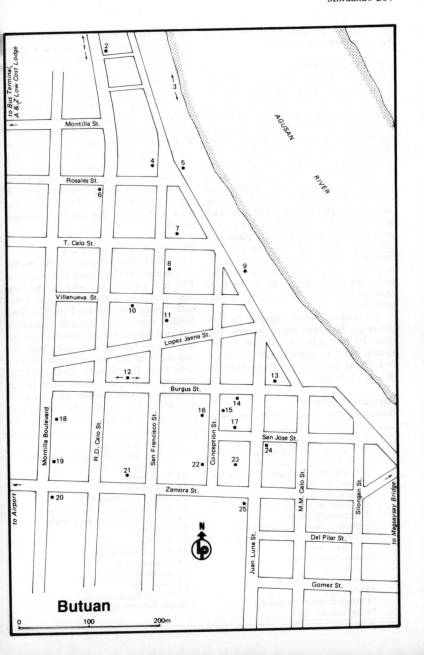

AGUSAN

RIVER

to Bus Terminal,
A & Z Low Cost Lodge

1

2

3

Montilla St.

4

5

Rosales St.

6

7

T. Calo St.

8

9

Villanueva St.

10

11

Lopez Jaena St.

12

13

Burgus St.

14

16

15

17

Conception St.

San Jose St.

18

24

19

22

23

20

21

Zamora St.

25

Montilla Boulevard

R.D. Calo St.

San Francisco St.

Juan Luna St.

M.M. Calo St.

Del Pilar St.

Silongan St.

Gomez St.

to Airport

to Magsaysay Bridge

N

Butuan

0   100   200m

and Cagayan de Oro. From Butuan to Balingoan takes two hours.

CAGAYAN DE ORO

Cagayan de Oro is a clean and friendly university city with numerous schools. The Xavier University Folk Museum on Corrales Avenue is worth having a look at. An old legend relates how the name Cagayan is derived from the word 'kagayha-an' which means shame. The legend tells of a Manobo tribe attacked by another tribe. The beaten villagers planned to retaliate but before this could be done their chieftan fell in love with the daughter of their enemy's chief and married her. Because of this his disgusted people referred to the place as a place of shame or 'kagayha-an'. The Spaniards changed the name to Cagayan to make it easy for them to pronounce and after discovering gold in the river through the village they named it Cagayan de Oro.

For entertainment Cagayan de Oro offers no less than eight cinemas and over 20 bars and the Marcos Sports Centre has a swimming pool. There's a folk pub at the corner of Tiano Brothers St and J R Borja.

Daytrips from Town

Interesting day trips include the Maca-hambus Caves which are 14 km southeast of Cagayan. Take a Talacag jeepney and make sure you bring a powerful light with you.

Another good day trip is to the pineapple plantation at Camp Phillip, 34 km out. Bachelor minibuses go there, on Wednesday and Saturday jeepneys go the further five km from Camp Phillip to the Del Monte Club House. You can get good food in the golf club. You may get to see the pineapple plantation. The Del Monte canning factory is at Bugo. If you want to spend a day at the beach try San Pedro Beach in Opol, seven km west of Cagayan. It's OK but no super beach.

Places to Stay — bottom end

The simple *Palace Lodge* on the corner of Panaca and Capistrano Sts costs just P10 per person. On Velez St the *Red Star Lodge* is a simple Chinese hotel with rooms with fan for P30. The *New Golden Star Inn* on Borja St is another straightforward but good hotel. Rooms are P32/38 for singles/doubles with fan and bath or P50 for an air-con double with bath. On the same street the *Casa Filipina Lodge* has rooms with fan at P18/30 or with air-con and bath at P45/60. It's a simple, clean hotel and there are some cheaper rooms in the

1 Red Star Lodging House, Kings
   Restaurant, Caprice Steak House
2 Salt & Pepper Restaurant
3 Tourist Office, Marcos Sports Center
4 Hotel Mindanao
5 Mabini Lodge
6 The Bungalow Restaurant
7 Ambassador Hotel
8 Coney Island Ice Cream Parlour
9 Shakey's Pizza Parlour, Magnolia
   Ice Cream
10 New Palace Lodge
11 Folk Pub
12 New Golden Star Inn
13 VIP Hotel
14 White Elephant Restaurant
15 Sampaguita Inn

16 Casa Filipina Lodge
17 Golden Spoon Restaurant, Imperial
   Palace Restaurant
18 Perlas Hotel
19 PAL Office
20 Golden Friendship Park
21 Xavier University Folk Museum
22 Philippine National Bank (PNB)
23 Post Office
24 City Hall
25 Fern's Grand Hotel
26 Riverside Park
27 Garden Restaurant
28 Gaston Park
29 Sunrise Restaurant
30 San Augustin Cathedral

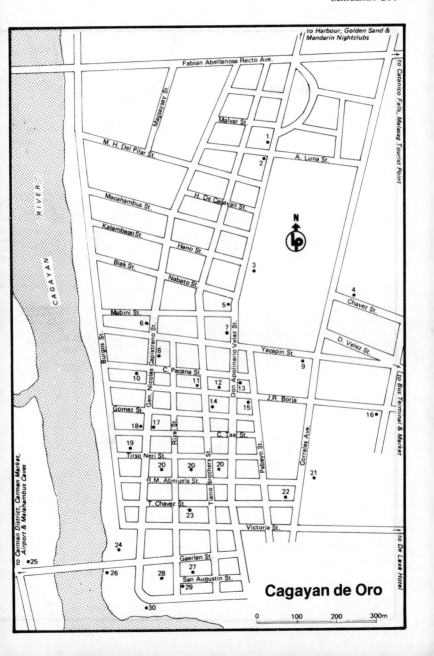

Cagayan de Oro

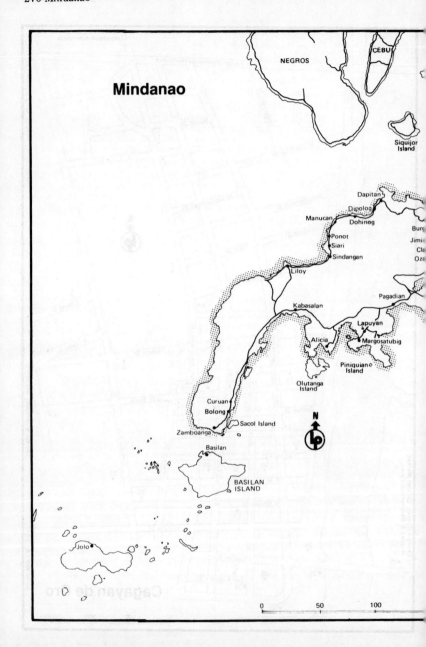

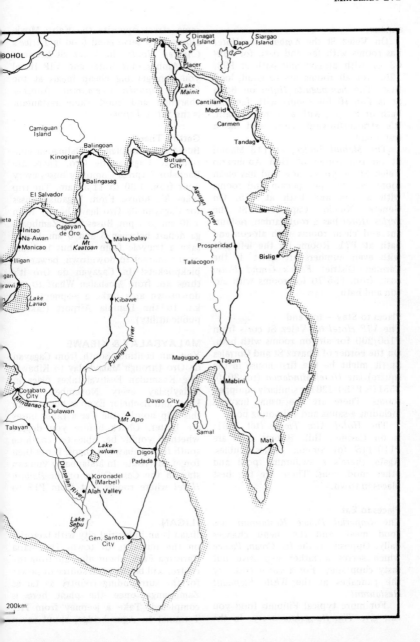

200km

annexe.

On Velez St the *Ambassador Hotel* has rooms with fan and bath for P39/63 or with air-con and bath at P93/126. Not all rooms are so good, look first. The *Sampaguita Hotel* on Borja St is P35/46 for rooms with fan and bath or P50/62 with air-con and bath. It's straightforward, clean and has a restaurant.

The *Mabini Lodge*, at 113 Mabini St on the corner of Don Apolinario Velez St, is pretty new and has clean rooms at P25 per person and rooms with air-con and bath at P75. On General Nicolos Capistrano St the *Perlas Hotel* has a roof garden, restaurant and clean rooms with air-con and bath at P71. Rooms on the left side with even numbers are quiet. In the Carmen District *Fern's Grand Hotel* costs from P55/70 for rooms with air-con and bath.

Places to Stay — top end

The *VIP Hotel* on Velez St costs from P160/200 for air-con rooms with bath. On the corner of Chavez St and Corrales St (it might be the first house in the square) the *Hotel Mindanao* (tel 3010, 3551) is P180/220 for similarly equipped rooms. There are the usual luxuries including a sauna and swimming pool.

The *Hotel Alta Tierra* (tel 3661) is on Carmen Hill. Rooms here are P110/145 for air-con singles/doubles. Again there's a swimming pool and other mod cons. These are the best places in town.

Places to Eat

The *Imperial Palace Restaurant* has good meals and the menu changes daily. Opposite is the *Ice Cream Palace* which serves a rather expensive but tasty chop suey. For a sweet treat try the pancakes at the *White Elephant Restaurant*.

For more typical Filipino food you can give *The Bungalow* a try. In the same street opposite the Kairo Movie House they serve good food in *Thrive's Chicken House*. In Velez St between the Ambassador Hotel and VIP Hotel you can get big cheap meals at the *Bagon Lipunen Restaurant*. Another charming and good value restaurant is the *Salt & Pepper*.

Getting There

Buses from Butuan via Balingoan continue to Cagayan de Oro. There are Bachelor Express Company buses every hour from 4.30 to 11.30 am. The trip takes 3½ hours. From Pagadian buses for Cagayan de Oro leave hourly from 4.30 am to 1 pm. Buses from Zamboanga depart between 5 and 6 am. If you take a tricycle from the bus terminal or the market to downtown, beware of pickpockets! In Cagayan de Oro it's three km from Mcabalan Wharf to the downtown area (take a jeepney), nine km to the Lumbia Airport (take a public utility).

MALAYBALAY & KIBAWE

You can continue south from Cagayan de Oro through Malaybalay to Kibawe. The Kaamulan Festival takes place in Malaybalay every November. Ceres Liner and Bachelor Express buses make this trip hourly, the Ceres Liner buses are better. Check before you depart whether you'll be able to continue south from Kibawe to Digos. If not then forget this route. In Malaybalay you can stay in the *Casa Crista* or the *Balbon Hotel* where rooms cost from P18 to 45.

ILIGAN

Iligan is an industrial city with factories on the outskirts of town. The Maria Christina Falls, about nine km from the centre, will be the main source of power for the surrounding country as far as Zamboanga once the plant here is completed. Take a jeepney from Pier Terminal to Agus bridge, about seven km. From here turn left behind the bridge and walk for about half an hour. The power station dominates the landscape and is likely to appeal more to the technically minded rather than nature lovers.

You can't swim in the pool and the river's a raging torrent and too dangerous to bathe in but the nearby Timoga Springs are fine. It's a large swimming pool supplied with fresh water from the tributary of the Agus River. Iligan is also a departure point for trips to Marawi and the Lake Lanao area, 33 km away.

Places to Stay
At *Jiddy Lodge* on Sabayle Avenue simple accommodation costs P10 per person. On Quezon Avenue, *Maxim Inn* is clean and good. Rooms with fan and bath are P28/35 or with air-con and bath P40/60. The *Altoro Hotel* on Tomas Cabili Avenue is P60/100 for rooms with fan and bath or P80/130 with air-con. It's also a clean and good hotel and is situated near the pier. On Mabini St the *Maria Christina Hotel* is the best hotel in the downtown area. Rooms with air-con and bath are P100/120. The *Village Hotel* is Iligan's best hotel but it is some distance out from the centre.

Places to Eat
Iligan has a surprising number of restaurants but most of them close about 9 p.m. You have a choice of Chinese or regular meals at the *Canton Restaurant* or you could try a good thick sandwich at the *Lions Restaurant*. The *Bar-B-Q* on the plaza is great for an evening meal. Or try the *Sugbakilan Beer Garden* for evening entertainment.

Getting There
There are several buses daily from Cagayan de Oro with Bachelor Express, Fortune Express and Diamond Express. The trip takes 1½ to two hours. From Zamboanga buses depart between 5 and 6 am. From Pagadian with Fortune Express the one way fare is P22.50. It's another trip on very bad roads and takes about five to six hours. This trip is OK security-wise.

LAKE LANAO & MARAWI
The region around Lake Lanao is a crisis zone so be careful and think twice before continuing on through Moslem territory to Cotabato. Marawi, 33 km south of Iligan, is generally OK though. This town is the spiritual and cultural centre for the Filipino Moslems. The country's second state university is also located here. The Mindanao State University is generally referred to as 'Misyu' from the initials MSU. Take a jeepney from downtown. Also located in Marawi is the RP-Libya Hospital, the biggest and most modern hospital in Mindanao.

Worth seeing in Marawi is the Aga Khan Museum with its exhibits of the Moslem culture of Mindanao. Don't expect an oriental bazaar in Marawi although you can buy brass products, tapestries and Indonesian crafts. Good handcrafted tapestries, at fixed prices, are available at the Art Shop of Dansalan College. Don't photograph Moslem women without asking permission first.

Places to Stay
You can stay in the expensive *Marawi Resort Hotel*. The guesthouse of the MSU is mainly used for students but ask the president of the Dansalan Collage, he might be able to help. You'll find the local tourist office in the Ford Guest House Number 2 of the MSU.

Getting There
From Iligan normal jeepneys to Marawi costs P6. Better ones (they're white) are P7 while taxis are P10 per person for four to six passengers.

PAGADIAN
The tourist idea of the province of

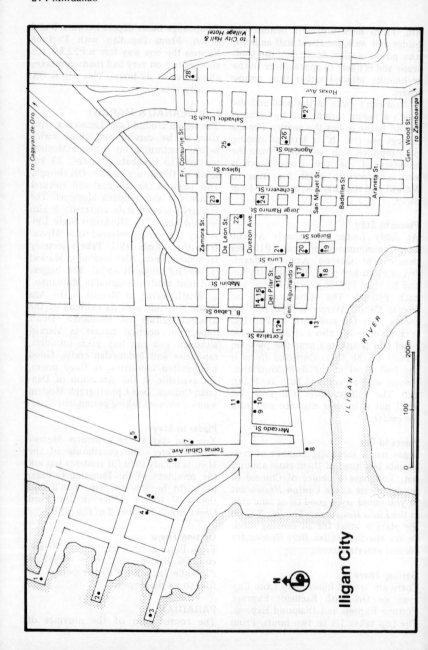

Iligan City

1 New Wharf	16 Plaza
2 North Wharf	17 Maria Christina Hotel
3 South Wharf	18 Post Office
4 William Lines, George & Peter Lines, etc	19 Malonhao Traveller's Kitchenette
5 Jiddy Lodge	20 Niga Restaurant
6 Altoro Hotel	21 Iceberg Cafe & Restaurant, Bahayan Restaurant
7 Marawi Terminal	22 Maxim Inn
8 Market	23 Sugbakilan Beer Garden
9 Lions Restaurant	24 PAL Office
10 Canton Restaurant	25 Church
11 Maranao Handicraft	26 Jelo's Icecream House
12 Police Station	27 J&L Supermarket
13 Philippine National Bank (PNB)	28 Fortune Bus Terminal
14 Maharaja Restaurant	
15 Bar-B-Q Inn	

Zamboanga del Sur is best captured by the description of Pagadian and the surrounding countryside given by the MOT as 'the land of lakes, caves, and water'. What could also be of interest is the small town of Lapuyan about 40 km from Pagadian, which is the home of the Subanon. Protestant American missionaries brought Christianity and the English language to this isolated ethnic minority group living in this rather hilly section of Mindanao. Subanon means river people (suba = river).

Places to Stay

On the National Highway the *Sea View Hotel* has rooms at P12 per person. The *Rainbow Hotel* on Mabini St is P15 per person for rooms with fan. On Jamisola St the *Zamboanga Hotel* has rooms with fan at P25/50 for singles/doubles or P60/80 with air-con and bath.

The *Peninsula* on Jamisola St is a rather better hotel, PAL have their office here. Doubles are P20, with bath P40 or with air-con and bath P60.

Getting There

From Iligan there are several buses daily from 3 am to 2 pm. Fortune Bus Company buses from Zamboanga go between 5 and 6 am. The trip takes between six and eight hours and costs

P35 — a hard dusty journey on bad roads.

It's better to take the overnight boat from Zamboanga. Check with the tourist office for times. Boats are supposed to leave Zamboanga on Saturday and Tuesday at 6 pm, arriving in Pagadian at 7 am the next morning. Fares range from P30 to 50 depending on the class.

PAL fly Zamboanga-Pagadian three or four times weekly.

OZAMIZ

Ozamiz is a port for ships to Cebu. A daily ship goes from Ozamiz to Iligan.

Places to Stay

The *Executive Lodge* on Port Rd is a simple hotel near the 'Lucky Girls'. Rooms are P12 per person. The *Grand Hotel* by the post office costs P50 — try to bargain. *Alinas Hotel* is more expensive at P70. Six km out at Clarin *Libert's Residence* is clean and quiet with rooms at P60/90 including breakfast.

Getting There

There's an hourly bus from Pagadian from 4.30 to 10 am. From Iligan there are many daily buses to Ozamiz via Kolambugan. The last ferry from Kolambugan to Ozamiz departs at 5 pm.

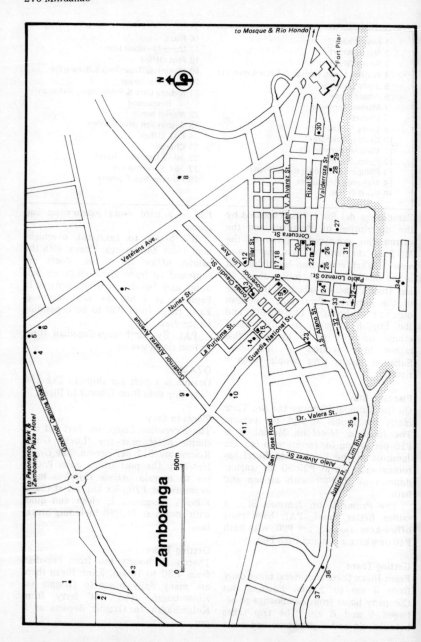

Zamboanga

OROQUIETA, DAPITAN & DIPOLOG

Oroquieta is the provincial capital of Misamis Occidental and the seat of the governor. Close to Dipolog, Dapitan is the site of Jose Rizal's period of exile from 1892 to 1896. The city waterworks and a grass-covered relief map of Mindanao, in the town square, were made by Rizal. A few km away from the city is the place he stayed with a dam be built to create a swimming pool. Other attractions in the area include an area where fruit bats roost and some good places for swimming.

Dipolog, the provincial capital of Zamboanga del Norte, gives an impression of being very clean and neat. There is a beach resort there now and the nearby island of Aliquay apparently has white sandy beaches and good coral reefs for snorkelling and diving.

Places to Stay

In Oroquieta the *Joy Restaurant & Lodge* has rooms at P15 per person. At the *Alma Hotel* a double with fan is P50.

In Dipolog the simple but family-style *Hotel Labrador* on Wilson St has rooms at P15 per person. The simple but clean *Queen Hotel* on Rizal Avenue has rooms with fan at P20/40. The *Arocha Hotel* on the corner of Quezon Avenue and Malvar St is new and very clean and has rooms with fan at P30/50 while rooms with air-con and bath are P90/110.

Getting There

From Ozamiz there are several buses daily making the one hour trip on good roads. The hourly buses from Pagadian from 4.30 to 10 am to Ozamiz continue to Dipolog. Buses for Dipolog from Zamboanga depart between 5 and 6 am but to be sure you had better enquire a day in advance about the exact departure time.

PAL flies Zamboanga-Dipolog four times weekly.

ZAMBOANGA

It's hard to ascertain why Zamboanga is lavished with such praise as 'the exotic pearl in the south of the Phil-

1 Airport	20 SKT Shipping Corporation
2 J's Pad, New Elvida Bar	21 George & Peter Lines
3 Zambayan Hotel	22 Sunflower Restaurant
4 Atin Atin Restaurant	23 Buses to Ayala & San Ramon
5 New Market	24 Philippines National Bank
6 Buses to Cagayan de Oro, Iligan & Dipolog	25 City Hall
7 Disco Inferno	26 Sweet Lines, Basilan Lines
8 Zamboanga General Hospital	27 Bel Air Hotel, Post Office (opposite)
9 Fil-Er Beer Garden	28 PAL Office
10 New Astoria Hotel & Restaurant	29 Tourist Office, Lantaka Hotel
11 Small Bars	30 Barter Trade Market
12 New Sultana Hotel	31 Post Office
13 Pasonanca Hotel	32 Market
14 Imperial Hotel	33 Jeepneys to Pasonanca Park & Taluksangay
15 Preciosa Tours	34 Wharf
16 Old Astoria Hotel	35 Alavar's House of Seafoods
17 Swiss Bar & Restaurant, Aristocats	36 Sunview Cocktail Lounge, Boulevard by the Sea
18 Sulpicio Lines	37 Bachelor's
19 New Zamboanga Hotel & Restaurant	

mosque in Rio Hondo

ippines'. A few Moslems in an otherwise typical Filipino city hardly makes
the place exotic. Furthermore the
colourful, and very expensive, sails of
the Vintas don't normally appear on
their boats apart from at festivals —
monotone sails are the normal wear.
You will, however, see these beautiful
sails many times in brochures and on
postcards.

Fort Pilar

A rather run-down Spanish fort on the
waterfront south of the city centre.
The altar, outside the fort, is notable.
From the fort battlements you can see
Rio Hondo, a little further east.

Rio Hondo

The Moslem water village is the site for
much new government-financed public
housing and is not terribly interesting.
You can wander along the causeways

that connect the houses in the village.

Barter Trade Market

After a major fire in Zamboanga the
Barter Trade Market is now at a new
site near the Lantaka Hotel. This
attempt to arrange a little government
control over the local penchant for
smuggling is not quite as fabulous as
the Zamboangans like to believe. The
fish market at the docks in the late
afternoon is very lively. In the alleys
of the bordering public markets,
between the fish market and J S Alano
St, there are lots of little flea-market
type shops.

Pasonanca Park

Situated 15 minutes by jeepney out of
Zamboanga, the park has given Zamboanga its alternative title of 'City of
Flowers'. The beautiful park has prize-
winning gardens, three swimming pools

and an amphitheatre but it's most famous for its tree house, supposedly built for honeymooners on a one night stand. It's completely furnished with two beds, stereo, fridge, fan, bath and telephone. Actually foreign visitors who apply to the mayor's office can stay — on honeymoon or not — but for one night only. Since it's open to visitors all day you wouldn't want to spend longer.

The park is also the setting for the exclusive Zamboanga Plaza Hotel and casino. Still in the process of being built is the Zamboanga Convention Centre. Approaching this across the suspension bridge you walk straight into a small primaeval forest.

Salva's Orchids (tel 2613) at 300 Tumaga Rd will be of interest to real flower enthusiasts.

Santa Cruz Island

Sea gypsies try to sell coral and shells from their outrigger canoes beside the Lantaka Hotel. You can also rent boats here and cross over to Santa Cruz Island. The 15 minute trip costs P70 per boat for the return trip. Alavar's House of Seafoods on Justice R T Lim Boulevard will get you there cheaper.

On the island there's a superb beach with good swimming and snorkelling. Booths on the island sell beer and other refreshments. There's a Moslem village here in a mangrove lagoon. There's no way there from the main beach but in the bush there's a small Samal cemetery.

Taluksangay

Situated 19 km north-east of Zamboanga the stilt-houses in this village are inhabited by Badjao while Samal live on the land. You can get a good view over the village from the police tower. Good seafood at the Bolong Beach Recreation Centre about 45 minutes by car along the east coast. The beach here is good and tours of the surrounding area can be arranged from here.

Sam Ramon

This prison and penal farm is 20 km west of Zamboanga and is a good place for buying handicrafts made by the prisoners. If there is no direct bus you can get there via Ayala. You won't mind hanging around for the connection if the same pleasant people are still running the sari-sari store at the large tree next to the police station.

vintas near Zamboanga

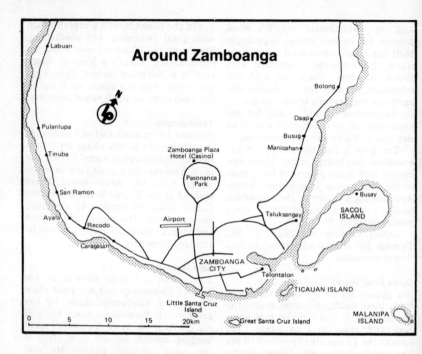

Around Zamboanga

On the way to San Ramon, about seven km from Zamboanga, is a Yakan weaving village on the right hand side of the road. There seven families follow the traditional weaving methods of the Yakan.

Places to Stay — bottom end

On Corcuera St the *Bel-Air Hotel* (tel 3598) is a simple, even primitive, hotel near the docks. Rooms with fan are P18/35 or a double with fan and bath costs P45. On L Magno St the *Old Astoria Hotel* (tel 3231) has rooms with fan at P30 per person or with air-con and bath at P40 per person. Rooms with fan and bath are a bit expensive. Meals are available but must be ordered in advance. On the same street the *New Zamboanga Hotel* (tel 2425) has rooms with fan and bath at P35/70 or with air-con and bath at P80/120. It's a good,

clean hotel and meals from the dining room are very reasonable; the best value rooms are on the upper floor.

On Pura Brilliantes St the *Imperial Hotel* (tel 3548) has rooms with fan at P30/55 or with air-con and bath at P55/90. It's not as good as the *New Zamboanga* but better than the cheaper hotels. The *New Pasonanca Hotel* on the corner of Almonte and Tomas Claudio Sts has singles with fan at P35, rooms with air-con and bath at P25/105. The rooms are clean but small and there's a good restaurant.

The *New Astoria Hotel* on Guardia Nacional St is clean and nice, singles with fan and bath for P55 or air-con rooms at P95/120. Also nice and clean is the *New Sultana Hotel* (tel 5531) on the corner of Governor Lim Avenue and Pilar St with rooms with fan and bath at P66/88 and rooms with air-con and bath at P110/143.

Places to Stay — top end

The *Lantaka Hotel* (tel 3931) on Valderosa St is pleasantly situated right on the waterfront. It has all the usual mod cons including a swimming pool and a very pleasant open-air bar. Rooms are US$22/28 for singles/doubles. The tourist office and PAL is also situated here.

Out at Pasonanca Park the *Zamboanga Plaza Hotel* is the most expensive in town. It's a large 250 room hotel with singles at P320, doubles at P360. Fully air-con it boasts everything from a restaurant and swimming pool to a disco, casino and pelota court.

Places to Eat

There are plenty of restaurants, snackbars, kitchenettes, bakeries and whathave-you around the centre of town. Try the *Hover Restaurant*, on the corner of Guardia Nacional and Pura Brilliantes, for good Chinese food. The *Bread & Butter* on Valderosa, almost next door to the city hall, is clean and cool. Ditto the *Shop-o-Rama Snack* on Pedro Reyes. On Rizal St the *Sunflower Luncheonette* is good for goat meat but the rice is too expensive.

Upstairs in the *New Zamboanga Hotel* you can get a complete meal for around P15. The *Swiss Bar & Restaurant* has European food and about 30 reasonably priced dishes on the menu. At *Alavar's* the seafood is good but rather expensive.

In the evening you can catch the sunset and eat at the bay-side places about a km along Justice R T Lim Boulevard — a beautiful place for sunset freaks. Try the *Boulevard Restaurant by the Sea*. Or spend up at the *Hotel Lantaka* where you can eat outside.

Nightlife

The *Swiss Bar* on Pablo Lorenzo St has a nice atmosphere, is reasonably priced and doesn't have loud music, go-go girls or other typically Filipino distractions.

The best nightclubs are outside the city and include the *Fishnet Pub House*, the *Sunset View Cocktail Lounge* and *Bachelor's Pub*. All have table and service charges and are situated near the athletic field. Then there's *J's Pad*, the *New Elvida* and the *Atin Atin Restaurant*, all in Cov Camins Rd where it usually kicks on late at night.

Simple beer bars are found on Governor Alvarez Avenue near the Astoria Hotel and in Tomas Claudio St at the *Zamboanga Inn*. Midnight is generally closing time in Zamboanga, however.

Getting There

From Pagadian there are buses hourly from 4.30 to 10 am. The trip takes six to eight hours and costs P35. It's a hard, dusty journey on bad roads and the overnight boat is probably preferable. The ship goes two or three times weekly and costs from P30 to 50 depending on the class. There are three or four flights weekly from Pagadian to Zamboanga.

From Iligan the Fortune Express Company operates a bus at 6.45 am daily. The trip takes 11 hours along a bad road.

From Cotabato a possible combination is the ship at 5 pm for Pagadian and from there a bus to Zamboanga. Supposedly you need a military permit before you can fly Cotabato-Zamboanga. The overland trip Cotabato-Pagadian goes through a crisis zone and destroyed bridges along the route may make it impassable. The best way to go is by the *MV Dona Marilyn* of Sulpicio Lines leaving Cotabato on Tuesday at 10 pm. The trip takes eight hours. Or there's the *MV Davao City* of William Lines which leaves on Saturday at 6 pm. This trip takes 12 hours.

From Davao there's a weekly ship which takes 18 hours or a number of PAL flights each week. From General Santos City there's only the *Don Eusebio* of Sulpicio Lines from the Makar Wharf. It departs on Fridays at 8 pm and takes 12 hours. This ship is often used for cruises and it's then difficult to find any other ship.

If you arrive in Zamboanga at the airport it's worth trying to get a ride in to the city with the flight crew in their minibus.

DAVAO

Davao is the fastest growing city in the Philippines after Manila. With a population of 700,000 it's also the second largest city in the Philippines. Its cosmopolitan population, comprising settlers from all over the country, has 2440 square km to sprawl over, although most are concentrated in the central area known as 'City Town'. Davao even has a Chinatown and a number of pleasant parks.

Davao's attractions include the Lon Wa Temple; three km out towards the airport it's the largest Buddhist temple in Mindanao. Five km out is the Shrine of the Holy Infant Jesus of Prague (good views of the city from up here).

Davao is renowned for its wide variety of tropical fruits — particularly the infamous durian. The durian, the fruit that 'stinks hellishly and tastes heavenly' is so esteemed in Davao that they even have a statue of the spikey fruit standing in front of the town hall. There are also many banana plantations around Davao, one is in Lapanday, about 15 km north of Davao.

The black sand Times Beach and Tamolo Beach, some km west of Davao, are not worth a visit, but Paradise Beach, north-east of the town, is better and has white sand.

Of interest to ornithologists is an eagle station not far from Davao. The Panamin office is in the Sasa district and from here you may be able to find out more about the Bagobos and Mansakas, two tribal groups who, according to the tourist office, are 'untouched by modern civilisation'. This seems a rather dubious statement since tours to see them are quickly arranged. The Bagobo community inhabit Wangan at the Wangan Creek about 30 km north-west of Davao and the Mansaka come from the Maragusan Valley east of Mabini but you have to go to Mati first, the capital town of Davao Oriental.

1 Agdao Public Market	19 Lotus Garden Restaurant
2 Pier (Santa Ana Wharf)	20 Davao Hotel
3 William Lines	21 Liram's Store
4 Sweet Lines	22 Philippines National Bank
5 Sulpicio Lines	23 City Hall
6 Magsaysay Park	24 Suan's Dim Sum House
7 Davao Bay Hotel	25 International Restaurant
8 Lechon Restaurants	26 Sawali Folk House
9 Davao Famous Restaurant	27 Panamin Office
10 Paradise Inn	28 New King Lim Restaurant
11 Surigao Bus Lines, Ceres Liner, Bachelor's Express	29 Merco Restaurant
	30 Sunya Lodge
12 Post Office	31 Davao Pension House
13 Boy Scout Terminal (jeepneys to the north)	32 Dennis
	33 Men Seng Hotel & Restaurant
14 Aldevinco Shopping Center (jeepneys to the south)	34 El Gusto Family Lodge
	35 Horizon Folk House
15 Imperial Hotel	36 Shakey's Pizza
16 Tourist Office, Apo View Hotel	37 Mintranco Bus Lines
17 Horizon Folk House	38 Yellow Bus, Tacurong Liner
18 PAL Office	39 Tourist Lodge

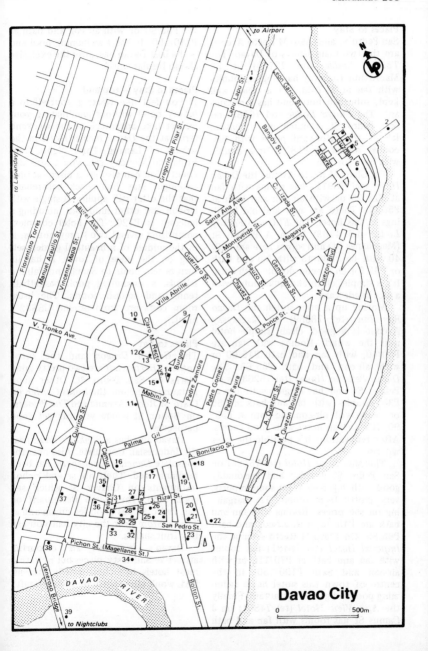

Davao City

0   500m

Places to Stay

San Pedro St and Claro M Recto Avenue are the two main streets of Davao. The *Tourist Lodge* (tel 78760) at 55 MacArthur Highway has singles/doubles with fan at P17/30. It's a clean, well kept, suburban hotel and has a restaurant. The *Sunya Lodge* (tel 76183) on San Pedro St is much more central. It's a straightforward place with fan-cooled rooms at P18/30 or a double with bath for P35.

On Claro M Recto Avenue the *Davao Hotel* (tel 78911) has rooms with fan at P18/25 or with air-con and bath at P50/60. There are new and old buildings in this hotel. The *El Gusto Family Lodge* (tel 4463) is on A Pichon St (Magellanes St) and rooms here are P20/40 with fan, P30/45 with fan and bath or P95 for an air-con double with bath. It's a simple, clean and quiet hotel with a nice inside yard.

Moving up a price notch the *Davao Bay Inn* (tel 78859) on Magsaysay Avenue is a good, clean, simple hotel near the wharf. Rooms with fan are P30/40, with fan and bath P45/60 or with air-con and bath P55/65. The *Davao Pension House* (tel 76263) is on Pelayo St and has singles with fan at P35, doubles with fan and bath at P65 or rooms with air-con and bath at P55/90. It's a clean hotel with good rooms. After renovations it's possible the rates will rise.

The *Men Seng Hotel* (tel 75185) on San Pedro St is clean and reasonably good with big beds from some reports, very grotty from others. Try bargaining on the prices. Rooms with fan and bath are P40/55, with air-con and bath P65/85. On Claro M Recto Avenue the *Imperial Hotel* (tel 78481) has rooms with fan and bath at P70/110 or with air-con and bath P100/150. In the centre of town this hotel has a swimming pool and garden restaurant. Finally the *Apo View Hotel* (tel 74861) on J Camus St has rooms with fan and bath for P65/90 or with air-con and bath at P110/150. It has a swimming pool and is the best Davao has, after the exclusive Davao Insular Hotel.

Places to Stay – top end

If you feel like treating yourself to a luxury hotel without annihilating your budget take advantage of the weekend tariff at the *Davao Insular Hotel* in the suburb of Lanang. Three nights from Friday to Monday gets you a 50% discount. You can also get a discount on a two-night stay but check beforehand that the offer still applies. A single with air-con and other mod-cons including a balcony is P120. The hotel complex, comprising several two-storey houses, is in the middle of a beautiful garden setting on the edge of town. It has its own beach, boats to Samal and Talikud Islands, a swimming pool, basketball, tennis and squash courts. The usual room costs are from around US$32 a night.

Places to Eat

The *Golden Dragon* and the *International Restaurant* are two pretty good places on San Pedro St. Other good restaurants include the *Lotus Garden* on Claro M Recto Avenue and *The Princess* on Bolton St where you can get good barbecues.

Davao also has a *Shakey's Pizza* near the Indonesian Consulate. Also near the consulate *Dencia's Kitchenette* has been recommended. There are several lechon restaurants on Chavez St which sell good food. The *Merco Restaurant* on San Pedro St has good ice cream and at *Lirah's Store* near the city hall you can buy fruit shakes.

Davao's fruitstalls are colourful, attractive and tasty places but note that most hotels ban those smelly durians. PAL won't allow them on their aircraft.

Nightlife
MacArthur Highway is the higher class nightlife area but there are simple bars along Emilio Jacinto St. *The Horizon*, *Sawali* (which also does good Filipino food) and *Dennis* are good places for folk music.

Getting There
From Zamboanga the William Lines ship *MV Manila City* sails each Friday. The trip to Davao takes 18 hours. PAL flies between the two cities four times weekly.

By bus from Cotabato it costs P32 and the road is good but there are lots of checkpoints. From Butuan there are daily buses with Mintranco, Bachelor Express and Ceres Liner. It's a six to seven hour trip on good roads. From General Santos City the last bus leaves at 4 pm.

AROUND DAVAO
Samal Island
This island, 45 minutes from Davao, is one of the town's major attractions due to the Aguinaldo Pearl Farm — but if you're expecting some sort of pearl diving atmosphere you'll be very disappointed. There's an expensive (but good) hotel here and a dreadful beach. On Sundays there is a regular boat at 9 am from the Santa Ana Wharf which returns at 3 pm. The fare is P15 return, to charter a boat costs P150.

Talikud Island
On this small island, near Samal Island, there is a cave and beautiful beaches. And sharks. You can stay with the mayor. There's a daily boat at about 10 am (although it may leave as late as 2 pm) from the Santa Ana Wharf (left side). The fare is P3 and the boat returns the next day — but check first.

Mount Apo
The highest mountain (2954 metres) in the Philippines can be climbed in four

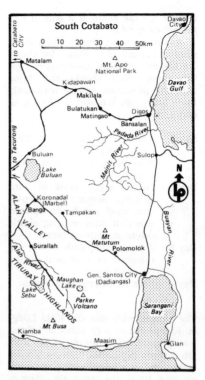

or five days. On your way to the top you'll pass waterfalls, hot springs, pools of boiling mud and you might even spot the rare Philippine Eagle. Digos or Kidapawan are starting points for the climb.

The tourist office in Davao has detailed information about Mt Apo National Park, the various routes and what sort of gear is recommended. In Digos, the office of the *Digos Times* (Mt Apo Climbers Association) can provide additional information about the ascent. Handy information is also available from Mr Plasabas, who lives in the house by the bus stop at the remarkable market in Kidapawan. Ben Mallorca, former mayor of Kidapawan, is also very helpful. He will arrange carriers and a guide for the climb at a cost of P25 per person per day.

A water canteen, boots and a warm sleeping bag are all necessary for climbing the mountain as the nights can get very cool. You should also bring adequate provisions and be reasonably fit — heavy smokers will not find it an easy climb!

Day 1   Jeepney to Illomavis from where you have a two to three hour walk to an overnight shelter.

Day 2   Six to eight hours of hard climbing. Spend the night outside which can be uncomfortable if it rains — bring plastic sheets or, better, a tent.

Day 3   A two hour climb to the top followed by a descent to the Day 1 shelter.

Day 4   Back to Kidapawan or Davao.

The woman who runs the Vista Lodge in Kidapawan is very good at helping you prepare for an ascent of Mt Apo. She advises her guests to try a simpler ascent (go to a neighbouring summit?) via New Israel, the mountain village of the Alpha & Omega sect, to which she belongs. This place is also famous throughout the area for its faith healer. From Kidapawan you catch a jeep to Bulactucan and then walk about two hours to New Israel. Occasionally a jeep goes all the way up but in bad weather this would be practically impossible. Accommodation is possible at the sect's guest house for a token

contribution and guides and porters can be hired in the village.

From New Israel you can walk to New Foundland in about five hours. It's a ghost town in the jungle which members of the sect intend to retreat to in the event of their predicted WW III in 1984. Here again overnight accommodation is available for a contribution. Then it's another eight hours to the summit where you can spend the night in a cave. From here the descent, in the direction of Illomavis, is very difficult. It's about eight or nine hours to the shelter and another two hours from there.

Places to Stay Accommodation is available in Kidapawan at the *Vista Lodge* which is very clean and offers double rooms with bath at P40 per person.

Getting There Take a Mintranco Bus to Digos or even further to Kidapawan (final destination Cotabato). The trip to Kidapawan takes two hours.

GENERAL SANTOS CITY (DADIANGAS)

Magindanaos Moslems and B'laans were still the sole inhabitants of this city right up to the beginning of the 20th century. The first influx of immigrants arrived in 1914 and 1915; more followed in the 1930s. In 1939 pioneers from Luzon and the Visayas under the leadership of General Paulino Santos built the settlement on the Silway River at Sarangani Bay. In 1965 Dadiangas was renamed General Santos City in his honour. Its economy is dependent on

1 Ram's Hotel	9 Golden City Hotel
2 Panamin Office	10 Public Market
3 Immigration	11 PAL Office
4 Police	12 Matutum Hotel
5 City Hall	13 Chan's Hotel
6 Philippines National Bank	14 Brillantes Pension House
7 Post Office	15 Ministry of Public Information
8 Bus Terminal	16 Pioneer Hotel

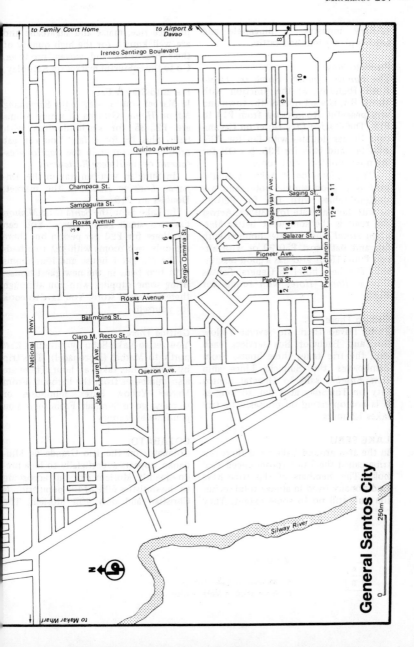

General Santos City

primary industry — pineapple and banana plantations and cattle.

Places to Stay

The *Family Country Home* on Lagao Road Highway, at the junction with Mateo Rd, is a bit outside the town and very peaceful. Rooms cost from P14 to P18. The *Golden City Hotel* on Cagampang St has doubles with fan for P25, with fan and bath for P35. It's OK for the price, not too many rooms.

Chan's Hotel on P Acharon Boulevard is a good simple hotel and has singles/doubles with fan for P20/25 or with fan and bath for P30/45. Across the road is the somewhat better *Matutum Hotel* where singles/doubles with fan and bath cost P50/90 or with aircon P90/115. It also has a good restaurant. The best hotel in General Santos City is *Ram's Hotel* with rooms for P185.

Getting There

From Davao there are several Yellow Bus and Bachelor Bus services each day; the trip takes three hours. From Zamboanga the Sulpicio Lines ship *Don Eusebio* sails to General Santos City on Thursday at 7 pm, so long as it is not operating on cruises. The trip takes 12 hours.

LAKE SEBU

In the area around Lake Sebu there is a tribe called the T'boli (pronounced Tea' boli). The members of this tribe have traditionally lived in almost total seclusion and still do to some extent. They produce rice, maize and sugarcane and are well known for the high quality of their brasswork and woven products. Go to the colourful market on Saturday.

Places to Stay & Eat

In Marbel you can stay in the *Samahang Nayon Home*, Osmena St where rooms are P25/35 for singles/doubles with bath, plus P8 for a fan. You can eat around the corner in the *Capitol Restaurant* or the *Breeze Restaurant*.

In Surallah you can stay in the *Ampayas Lodging House* at the market. Doubles are P18.

In Lake Sebu the *Santa Cruz Mission* has two small guest houses. You can stay here for P20 per person but there are only two rooms with just two beds in the old guest house and four rooms with two beds in the new guest house. Bring some supplies with you although there is a small store. You have to cook for yourself.

Getting There

You get to Lake Sebu by travelling first north to Marbel (Koronadel). The trip by Yellow Bus takes an hour. There are also minibuses from the harbour. From Marbel Yellow Buses, minibuses or jeepneys go to Surallah. From there you continue by jeepney.

COTABATO

Cotabato, on the Rio Grande de Mindanao, appears superficially to be a predominantly Moslem city but according to the statistics 60% of the population is Christian and only 40% Moslem. The

Mindanao

a   Mosque on Lake Lanao
b   Brass shop in Marawi City

Moslems are known as Magindanaos — from the district of the same name around Cotabato.

Places to Stay
At *Sariling Atin* on Figueroa St rooms cost P11 without a window, P14 with. A fan costs another P3. You can also check the *Imperial Hotel.*

Getting There
The Maguinado Express or the J D Express from Marbel take three hours to cover the 192 km of new road. From Davao there are many buses every day and the air-con bus departs shortly after 7 am. This is a difficult Moslem area so it's advisable to travel in daytime. From Marawi there's a minibus in the morning at 7 am and the last jeepney leaves at 4 pm. The trip takes about eight hours but make enquiries before setting off through the danger zone to Cotabato. If it appears dangerous it may be wiser to backtrack to Iligan.

A ship from Pagadian goes at 5 pm daily and the trip takes seven to nine hours and costs P33.50. It's a rather small boat so be prepared for a lot of people throwing up! You must be careful if you mean to leave the boat or the harbour at night. In any case it's much safer to visit the town in the daytime. From Zamboanga the *MV Dona Marilyn* of Sulpicio Lines departs Mondays at 10 pm for Polloc harbour at Cotabato. The trip takes eight hours. The *MV Davao City* of William Lines leaves Zamboanga on Friday at 10 pm. This trip takes 12 hours.

TRANSPORT FROM MINDANAO
To Basilan Six times a day a large Basilan Shipping Lines ship goes from Zamboanga to Isabela. Sailing times are 6.30, 9.30, 11 am and 1, 3.30 and 5 pm. The voyage takes 1½ hours. A ship leaves Zamboanga for Lamitan every afternoon.

To Bohol On Friday and Sunday at noon a ship of Trans Asia Shipping Lines goes from Cagayan de Oro to Jagna. The trip takes six to eight hours. On Monday at noon the *MV Asia Philippines* leaves Cagayan de Oro for Tagbilaran. It's a seven hour trip. The same company also operates a ship from Butuan to Jagna on Mondays, Wednesdays and Saturdays.

Sweet Lines has ships on Wednesday and Sunday at 7 pm from Cagayan de Oro to Tagbilaran. Again it's a six to eight hour trip. The *MV Cebu City* of William Lines leaves Ozamiz on Tuesday at 1 pm for Tagbilaran.

To Camiguin At 8 and 11 am and 3 pm a ship makes the 1½ hour trip from Balingoan to Binone. Mondays and Fridays a ship leaves Cagayan de Oro at midnight for Binone. It's a five to six hour trip.

To Cebu From Butuan, Cagayan de Oro, Iligan and Ozamiz several ships weekly (about daily in fact) sail to Cebu City. Enquire at the offices of Aboitiz Lines, George & Peter Lines, Escano Lines, Sulpicio Lines, Sweet Lines, William Lines and Carlos Gothong Lines.

People of the South

a Badjao woman with gold teeth
b T'boli woman

Each Wednesday at 12 midnight a Kasamahan Lines ship goes from Surigao to San Juan on Leyte and on to Cebu City. On Tuesday, Thursday and Sunday at 8 pm a ship of Sweet Lines goes from Surigao to Cebu City while a George & Peter Lines ship departs on Monday, Wednesday and Friday at 7 pm. They also operate a ship from Oroquieta to Cebu City on Wednesday at 8 pm.

William Lines have the *MV Cebu City* from Ozamiz to Cebu City on Sunday at 10 pm. The Sulpicio Lines ship *Dona Paulina* goes from Cagayan de Oro to Cebu City on Friday at 8 pm. The *Don Ricardo* of the same company operates the same route at 7 pm on Tuesday, Thursday and Sunday. Also a Sulpicio Lines ship, the *Don Enrique*, sails at 8 pm on Wednesday from Davao for Cebu City.

George & Peter Lines have a ship from Zamboanga for Cebu City via Dumaguete on Tuesdays, Thursdays and Saturdays at 6 pm.

PAL have numerous flights between Mindanao and Cebu City. There are flights from Alah Valley (twice weekly), Bislig (three times weekly), Butuan (daily), Cagayan de Oro (daily), Cotabato (four times weekly), Davao (daily), Dipolog (four times weekly), General Santos City (four times weekly), Iligan (three times weekly), Ozamiz (twice weekly), Pagadian (four times weekly), Surigao (five times weekly), Tandag (twice weekly), and Zamboanga (daily).

To Leyte The *Cardinal Ferry* goes daily at noon from Surigao to Liloan. The trip takes 3½ hours and at 4 pm the ship continues to Maasin, another 2½ hours on. Until the new port is complete — it will probably be finished in 1984 — there might be only bancas leaving daily from the river mouth in Surigao for Liloan. Travel time is five hours.

Trans Asia Shipping Lines go on Friday and Saturday from Butuan to Maasin. Each Wednesday at midnight there's a Kasamahan Lines ship from Surigao to San Juan.

To Luzon A direct William Lines ship, the *MV Manila City*, between Zamboanga and Manila operates on Sunday at 11 pm. It's a good ship and the trip takes about 30 hours. There's also a direct service with the Sweet Lines *MV Sweet Land* which leaves on Wednesday at 2 pm and also takes about 30 hours.

The *MV Don Eusebio* of Sulpicio Lines departs from Zamboanga for Manila via Iloilo on Panay at 6.40 pm on Saturdays. In the opposite direction this ship takes a different route. The *MV Dona Florentina* of Negros Navigation Lines goes on Sunday at 7 pm via Iloilo on Panay (stopping there for about two hours) from Cagayan de Oro to Manila. Again the trip takes about 30 hours.

PAL flies daily from Cagayan de Oro, Zamboanga and Davao to Manila.

To Negros George & Peter Lines have a ship on Tuesday, Thursday and Saturday at 6 pm from Zamboanga to Dumaguete. The trip takes 18 to 20 hours. They also operate Tuesday and Thursday at 6 pm and all other days at noon from Dipolog to Dumaguete. The trip takes five hours. The name of the port of Dipolog is Dapitan Port and it is located between Dipolog and Dapitan. Tricycle fare from Dipolog is P5.

To Panay The Sulpicio Lines ship *MV Don Eusebio* goes on Saturday at 6.30 pm from Zamboanga to Iloilo. The trip takes 15 hours and the ship continues to Manila after a four hour stop. Note that when the *Don Eusebio* is operating on cruises this service is suspended. The *MV Davao City* of William Lines leaves Zamboanga on Sunday at 11 am for Iloilo. The trip takes 21 hours. The Negros Navigation Company ship *Dona*

Florentina goes on Sundays at 8 pm from Cagayan de Oro to Iloilo.

To Siquijor Every Sunday and Thursday at 3 pm the *MV Sweet Sound* of Sweet Lines departs from Plaridel for Larena. The trip takes eight hours.

To Sulu Islands Every day ships will sail from Zamboanga at least as far as Jolo and some go to other ports as far as Sitangkai. Ask on the harbour and at the office of the Sampaguita Shipping Lines in Valderossa St, at the Magnolia Shipping Lines office in J S Alano St (diagonally left, opposite the PNB), and at the SKT Shipping Corporation. SKT has the largest ships and the most reliable and regular timetables. The *MV Queen Helen*, listed below, was burnt out while at sea in mid-82 but there will probably be a replacement by now. One way fare Zamboanga-Jolo is P35. It's preferable to leave your name with the tourist office for security reasons. This is the timetable for the three SKT ships prior to the accident.

		MV Lady Ruth	*MV Queen Helen*	*MV Dona Isabel*
Zamboanga	dep 7 pm	Monday	Thursday	Saturday
Jolo	arr 4 am	Tuesday	Friday	Sunday
Jolo	dep 10 am	Tuesday	Friday	Sunday
Siasi	arr 2 pm	Tuesday	Friday	Sunday
Siasi	dep 6 pm	Tuesday	Friday	Sunday
Bongao	arr 2 am	Wednesday	Saturday	Monday
Bongao	dep 9 am	Wednesday	Saturday	Monday
Sitangka	arr 1 pm	Wednesday	Saturday	Monday

PAL has daily flights from Zamboanga to Jolo and on Tuesdays, Thursdays and Saturdays from Zamboanga via Jolo to Tawi-tawi.

Palawan

The south-west island of Palawan is 397 km long but averages only 40 km wide. It divides the Sulu Sea from the South China Sea and the province includes 1768 smaller islands as well as the main one. The largest of these islands are Busuanga Island, Culion Island, Coron Island, Cuyo Island, Dumaran Island, Bugsuk Island, Balabac Island, and Cagayan Island.

At 2073 metres Mount Mantalingajan is the highest mountain in the region. Most of Palawan is covered with mountainous jungle with only a few coastal regions devoted to agriculture. Rice, coconuts, bananas and ground-nuts are cultivated, but fishing is the mainstay of the economy. Near the coast of north Palawan are the richest fishing grounds of the Philippines. The area between Coron Island, Cuyo Island, and Dumaran Island, but especially in Taytay Bay, provides 60% of the total Filipino fish catch. Forestry is also an important local industry. And since the discovery of oil in commercially viable quantities on the north-west coast development of the industry looks promising.

At El Nido the rocks harbour swallows' nests, which are used to make that famous oriental delicacy, birds' nest soup. The Palawan jungles also shelter plants and animals not found anywhere else in the Philippines. These include the iron tree, the mouse deer, the king cobra and many rare butterflies and parrots.

Palawan is quite thinly settled with much of the population coming from the Visayas. The population of the province is only about 370,000. Through offers of cheap land it is hoped to attract more settlers. There are various groups indigenous to Palawan, some having had little contact with Europeans. The Tagbanua of northern Palawan are a seafaring tribe with only temporary settlements. The Tau't Batu, only discovered in 1978, still live much as they must have 20,000 years ago. Their area in the Singnapan Basin, some km east of Ransang in southern Palawan, is absolutely off limits and you should respect it.

The larger tribal groups include Negrito-like Bataks and Palawenos. Attempts to settle these nomadic hunters into an agricultural lifestyle have always been resisted. Some of them now go to school but they almost always return to the jungles. The Bataks are very shy and if you want to find them and visit their villages you will need time, patience and a capable guide.

There are no spectacular sights to speak of in Palawan apart from the underground river and the Tabon Caves. It's the friendly people, untouched natural scenery and beautiful beaches which make a visit to Palawan worthwhile. A diving mask is an absolute necessity for a Palawan visit.

In the April-May summertime there are many Japanese visitors to Palawan — they come in search of the rare and beautiful butterflies. You will meet many natives wanting to sell butterflies, they even raise them! Palawan is also a paradise for seafood lovers. You could try a different fish dish every day of your stay in Palawan. Or crabs, mussels, sea urchins, lobsters and even jelly fish. There is a possibility that south Palawan may be temporarily closed to foreigners. Make the best of it, the northern part will still be worth a visit.

Tours & Transport

It is somewhat difficult to find tours and accommodation in Palawan. Away from the capital, Puerto Princesa, you are often dependent on the friendly people but in any case the local mayor will arrange accommodation for you. Transport between the villages is terrible. The only 'road' is from Brooke's Point through Puerto Princesa to Roxas and it isn't even surfaced. Any travel on byroads requires lots of time and/or money.

Jeepneys and boats will always try to get you to pay for a 'special ride'. If you can't wait and must take a 'special' you'll find that the vehicle soon packs out with passengers coming along for a free ride — at your expense. In the wet season a few days of rain totally shuts down bus transport. You are then dependent solely on boats and you'll have to dig very deeply into your pockets to pay.

Health Warning

Away from the capital medical services are poor. Even if there is a doctor there is usually no pharmacy with prescribed medicines. In case of illness you should head straight for Puerto Princesa. Malaria is very widespread on Palawan, particularly in the south, so don't forget your anti-malarials and always sleep under mosquito netting and wear repellent. If you get a fever you should always consider malaria and head for Puerto Princesa. Doctors there know more about the diagnosis and treatment of malaria then they do in Manila. In 1978 almost 12,000 cases of malaria were officially registered. To ease your mind, it's nice to know that during the dry season — when most of us visit the Philippines — Palawan is not infested with mosquitoes. The plague usually begins in the rainy season.

During the summer months all the coastal waters can be alive with deadly species of jellyfish — salabay — so be careful when you swim.

PUERTO PRINCESA

Puerto Princesa is a relatively recent city with about 60,000 inhabitants. Practically all the houses are made of stone and the town is dominated by the cathedral. Although there are always new houses being built you still find strikingly beautiful examples in the old style. At the waterfront there are fishermen's huts built out over the water. The atmosphere on the wharf at sunset is good fun. There are also some interesting places for divers in Puerto Princesa Bay. For P100 a day you can charter an outrigger and sail, swim, dive and fish in the bay.

White Beach, near the airport, is good for sunbathing but you can only swim here at high tide. Keep a watchful eye on your belongings on this beach as petty thieves have been attracted by the tourists here. You can get to White Beach by tricycle. At the ice plant, before the airport, is an old gate, get off here and then walk about 10 minutes down the path to the beach. In the dry season you can tricycle all the way to the beach.

You can even see Palawan by helicopter if you have money to burn, enquire at the Hyatt Hotel. Each year from 7 December there's a week long festival which includes concerts in Mendoza Park, Caracol boat processions, competitions and other events.

Diving

Palawan is becoming more and more popular for underwater enthusiasts. For organised trips Aqua Venture, 60 Taft St and Island Divers (ask for Norman Songco) on Rizal St near Edwin's Food Palace are both competent. Complete outfitting costs US$30 per day. Diving tours for two or more divers costs US$42 per person per day. For this you get transport, two tanks, backpack,

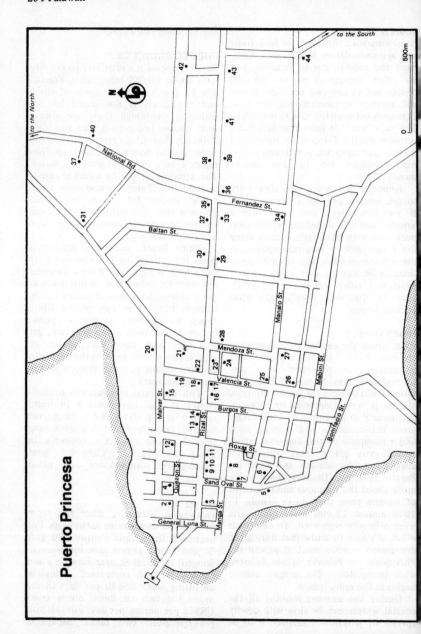

Puerto Princesa

to the South

to the North

to the North

National Rd.

Fernandez St.

Baltan St.

Mendoza St.

Valencia St.

Burgos St.

Roxas St.

Sand Oval St.

General Luna St.

belt, two dives a day and a meal. You can also get tanks and backpack from Mr Gus Go in Sand Oval St. Mr Macolor, the chief of the Bureau of Fisheries, is a good man to see about diving possibilities. He knows the good places and how to get to them.

Information
The tourist office has a counter at the airport and an information officer for Puerto Princesa at the City Hall. For other islands see the friendly and helpful tourist promotion officer, Mrs Ellen Hagedorn, at the Planning Department in the Provincial Capitol Building. Puerto Princesa has a Philippine National Bank branch where you can change travellers' cheques and it also has the only post office on the whole island.

At Ensomo Studio & Photo Supply, Rizal St — between Hidden Valley and the Dynasty Hotel — you can not only buy excellent postcards but also hire motorcycles. A Kawasaki 125 costs

P120 a day. George Marcelo will also take his Honda 125 out of his tricycle for the same price and he has a jeep available for P350 per day.

Places to Stay — bottom end
Mrs Abordo at 36 Sand Oval St still rents rooms at P15 per person. It's probably the cheapest place in town. The *Duchess Pension House* on Valencia St is run by pleasant people — Joe and Cecille are good sources of travel information. The food here is good but try to order in advance. The rooms are clean, fan-cooled and cost P25 per person.

Yayen's Pension on Manalo Extension is also run by pleasant people and has clean rooms. They cost P35/55 for singles/doubles with fan; P70/90 with fan and bath or P120/130 with air-con and bath. There's good food in the coffee shop and they own a small island with two cottages in Honda Bay.

Civen's Inn on Mendoza St has rooms with fan for P50/70. It's got a peaceful

1 Wharf
2 Palawena Hotel
3 Cathedral
4 Ignacio Restaurant
5 Mrs Abordo
6 George Marcelo
7 Panamin Office
8 Aqua Venture Scuba Diving
9 Oriental Maritime Shipping Lines
10 Fishery Bureau
11 A&D Refreshments
12 Holy Trinity College
13 Hidden Valley
14 Dynasty Hotel
15 Public Market
16 Post Office
17 Circon Lodge & Restaurant
18 PAL Office, Rafol's Pension House, Philippine National Bank (PNB)
19 Bowling Lanes
20 Ice Cream House
21 Civens Inn
22 Edwin's Food Palace & Disco, Metro Bank
23 Mendoza Park
24 City Hall, Tourist Office
25 College
26 Duchess Pension House
27 Badjao Ice Cream Parlour, MM Canteen
28 Swimming Pool
29 Leah's Bahay Kamayan, Magnolia Ice Cream Kiosk, Karla's Antiques
30 Golden House Restaurant, Yakiniku Restaurant, World Vision
31 Provincial Hospital
32 Cardinal Ferry Office
33 Kamayan Restaurant
34 Miriam Bus Terminal
35 William Lines
36 Provincial Capitol, Tourist Office
37 Rafol's Hyatt Hotel
38 Land-Rover Bus Terminal
39 Badjao Inn & Steak House
40 Bulakenia Beer Garden
41 Palawan Hotel
42 Airport
43 Kadlao Disco
44 Yayen's Pension House & Coffee Shop

location but the rooms are only relatively clean and the service is poor. On Conception St the *Palawena Hotel* is also not so good. The rooms are clean and there's a restaurant but the street is noisy and it's rather unfriendly. Rooms with fan are P45/70 or a double with air-con and bath costs P170.

On Rizal St the *Dynasty Hotel* is P70 for rooms with fan, P140 for rooms with air-con and bath. On the same street, near the airport, the *Badjao Inn* is a good clean hotel with rooms with fan and bath at P35/55 or with air-con and bath at P80/90. Air-con rooms in the new annexe are twice as expensive. The *Steak House* restaurant is also here. At Mendoza Park on the corner of Rizal St and Valencia St the *Circon Lodge & Restaurant* is clean with singles/doubles with fan at P60/75 and doubles with air-con and bath at P135.

Places to Stay — top end

Still on Rizal St the *Palawan Hotel* is a very good hotel near the airport. Rooms with air-con and bath are P135/170. *Rafol's Pension House* is also on Rizal St but the service is poor and it's overpriced. Baths are shared between two rooms. With air-con the rooms cost P145/170.

On National Rd, the *Hyatt Rafols Hotel* is the best in town. It's got a swimming pool and is not totally overrun with tour groups. Rooms cost P300/330 for singles/doubles with air-con and all the usual mod cons.

Places to Eat

The *Golden Horse Restaurant* on Rizal St does Chinese and Filipino food. Also on Rizal St the *Kamayan Restaurant* also does Filipino food but it's rather expensive although it has a beautiful large terrace and a treehouse.

Other Rizal St restaurants include *Bahay Kamayan* where the food is Filipino and you have to eat with your fingers. The *Badjao Steak House*, still

on Rizal St, is popular with oil-workers who come here for its international food. A final Rizal St eating place is the *Yakiniku Restaurant* where the food is Japanese and the prices are rather high.

Edwin's Food Palace on Valencia St does good value Chinese food. There's a disco here in the evenings. The *Ignacio Restaurant* on Quezon St is a simple restaurant with good Filipino food — try the beef mami or the bola-bola.

Nightlife

Every Saturday the *Hyatt* puts on folk music by the swimming pool and provides a big buffet for P35 per person. Afterwards many locals continue to their favourite disco. Simpler and better value is the *Bulakenia Beer Garden* on the other side of the street. On National Rd there are a few other places like this. For nightlife downtown there's the *Hidden Valley*. You can even go bowling in Puerto Princesa.

BROOKE'S POINT & URSULA ISLAND

Ursula Island is a special attraction for bird-watchers as thousands of birds nest on this small, uninhabited island. At dusk they return from seeking food on other islands. According to the locals there are no longer as many birds on Ursula as there used to be, however, it's still worth a visit. Also of interest to ornithologists is the Tubbataha Reef wih its countless gulls. Some of the bird species of Ursula have shifted their nesting places over here.

Places to Stay

In Brooke's Point *Villa Senior* offers simple accommodation at P20 per person and good food. It's better than the *Sunset Garden*. The *Silayan Lodge*, owned by the friendly Dr Fabellon and his wife Alice, is cheap and clean with rooms at P18 per person.

In Rio Tuba there are a number of

places at the pier where you can stay and eat. The cost of lodging is rarely fixed, it all depends on how you present yourself to the locals and how well you can bargain.

Getting There
From Puerto Princesa to Brooke's Point

there are several buses daily from the market. The trip takes seven to eight hours.

There are several ways of getting to Ursula Island. A large outrigger leaves once a day at 8 am from Brooke's Point for Rio Tuba. Alternatively you can go to Batarawa — from Brooke's Point —

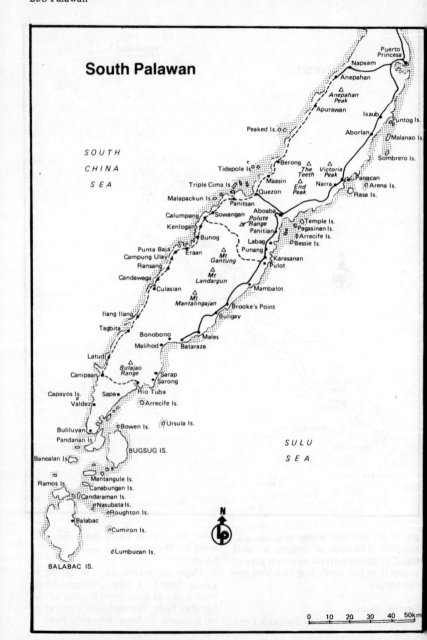

South Palawan

SOUTH

CHINA

SEA

SULU

SEA

Puerto Princesa
Napsam
Anepahan
Anepahan Peak
Apurawan
Isaub
Puntog Is.
Peaked Is.
Aborlan
Malanao Is.
Sombrero Is.
Berong
The Teeth
Victoria Peak
Tidepole Is.
Maasin
End Peak
Panacan
Triple Cima Is.
Quezon
Narra
Arena Is.
Malapackun Is.
Panitsan
Rasa Is.
Calumpang
Sowangan
Aboaba
Polute Range
Temple Is.
Kenlogan
Panitian
Pagasinan Is.
Bunog
Labag
Arrecife Is.
Punta Baja
Eraan
Punang
Bessie Is.
Campung Ulay
Mt Gantung
Karasanan
Ransang
Pulot
Candawaga
Mt Landargun
Culasian
Mambalot
Mt Mantalingajan
Brooke's Point
Ilang Ilang
Buligay
Tagbita
Males
Bonobono
Malihod
Bataraza
Latud
Bulajao Range
Canipaan
Sarap
Sarong
Capayos Is.
Sapa
Rio Tuba
Valdez
Arrecife Is.
Buliluyan
Bowen Is.
Ursula Is.
Pandanan Is.
Banealan Is.
BUGSUG IS.
Mantangule Is.
Ramos Is.
Canabungan Is.
Candaraman Is.
Nasubata Is.
Roughton Is.
Balabac
Cumiron Is.
BALABAC IS.
Lumbucan Is.

N

0 10 20 30 40 50km

and take an outrigger from here to Rio Tuba. Once here you can charter an outrigger to go to Ursula Island but be warned, they may ask up to P500!

Another route to Rio Tuba is along the west coast of southern Palawan. Between Quezon and Canipaan there are two boats going regularly (from time to time). The journey takes about three days including loading and unloading cargo in a few Barangays along the coast. The cost of the boat ride is P75 including food (rice and fish, coffee). You can either sleep on the boat, which is usually anchored in a bay near settlements, or you can go ashore and stay for free with the Barangay captain or better yet in a marine detachment. Between Canipaan and Rio Tuba there is a trail which should not take more than six hours to walk. It is possible to hire a guide in Canipaan, ask the Barangay captain.

QUEZON & THE TABON CAVES

Quezon is the jumping-off point for the Tabon Caves which are about 30 minutes away by boat. Human bones from the stone age have been found in the caves and it is assumed that they served as a burial ground for the original inhabitants. Altogether there are 29 caves of which the Tabon Cave is the largest and the Diwata Cave, 30 metres above sea level, is the most beautiful and the highest standing. Ask in the National Museum in Quezon about a guide.

Places to Stay

The *Jurahida Inn* has rooms at P12 per person. At *Edelen's Hometel & Bakery* rooms are P40 per person including food — clean and friendly service.

Getting There

A bus goes from the Puerto Princesa market in the morning. The trip takes five to seven hours.

IWAHIG

Set in 37,000 hectares of undulating rice fields and orchards, Iwahig is a penal settlement which has about 4000 inmates. They're known as 'colonists' and a small number of prisoners, 55, have their families with them. Twenty have been able to settle on their own land here after carrying out their sentences. The jail supports itself through agriculture, fishing and handicrafts; it is not state subsidised. It is believed that the reversion rate of released prisoners from Iwahig is much lower than at other jails as a result of the more liberal conditions. It's about 23 km south of Puerto Princesa and visitors are welcome — particularly in the souvenir shop.

Getting There

A jeepney goes from the public market in Puerto Princesa early in the morning and another comes back in the afternoon.

BALSAHAN

There is a resort right on the river at Balsahan where the locals go to relax and sometimes to celebrate family occasions. To get there take a morning jeepney to Iwahig. The trip to Balsahan is not regular so make enquiries about it, it may also cost P2 extra. If you don't want to return with the mid-day jeepney you can walk to the main road and hail a bus in the late afternoon. Between 1 and 1.30 pm you should be able to pick up the jeepney on its return journey to Puerto Princesa.

SANTA LUCIA

Santa Lucia is a sub-colony of Iwahig and has a hot spring but it's a 14 km round trip walk. It's a favourite place for weekend excursions. Don't go on Mondays when they clean the pool.

Getting There

From Puerto Princesa harbour boats shuttle back and forth according to demand. They leave as soon as they're full and the trip costs P2.

BAHELI

Baheli (also known as Bahile) is famed for its underground river which has been traced back under the heart of the St Paul National Park for about eight km. It is navigable for much of this length if not in flood and includes, in addition to the main tunnel, some very large cathedral-like caverns. Both bats and swiftlets inhabit the caverns; if you can hear their squeaks they will be swiftlets.

Mr Layacan is the man to see for boat charters to visit the caves. Food and accommodation in his house should be included in the charter price but clarify that beforehand! Alternatively you can try Mr Rey Correa. You depart at 5 am and should take food for yourself and the boat people. After about three hours you reach a small bay where you find the river entrance. A small outrigger boat is quickly built from poles and boards which have been brought along. This is used to explore the underground river for several hours. Take along a camera and torch (flashlight), a kerosene lamp will reveal the innumerable bats.

If surf is breaking at the beach then disembarkation becomes tricky and visitors should have waterproof bags for cameras and valuables. It is essential that visitors remove all rubbish and food from this area and take it back with them. There are no collection facilities at this spot. In future years it may be possible to gain access via a walking track from the village of Sabang, not far from Baheli, thus obviating the uncertain and expensive boat ride.

Getting There

From Puerto Princesa jeepneys go from the public market — look for 'Bahile'. Avoid expensive 'special rides'. You can get there by road during the rainy season as well as the dry and the usual price is about P10.

Once in Baheli you usually have to charter a boat to get to the underground river. The cost of a day's charter of a pumpboat is commonly around P450. There are a number of owners who will charter boats. If in doubt try Mr Layacan or Mr Correa. Mr Layacan also has a rest house where you can stay overnight.

An alternative means is to ask in Baheli about transport to Tagabinit and for directions for the walk to Cabayugan. Generally an outrigger leaves Baheli for Tag Nipa at about 1 pm. It should take 1½ hours but it could take longer so be prepared. From Tag Nipa the walk to Cabayugan takes another 1½ hours. Then from Cabayugan to Sabang is another longish walk — about two hours. In both Cabayugan and Sabang private accommodation is available, ask around. From Sabang walk along the beach and over a hill until you reach the park ranger's house. Ask about a guide here as the last stretch to the mouth of the river is difficult terrain. It takes about two hours from Sabang to the underground river.

TAGBUROS & HONDA BAY

Honda Bay, off Tagburos, is about 10 km from Puerto Princesa and offers good diving conditions. Try to find Bong, the owner of the *Norma*, he will take you out diving for a fair price — he has a good reputation for being reasonable. It should cost roughly P100 to 150 a day. When chartering boats make your instructions very clear and determine the price beforehand. If you intend to go 'island hopping' make sure the boat carries enough fuel.

Many of the islands have shallow reefs and good beaches for camping. You must be self-sufficient in food, fuel and water if you intend to camp. Only snorkelling gear is needed since many of the reefs are close in. There is an excellent coral reef between Canon and

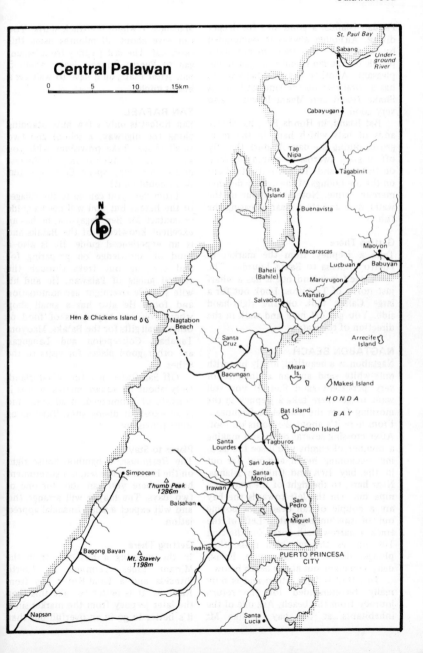

Central Palawan

0 5 10 15km

St. Paul Bay

Sabang

Underground River

Cabayugan

Tag Nipa

Tagabinit

Pita Island

Buenavista

Maoyon

Macarascas

Lucbuan

Babuyan

Baheli (Bahile)

Maruyugon

Manalo

Salvacion

N

Arrecife Island

Hen & Chickens Island

Nagtabon Beach

Santa Cruz

Meara Is.

Makesi Island

Bacungan

HONDA BAY

Bat Island

Canon Island

Santa Lourdes

Tagburos

San Jose

Santa Monica

Simpocan

Thumb Peak 1286m

Irawan

San Pedro

Balsahan

San Miguel

PUERTO PRINCESA CITY

Bagong Bayan

Mt. Stavely 1198m

Iwahig

Napsan

Santa Lucia

Pandan Islands, a good area for deeper diving. Although always recommended by the tourist office there are not many people on Pandan Island — it's quiet and pleasant. Another nearby island which has a coral reef on the landward side is Snake Island and Meara Island is also very good.

Bat Island, in Honda Bay, has thousands of bats which hang in the mangroves during the day. At dusk they fly off in giant swarms to search for food on the mainland. Tagburos itself is built on the ore tailings of the nearby defunct mercury mine. Note the colour of the water here and steer clear of eating the fish.

Getting There

Take a jeepney from the market in Puerto Princesa to Santa Lourdes. The town itself is inland but it has a wharf just north of Tagburos. Look out for a large Caltex tank on the right-hand side. You get off here and walk in the direction of the water.

NAGTABON BEACH

Nagtabon is a beautiful, lonely bay with milk-white sand and an abundance of very persistent sand flies. If you still want to go there take a jeepney in the morning from the market to Bacungan. From here it's about 2½ hours on foot. After crossing several rivers and making a number of climbs you'll see the shining, beckoning beach and not far out in the bay Hen and Chicken Islands. Near here, to the right of the track, is a nipa hut. On the left towards the bay are a couple of tall dead trees poking out of the undergrowth. Left of the track a narrow path forks for the first 100 metres through high grass, then plunges down into the jungle. Eventually you come out at the beach below.

This trail is fairly steep and is only really recommended for the return journey from the beach. Ask one of the inhabitants at the bay — like Mr

Martinez — where the track starts. You can save about 30 minutes using this short cut. The last jeepney from Bacungan to Puerto Princesa leaves about 5 pm. After that you'll have to wait for a bus or hitch.

SAN RAFAEL

San Rafael is only a few huts, standing along the highway, a school and two small shops. Take provisions with you as there is not much to buy. In the rest house they may speak English — but don't count on it!

From here you can go to the villages of the Bataks but you will need a guide — contact Mr Ben Pagayona, he has an excellent knowledge of the Bataks and is an experienced guide. He is also a fund of knowledge on preparing for and carrying out treks through the central jungle of Palawan. He and his wife provide overnight accommodation and food. He also has a small shop where you can buy items of food or other small gifts for the Bataks. Maoyon, Tanabag, Concepcion and Langogan are other good places for visits to the tribes.

Off San Rafael is a tiny coral island. Only about 50 square metres in area it consists of submerged, dead coral and is an excellent diving spot. Take along some provisions.

Places to Stay

The *Resthouse*, a bamboo house right on the beach by the sea, is a government house where you can stay for one or two days. The mayor will arrange this and will expect a small financial appreciation.

Getting There

In the morning a bus goes from the Miriam Lines Terminal in Puerto Princesa and a Land-Rover bus from Rizal St. It is better to take this than the later jeepney from the market since it's better to go in an overfull bus than an overfull jeepney! The trip takes two hours.

If you want to continue further from San Rafael to Langogan and Roxas or back to Puerto Princesa you must catch the appropriate bus at about 9 am on the highway. Another bus comes at mid-day. Travel time is about four hours.

ROXAS

Roxas is a beautiful small town right on the sea with bamboo huts under palms but no beaches. There are a few power co-operatives but most houses are lit by candles or kerosene lamps. When walking about the town note the effects of past sand mining which is in fact still going on. One rumour has it that the whole town will eventually be moved. Sand-laden barges can be seen anchoring in the bay. There are beaches north of here, before the market. An American woman doctor works in the hospital.

From Roxas pumpboats can be chartered to take visitors to the many islands offshore for camping or diving. Green Island has the largest reef, 20 km in circumference, but other islands are much closer. Green Island used to have a seaweed farm. If you go there be sure to take food with you.

Some km out of Roxas towards Port Barton is the now deserted tourist resort of Matalangao with its abandoned huts, silted-up pools and damaged causeways. The small hydro-electric plant has been demolished by floods. It is an interesting place for a few hours, on a delightful stream. Ask the Port Barton driver for directions.

Places to Stay & Eat

There are two guest houses but the facilities are basic. The *Rover Inn* is near the bus station and costs P15 per person. It belongs to the bus owner and has a loud disco! Opposite the market and

Waterfront at Roxas

with views over the sea is the *Gemelyn* but it's too expensive at P20 per person. A reasonable place to eat is *Tito's Canteen*. You can buy fresh fish and fruit at a good price in the market.

Getting There
It's a three to four hour bus trip from San Rafael to Roxas. With a little luck the bus from Puerto Princesa will come through San Rafael early in the morning. If you want to continue further to north Palawan you have to go by boat because the road ends at Roxas. Ask in the hotel or at the public market whether and where a boat goes. It's likely to be an expensive affair.

TAYTAY
Taytay is the former capital city of Palawan. The ruins of the old fort, built by the Spanish in 1622, are still in evidence. There is also an early church here — about 300 years old. Taytay has a hospital and numerous shops which offer good buys. A few — such as NNDV's Rendezvous — are owned by Mr Leonardo Publico, head ranger and husband of the current vice-mayor. With him acting as intermediary you can fix up cheap accommodation at one of the student houses.

He might also drive you, on the only road in the entire area, to Embarcadero — about seven km away. From Embarcadero outrigger boats occasionally travel along the forest river to Malampaya Sound on the west coast and also to Liminangcong. If you'd like to spend a few days in the forest go to Lake Danao, just a few km south of Taytay. The jeepney ride takes about 30 minutes. You can stay there in a Government Resthouse hut for P10 per person. Get in touch with the forest ranger.

Getting There
When the highway from Roxas to Taytay is eventually completed public transport may improve. At the moment

jeepneys only cover half the distance, and that only sporadically. Four-wheel drive is still the only reliable means of transport. Travelling by boat is both expensive and time consuming, since you either have to charter one or wait for one. Also the regular boat makes numerous stops along the way.

LIMINANGCONG
During the north-east monsoon this is a fishing centre and also a jumping-off point for boats travelling to the northern islands. Ask the shopkeepers about connections to the islands; they usually know more about them than the coast guard. The people from here are both friendly and helpful, but take care for there are still pirates working around these islands.

PORT BARTON
Port Barton consists of only a few houses on Pagdanan Creek by the beautiful beach. You can rent outriggers here for P100 to 120 a day to sail to one of the superb offshore islands. There's good snorkelling at the 'aquarium', at Albagin Island and around Exotic Island. Nearly all the beaches here have white sandy shores.

There are also several good waterfalls and some virgin jungle in the area. The lovely Honeybee Valley is located towards Caruray. A day trip to the underground river costs P400.

Places to Stay
Elsa's Beach House has singles at P15, doubles with balcony for P30. It's a big, beautiful house right on the beach and run by nice people. Very good food too. You can also find cottages here for P25.

Getting There
Jeepneys from Roxas depart from the public market when they have a full passenger load at any time of day. The wait can last a few hours but the trip

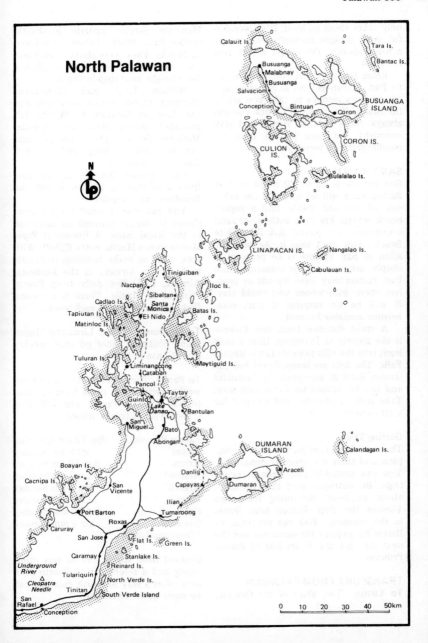

North Palawan

N

Calauit Is.

Tara Is.
Bantac Is.

Busuanga
Malabnay
Busuanga
Salvacion
Conception   Bintuan   Coron

BUSUANGA
ISLAND

CULION
IS.

CORON IS.

Bulalalao Is.

LINAPACAN IS.

Nangalao Is.

Cabuluan Is.

Tiniguiban

Nacpan   Iloc Is.
Sibaltan
Cadlao Is.   Santa
              Monica   Batas Is.
Tapiutan Is. El Nido
Matinloc Is.

Maytiguid Is.

Tuluran Is.

Liminangcong
Cataban
Pancol
Guinlo   Taytay
          Lake
          Danao   Bantulan
San
Miguel   Bato
          Abongan

DUMARAN
ISLAND

Calandagan Is.

Danlig   Araceli
Capayas
Ilian
Tumarbong
Dumaran

Boayan Is.

Cacnipa Is.
              San
              Vicente
Port Barton
          Roxas
Caruray   San Jose
          Caramay   Flat Is.   Green Is.
                      Stanlake Is.
Underground   Reinard Is.
River
△ Cleopatra Tulariquin North Verde Is.
  Needle   Tinitan   South Verde Island
San
Rafael
Conception

0   10   20   30   40   50km

only takes about an hour. It's a wonderful drive straight thorough dense jungle across Palawan. Try to get a seat near the front.

From San Rafael if you want to get to Port Barton get off at San Jose and try to get a jeepney to take you across the island. If this doesn't work you can always get a ride to Roxas and stay overnight but you should have no trouble getting a jeepney.

SAN VICENTE

San Vicente is 15 to 20 north of Port Barton on a spit of land. On the other side of the spit you'll find a superb beach several km long with white sand sometimes even waves! Ask for 'White Beach', you can't miss it. Accommodation in San Vicente is no problem — simply ask around, or someone from Port Barton may have friends or relatives there with whom you could stay. It will be no surprise if huts soon become available for rent.

A short distance from San Vicente is the airstrip at Inandeng. Here a road leads into the hills towards Little Baguio Falls. The falls are insignificant but the stream itself is exceptionally beautiful and can be walked up for a long way. Take some sandwiches and a tripod for your camera.

Getting There

The road from Port Barton is now complete and there are irregular departures. You can probably also arrange special trips. By outrigger boat the trip takes about an hour. Returning from San Vicente the Port Barton boat leaves in the morning. You can continue to Roxas by jeepney the same day and the next day get the 6 am bus to Puerto Princesa.

TRANSPORT FROM PALAWAN
To Luzon Two ships of the Oriental Maritime Service operate a shuttle service from Puerto Princesa via Cuyo to Manila. They leave about weekly and the trip takes three days including a five to eight hour stop in Cuyo.

William Lines and Magasagana Shipping operate weekly via Coron and San Jose on Mindoro to Manila. It's probably better than the Oriental Maritime Service. The departure time can vary due to long, undetermined stays in the harbour.

Once weekly the *MS Bataan* goes from Liminancong to Manila but the departures are irregular.

You can charter small aircraft from Coron to Manila through Mr Baracoso in the Rural Bank. A five-seater Piper Manila-Coron-Manila costs P2800. With luck you can make bookings in Manila with Pacific Airways at the Domestic Airport. PAL flies daily from Puerto Princesa to Manila. There is a second flight on three days of each week.

To Mindoro William Lines and Magasagana Shipping Lines go once weekly from Coron to San Jose.

To Panay The *Cardinal Ferry* goes once weekly with many stops from Palawan to San Jose on Panay. The following schedule is not totally reliable.

Puerto Princesa	dep 12 am Saturday
Roxas	arr 6 am Sunday
Roxas	dep 10 am Sunday
Araceli*	arr 3 pm Sunday
Araceli*	dep 5 pm Sunday
Cuyo	arr 11 pm Sunday
Cuyo	dep 10 am Monday
San Jose	arr 4 pm Monday
*Dumaran Island	

Onward from Roxas can be very interesting and a return trip to Puerto Princesa, after a stay in North Palawan, can be made quite superfluous.

Index

Abbreviations
    Basilan (Ba)
    Batan Islands (BI)
    Bohol (Bo)
    Camiguin (Ca)
    Catanduanes (Ct)
    Cebu (Ce)
    Leyte (Le)
    Lubang (Lu)
    Luzon (L)
    Marinduque (Mq)
    Masbate (Ma)
    Mindanao (Mo)
    Mindoro (Mr)
    Negros (N)
    Palawan (Pw)
    Panay (Py)
    Romblon (R)
    Samar (Sa)
    Siquijor (Sq)
    Sulu Islands (SI)

Abatan (L) 116
Abra de Ilog (Mr) 173
Abuyog (Le) 205
Agno (L) 103
Agno River (L) 11
Agoo (L) 121
Agoucillo (L) 95
Agus River (Mo) 273
Agusan River (Mo) 11, 266
Alabang (L) 97
Alaminos (L) 94, 103-104
Albagin Island (Pw) 304
Albay (L) 142
Alcada (N) 212
Aliquay (Mo) 277
Allen (Sa) 239, 241
Alligator Bay (L) 94
Alona Beach (Bo) 175
Ambil Island (Lu) 157
Ambulong Island (Mr) 171
Anahawan (Mo) 263
Angeles (L) 108
Angol (Py) 230, 231
Angono (L) 31, 33
Anini-y (Py) 232
Apalit (L) 32
Aparri (L) 130
Apayao River (L) 16
Apo Island (N) 214, 216
Apo Reef (Mr) 53, 171
Apunan (R) 235
Ardent Hot Spring (Ca) 252
Arevalo (Py) 222, 232
Argao (Ce) 194
Aringay (L) 121
Aroma Beach (Mr) 170, 171
Asin Hot Springs (L) 111
Atimonan (L) 133
Aurora Memorial Park (L) 101
Ayala (Mo) 279

Babuyan Islands (L) 129
Bacarra (L) 126
Baclayon (Bo) 178

Bacolod (N) 207, 208-212
Bacungan (Pw) 302
Bacuyongan River (N) 217
Bagac (L) 91
Bagacay (L) 136
Bago (N) 207
Baguio (L) 33, 108-113
Bahau (L) 138
Baheli (Pw) 300
Balabac Island (Pw) 292
Balabag (Py) 229, 230, 231
Balanacan (Mq) 161
Balanga (L) 91
Balaquilas (Lu) 157
Balayon (L) 32
Baler (L) 101
Baler Bay (L) 101
Balete Beach (Mr) 166
Balingoan (Mo) 266-268
Balsahan (Pw) 299
Banago (N) 219
Banaue (L) 8, 21, 118-120
Banga (Py) 228
Banga'an (L) 118
Banilad (Ce) 187
Barili (Ce) 192
Barrio Lantangan (Py) 225
Barrio Piaoa (Py) 226
Bas Diot Beach (Ce) 193
Basco (BI) 151, 152
Basey (Sa) 201
Basilan (Ba) 246-249
Basilan Island (Ba) 25, 33
Basilan Strait (Ba) 246
Bat Island (Pw) 302
Bataan Peninsula (L) 9, 30, 91
Batac (L) 126
Batad (L) 120
Batan Islands (BI) 151-153
Batangas (L) 96, 98-99
Bataraza (Pw) 297
Bathala Caves (Mq) 159
Bato (Ce) 194
Bato (Ct) 154
Bato (Le) 205
Bato Ili (Mr) 171
Bauang (L) 121-122
Bayawan (N) 216, 218
Baybay (Le) 204
Bayombong (L) 32, 118, 120
Belongbong Falls (Ct) 154
Beverley Hills (Ce) 183
Bikini Beach (Bo) 175
Bilatan (SI) 256, 262
Biliran Island (Le) 206
Binalbagan (N) 207, 217
Binanuahan Falls (Ct) 154
Bingag (Bo) 177
Binone (Ca) 253
Bitik (Mq) 159
Bitoon Beach (Le) 205
Bitu Falls (R) 236
Blanca Aurora Waterfall (Sa) 239
Blue Beach (L) 106

Boac (Mq) 159
Boac River (Mq) 159
Bocaue (L) 32
Bohol (Bo) 175-181
Bolinao (L) 105-106
Bolong Beach (Mo) 279
Bonbon (Ca) 252
Bonbon Beach (R) 235
Bongabong (Mr) 170
Bongao (SI) 255, 256, 258-262
Bontoc (L) 113-118
Bontod Island (Bo) 175
Bonuan (L) 106
Bool (Bo) 178
Boquete Beach (Mr) 166
Boracay Island (Py) 220, 229-232
Borongan (Sa) 239, 241
Botolan (L) 101
Brooke's Point (Pw) 293, 296-299
Budiao (L) 143, 145
Buenavista (Py) 223
Bugasan III (Sa) 200
Bugnay (L) 115
Bugo (Mo) 268
Bugsuk Island (Pw) 292
Bulactucan (Mo) 286
Bulalacao (Mr) 171
Bulan (L) 148
Bulusan (L) 148
Bunabunaan (SI) 262
Bundulan Point (Py) 223
Burias Island (Ma) 162
Busuanga Island (Pw) 292
Butauanan Island (L) 136
Butuan (Mo) 266
Buyuhan (L) 142
Bwansa (SI) 8

Cabalagnan (N) 212
Cabanatuan (L) 101
Cabayugan (Pw) 300
Cabua-an Beach (Ca) 250
Cabugao (Ct) 154
Cabugao Norte (Py) 226
Cabugao Sur (Py) 226
Cagayan Island (Pw) 292
Cagayan River (L) 11
Cagayan Sulu (SI) 255
Cagayan de Oro (Mo) 263, 268-272
Cagayan de Tawi-tawi (SI) 255
Cagsawa (L) 143, 145
Cajbo-aya (R) 236
Cajidiocan (R) 237
Calabagio (Ct) 154
Calabagnan (Py) 223
Calamba (L) 91, 94, 96
Calapan (Mr) 164, 169-170
Calatrava (R) 237
Calayan Island (L) 129
Calbayog (Sa) 241
Calintaan (Mr) 171
Caliraya Lake (L) 95

Callao Caves (L) 130
Caloocan (L) 66
Camalaniugan (L) 131
Camalig (L) 145
Camanci (Py) 231
Camera Island (L) 101
Camiguin (Ca) 250-254
Caminavit Port (Mr) 173
Camotes Islands-(Le) 204
Camp Amparo (L) 142
Camp Look Out (N) 216
Camp Pepito (L) 142
Camp Phillip (Mo) 268
Cangalwang (Sq) 243
Canipaan (Pw) 299
Canlaon Volcano (N) 207, 212
Canon Island (Pw) 300
Cape Encanto (L) 101
Capones Island (L) 101
Carmen (Bo) 181
Caruray (Pw) 304
Cataga Falls (R) 237
Cataingan (Ma) 163
Catanduanes (Ct) 154-156
Catarman (Sa) 253
Catarman (Sa) 239, 241
Catbalogan (Sa) 239, 241
Caticlan (Py) 232
Cauayan (L) 130
Cavite (L) 9, 94
Cebu (Ce) 28, 182-197
Cebu City (Ce) 182-192
Celebes Sea (SI) 255
Cervantes (L) 116
Chamban (R) 235
Chicken Island (Pw) 302
Chico Valley (L) 131
Chocolate Hills (Bo) 179-181
Claveria (L) 129-130
Concepcion (Pw) 302
Cono Beach (Lu) 157
Coral Island (L) 148
Coron (Pw) 306
Coron Island (Pw) 292
Corregidor Island (L) 9, 31,
  91-92
Cotabato (Mo) 273, 281, 288-
  289
Cotmon (L) 145
Cresta de Gallo Island (R) 238
Culasi (Py) 233
Culion Island (Pw) 292
Currimao (L) 124
Cuyo Island (Pw) 292

Dabdaban (R) 236
Daco La Janoza (Mo) 263
Dadiangas (Mo) 286-288
Daet (L) 133, 136
Dagupan (L) 106-107
Daliran Cave (Py) 223
Dananao (L) 115
Danjugan Island (N) 207-208
Dapa (Mo) 263
Dapitan (Mo) 9, 277
Daraga (L) 145
Dasol Bay (L) 103
Dau (L) 91
Davao (Mo) 32, 263, 282-285

Davao Bay (Mo) 22
Davis (Bo) 177
Del Carmen (Mo) 263
Dibut (L) 101
Digisit Springs (L) 101
Digos (Mo) 272, 285
Dinagat Island (Mo) 266
Dingras (L) 126
Diniwid (Py) 231
Dipaculao (L) 101
Dipolog (Mo) 277
Diwata Cave (Pw) 299
Doljo Beach (Bo) 175
Dulangan (Mr) 166
Dumaguete (N) 207, 214-216
Dumaguit (Py) 233
Dumaran Island (Pw) 292

Easayon (L) 124
El Nido (Pw) 292
Elephante Cave (Py) 225
Embarcadero (Pw) 304
Ermita (L) 66, 67
Esperanza (Ca) 251
Estancia (Py) 226
Exotic Island (Pw) 304

Forbes Park (L) 66, 71
Fuga Island (L) 129

Gabu (L) 128
Gandara (Sa) 239
Garcia Hernandez (Bo) 179
Gasan (Mq) 27, 159
Gaspar Island (Mq) 161
General Luna (Mo) 263, 264
General Santos City (Mo) 286-
  288
Gigante Islands (Py) 225
Gigante Norte (Py) 225
Gigante Sur (Py) 225
Gigmoto (Ct) 154
Government Island (L) 105
Granada (N) 212
Green Island (Pw) 303
Gubat (L) 148
Guihulngan (N) 216, 218
Guimaras Island (Py) 212, 223-
  225
Guimbal (Py) 232
Guinaag (L) 115
Guinsiliban (Ca) 253
Guiuan (Sa) 241
Gulf of Lagonoy (L-Ct) 154
Gumaca (L) 133
Guyam (Mo) 263

Hadson Beach (Ce) 191
Halike Beach (Mr) 166
Hen Island (Pw) 302
Hibok-Hibok Volcano (Ca) 250
Hilecon (N) 217
Hilongos (Le) 204
Hilosig (Le) 205
Hinagdanan Cave (Bo) 177
Hinobaan (N) 207, 216, 217,
  218
Homonhon (Sa) 9, 239
Honda Bay (Pw) 300-302

Honeybee Valley (Pw) 304
Hoyop-Hoyopan Caves (L) 145
Hundora Beach (Mr) 166
Hundred Islands (L) 105

Iba (L) 103
Ibarra (Le) 205
Igang Beach (Ct) 154
Igbaras (Py) 232
Iligan (Mo) 272-273
Ilin Island (Mr) 171
Illomavis (Mo) 286
Iloilo City (Py) 28, 29, 220-22
Iloilo Strait (Py) 223
Inandeng (Pw) 306
Inarihan Dam (L) 139
Intramuros (L) 67, 69
Iriga (L) 133, 139-140
Irosin (L) 148, 150
Isabela (Ba) 248
Isabela Harbour (Ba) 248
Itbayat Island (BI) 152-153
Itum (Ca) 251
Ivana (BI) 152
Iwahig (Pw) 299

Jagna (Bo) 179, 181
Jolo (SI) 23, 255, 258
Jordan (Py) 29, 223
Juban (L) 148

Kabankalan (N) 217, 218
Kabibitan (R) 237
Kalibo (Py) 28, 220, 228
Katibawasan Waterfall (Ca)
  252, 253
Kawasan Falls (Ce) 193
Kawayan Beach (N) 216
Kawe-Kawe Falls (R) 237
Kiamba (Mo) 24
Kibawe (Mo) 272
Kidapawan (Mo) 285
Kiyab Pool (Ca) 253
Kolambugan (Mo) 275
Koronadel (Mo) 288
Kuguita (Ca) 252

La Carlota (N) 207
La Laguna Beach (Mr) 166, 167
La Paz (L) 128
La Trinidad (L) 111
Laa (SI) 256
Labo (Mq) 159
Lagawe (L) 120
Laguna de Bay (L) 94
Lahug (Ce) 183, 187
Lake Balinsasayanao (N) 217
Lake Bato (L) 140
Lake Buhi (L) 26, 139
Lake Bulusan (L) 148
Lake Danao (N) 217
Lake Danao (Pw) 304
Lake Imelda (Le) 204
Lake Imelda National Park (Le)
  204
Lake Lanao (Mo) 22, 263, 273
Lake Mahagnao (Le) 204
Lake Naglagbong (L) 148
Lake Paoay (L) 128

Lake Sebu (Mo) 24, 288
Lambingan Falls (R) 237
Lamitan (Ba) 248
Lamon Bay (L) 133
Lanang (Mo) 284
Langogan (Pw) 302
Langub Cave (Py) 226
Laoag (L) 126-129, 153
Laoag River (L) 126
Lapanday (Mo) 282
Lapinin Island (Le) 206
Lapu-Lapu (Ce) 190
Lapuyan (Mo) 275
Larena (Sq) 243
Las Pinas (L) 93-94
Lazi (Sq) 244
Legaspi (L) 133, 140-147
Lemery (L) 97
Leyte (Le) 8, 200-206
Leyte Nature Trail (Le) 204
Liagao (L) 142
Lian (L) 98
Liloan (Ce) 194
Liloan (Le) 205
Liminangcong (Pw) 304
Lingayen (L) 106-107
Lingayen Beach (L) 106
Little Baguio Falls (Pw) 30
Little Balateros Cove (Mr) 16
Loay (Bo) 179
Loboc (Bo) 179
Long Beach (Mr) 166
Looc (Lu) 157
Looc (R) 237
Loreto (Mo) 266
Los Banos (L) 10, 94
Lubang (Lu) 157-158
Lubuagan (L) 131-132
Lucap (L) 103-104
Lucban (L) 31, 96, 133
Lucena City (L) 96, 133-136
Lumbacan (Mo) 266
Lumbia Airport (Mo) 272
Luzon (L) 91-150

Maac (Ca) 253
Ma-ao (N) 212
Maambong (Bo) 179
Maasin (Le) 205
Mabini (Mo) 282
Mablaran Falls (R) 237
Macahambus Caves (Mo) 268
Mactan Island (Ce) 8, 30, 190
Magdapio Waterfalls (L) 94
Magdiwan (R) 237
Magsaysay Island (Ca) 253
Magting (Ca) 253
Maguiguis (L) 103
Mahapalag (Le) 205
Mahayahay Beach (Ca) 252
Mahinog (Ca) 253
Mainit (Ce) 194
Mainit (L) 115
Malabatay (N) 216
Malabsay Falls (L) 139
Malampaya Sound (Pw) 304
Malamui Island (Ba) 248
Malandog (Py) 30
Malango (L) 115

Malate (L) 66, 67
Malay (Py) 232
Malaybalay (Mo) 29, 272
Maligcong (L) 115
Malobaon (L) 33
Maluso (Ba) 248
Mam-on (Mo) 263
Mambajao (Ca) 250
Mambucal (N) 212
Mamburao (Mr) 164, 173
Mangayad (Py) 231
Manila (L) 9, 66-90
Manila Bay (L) 9, 66, 69, 71, 94
Maniuayan Island (Mq) 159
Manoc Manoc (Py) 229
Mansalay (Mr) 170
Mantayupa Falls (Ce) 192
Manuk Manka (SI) 262
Maoyon (Pw) 302
Mapula (R) 235
Maqueda Channel (L-Ct) 154
Maragusan Valley (Mo) 282
Mararison Island (Py) 233
Marawi (Mo) 22, 273
Marbel (Mo) 288
Maria Bay (Sq) 244
Maria Christina Falls (Mo) 272
Maribago (Ce) 191
Maribojoc (Bo) 178
Marigondon (Ce) 190
Marinduque (Mq) 159-161
Mariveles (L) 91
Masbate (Ma) 162-163
Masiga (Mq) 161
Matabungkay (L) 97-98
Matalang River (L) 16
Matalangao (Pw) 303
Mati (Mo) 282
Matnog (L) 133, 150
Matutinao (Ce) 193
Mayon Volcano (L) 11, 133, 142-145
Mayoyao (L) 119
Mcabalan Wharf (Mo) 272
Meara Island (Pw) 302
Melco Beach (Mr) 170
Mendoza Park (Pw) 293
Mercedes (N) 136
Meridian Channel (SI) 262
Miagao (Py) 232, 233
Minalolan Reef (Sq) 244
Mindanao (Mo) 263-291
Mindoro (Mr) 164-174
Mindoro Beach (L) 124
Moalboal (Ce) 193
Molo (Py) 220
Mormbo Beach (Bo) 177
Morong (L) 91
Mountain Beach (Mr) 166
Mountain Province (L) 19
Mt Apo (Mo) 11, 263, 285-286
Mt Arayat National Park (L) 108
Mt Asog (L) 140
Mt Bongao (SI) 258
Mt Bulusan (L) 148
Mt Guiting-Guiting (R) 237
Mt Halcon (Lu) 157

Mt Iglit (Mr) 171
Mt Iriga (L) 133, 140
Mt Isarog (L) 133, 139
Mt Isarog National Park (L) 139
Mt Malisimbo (Mr) 166
Mt Mantalingajan (Pw) 24, 292
Mt Pinatubo (L) 103
Mt Pulong (L) 11
Mt Samat (L) 91
Mt Makiling National Park (L) 94

Naasag (Ca) 251, 252
Nabas (Py) 232
Nabontalan Falls (L) 139
Nadsadan Falls (Py) 232
Naga City (L) 32, 133, 138-139
Nagarao Island (Py) 212, 223, 225
Nagtabon Beach (Pw) 302
Nalsoc Caves (L) 103
Nasugbu (L) 98
Nauhang (N) 216, 217, 218
Naval (Le) 206
Negros (N) 207-219
New Foundland (Mo) 286
New Israel (Mo) 286
New Washington (Py) 233
Nogas Island (Py) 232
Novaliches L) 28
Nueva Valencia (Py) 223
Numcia (Mo) 263

Obando (L) 31
Odiongan (R) 237
Olango Island (Ce) 192
Old Siruma Island (L) 136
Olongapo (L) 91, 93
Opol (Mo) 268
Opon (Ce) 190
Ormoc (Le) 204
Oroquieta (Mo) 277
Oton (Py) 222, 232
Ozamiz (Mo) 275

Paete (L) 95
Pagadian (Mo) 273-275
Pagdanan Creek (Pw) 304
Pagsanjan (L) 33, 94-96
Pakil (L) 33
Palaui Island (L) 130
Palawan (Pw) 292-306
Palo (Le) 200
Paluan (Mr) 173
Palumbanes (Ct) 154
Palumbanes Islands (Ct) 154
Pamilacan Island (Bo) 177, 178
Panagsama Beach (Ce) 193
Panaon Island (Le) 205
Panay (Ct) 154
Panay (Py) 220-234
Pandan (Ca) 252
Pandan (Py) 233
Pandan Island (Pw) 302
Pandin Lake (L) 99
Pangil (L) 124
Panglao Island (Bo) 175
Pangutaran (SI) 255

Panhulugan I (Sa) 200
Paoay (L) 126
Paradise Beach (Mr) 166
Pasay City (L) 67
Pasiagan (SI) 258
Pasig River (L) 66, 69, 70
Pasonanca Park (Mo) 278-279
Pasuquin (L) 126
Patal Pinto (L) 103
Pateros (L) 32
Pavia (Py) 31, 222
Pawikan (Py) 225
Penablanca (L) 130
Pescador Island (Ce) 193
Pilar (Mo) 263
Pili (L) 139
Pinitan (L) 136
Polloc (Mo) 289
Polomolok (Mo) 24
Porac (L) 103
Poro (Le) 204
Poro Island (Le) 204
Porongpong (Ct) 154
Port Barton (Pw) 304-306
Port Currimao (L) 124
Puerto Galera (Mr) 164-169
Puerto Princesa (Pw) 293-296
Puerto Princesa Bay (Pw) 293
Pulitan (L) 31
Pulupandan (N) 218
Pundaquit (L) 101
Punta (L) 136
Punta Tabok (Py) 228
Putsan Beach (L) 148

Quezon (Pw) 299
Quezon City (L) 29, 33, 66
Quezon Island (L) 105
Quezon National Park (L) 133
Quiapo (L) 27, 70

Rainbow Falls (L) 94
Ransang (Pw) 292
Red Beach (Le) 200
Rio Grande de Mindanao (Mo)
    11, 288
Rio Grande de Pampanga (L) 11
Rio Hondo (Mo) 278
Rio Tuba (Pw) 296, 299
Rizal Beach (L) 148
Romagangran (N) 212, 223
Romblon (R) 235-238
Romblon Island (R) 235
Roxas (L) 130
Roxas (Mr) 170
Roxas (Pw) 293, 303-304
Roxas (Py) 228

Sabang (Pw) 300
Sabang (R) 235
Sabang Beach (Mr) 166, 167
Sabangan Beach (L) 103
Sablayan (Mr) 171, 173
Sabtang Island (BI) 152
Sagada (L) 118
Sagay (N) 207
Salang Do-Ong (Sq) 244
Salinas (L) 120
Salomague Island (Mq) 159

Samal Island (Mo) 285
Samales (SI) 255
Samar (Sa) 239-242
Samboan (Ce) 194
Sampaloc Lake (L) 99
San Andres (R) 237
San Antonio (L) 101, 103
San Antonio (Sq) 244
San Augustin (R) 236
San Carlos (N) 207, 213
San Fabian (L) 106
San Fernando (Pampanga) (L)
    29, 33, 108
San Fernando La Union (L) 120-
    121, 153
San Isidro (L) 31
San Isidro (Mr) 166
San Isidro (Py) 223
San Isidro (Sa) 241
San Joaquin (Py) 232
San Jose (Mr) 164, 171
San Jose (N) 217
San Jose de Buenavista (Py)
    30, 220, 233
San Juan (L) 121
San Juanico Strait (Le-Sa)
    200, 239
San Miguel (L) 70, 93, 103
San Miguel Bay (L) 133, 136-
    138
San Nicolas (L) 97, 126
San Pablo (L) 94, 99
San Pedro Beach (Mo) 268
San Rafael (Pw) 302-303
San Ramon (Mo) 279
San Sebastian (Ce) 194
San Vicente (BI) 152
San Vicente (L) 130
San Vicente (Pw) 306
Sanga Sanga (SI) 258
Santa Ana (L) 130
Santa Cruz (L) 96, 97
Santa Cruz (Mq) 27, 159
Santa Cruz Island (Mo) 279
Santa Domingo (L) 147
Santa Fe (L) 130
Santa Fe (R) 237
Santa Filomena (L) 129
Santa Lourdes (Pw) 302
Santa Lucia (Pw) 299-300
Santa Rosa Island (Ce) 192
Santander (Ce) 194
Santo Nino Cold Springs (Ca)
    253
Sarangani Bay (Mo) 286
Sariya (L) 31
Sarrat (L) 126
Seksi Beach (L) 126
Siargao Island (Mo) 26, 263-
    266
Siasi (SI) 255, 256, 258
Sibutu (SI) 255, 256
Sibuyan Island (R) 237
Sicogon Island (Py) 220, 225
Sierra Lake (L) 95
Sierra Madre (L) 101
Sigma (Py) 228
Silay (N) 207, 213
Silliman Beach (N) 214

Silway River (Mo) 286
Simunul (SI) 262
Singnapan Basin (Pw) 292
Sipangkot (SI) 256
Sipaway (N) 213
Siquijor (Sq) 243-245
Sirawgan Beach (L) 147
Siruma (L) 136
Sitangkai (SI) 256, 262
Sitio Sangke (N) 217
Small La Laguna Beach (Mr)
    166, 167
Snake Island (Pw) 302
Sogod (Ce) 192
Sogod (Le) 205
Sogod Beach (L) 148
Sohoton National Park (Sa)
    200-201, 239
Solano (L) 8
Sorsogon (L) 148-150
South Cotabato (Mo) 23
St Paul National Park (Pw) 300
Suba (L) 128
Suba Beach (L) 128
Subic (L) 93
Sulu Islands (SI) 16, 18, 23,
    255-262
Sulu Sea (SI) 255, 292
Sumadel (L) 115
Sumilon Island (Ce) 194, 214
Sumilon Marine Park (Ce) 194
Surallah (Mo) 24, 288
Surigao (Mo) 263

Taal Volcano (L) 96-97
Tabaco (L) 156
Tabinay Beach (Mr) 167
Tablas Island (R) 236
Tablas Plateau (N) 207
Tabon Caves (Pw) 292, 299
Tabuk (L) 115, 131
Tacloban (Le) 200-202
Taclon (Py) 223
Tadlac (L) 94
Tag Nipa (Pw) 300
Tagabinit (Pw) 300
Tagaytan (L) 96-97
Tagbac (Lu) 157
Tagbilaran (Bo) 8, 175-178
Tagburos (Pw) 300-302
Taggat (L) 128-129
Tagudin (L) 116
Takal (L) 136
Talacag (Mo) 268
Talikud Island (Mo) 285
Talipanan Point (Mr) 166, 167
Talisay (Ce) 192, 194
Talisay (L) 96
Talosa (Le) 200
Taluksangay (Mo) 279
Tamaraw Beach (Mr) 166
Tamaraw Waterfalls (Mr) 166
Tambuli Beach (Ce) 191
Tamolo Beach (Mo) 282
Tampi (N) 217, 218
Tanabag (Pw) 302
Tanauan (L) 96
Tanggue Beach (Ce) 192
Tangub Hot Spring (Ca) 252

Tanguine Lagoon (Ca) 253
Tapul (SI) 255
Tapul Island (SI) 8
Tawi-tawi (SI) 255, 258
Taytay (Pw) 304
Taytay Bay (Pw) 292
Tejero (N) 216
Ticao Island (Ma) 162
Tigbauan (Py) 232
Tilik (Lu) 157
Times Beach (Mo) 282
Timoga Springs (Mo) 273
Tinagong Dagat (R) 237
Tinglayan (L) 115
Tiniphagan Cave (Py) 225
Tinuray Highlands (Mo) 24
Tiwi (L) 133, 147-148
Toledo (Ce) 182, 192
Toledo (N) 207
Tondo (L) 66
Tong Tong (SI) 262
Tongo Beach (L) 136
Tontonlac Falls (Bo) 179
Torrijos (Mq) 160
Tree House Beach (R) 235

Tres Reyes Islands (Mq) 161
Tubbataha Reef (Pw) 53, 296
Tubigon (Bo) 181
Tudela (Le) 204
Tugdan (R) 237
Tuguegarao (L) 130-131
Tulgueo (L) 115
Tumiangan (L) 132
Tumindao (SI) 256
Tumindao Channel (SI) 262
Tungkalang (SI) 258
Tungonan (Le) 204
Tungonan Hot Springs (Le) 204
Turtle Cave (Py) 225
Turtles Nest Beach (Ca) 252
Tuwasan Falls (Ca) 253
Twin Lake (N) 217

Ubay (Bo) 179, 180, 181
Union (Mo) 264
Ursula Island (Pw) 296-299

Valencia (N) 216
Valladolid (N) 212, 225
Victorias (N) 207, 213

Viga (Ct) 154
Vigan (L) 122-126
Vigo (Lu) 157
Villar (L) 103
Virac (Ct) 154

Waikiki Beach (L) 129
Wangan (Mo) 282
Wangan Creek (Mo) 282
White Beach (Ba) 248
White Beach (L) 106
White Beach (Mr) 166
White Beach (Pw) 293
White Beach (Py) 230, 231, 232
White Island (Ca) 252
White Sand Beach (Mr) 166, 167

Y'ami (BI) 151
Yambo Lake (L) 99
Yapak (Py) 229, 230
Yumbing (Ca) 252

Zambales Mountains (L) 103
Zamboanga (Mo) 29, 277-282
Zamboanguita (N) 216
Zaopote (L) 97

Update Supplement

A number of readers' suggestions came in too late to be included in the main text:

INTRODUCTION
Visas If you over-stay your 59 day visa you'll probably get hit at the airport for a P82 fine, the same as a visa extension.

Diving Aquaventure, 2178 Natrinco Building, Pasong Tamo, Makato (near Goldilocks) or the Scuba Center, 722 Vito Cruz, Malate are good for diving gear.

Air Travel Finding a PAL domestic timetable in the Philippines can be very difficult. You'll probably have to copy one if you need a schedule.

Car Rental Rental cars tend to be in very poor condition wrote one traveller who recommended checking a car over carefully, particularly if you're planning to drive up to Baguio and Bontoc from Manila.

MANILA
Faith Healers Orbit Tours, Ramada Midtown Hotel, Ermita (tel 50 3966) will arrange visits to faith healer Alex Orbito or other Manila healers.

NORTH LUZON
Bontoc Emma Poloc, usually known as Mrs Massa Poloc, is not at the Pines Kitchenette as reported in the main text. You can find her via her son at the billiards hall. She's an Igorot, a real character and a fund of information on local customs and events. She's particularly good to visit Bugnay with, which is a pretty little village and relatively unspoilt.

Sagada A rave from one writer for *Julia's Guest House* — lots of flowers, excellent food, very friendly, lots of information, a good meeting place. Sagada is a nicer place to stay than Bontoc, continued the same person. The caves are just down the road past Julia's.

Banaue If you want to stop between Manila and Banaue the *Olympic Motel*, three km out of town on the Manila side of San Jose, is a good place to stop. There are five hotels in Cabanatuan.

MINDORO
San Jose The *Chef Restaurant* on Lapu Lapu St near the market has good food and is a cool refuge from the heat and noise.

Roxas Melco Beach, Dangay is a good place to stay and is very friendly.

PALAWAN
Introduction There are no banks or post offices outside of Puerto Princesa wrote one traveller. You can now find post offices in the smaller towns wrote another. There are now local medical centres where you can get treatment for malaria in villages in Palawan.

Puerto Princesa The *Duchess Inn* has a book where travellers write their experiences, lots of useful information. Do not pay more than P1 for tricycle rides around town.

Quezon A sleepy although friendly town. Contact the museum before you go out to the caves as they are generally kept locked. A pumpboat costs P80 return. You can take a pumpboat from Quezon to Tamlagon Island for P50 to 100. A great place to visit although it can be difficult to get boats out there in the afternoon because the sea is generally rougher then. There's a couple of nipa huts on the island which you can rent but you have to bring food with you.

The *SP Guest House* is pleasant and clean but no meals are available reported one traveller who was also impressed by Edelen's. The *Tabon Beach Resort*, you can walk there or take a tricycle, is a brand new place with pleasant nipa huts and a restaurant. Rooms cost from P40. The *Panganiban Restaurant* has good, simple food but you have to eat early or they'll run out.

From Puerto Princesa buses to Quezon (and Brooke's Point and Roxas) leave from the market on the corner of Malvar and Valencia Sts. Alternatively you can bus to Narra and take a jeepney from there to Quezon.

Baheli & the Underground River One traveller wrote of the great difficulties and expense involved in visiting the underground river. Another wrote that you can often find inclusive day tours from Puerto Princesa and these can be good value. He paid P50 per head and that included an excellent lunch. 'It's spectacular and not to be missed' he continued. Rita Island, near Baheli, is a good stop-over with a beautiful coral reef and lots of fish.

Honda Bay Mr Vittorio Bong is a good contact for island-hopping trips from Santa Lourdes but be very precise about what you want — lots of islands, snorkelling, fish. There's no shade on Snake Island but a beautiful reef. There are some abandoned nipa huts or you can camp on this and other islands but you must bring food and water.

Taytay Reports indicate that the Roxas-Taytay road is now all weather and a pilot road (dry season only and with no regular transport) is also through from Taytay to El Nido. You can charter a boat from Taytay to Elephant Island. El Nido is difficult to get to but has great snorkelling, trips to nearby islands and even jungle hikes. 'The highlight of north Palawan'. You can get there by pumpboat from Taytay or Abongan via Liminangcong but you may have to wait several days or pay a lot for a special trip.

Cuyo If you get here, off to the northeast of the main island of Palawan, stay with Mr Lucas. Cuyo is a quiet and friendly place and has some good boat connections to other islands of the Philippines. No place to change travellers' cheques here.

320

Lonely Planet travel guides
Africa on the Cheap
Australia — a travel survival kit
Alaska — a travel survival kit
Burma — a travel survival kit
Bushwalking in Papua New Guinea
Canada — a travel survival kit
Hong Kong, Macau & Canton
India — a travel survival kit
Japan — a travel survival kit
Kashmir, Ladakh & Zanskar
Kathmandu & the Kingdom of Nepal
Korea & Taiwan — a travel survival kit
Malaysia, Singapore & Brunei — a travel survival kit
Mexico — a travel survival kit
New Zealand — a travel survival kit
North-East Asia on a Shoestring
Pakistan — a travel survival kit
Papua New Guinea — a travel survival kit
The Philippines — a travel survival kit
South America on a Shoestring
South-East Asia on a Shoestring
Sri Lanka — a travel survival kit
Tramping in New Zealand
Trekking in the Himalayas
Thailand — a travel survival kit
Turkey — a travel survival kit
USA West
West Asia on a Shoestring (formerly Across Asia on the Cheap)

Lonely Planet travel guides are available around the world. If you can't find them, ask your bookshop to order them from one of the distributors listed below. For countries not listed or if you would like a free copy of our latest booklist write to Lonely Planet in Australia.

Australia Lonely Planet Publications, PO Box 88, South Yarra, Victoria 3141.
Canada Milestone Publications, Box 2248, Sidney British Columbia, V8L 3S8.
Denmark Scanvik Books aps, Store Kongensgade 59 A, DK-1264 Copenhagen K.
Hong Kong The Book Society, GPO Box 7804, Hong Kong.
India UBS Distributors, 5 Ansari Rd, New Delhi.
Israel Geographical Tours Ltd, 8 Tverya St, Tel Aviv 63144.
Japan Intercontinental Marketing Corp, IPO Box 5056, Tokyo 100-31.
Malaysia MPH Distributors, 13, Jalan 13/6, Petaling Jaya, Selangor.
Nepal see India
Netherlands Nilsson & Lamm bv, Postbus 195, Pampuslaan 212, 1380 AD Weesp.
New Zealand Caveman Press, PO Box 1458, Dunedin.
Papua New Guinea Gordon & Gotch (PNG), PO Box 3395, Port Moresby.
Singapore MPH Distributors, 116-D JTC Factory Building, Lorong 3, Geylang Square, Singapore, 1438.
Sweden Esselte Kartcentrum AB, Vasagatan 16, S-111 20 Stockholm.
Thailand Chalermnit, 1-2 Erawan Arcade, Bangkok.
UK Roger Lascelles, 16 Holland Park Gardens, London W14 8DY.
USA (West) Bookpeople, 2940 Seventh St, Berkeley, CA 94710.
USA (East) Hippocrene Books, 171 Madison Ave, New York, NY 10016.
West Germany Buchvertrieb Gerda Schettler, Postfach 64, D3415 Hattorf a H.